PROBLEM SOLVING FOR INFORMATION PROCESSING

PROBLEM SOLVING FOR INFORMATION PROCESSING

Maureen Sprankle

College of the Redwoods

Prentice Hall

Upper Saddle River, New Jersey
Columbus, Ohio

Library of Congress Cataloging in Publication Date

Sprankle, Maureen.
Problem solving for information processing / Maureen Sprankle.
p. cm.
Includes index.
ISBN 0-13-025599-8
1. Application software. 2. End-user computing. 3. Problem solving—Data processing.
I. Title

QA76.76.A65 S73 2002
004—dc21 2001021569

Vice President and Editor in Chief: Stephen Helba
Assistant Vice President and Publisher: Charles E. Stewart, Jr.
Assistant Editor: Delia K. Uherec
Production Editor: Alexandrina Benedicto Wolf
Production Coordinator: Carlisle Publishers Services
Design Coordinator: Robin G. Chukes
Cover Designer: Galen Ludwick
Cover image: Kevin McTigert
Production Manager: Matthew Ottenweller

This book was set in Times by Carlisle Communications, Ltd. It was printed and bound by The Banta Company. The cover was printed by The Lehigh Press, Inc.

Prentice-Hall International (UK) Limited, *London*
Prentice-Hall of Australia Pty. Limited, *Sydney*
Prentice-Hall Canada, Inc. *Toronto*
Prentice-Hall Hispanoamerican, S.A, *Mexico*
Prentice-Hall of India Private Limited, *New Delhi*
Prentice-Hall of Japan, Inc., *Tokyo*
Prentice-Hall Singapore Pte. Ltd.
Editora Prentice-Hall do Brasil, Ltda., *Rio de Janeiro*

Prentice Hall

10 9 8 7 6 5 4 3 2 1
ISBN 0-13-025599-8

This book is dedicated to my wonderful husband, Norm, for his years of constant love and support.

Preface

Applications software has become more complex and more sophisticated over the years. Today, students should think in terms of how to process information to solve a problem. Problems for the end user are many times complex and require more than one type of software to achieve an efficient solution. Information processing involves problem-solving techniques and preplanning before approaching the computer. This book presents problem-solving techniques for applications including word processing, graphics, presentation graphics, desktop publishing, spreadsheets, relational database management systems, and the integration and automation of these applications.

Students will explore problem solving using applications for a project involving one or more types of software. They will study a problem and learn the best types of software to use for developing components of the solution instead of limiting the solution to just one specific type of software. When students view a problem through the use of multiple packages, they are thinking in terms of *information processing*

This book was written for the beginning to intermediate applications students and may be used in conjunction with another text, or as a textbook in problem solving in applications or information processing classes. It is generic in nature, as no one brand of applications is presented. The book is written to help students find the best solution to a problem, and not on how to accomplish a task using a specific brand of software. If students are able to understand the concepts of various types of software, they can transfer that knowledge to any specific brand.

The text presents several types of applications concepts, as well as guidelines for problem design. It also provides specialized planning guides for problem development that follow the six steps of problem solving presented in Chapter 1. There are examples and case studies for each type of software presented in designated chapters. These are for students to follow and complete on a computer, if appropriate to the class. Problems at the end of the chapter—developed for personal and business use— allow students to develop their own solutions.

Organization

The book is divided into six units. Each is separate and may be presented in class in a different order from that presented in the book. Unit One presents information on problem solving, types of applications, installing and learning new software, and commonalities among software. Unit Two presents design concepts, graphics concepts, presentation graphics concepts, and case studies. Unit Three presents concepts and case studies for word processing and desktop publishing. Unit Four presents concepts and case studies for spreadsheets, including a chapter on mathematical concepts and functions for use with the development of spreadsheets. Unit Five presents concepts and case studies for relational database management systems. Unit Six presents concepts of documents processing and integration of types of software, programming concepts for use with applications, and concepts of automating a project. Included in the appendices are the ASCII Code, copies of the planning guides, and Otto the Robot who helps students with beginning programming concepts.

Acknowledgments

I would like to thank those who reviewed the manuscript and offered suggestions and constructive comments. In particular, I thank Stephen Dawe, West Georgia Technical Institute; John P. Russo, Wentworth Institute of Technology; Thomas A. Duer, New Hampshire Community Technological College; Gouri Banerjee, Emmanuel College, MA; David P. Beach, Indiana State University; and David Harris, College of the Redwoods, CA.

In addition, I wish to thank assistant editor Delia Uherec and production editor Alex Wolf at Prentice Hall, and Kelli Jauron at Carlisle Publishers Services for their care and patience during the writing and production process.

I would also like to thank Kevin McTigert, a College of the Redwoods multimedia student, for creating the cover image.

Maureen Sprankle

Contents

UNIT ONE

GENERAL CONCEPTS OF PROBLEM SOLVING FOR INFORMATION PROCESSING

Chapter 1

Introduction to Problem Solving

Overview

Types of Problems
Six Steps to Problem Solving
Problem Solving in Everyday Life
Problem Solving with Computers

Objectives

When you have finished this chapter, you should be able to:

1. Describe the types of problems that can be solved by a computer.
2. List and use the six problem-solving steps to find the best solution for a problem.
3. Create and describe a solution for a problem with a given knowledge base.

Problem solving is the act of selecting and setting up a method to find the best solution for a problem. The **solution** for a problem is the processes involved to solve the problem. People make decisions every day to solve problems that affect their lives. The problems may be as unimportant as what to watch on television or as important as choosing a new profession. If they make a bad decision, then they have wasted time and resources.

It is important to know how to make the best decisions. Problem solving using the computer requires the same thought processes as for determining solutions in everyday life. This book is written to help you understand how to solve such problems on a computer. To understand how to create a solution on a computer, we will first examine a problem in everyday life—since we are most familiar with everyday problems. Then we will discuss problem solving using a computer. If you can understand how to process a solution in your own mind, then you will be able to understand how to process the same solution on a computer.

The computer is a tool to help solve a problem, whether it is writing a letter or creating a database for a company. Preplanning a solution should save time in the long run. As with any project, it is better to plan the entire process first. For example, architects create plans before they build a house or an office building, and companies plan assembly lines before they start to construct a car.

The job of an engineer is to design and plan. When you solve a problem on a computer, you become the engineer or the architect who designs and plans the solution. The same thought process and care should take place when designing and planning a document, a slide show, a spreadsheet, or a database as when building a house, designing a toy, or purchasing a car. The prospect of designing and planning a computer solution may sometimes seem tedious, but if done right, it should save time and frustrations when finishing the product on the computer.

Six Steps to Problem Solving

There are six basic steps used in problem solving. An understanding of each of the following steps is important to find the best solution for a problem.

Identify the problem

1. *Identify the problem.* The first step in problem solving is to identify the problem. It is hard to solve a problem if you cannot properly identify it. In the classroom situation, most problems have been identified for you and given to you in the form of written assignments or problems out of the book. However, when you are doing problem solving outside of the classroom, you should identify the problem before you start to solve it. To begin, write a short paragraph, sometimes called an abstract or a problem statement, to describe the problem.

Understand the problem

2. *Understand the problem.* Before continuing toward the solution, try to understand what is involved in the problem. This includes understanding the audience and the knowledge base of the problem requirements, the developer, and the audience. If you are creating a spreadsheet on the cost of building a house, then you must first have as part of your knowledge base a working knowledge of what the cost of building a house entails. If you are setting up a solution for another person, then you must know the knowledge base of that person. Different terminology and graphics might be used depending on this knowledge base. For example, you would use a more detailed set of instructions with different terminology to tell someone how to find a restaurant in your city if he has a limited knowledge of the city than if he knows the city well. When you work with a computer, its knowledge base is very limited, very exact, and requires you to solve the problem using the knowledge base of the software that you are using. This knowledge base differs among software packages.

Identify alternative solutions

3. *Identify valid alternative methods to solve the problem.* The list of alternatives should be as complete as possible. You may want to talk to other people to find other solutions than those you have identified. Alternative solutions must be acceptable ones. For example, you could go from Denver to Los Angeles by way of New York; however, this probably would not be an acceptable solution, unless you also needed to go to New York. The more alternative solutions you have, the better your chance of selecting the best solution.

Select best solution

4. *Select the best method to solve the problem from the list of alternative solutions.* In this step you need to identify and evaluate the pros and cons of each possible solution before selecting the best one. To do this, you must first select criteria for the evaluation. These criteria will serve as the guidelines for evaluating each solution in order to find the best one.

Plan the solution

5. *Plan the solution.* Your plan should include the requirements of the problem as well as any instructions, a list of things to do, sketches, and so on. The plan should stay within the knowledge base of the individual, the nature of the audience, and the capabilities and limitations of the computer as defined in step 2. These restrictions can be very limiting especially when working with computers. Planning guides to help plan solutions to problems are included in later chapters.

Evaluate the solution

6. *Evaluate the solution.* To evaluate or test a solution means to check its result to verify if it is correct, if it meets the requirements specified in the problem statement, and if it satisfies the needs of the client. A set of criteria is needed as a guide to evaluate the solution, and should be part of your plan. For example, when a person needs a piece of furniture to sleep on, buying a cot may be a solution, but it may not be satisfactory or meet the requirements of the problem statement. The criteria for evaluation might include the following: is the piece of furniture comfortable, is it within a budget, and will it fit the decor of the room? If the result of the solution for a problem is either incorrect or unsatisfactory, then the problem solver must revise the solution or start the process again.

If any one of these six steps is not completed well, the results may be less than desired.

Problem Solving in Everyday Life

People solve problems daily at home, at work, or wherever they go. Problems at home may include what to cook for dinner, what movie to see, what car to buy, or how to sell a house. At work, the problems may involve dealing with fellow employees, work policies, management, or customers. The better the decisions an employee can make, the more valuable that person is to the company. In each case, the six steps to problem solving should be followed. Most people use them without even knowing it.

For example, take the problem of what to do this evening.

1. *Identify the problem:* How do you and your friends or family want to spend the evening?
2. *Understand the problem:* Even with this problem, the knowledge base of you and your friends should be considered. Select only the solutions that everyone involved would know how to do. You probably would not select, as a possible solution, playing a game of chess if you or any of your friends do not know how to play chess or if there are more than two of you, since only two can play.
3. *Identify alternative solutions:*
   - **a.** watch television
   - **b.** invite other friends over
   - **c.** play games
   - **d.** go to the movies
   - **e.** rent a video
   - **f.** play miniature golf
   - **g.** go to an amusement park
   - **h.** go to a party

   The list is complete only when you and your friends have exhausted all possible alternatives.
4. *Select the best solution:*
   - **a.** Select the criteria for evaluation of the solutions, such as a maximum amount of money, distance, or time involved.
   - **b.** Eliminate unacceptable alternatives, such as those that cost too much or do not interest one or more of the individuals involved.
   - **c.** Specify the pros and cons of each of the remaining alternatives.
   - **d.** Evaluate the pros and cons in terms of the criteria set up in step a. Select the best solution according to these criteria.

5. *Plan the solution (evening):* Prepare a list of actions related to the best solution, the result of which is a fun evening.
6. *Evaluate the solution:* Did you and your friends have a fun evening?

By going through these steps, the problem solver can be assured that he arrived at the best solution and will achieve the desired results. When dealing with everyday problems, you may elect to not write everything, but you should go through the steps in your mind.

Let us consider the steps involved in making a cup of cocoa.

1. *Identify the problem:* How do you make a cup of cocoa?
2. *Understand the problem:* Identify the knowledge base of the person who will be making the cocoa. This person needs to know the following: a refrigerator, milk, cupboard, microwave, minutes, marshmallows, package of cocoa, spoon, and a cup. This list should include any knowledge required to execute the list of instructions in step 5 below. There are certain assumptions we can make, such as a common language, the ability to move, and the ability to reach needed items. Along with the knowledge base of the person, you have to know how to make a cup of cocoa so that you can tell someone else how to do it.
3. *Alternative solutions:* List some alternative solutions, such as to use a stove, a microwave, prepackaged cocoa, or to make your own recipe, or use bulk cocoa. You want to make this list as complete as possible.
4. *Select the best solution:* After evaluating all pros and cons, we will use a microwave and prepackaged cocoa, because these are the easiest to use and are what we have to use.
5. *Plan the solution:*
   a. Go to refrigerator and get out the milk.
   b. Get a cup from the cupboard.
   c. Get a package of cocoa from the cupboard.
   d. Pour the cocoa into the cup.
   e. Fill the cup almost to the top with milk.
   f. Stir the cocoa and milk with a spoon.
   g. Put the cup with the cocoa mixture into the microwave.
   h. Set the time for 2 minutes.
   i. Start the microwave.
   j. When done, take the cocoa out of the microwave and enjoy.
6. *Test the solution:* The criteria for evaluation may include the following: Is the cocoa hot enough? (yes) Is it too hot? (no) Is there enough milk? (yes) Is there too much milk? (no) Is it good? (yes) If any of these questions are answered by a response other than the one in the parentheses, then the solution needs to be modified. If the solution is bad, then restart the process with step 1.

These are the steps you would probably go through when you tell someone how to make a cup of cocoa even if you have not really thought about it. We should think about the processes of how we solve problems in everyday life so that we can then transfer them to the computer, because the process is basically the same. When we understand how to solve problems for ourselves, then we can begin to understand how the computer can solve problems.

Problem Solving with Computers

When working with computers, your assumptions can get you into trouble. Try not to assume anything other than the fact that there is a common language between you and the computer of which the computer is in control. That is, you must use the language of the computer, because the computer will not adapt to your language. You should learn the **syntax,** or the rules and regulations, of your software. Even though there are commonalties among software, each has its own set of commands, menus, toolbars, and uses. You should try to learn the commonalties along with the differences.

The computer is a tool to help you solve a problem. The six problem-solving steps may be used on the computer as well as in everyday life. Let us examine the six problem-solving steps involved in working with computer software.

1. *Identify the problem:* When you are working in a classroom situation, the problem will be identified for you. If you are working in a job situation, however, the problem will not be identified. In this case, you will write a short paragraph to identify the problem. This paragraph should include a statement of the problem, an analysis of the audience, and a list of the required outcomes. Have your client or your supervisor read and agree upon this problem statement.
2. *Understand the problem:* You must understand the problem and have all the information about the problem before you can solve it. To help better understand the problem and to ensure that you have all required information, use a **problem analysis chart (PAC).** Figure 1.1 shows the four parts of the PAC form. There are 4 parts to this form.

   The PAC

   - *Given data.* This section is for you to write all known data required for the problem.
   - *Required results.* This section is for you to write all items that need to be calculated and printed. These entries will answer the question as to why you are solving the problem.
   - *Processes and equations.* This section is for you to record all the needed equations and processes such as sorting or selecting that are required to process data to get the required results.
   - *The audience.* This section is for you to evaluate the audience. For example, who is the audience, how old is the audience, what is the knowledge base of the audience, and anything else that will define this group.

   The PAC allows you to discard the superfluous words and glean the data from the problem.
3. *Identify valid alternative methods to solve the problem:* This step may take some time. You will need to stretch your imagination, open your mind to new ideas, and talk with others about alternative solutions. You must realize that on the computer you are processing information and not simply learning button-pushing. The computer is a tool to help you solve problems. As discussed, the way the computer processes information is similar to the human process. The main problem is that we do not always realize how we process information. Part of this step is analyzing what type of software should be used to solve the problem.
4. *Select the best method to solve the problem from the list of alternative solutions:* Create a list of criteria for selecting the best solution. Review the list of solutions from step 3 and identify three or four of the best solutions. From

Given Data	Required Results
Processes and Equations	**The Audience**

Figure 1.1 Problem Analysis Chart (PAC)

these, write pros and cons of each solution using your list of criteria. Finally, decide which is the best.

5. *Plan your solution:* When working with computer software, your plan will vary depending on the type of software you select. These various problem-solving techniques will be discussed in other chapters. Part of your solution should include answers to the following questions:
   - What software package(s) will you use?
   - Where will you get the data?
   - Where and how will you store the data?
   - How will you design the required document(s), data files, and screen(s)?
   - How will you integrate files?
   - How will you proceed to solve the problem on the computer?

These questions will also be directed to different types of software in later chapters. Problem-solving planning guides will be introduced with each type of software to help in the development of a solution.

6. *Evaluate the solution:* Look at the document and see if the finished product fits the requirements listed in steps 1 and 2. If there are calculations, use sample data to manually check the results. If the results are wrong, then go back and correct mistakes. Develop a list of evaluation criteria as part of the solution plan.

We will revisit these steps for each type of software and discuss how to apply these steps to develop a solution plan.

Summary

Problem solving occurs every day in our lives. The six steps to solving a problem are as follows:

1. Identify the problem.
2. Understand the problem.
3. Identify valid alternative ways to solve the problem.
4. Select the best way to solve the problem from the list of alternative solutions.
5. Plan your solution.
6. Evaluate the solution.

These steps can be used in everyday problems and for problems that can be solved on a computer. We must use these steps to increase our productivity and to decrease our frustration level while working on the computer. To accomplish this, we need to first understand how we solve problems in everyday life before we can understand the problem-solving methods for directing the computer to accomplish our needs.

Key Words

problem analysis chart (PAC)	solution
problem solving	syntax

Questions

1. What are the six steps to problem solving?
2. Name three problems that might arise at home, at school, or in a business setting that you think could be solved more efficiently with computer assistance.

Problems

1. Develop the knowledge base for the user and the developer (problem-solving step 2) with a set of instructions (problem-solving step 5) for each of the following tasks.

   a. sharpening a pencil
   b. walking from the classroom to the student lounge, your dorm, or the cafeteria
   c. starting a car (Your instructions should include what to do if the car does not start.)
   d. getting a glass of water from your kitchen

2. Develop the knowledge base required to create instructions for the following problems:
   a. balancing your checkbook
   b. driving a car
   c. repairing a car
   d. building a house
   e. calculating the cost of using your car for one month

3. Develop the knowledge base assumed in order to execute the instructions for the items in problem 2.

4. Write step-by-step instructions on how to find the largest of three numbers.

Chapter 2

Introduction to Computer Software

Overview

Computer Tools for the End User
Basic Terminology
Internet Browsers
Word Processing
Desktop Publishing
Spreadsheets
Presentation Graphics
Relational Database Management Systems
Multimedia
Languages
Support Software
Defining Information (Document) Processing
Installing a New Software Package
Learning a New Software Package

Objectives

When you have finished this chapter, you should be able to:

1. List and define the major types of software.
2. Differentiate between uses of the major types of software.
3. Explain how and why to install a software package.
4. Explain how to learn a new software package.

Personal computers started a revolution in the computer industry during the late 1970s. Until then, computers were used only by large businesses because of the initial capital outlay, their size, and operating cost. The advent of personal computers made them affordable for almost anyone. Many people who were interested in using personal computers had no desire to program them. The computer industry responded to this need by introducing **software** for the **end user.** Today everyone who owns a computer uses software. Computers are commonplace in all parts of our lives: at home, at school, at work, and even on vacation. Just as our grandparents and great grandparents had to learn how to use inventions such as the telephone and the car, and get used to other new forms of communication such as the radio and television, we have to learn how to use the computer. The computer is becoming as much of a necessity in our lives as the telephone and the car.

Computer technology involves more complex uses than a car or telephone. The computer should be a tool to help solve problems or be used for recreation. It should increase our productivity and save us time. Because of the complexity of the computer, however, the end user should understand how to use the computer efficiently. This includes knowledge of computer tools, use of the correct tool, and use of problem-solving techniques.

This chapter reviews the basic computer tools for the end user and the knowledge required to make them work. Later chapters will discuss the problem-solving techniques of using the tools and the use of the correct tool for the problem to be solved.

Computer Tools for the End User

Vertical Software

Horizontal Software

Computer tools for the end user are the various types of software packages developed to increase productivity. Software developed for computers other than the personal computer market is designed and maintained for a single purpose. Corporations hire a team of computer programming specialists, who either program applications from scratch or purchase programs from vendors and then modify them to fit the needs of the corporation. The team maintains the program for the corporation. This type of software is called **vertical software,** because it is limited to the number of applications in which it can be used. When personal computers first came on the market, the only software available on the computer was the operating system and a language called BASIC. Users had to program their own applications. Soon, however, consumers made it known to the computer industry that they did not want to program, but instead use software that was already programmed. The industry responded to this request and started to produce **user-friendly software,** which is relatively easy to use, and can be utilized for a variety of applications instead of being application specific. This type of software is called **horizontal software,** because it spans many kinds of applications. Another term for horizontal software is **productivity software,** referring to the fact that it should increase the user's productivity.

Vertical software may also be purchased for personal computers. Normally, vertical software is bought through a software business that hires computer programming specialists to complete the program for a specific use in a business. This software is sometimes called a turnkey system, because the end user simply turns on the computer to use the software. Examples of this type of software include such programs as an accounting package for a dental office, a real estate estimating package for a broker, or a client-tracking program for a lawyer's office. The packages have specialized uses and are normally more expensive than horizontal software that is written for personal computers. These programs may cost thousands of dollars.

Although horizontal software is relatively inexpensive, a company requires someone in the office who can develop the needed processing on the computer. The typical types of horizontal software programs include internet browsers, word processing, desktop publishing, graphics, spreadsheets, presentation graphics, and database management systems. In this book we will discuss problem solving only for horizontal software, not for vertical software. We will discuss the types of horizontal software and provide in-depth coverage of each. See Figure 2.1a–f for sample documents produced from some of the following types of software.

Basic Terminology

Hard Copy and Soft Copy

Certain terms must be defined before we can discuss software. Two such terms are **hard copy** and **soft copy** output. Hard copy refers to information that is printed in some form. It is a document that users can read and take away from the computer with them. Soft copy output refers to information that is shown on a computer that is readable, but may not be taken away from the computer. This copy is usually displayed on a monitor.

Data and Information

The terms **data** and **information** are easily confused and many times interchangeable. In this book, the term *data* will refer to unorganized facts, and the term *information* will refer to organized facts. Usually data are input into the computer and output refers to information; however, at times information becomes data for another application.

File

A **file** on a computer is a group of related information that is saved for future use. The file may contain instructions to the computer about data such as text, graphics, sound, or video. Files are saved to one of the many storage media such as the hard drive, floppy disk, zip cartridge, or CD-ROM. Chapter 3 will discuss the importance of file maintenance on your computer.

Information Processing

Information processing is the processing of data into information using one or more software packages to achieve an aesthetically designed document. First in mind should be that we are processing information on the computer. Our plan should include how to best process the data using one or more software packages to complete a solution to a problem. We should avoid thinking in limited terms of using only one package in our attempt to find a solution and thus eliminate button-pushing and trial and error. Information processing requires preplanning before we sit at the computer.

Internet Browsers

Internet browsers allow the end user to "surf the net." Computer research and shopping among other things have become important to individuals and businesses in recent years. Schooling is becoming an important part of the Internet with colleges adding distance learning classes via the Internet. College information, registration for classes, home pages for students and instructors, class information, assignments, and grades are available to students on the Internet. You can find just about anything you want to know on the Internet. Information is located through the address of the site, also called a uniform resource locator (URL). If you do not know the URL, then you may use a search engine to locate sites that contain the specified information. Because there is so much information at our fingertips, however, it may take time to narrow the search in order to find the desired information. The key is to know what word(s) to tell the search engine to search for. See Figure 2.1a for an example of an Internet site.

Word Processing

Word processors are text editors. See Figure 2.1b for an example of a document developed in a word processor. Using this software, end users may enter text into the computer and format it in a variety of ways. The majority of the work done on a computer, aside from recreation and Internet use, is word processing. This software is usually the first

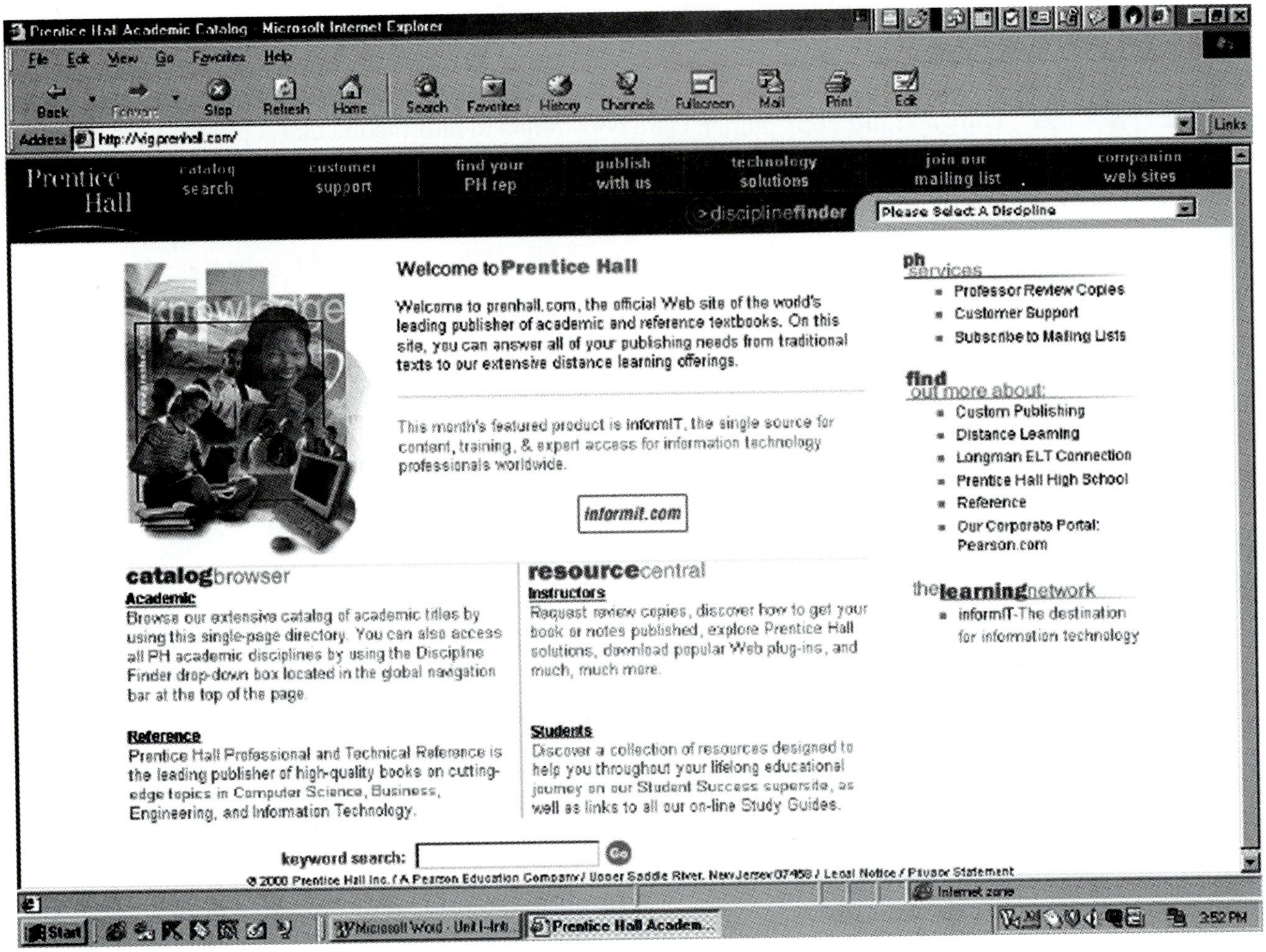

Figure 2.1a Internet Site Example

Word-Processing Example

This is an example of word processing. You have many features with word processing, including character enhancements such as **boldface,** *italicize*, <u>underline</u>, and alignments:

Right alignment

Center alignment

• Bullets

Borders around text.

Columns, tabs, and many more features. You may also import graphics:

Figure 2.1b Word-Processing Example

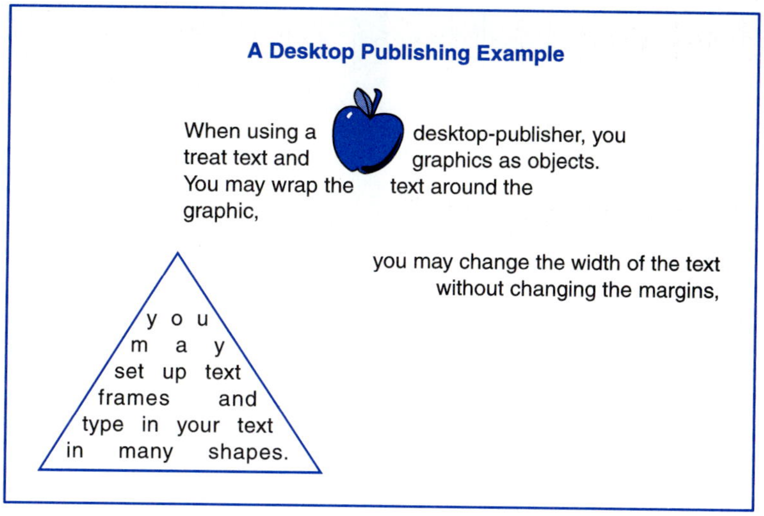

Figure 2.1c Example of Desktop Publishing

productivity package users learn. Because of the numerous features of today's word processors, however, it takes planning to complete a document efficiently for use today and also for modification in the future.

Desktop Publishing

Desktop publishers are composition programs. See Figure 2.1c for an example of a document developed in a desktop publisher. This software has the ability to place text and graphics on a page in an efficient way. These programs are not word processors in the sense of having all of the features of a word processor. Conversely, word processors are not true desktop publishers, even if they claim to be, because a word processor does not have the features that allow the easy placement of text and graphics that float on the page. Other features of desktop publishers that word processors do not have are the pasteboard to store objects, blue lines for guides, and the ability to easily modify margin, column, and ruler guides or to ignore them if necessary. The problem that end users have with desktop publishing is learning how to create well-designed documents that are aesthetically pleasing to the eye, communicate the message, and are easy to create. This takes preplanning and a knowledge of good design concepts.

Spreadsheets

Spreadsheets are basically electronic calculators. These programs allow the end user to easily enter text, numbers (or values), and mathematical expressions (or formulas) that are automatically calculated and recalculated every time the spreadsheet is updated. See Figure 2.1d for an example of a spreadsheet. Notice that there are two spreadsheets, one showing the calculated values and the other showing the formulas. The problem that end users have with spreadsheets is developing formulas and incorporating them into a user-friendly design. To accomplish this, end users must preplan, using their knowledge of how to develop formulas and of good design concepts. Of all the computer software

	A	B	C	D	E	F	G	H	I	J
1	An Example of a Spreadsheet Shown with Calculations									
2										
3	Calculation of Your Grade Point Average for the Semester									
4										
5	**Class**	**Grade**	**Units**	**Grade Points**						
6	History	A	3	12						
7	Computer Science	A	4	16						
8	English	B	3	9						
9	Physics	C	4	8						
10	Totals		14	45						
11										
12		Grade Point Average=	3.21							
13										
14										
15										
16	An Example of a Spreadsheet–Showing Equations									
17										
18	Calculation of Your Grade Point Average for the Semester									
19										
20	**Class**	**Grade**	**Units**	**Grade Points**						
21	History	A	3	=IF(B21="A",4*C21,IF(B21="B",3*C21,IF(B21="C",2*C21,IF(B21="D",C21,0))))						
22	Computer Science	A	4	=IF(B22="A",4*C22,IF(B22="B",3*C22,IF(B22="C",2*C22,IF(B22="D",C22,0))))						
23	English	B	3	=IF(B23="A",4*C23,IF(B23="B",3*C23,IF(B23="C",2*C23,IF(B23="D",C23,0))))						
24	Physics	C	4	=IF(B24="A",4*C24,IF(B24="B",3*C24,IF(B24="C",2*C24,IF(B24="D",C24,0))))						
25	Totals		=SUM(C21:C24)	=SUM(D21:D24)						
26										
27		Grade Point Average=	=D25/C25							
28										
29										

Figure 2.1d Example of a Spreadsheet Showing Calculated Formulas and Showing the Formulas

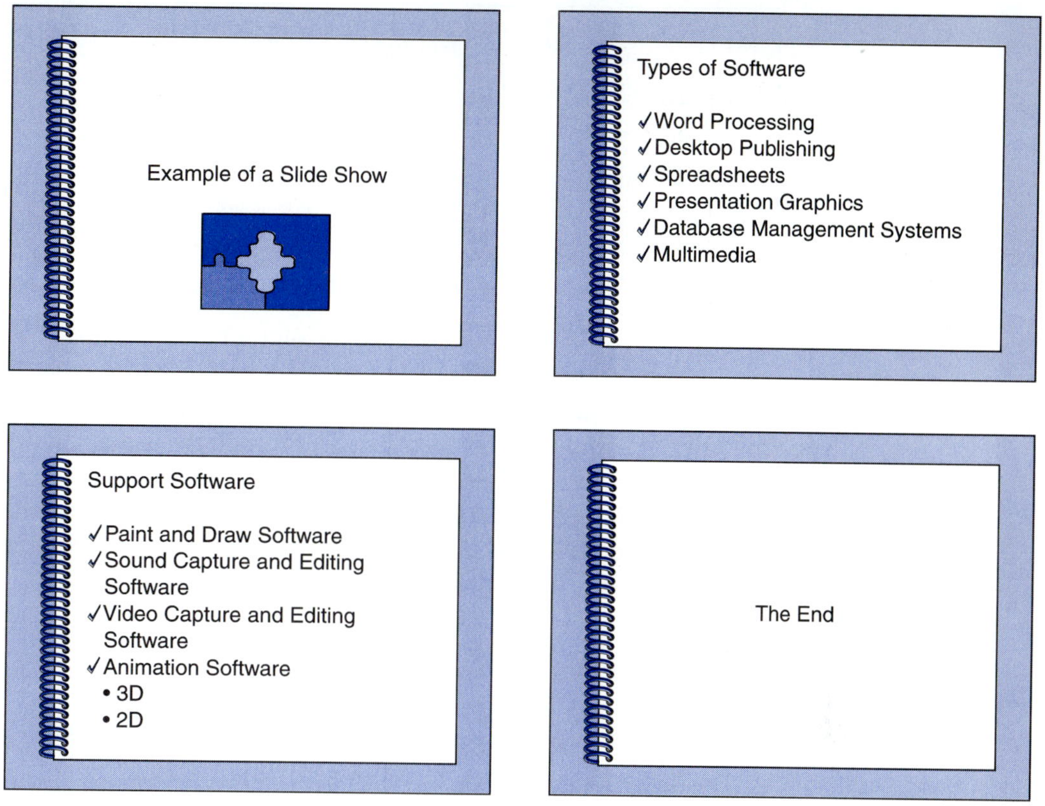

Figure 2.1e Example Slide Show

packages, spreadsheets are probably the most critical to have correct. A wrong equation in costing a job can be disastrous to a company.

Presentation Graphics

Presentation graphics packages allow the user to easily develop an electronic slide show. See Figure 2.1e for an example of a printed slide show. Visual aids developed to accompany a speech have long been known to enhance a speaker's presentation, although the graphics have traditionally taken time to develop and maintain. Presentation graphics packages solve these problems. Electronic slide shows are fairly easy to assemble and are easy to maintain electronically. End-user's problems with presentation graphics packages lies in the proper order of the slides, the design of the slide show, the right amount of words to place on one slide, and the correct use of graphics to enhance the show.

Relational Database Management Systems

Relational database management systems (RDBMS) are electronic file cabinets, or card files. See Figure 2.1f for an example of a report from a RDBMS. These programs allow the end user to easily store data, organize that data, and produce hard copy and/or soft copy output. Database management software is usually the last type of software people

Grades

Class	Units Grade
Computer Science	4 A
English	3 B
History	3 A
Physics	4C

Figure 2.1f Example of a Relational Database Management System Report

learn to use, basically for three reasons. First, the data need to be organized initially. Second, the data need to be entered, usually through the use of a keyboard which takes time. Third, the database file needs to be maintained, a task that most users do not like. To efficiently use a RDBMS, the user needs to know what data should be kept, how the data are to be organized, and how and what information should be reported.

Multimedia

Multimedia software packages are popular on the market. Multimedia software is used to combine text, graphics (clipart, pictures, etc.), sound, video, and animation into an interactive presentation of information. Presentation graphics programs have the ability to produce multimedia presentations. Some multimedia programs are designed for the multimedia producer only, to develop games and educational software, for example. Multimedia projects are developed for use on the Web; others are used in business for training and advertising.

Languages

Computer languages such as Visual Basic or macros are used to customize a project developed with application software. Languages allow the developer to create instruction sets that may be executed repeatedly and are saved with the project. These instruction sets automate the project by completing a task such as adding data, deleting data, printing a report, or accessing an internet site, through the use of a button, a hot spot, or a series of keystrokes. The addition of these instruction sets increases the user friendliness of the project.

Support Software

In today's world of computer technology and multitudes of software for our use, end users will learn about and use many products to create most documents. Many of the programs mentioned require support software packages to complete the requirements of the document being produced. Support software packages produce files that may be either imported into productivity software to enhance the required document or be used in tandem with the productivity software to make the designed application user friendly. Support software includes draw and paint packages, video capture and editing packages, and sound capture and editing packages.

Defining Information (Document) Processing

It is important to understand the basic functions of many types of horizontal software programs in order to produce the best documents in the least amount of time. An important rule is to select the right tool for the job. This leads to efficient information processing, sometimes called **document processing.** As mentioned, information processing refers to the import and export of files between software packages to produce the final document. For example, you may want to produce a letter that requires a logo from a graphics package and a spreadsheet from a spreadsheet program. You would create the logo and the spreadsheet in another software package and then import the files into a word processor to create the letter. This task is information processing. When you perform this task, you have chosen the best tools for the job: a graphics package for creating the logo, a spreadsheet package to create the spreadsheet, and a word processor to create the letter. During the ensuing chapters we will discuss how to choose the right software package. You must know the function of each package in order to choose the right one to use.

Installing a New Software Package

Licensing Agreement

When you purchase a new software package, you are not buying the software. You are only purchasing the right to use it. Along with the software comes a **licensing** agreement. As you open the package you are in essence signing a contract with the software development company as to how you may use the software. Be sure to read this agreement.

Inside the package you will find the following parts:

1. One or more diskettes or CD-ROMs containing the programs, computer-based tutorials, and any other files necessary to use the package
2. One or more manuals that provide instructions for using the software, manual-based tutorials for learning the package, installation instructions, and other information for the end user
3. Advertisements for other software, hardware, online systems, etc. (These you can read and use or opt to throw away.)
4. The registration card to be sent in to the vendor saying that you are the registered user for this package. (In many packages, you have the option of registering online.)
5. Your software licensing agreement which explains the limitations for using the software package

Installation Wizard

Read the licensing agreement and the installation instructions first. Next, install the software package. **Installation** has several jobs:

1. It copies the software to the storage device of your choice, usually your hard drive.
2. It communicates the configuration of your hardware to the software package.
3. It installs other files and software packages that are either needed by or that accompany the software that you purchased.

Installation is fairly simple today because most packages use an installation wizard. A **wizard** is a set of instructions built into the software package to easily guide you through a task. An installation wizard, then, is designed to easily guide you through the installation process. First read and then follow the directions carefully. Since part of the installation is to communicate your hardware configuration to the software package, when you buy new hardware you may need to reinstall your software. Before you reinstall software, run the uninstall program. This program deletes all files associated with the software. When you install your software, files are copied to various folders on your storage devices, which will need to be deleted. The uninstall program does this task for you. You can then proceed to reinstall your software.

Learning a New Software Package

After you have installed the software package, you must learn how to use it. You want to decrease your frustration time as much as possible and to approach the learning process in a systematic way. Do not try to learn everything about the package at one time. Following are some recommended steps to approach the learning of a new software package.

1. Look through the manuals to get an overview of the sections for future reference. Most manuals are also online in the form of help menus. You should learn how to use this feature. Find the indexes and the table of contents in the manuals. Try to find information by using these tools.
2. If there is a computer-based tutorial, run this next. These **tutorials** will show you the program's capabilities. Do not try to take notes or remember everything. Use the tutorial as an overview of the program.
3. If there is a tutorial as part of the manual, complete it next. A manual-based tutorial will allow you to make mistakes and correct them as you work through the instructions. Manual-based tutorials usually are provided in a "cookbook style," which presents a list of instructions to follow to learn how to complete a specific task. Follow the directions carefully. Do not skip parts even if you think you already know them. If no manual-based tutorials exist, you may elect to purchase a trade book written on the package. These usually have tutorials as part of the book. As you complete the tutorials, observe the functions that you already know from another program, such as save or print. This should give you confidence, and soon you should realize that you already know some of this new package.
4. After completing the tutorial or parts of it, try the same steps with a document of your own. The more you practice using the software features, the more you will increase your productivity. When you have questions or problems, use the help menu to find an answer. Many packages today also have wizards to walk you through procedures. Explore what is available in your new package.
5. Every time you use the package, plan to add one new feature to your repertoire of knowledge such as the thesaurus, columns, report manager, and so forth. Do not try to learn everything about the package at one time. A full-featured software package has too many features. On the other hand, do not be satisfied with the basics. Keep trying out new features one at a time.

If you follow these few steps you will be happier knowing how to use your new package, and you will not be overwhelmed by all of its wonderful features.

Summary

End users utilize computer tools to help find solutions to problems. Software may be vertical, which is designed for a specific use, or horizontal, which is designed for multiple uses. Horizontal computer tools include word processing, desktop publishing, spreadsheets, presentation graphics, database management systems, multimedia, and other support software. Through the use of these software packages, end users may design and create a solution to a problem through the concept of information processing, which is the integration of multiple packages to achieve the needed outcome. Users must learn how to use the right tools to complete the job, which may include using many software packages.

Before end users can use a software package, they must install the software on their own machine and thus accomplish three things:

1. Copy the software to the storage device of choice, usually the hard drive.
2. Communicate the configuration of hardware to the software package.
3. Install other files and software packages that are either needed by or accompany the selected software.

After installing the software, end users must learn how to use it. This entails reviewing the manuals, reviewing online tutorials, completing manual tutorials, experimenting with the different features, and adding new features to their repertoire each time they use the package.

Key Words

Data
Desktop publisher
Document processing
End user
File
Hard copy
Horizontal software
Information
Information processing
Installation (of software)
Internet browser
License
Licensing
Presentation graphics
Productivity software
Relational database management systems (RDBMS)
Soft copy
Software
Spreadsheet
Tutorials
User-friendly software
Vertical software
Wizard
Word processor

Exercises

1. Name and explain the functions of five different types of horizontal software.
2. What is the difference between vertical and horizontal software?
3. What is another name for horizontal software?
4. What does installing software mean?
5. What is a wizard?
6. How should you proceed to learn a new software package?

Chapter 3

Commonalities and Problems with Software

Overview

File Management
Compatibility Issues
Common Features

Objectives

When you have finished this chapter, you should be able to:

1. Understand and plan the basic concepts of file management including file structure.
2. Understand and solve compatibility problems with files.
3. Describe the common features of horizontal software.

As an end user, you will discover that most horizontal software has common features and problems. Since these commonalities are used in most software packages, it is important to learn and understand them. If you do, then you will find that you have already learned similar features for just about any new software package you purchase and you will know how to solve some basic problems that occur in other software packages. Thus, each software package becomes easier to learn.

This chapter will also highlight the importance of **file management.** We will answer the question: How do I organize my files so I can retrieve the one I need as fast as possible? We will tell you how to find a file that you have lost and discuss problems with file compatibility. In the last part of the chapter we will discuss some features that are common among almost all horizontal software packages. The topics in this chapter are important to the end user because they include the basic problems of computer usage.

File Management

A computer may have thousands of files located on media for the various storage devices (hard drive, floppy disks, zip cartridges, CD-ROMs). There are basically two types of files, program files and data files. **Program files** contain the instructions to tell the computer what to do. **Data files** contain the products of the software such as a word-processed document, a spreadsheet, a picture, or a database.

File Extensions

Some programs use **file extensions,** which identify the type of information a program contains and, many times, the software package in which it was created. The extension designates the format, or the way the information was saved. Other **operating systems** save this information as part of the file or as part of the file information section of the media. If file extensions are used, Table 3.1 lists some common ones and the formats associated with each. For example, an extension of .exe represents an executable file. These files are program files, such as Word, Excel, and Access. The extension of .doc indicates that the file is a data file and originated as a Word document. By knowing these file extensions, you can recognize file types in a listing and perhaps have a better understanding of compatibility issues. The different file types and issues will be discussed later in this chapter.

Folders

It is essential to organize files to be able to find them again. Think about your storage devices as you would a file cabinet. If you put each letter or report in drawers without any order, it would take you a long time to find a particular letter. However, if you put these documents in **folders,** label the folders, and put the folders in alphabetical order, then it would take very little time to find the needed document, assuming you put them in the correct folder. The same is true for your computer.

Moving Files

You may move your files from one folder to another on the same medium or to other media. When you move a file from one folder to another folder, you may select the file and drag the icon or file name from one folder to another. The selection of an item by pointing to the object and depressing the mouse button, dragging the object to another location, and then releasing the mouse button is called a drag-and-drop procedure. When you move a file from one folder to another folder on the same medium, it removes the file from the original folder and copies it into the new folder. This process is similar to a cut and paste procedure. If you want a copy to remain in the original folder, then you must go through a copy and paste procedure. When you move the file to a folder on another medium, it copies the file into the new folder but retains the file on the original medium. This process is similar to a copy and paste procedure.

The Desktop

Before we discuss files, you need to understand the desktop on your computer. The **computer desktop** is the screen that you see after you start the computer. It contains program icons, menus, and other icons depending on the operating system of the computer. The operating system contains the programs that allow you as an end user to communicate with the computer in a user-friendly environment.

Compare the virtual computer desktop with a real desktop, that is, the top of your desk. What do you keep on top of your desk? Probably the things you use frequently: file folders, equipment, such as a word processor, a calculator, pens, pencils, and drawing paper. On your virtual desktop, you may have the same items: electronic folders, a word processor, a calculator, other software, and so on. The exception is that on your virtual desktop you have the option to have a "shortcut" or an "alias" to your word processor, your calculator, your spreadsheet software, your paint program, and your data folders.

Shortcut or Alias

A **shortcut,** or **alias,** is an icon on the desktop that has the location of the item attached to the icon. By double-clicking on the icon, the computer will locate the attached file and open it. By opening the file, the computer will process an execution of a program if the shortcut is to a program file. However, if the file is a data file, the computer will find the program file that is associated with the data file and first process an execution of that program and then bring the data file into the program. This procedure is timesaving. To begin, decide which shortcuts you want on your desktop. Your first inclination will be to put everything on your desktop; however, this would only confuse the issue. If you have too many shortcuts, then it gets cluttered—similar to your real desk. You should be selective about what you decide to place on the desktop, because an organized

Table 3.1 File Extensions and Corresponding Formats.

Extension	Format
Program Files	
.exe	Program Execution Files
Text Files	
.txt .rtf .asc	Text Files—compatible with most software Rich Text Format—compatible with most software ASCII format—Similar to Rich Text Format
Graphics Files	
.bmp .jpg .gif .tif	Bit mapped graphic Jpeg Graphic Tagged image file format—usually a scanned image
Video Files	
.avi .mov .mpg	Windows-based video Quick Time Movies Compressed Video File
Sound Files	
.wav .mdi	Wave files Midi files
Web Files	
.htm	HTML
Horizontal Software	
Data Files	
.doc .mdb .xls .xlw .ppt .p65	WORD data file ACCESS data file EXCEL data file EXCEL worksheet data file POWERPOINT data file PAGEMAKER 6.5 data file
Compressed Files	
.zip .rar	WinZip file compression RAR file compression

computer desktop should increase your productivity. Each operating system has a specific way to add items to your desktop, usually through a menu item or a drag-and-drop procedure. The operating system also has a way to delete items from the desktop.

There are some cautions you should understand when placing files on the desktop. First, when working on a computer on which others also work, you should be in mutual agreement as to what should be placed on the desktop. Second, it is easier to accidentally delete files from the desktop than from a directory. Third, you should always use shortcuts to data files and not save them directly to the desktop. If the operating system needs to be reinstalled then you may lose your data. In either case, backups should be frequently updated.

The desktop has one or more menus—either pull-up or pull-down menus. These menus allow you to interact with the operating system. You may add things to the desktop, specify preferences, install programs, execute programs, find recent documents in the workings, find past documents, and so on. Take some time to find out what you can do with your desktop and customize it to your liking.

File Organization

Folders are organizers. You may put files or other folders within a folder just as you would put letters or reports in a folder in your file cabinet. When you install a software package, the installation program will create a folder for many of the program and data files associated with the software package. At the time of installation, you may change the name or location of the folder if you so desire. After you install your software, you should not change the name or location of these folders unless you reinstall the software, because, depending on the software, many times during the installation the location of these files are identified to associated programs. You may, however, change the names and the locations of the folders you create for your data files at any time. One exception relates to linked files, which will be discussed later in the book.

To increase productivity and decrease the frustration level, organize your files within folders and name them according to their contents. File organization should be according to the function of the file. For example, locate all of your English homework in one folder and your history homework in another folder. These folders may be organized into a school folder. See Figure 3.1. Figure 3.2 shows another view of the relationship between folders.

File Structure Planning Diagram

Figure 3.3 presents a file structure planning diagram. You may use it to plan what you will name your folders and how you will organize them. Figure 3.4 shows a completed diagram. Whether you use the view as found in Figure 3.1 or in Figure 3.2, this file structure planning diagram should work for you. Notice that this is for the folder named "My Data" on the hard drive. Within this folder are folders named School, Work, Personal, and Miscellaneous. In the School folder are folders named Fall 2001 and Spring 2002. In the Fall 2001 folder there is a folder for each class a student is taking, for example, English, Mathematics, History, and Computer Science. As you develop data files for English, you will save them in the English folder and save new math files in the Mathematics folder, and so on. When your English paper needs to be reworked, you can easily find it in the English folder.

Naming Your Files

Data files should be named so that the user can remember what the file contains without looking at it, such as History Homework #1 stored in the History folder and English 100 Final Report stored in the English folder. Your folder name should be short enough to remember and long enough to identify the contents of the file. A little planning, management, and time can save hours in the future. You may think you will remember what a data file named "AS55" contains; however, a month or two later it may become obscure, especially when you have developed many other files in the meantime. If you are naming files that have file extensions, do not use the period in the name as this indicates that the extension is following. Use the underline character or the dash instead of a period. File names should start with a letter. Avoid the use of numerous symbols. Check with your operating system as to limitations when naming files.

File Paths

The **path** of a file is the way the computer locates the file. It includes the storage device and all folders that are part of where the file is located. All folders in a path are nested; that is, one folder is inside the previous folder. For example, the path of an English 100 Assignment 1 file might be:

D:\School\English\English 100 Assignment 1.doc or

Sprankle: School: English: English 100 Assignment 1

Figure 3.1 File Structure

- a\ (the floppy drive)
- c\ (the hard drive)
  - program 1
  - program 2
  - program 3
  - program 4
  - My data
    - School
      - Fall 2001
        - English
        - Mathematics
        - History
        - Computer Science
      - Spring 2002
        - Economics
        - Management
        - Networking
        - Spreadsheets
    - Work
      - XYZ Corporation
      - Salespeople
      - Z-Rocks Corporation
      - Correspondence
      - Miscellaneous
    - Personal
      - Budget
      - Correspondence
      - Miscellaneous
    - Miscellaneous
- d\ (zip drive)
  - School
    - Spring 2002
      - Economics
      - Management
      - Networking
      - Spreadsheets
  - Work
    - XYZ Corporation
    - Salespeople
    - Z-Rocks Corporation
    - Correspondence
    - Miscellaneous

TIPS

1. Create a logical organization for your files. Use the planning guide in Figure 3.2 to help you build a file structure. (A copy of this guide is found in Appendix B.)
2. Name your files according to their content.
3. When you initially save your document or save it under a different name, be sure to save it to the appropriate folder.

Figure 3.2 Another View of File Structure

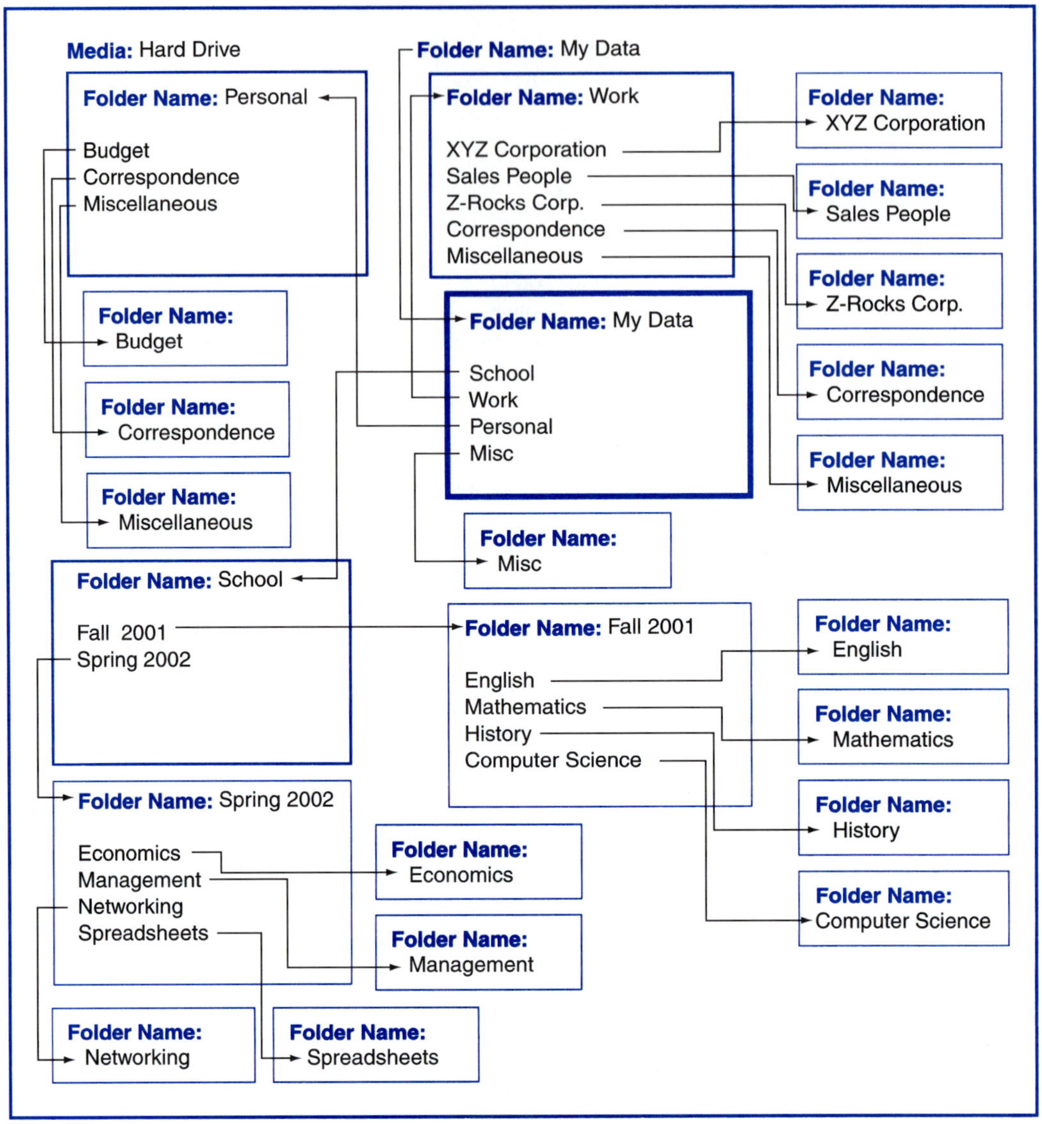

D:\ and Sprankle indicate the storage device where the storage media are located, such as a hard disk or a zip drive. School is the outer folder; English is a folder found in the School folder; and English 100 Assignment 1.doc is a document found in the English folder. Understanding a file's path will help you understand the file structure of a computer and how to find the files you need. Check with your operating system as to the notation of the path.

Finding a File

Please check to make sure your document is saved in the appropriate folder when you initially save your data file or when you save it under a different name. When you are hurried or simply forget to check, the computer saves the file in an unknown folder. When you return to retrieve it, you will not find it. Then, you will want to use the Find command in the operating system to locate the missing file on a storage device medium. If you remember the exact name of the file, then you may type that name into the input

Figure 3.3 File Structure Planning Diagram

File Structure for: ______________________

Folder Name: ______________________ Storage Media ______________________

Folder Page: ______________________ Date: ______________

Folder Name	Contains Folders	Contains Folders

Figure 3.4 Completed File Structure Planning Diagram

File Structure for: Maureen Sprankle

Folder Name: My Data

Folder Page: 1

Storage Media: Hard Drive

Date: September 1, 2001

Folder Name	Contains Folders	Contains Folders
School	Fall 2001	English
		Mathematics
		History
		Computer Science
	Spring 2002	Economics
		Management
		Networking
		Spreadsheets
Work	XYZ Corporation	
	Salespeople	
	Z-Rocks Corporation	
	Correspondence	
	Miscellaneous	
Personal	Budget	
	Correspondence	
	Miscellaneous	
Miscellaneous		

box labeled "Named" in the Find window. Because few of us can remember the exact name, you may type in any characters that are contained in the file into the box labeled "Containing text." Select the storage media or folder where you wish to find the file, and then let the computer find it for you. Once you have found the file you will want to move it to an appropriate folder.

There are other limiting options you may want to use such as data constraints, file type constraints, and size constraints. The computer will return a list of all files that fit the constraints you have chosen. Your file should be in this list. If not, then you need to expand or otherwise modify the constraints, or search a different storage medium. If the file is not found on any of your storage media, then you may have saved it on a computer at school or work, or under an unfamiliar name. Perhaps you neglected to save your document. If you are unable to find a document, you will need to re-create it. This fact explains why it is important to be careful when saving your document by naming it correctly and saving it in a proper folder. It is wise to save often. You never know when the electricity will go off or when a circuit breaker might trip.

Backup Copies

It is important to keep backup copies of all data files. A **backup copy** is a copy of the files saved on another storage medium. When you purchase a storage medium, always buy two, one for everyday use and the other to serve as a backup copy in case the original becomes corrupted in some way. Data saved on storage media can become corrupted for a variety of reasons. If you do not have backup copies, then you will need to re-create all of your corrupted files—which may be a huge task. Become habitual about making backup copies of your files on a regular basis such as daily, weekly, or when you make important changes. If your working storage medium becomes corrupt, then use your most recent backup copy. It takes only one time for your storage medium to become corrupt to make you a believer in backup copies.

You may want to make a backup copy of your hard disk including program files. If your hard disk becomes corrupted, you may recover all of your files through the backup including your program files. If you do not have a backup of your hard disk, you will need to reinstall all of your program files. Be sure to archive any files you may need at a future date. Keep several storage media for this purpose. Label the media carefully and copy the files to be archived to the correct medium. Archived files are especially difficult to find if you do not carefully organize them. You never know when you will need that English paper again or information about a past client.

Compatibility Issues

File Compatibility

One major computer problem is compatibility of data files. Using one data file as a component of another document is called **importing, inserting,** or **placing** data files. These terms are synonymous. For example, when a graphic is needed in a word-processing document, the graphic file is imported (inserted or placed) into a word-processing document. The imported document becomes part of the word-processing document file without destroying the original file. A copy of the imported file is simply placed into the working file. Chapter 17 highlights object linking (OLE), placing the location of one file into another file; and embedding, copying one file into another file. For now we will think of importing as embedding which is a copying procedure.

Because of the many formats in which data files can be saved, importing files may become a problem. Each software package has specific formats that the program will allow to be imported. You may have a graphic file in a format that your word processor will not allow and therefore you may not use the desired graphic without first converting it to a format that is compatible with your word processor. For example, you would open your graphic file in the program in which it was created, save the graphic in a compatible file format, and then import the newly saved graphic file into your word-processed document. This may require you to save the graphic file in many formats to accommodate multiple future uses or go back to the program in which the file originated and save the desired graphic in a compatible format. This is only one solution. Another is to buy a conversion program that will convert graphic files from one format to another. If all else fails, sometimes the copy and paste technique will work. Regardless of the process, you should learn the procedures and techniques of importing a file.

TIPS

1. Learn the common format extensions.
2. Learn the common importing formats that the programs you use require. If you use the imported file once, it is often easier to open the file to be imported, copy it, and then paste it into the receiving document—assuming you have the program in which the file originated.
3. Use a file conversion program to convert from one format to another. Investigate the conversion program to be sure the conversions are those you need.

Version Compatibility

Another problem with compatibility of data files is between different versions of the same software package. If you are working on one version at home but your school has another version, then you may have a problem. Most packages are usually upward compatible, meaning a data file created in an older version may be used in a newer version; however, most packages are not downward compatible, so a data file created in a newer version cannot be used directly in an older version. Therefore, when you are working in the newer version, you may want to save it in the format of the older version. This means that you may lose some of the features from the newer version that the older version does not have, but you can now use the file at home and at school.

Operating System Compatibility

Another problem with compatibility is between platforms. A **platform** is a type of operating system such as Windows, MAC, and OS2. For example, the problem occurs when you take a data file that was created on the Windows platform and try to use it on a MAC platform or vice versa. Some operating systems allow the exporting of data files in a different platform format. Some programs convert from one platform format to another. You will need a program that will import the converted file on the new platform. For example, if you have developed a word-processed file in Word on one platform and want to use it on another platform, then you must have a program on the second platform that will import a Word document.

Many programs advertise that they are cross-platform programs, which means that data files may be used in the same program on both platforms with few changes required; however, you must have purchased programs for both platforms. Having cross platforms does not allow you to install a Windows version on a Mac platform or vice versa. Even with cross-platform software, minor changes will still need to be made. The fonts are slightly different on each platform even if they have the same name. The color palette may differ slightly. You must proofread each part for design considerations. An advantage of cross-platform software is that you do not have to re-create the data file on the other platform and you only need to spend a little time cleaning it up, so it does save time.

Common Features

Common features exist between packages, so if you learn these features in one package, you will know them for other packages as well. See Table 3.2 for an overview of common features. Following are expanded descriptions of these features.

New

New: Creates an empty document, a clean page in a word processor, a clean canvas in a graphics program, a grid with no entries in a spreadsheet.

Open

Open: Retrieves a data file from a storage media (hard drive, floppy disk, zip cartridge). You must specify the medium and the folder where the data file is located.

Close

Close: Makes the file unavailable from memory. If you have not saved data, all will be lost. Be sure to carefully read any window that appears.

Save/Save as

Save/Save As: Places a copy of the document as it appears in memory on a storage device. You must specify the medium and the folder where you want the data file to be stored. After the initial save, the Save command is actually a Replace command. It resaves the document as it appears in memory in the place on the storage medium where it was initially saved. The Save As command allows you to save the document that is presently in memory under a new name and/or a new location. You must specify the medium and folder in which you want it saved. After the computer has completed a Save As, each time you use the Save command the document will be saved to the location of this new name. The old document will not be updated.

Print/Print Options/Print Preview

Print/Print Options/Print Preview: These three commands pertain to obtaining a hard copy of your data file. The Print command sends the document to the printer to be printed. What actually happens is a copy of the document is sent to

Table 3.2 Common Features

Feature	Explanation
New	Creates an empty document
Open	Retrieves a document from storage
Close	Erases the document from memory
Save/Save as	Copies the document from memory to storage
Print/Print Options/Print Preview	Prints a hard copy of your document
Cut/Copy/Paste	Cuts or copies selected material to another location
Undo/Redo	Undoes and redoes tasks
Find/Find Replace	Finds a selected item. Finds and replaces a selected item.
Headers/Footers	Designates text in top or bottom margins
Character Formatting	Enhances text
Spell Checker	Checks for spelling errors
Draw and Paint Features	Allows users to draw graphics in a document
Object-Oriented-Programming Language Interface	Interfaces to a language to add flexibility and automation
Web Features	Provides internet development features
Import (Insert or Place)	Copies a file from another program into the document
Export	Saves the document in a different format
Toolbar selection	Provides choice of toolbars
Zoom	Views the document in different sizes

the hard drive. The operating system then sends parts of the document to the printer to be printed as you continue to work on the computer. You must have enough space on your hard drive to hold your document to be printed. If you do not, then you will not be able to print the document. With the increasingly large storage devices of today, this problem is no longer a major issue. The Print Options command allows you to choose options as to how to print the document. These options may include orientation, sizing, collating, reverse printing of pages, and color options. Print Preview allows you to look at the whole page to see how it looks. It will also show you what is on each page. It is best to execute Print Preview before you print. It will save time and materials.

Cut/Copy/Paste

Cut/Copy/Paste: These are among the most valuable tools you will use in developing your data files. The Cut command copies the selected material to the clipboard and then deletes the material from memory. The clipboard is a section of memory that holds the cut or copied material. The Copy command copies the selected material to the clipboard but does not delete it from the memory. The Paste command copies whatever is on the clipboard to the place where the cursor is located. Paste does not delete the material from the clipboard. With the exception of spreadsheets, the data on the clipboard will remain there until other material is placed on it or until the computer is turned off. You may paste the material in the document on which you are working or in another document in a different program. It is an easy way to transfer material from one document to another.

Undo/Redo

Undo/Redo: Undo and Redo are your salvation commands. Undo undoes whatever you have just done. You may have deleted the wrong item. Undo will bring it back. The Redo command redoes the undo. If you really did want to delete it, Redo will do just that. Most programs have a queue of undoes and redoes to allow you to undo something you did five or six steps ago. You may go backward and undo everything you did until you get to the desired undo, or you may choose the undo you want from a list.

Fing/Find Replace

Find/Find Replace: These commands allow you to find an item and transfer it to a certain place in the document or to replace the item with something else. Maybe you spelled a client's name wrong throughout a letter—perhaps five or six times. You would then use the Find and Replace command. For example, you would find *Smith* and replace it with *Smythe.*

Headers/Footers

Headers/Footers: A header lies in the top margin area. A footer is one or more lines of data placed in the bottom margin area and is the same on all pages. Headers and Footers commands allow you to change the date, the page number, or text such as the name of the chapter or the name of the company. Look at the bottom of this book to see footers. Other books may contain headers. These elements are useful for page numbers, the date, and the time of day the document is printed, especially in the development of the document.

Character Formatting

Character Formatting: Chapter 4 will discuss the various ways to format characters. Most programs allow you to display the text to your liking.

Spell Checker

Spell Checker: The spell checker will check all or selected words in a document in its dictionary. Even if the word is spelled correctly or the word is not included, it will display a message that it cannot find the word and then give you suggestions for change. It will not find errors such as *it* for *is* or *at* for *it* or *deer* for *dear.* It only checks to see if the word is in the dictionary. You have the capability to build your personal dictionary of words that are not in the computer's dictionary. This feature is especially helpful if you are in a field that has many uncommon terms, such as the medical or law profession. Most dictionaries contain approximately 55,000 words including some common proper nouns. Be sure to proofread any document that you have developed even if it has been spell checked.

Draw/Paint Features

Draw/Paint Features: Most packages today have built-in draw or paint features. Chapter 5 details these features.

Object-Oriented-Programming Language Interface

Object-Oriented-Programming Language Interface: If you want to automate your spreadsheet, database, or other software packages, then you would use an object-oriented-programming language such as Visual Basic to add interaction to your data files. This topic is discussed in depth in Chapters 18 and 19.

Web Features

Web Features: The internet has become an integral part of computers today. Therefore, many people want the ability to have their documents exported in a format that is Web compatible. Most software packages have this feature. Because research on the internet is highly effective, another Web feature in most programs is the ability to access the Web directly from a document.

Import/Insert/Place

Import (Insert or Place): This feature allows you to copy another file into the document in which you are working. The imported file must have a compatible format to your working program.

Export

Export: This feature allows you to save your document in other formats, such as saving a Word document as an HTML file or a text-only file.

Toolbar Selection

Toolbar Selection: Each software package has many toolbars to make your work more productive. You may choose from as many as 15 different ones. You will probably use only three or four toolbars at one time because they take up space in your working area on the screen. Some toolbars are in the form of a window and are listed under the window menu. Some toolbars and windows have menus attached to them. You may also customize your own toolbar. Toolbars differ among software packages and many times within a software package. Be sure to investigate all toolbars available to you.

Zoom

Zoom: This feature allows you to view your data at a different magnitude. You may zoom in to make the document larger or zoom out to make it smaller. You may also choose a percentage of size to view.

Most packages have many ways of doing the same thing. You may choose to use a menu item, a button, a menu on the toolbar, or equivalent keystrokes. For example, Save is normally in the File menu; however, it is also found on the standard toolbar or you can use the control (Ctrl) key and the *s* key simultaneously. You should try all of them and see which you like to use.

Summary

File management is an important aspect of using the computer. Data and program files should be organized into folders for easy retrieval. Extensions on files usually indicate the type of format and often times the software package in which it was created. Knowing the common extensions can increase productivity by being able to recognize files in a list. The desktop of your computer is the screen that is available to you when you start your computer. From this desktop, you may execute programs, find files, change settings and preferences on your computers, in addition to many other things. If you lose a file, you may locate it through the Find feature.

Using a computer involves many compatibility issues. Included in these issues are file format compatibility, software version compatibility, and platform or operating system compatibility.

Software packages provide many common features, including character formatting, close, cut/copy/paste, draw/paint, export, find/find replace, headers/footers, import (insert or place), new, object-oriented-programming language interface, open, print/print options/print preview, save/save as, spell checker, toolbar selection, undo/redo, web features, and zoom.

Key Words

Alias
Backup copy
Character Formatting
Close
Common Features
Computer desktop
Cut/Copy/Paste
Data file
Draw/Paint Features
Export
File extensions
File management
Find/Find Replace
Folder
Headers/Footers
Import
Import (Insert or Place)
Insert
New
Object-Oriented-Programming Language Interface
Open
Operating system
Path
Place
Platform
Print/Print Options/Print Preview
Program file
Save/Save as
Shortcut
Spell Checker
Toolbar Selection
Undo/Redo
Web features
Zoom

Exercises

1. Why is it important to organize data files?
2. What are the two parts of a file name?
3. Given the content in the following five files, how would you name each file?
    a. English 1A term report
    b. spreadsheet for an Economics 1 class developed as part of Assignment #1
    c. letter to a good friend named Mary Smith
    d. personal budget
    e. course grades while you are enrolled in school

4. What would be the file type for the following extensions?
   a. .exe
   b. .bmp
   c. .avi
   d. .jpg
   e. .txt
   f. .rtf
5. What is a shortcut or an alias?
6. What is the purpose of folders?
7. How would you find a data file if you only know that the first part of the name contains History?
8. Name and explain three compatibility issues when working with computers.
9. Using one compatibility issue named in question 8, explain how to solve this problem.
10. Name and explain five common features in most computer software packages.
11. Why do you think it is important to make backup copies of your data files?

Problems

1. Using the file structure planning diagram, develop a file organization for your data files on a new storage media (floppy disk, zip cartridge, or whatever you use). These files should include school files, personal files, and work files.
2. You are using one disk for all of your schoolwork. Develop a file structure plan for this disk. Use the classes you are taking.
3. What is the file naming convention you will use for your school files?

UNIT TWO

GRAPHICS AND DESIGN

Chapter 4

Design Concepts

Overview

Typography

- **Fonts**
- **Leading**
- **Size**
- **Alignment**
- **Letter Width**
- **Font Enhancements**
- **Horizontal Spacing**
- **Font Types**
- **Serif versus Sans Serif**
- **Font Uses**

Guidelines for Well-Designed Projects

- **Guidelines for the General Layout of a Project**
- **Guidelines for Text**
- **Guidelines for Adding Graphics**
- **Guidelines for Adding Color**
- **General Guidelines**

Objectives

When you have finished this chapter, you should be able to:

1. Select fonts to enhance understanding and retention of information from a project.
2. Use color to enhance a project.
3. Design the layout of a project so that its message is not lost.
4. Design a project that is pleasing to the eye.
5. Use artwork to enhance the understanding and retention of information in a project.

Chapter 4 is one of the most important in this book. A project may be a failure due to poor design or a success due to good design. This is true when working with all types of software. In this unit the term *project* will refer to the finished product from any type of software. It is just as important to have a well-designed spreadsheet as it is to have a well-designed slide show or report. With the vast amount of fonts and artwork available on the computer, it is easy to create a project that has lost the message in the glitz, uses fonts that are inappropriate and hard to read, and loses eye appeal. This chapter will answer such questions as which font should I use for this project, what graphics should I include, where do I place the graphics, what size of font should I use, where should I use color, how do I design a project that people will use, plus many more design questions.

The first part of this chapter presents a discussion of typography, the art of using type in the creation of projects, including character enhancements. The last part of the chapter presents design guidelines for creating a well-designed project. Guidelines presented in this chapter are not as in-depth as in an advanced graphic design manual, but they do include design concepts necessary for an end user to create a well-designed project.

Typography

Computer Typography

Typography is the art of printing with type and involves the style and layout of printed material. We will limit this definition to typography as it pertains to the computer. Our modified definition of the term *computer typography* is the art of using electronic fonts and their enhancements in the layout of text on a page. New words that accompany computer typography are defined in this chapter. Many of these terms have their origin from printing technology. Some of those have been modified for the computer. These differences are discussed as the chapter progresses. Text is used in almost all software packages and therefore typography is relevant to almost all projects. Table 4.1 presents a list of typography terms and concepts discussed in this section.

Table 4.1 Typography Terminology

Term	Definition
Alignment	Where characters are aligned, including left, right, center, and justify
Bit mapped fonts	Fonts that are designed according to the pixel locations designating the design of the letters
Font enhancements	Boldface, italicize, underline, strike through, shadow, outline, emboss, engrave, subscript, and superscript
Fonts	The design of a set of characters
Horizontal scaling	The increase or decrease of the horizontal size of characters
Kerning	The adjustment of pulling one letter closer to another letter
Leading	The adding of space between lines of text
Letter width	The width of the individual letters which makes one font wider than another font
Pixelation	The ragged edges of graphics
Points	One point equals 1/72 of an inch; a measurement of font height
Scalable fonts	Fonts that are designed through the use of algorithms
Size	The height of a font
Tracking	The variance of spacing between letters
Typeface	The design of a font

Fonts

Fonts

A **font** is a set of characters with a common design. A character is a letter, a number, or a special symbol. Traditionally the term *font* involves three aspects: the design of the characters, the size of the characters, and the certain enhancements such as bold, italicized, and bold-italicized. This definition of font originates from typesetters, people who set type for printing presses before any automatic typesetting was developed. Typesetters used a set of lead cast characters, a font, for each design and size. Therefore, a font would have a name such as Times, a size such as 12 points (**size** is measured in points and is defined as 1 point equals 1/72 of an inch), and an enhancement such as bold. We will discuss point size later in this chapter.

Bit Mapped Font

When fonts were first transferred to the computer, the definition did not change. The fonts were set up as an electronic version of the lead cast characters. Each character was defined as a set of dots, called pixels, on the screen. These fonts are called **bit mapped fonts.** See Figure 4.1 for an example of the bit mapped character uppercase *A*. In the past when you purchased a font, it was of a specific design, size, and enhancement. Vendors once advertised 240 fonts for seeming very little money. However, if there were 10 sizes and four enhancements, you really received only six different character designs since there were 40 fonts for each one. If you wanted another size, you were out of luck because bit mapped fonts do not scale to other sizes without some pixelation. **Pixelation** is the ragged effect visible on some graphics and fonts when scaled. The fact that one typeset design required so much memory limited the number of character designs for use on the computer. An additional problem was in printing. The computer's printer required knowledge of each font in its memory. If the font was not in the printer memory, then the printer would revert to the default font which probably was less than satisfactory.

Pixelation

Scalable Fonts

Since there were so many problems with traditional fonts, scalable fonts were created. A **scalable font** has a set of instructions, called an algorithm, for the creation of each character. These instructions include parameters for the changing of the size and the basic enhancements. The instructions take up more room in memory than one of the traditional fonts, but, since each character is scalable, there is only a single font set for each character design instead of 40. This new capability changed the definition of fonts as we knew it. Now, when 50 fonts are advertised, you get 50 different type designs. When you purchase scalable fonts, one font is defined as one character design with multiple sizes and enhancements. Scalable fonts are most common today. When fonts are used in an application, however, the end user designates the font design, size, and enhancements separately.

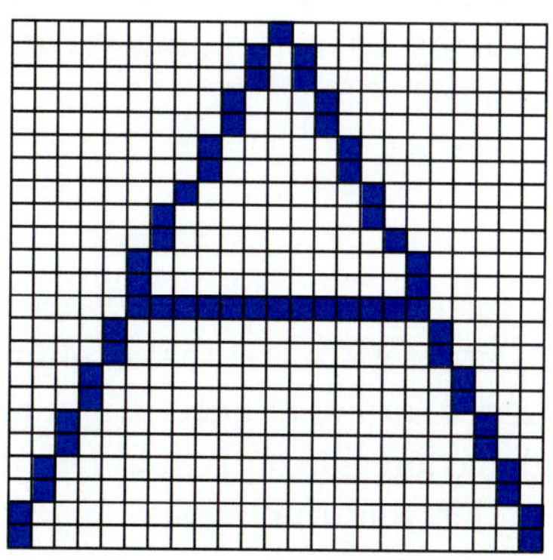

Figure 4.1 Bit Mapped Font

TRIVIA

Why do we call the capital letters, "uppercase," and the small letters, "lowercase"?

When typesetters used individual characters to create a page of type (set the type in the proper place), the characters were in large wooden trays called cases, with a section for each character. The capital letters were in a different case from the small letters. These cases were set on a stand one above the other. The capital letters were in the "upper case" and the small letters were in the "lower case," hence **uppercase letters** and **lowercase letters** today.

Typeface

Most application software uses common terminology when referring to fonts. This terminology is defined before a discussion of design can take place. **Typeface** is the basic design of the font character set. The typeface is given a name that becomes the name of the font, such as Arial or Times New Roman. The typeface is recognizable even if it has been modified through enhancements such as boldface or italicize.

Leading

Leading

Leading is extra space that is added between lines. The term *leading* originated from the extra pieces of narrow lead spacers that were used by typesetters to add extra space between the lines of type. To increase the amount of space between lines or paragraphs, you increase the leading. You may also decrease the amount of space by decreasing the leading. When the leading is decreased enough, the bottom of one character line will be placed on top of the line directly beneath. If you decrease the leading too much, the lines will be printed on top of each other.

Size

Size

Points

The **size** of a font is the vertical height of the characters, not the horizontal width. This fact is sometimes confusing because the actual height of the same character in two different fonts may be different. Again, this terminology dates back to the printing technology before computers. The size actually referred to the height size of the metal blocks on which the characters were created. In electronic terms, the size is measured from the top of the tallest letter of the font in one line to the top of the tallest letter of the font in the next line, without leading. See Figure 4.2. The size is normally measured in either *points* or *picas.* There are a few applications where you may use inches. A point is 1/72 of an inch. A pica is equal to 12 points. Therefore, 6 picas equal 1 inch and 72 points equal 1 inch. Normal reading text is usually 10 or 12 points. Sizes vary from 6 points to over 100 points in most software packages.

Alignment

Alignment

Alignment of text, sometimes called justification, refers to where the text is aligned on the page. See Figure 4.3. Left alignment refers to text that is aligned on the left margin. The right side of the line of text is ragged, or not aligned. Right alignment refers to text that is aligned on the right margin with the left side ragged. Center alignment refers to text that is aligned in the center with both left and right sides ragged. Justified, sometimes called full justification or justification alignment, refers to text aligned on both the left and

Size:

24 Pts.

Font Size
Font Size

Figure 4.2 Font Size. This font size is 24 points.

This is an example of Left Alignment.

This is an example of Right Alignment.

This is an example of Center Alignment

This is an example of justify alignment of text in a project.

Notice the extra white space.

Figure 4.3 Alignment Examples

right margins. Traditionally, text used justified alignment. Today, however, the trend is toward left justification because of the decrease in white space in a line. Most people think that left justification is more aesthetically pleasing to the eye and is easier to read. Formal presentation of text—for example, in a book—still uses justified alignment.

Letter Width

Letter Width

Letter width varies from font to font. See Figure 4.4. Notice the differences between the width of the letters and the height of the letters. All fonts are specified at a size of 12 points. Notice that the Comic Sans MS font uses more leading in its design. The amount of space on a page that text requires depends on many things, one of which is the font chosen. If your professor asks for a five-page report and yours only fits on four pages, you may be able to find a wider font that will expand the text to five pages. Or if your report is six pages long, you may find a font that is narrower and end up with five pages. This process will be discussed further in Chapter 6.

This is an example of Times New Roman font.
This is the second line of Times New Roman font.
This is an example of Ariel font.
This is the second line of Ariel font.
THIS IS AN EXAMPLE OF COMIC SANS MS FONT.
THIS IS THE SECOND LINE OF COMIC SANS MS FONT.

Figure 4.4 Example of Font Widths with Size of 12 Points

Font Enhancements

Font Enhancements

There are many font **enhancements** available to use. See Figure 4.5. These include but are not limited to boldface, italicize, underline, strike through, shadow, outline, emboss, engrave, subscript, and superscript. **Boldface** widens the lines in the text characters to make the text darker. **Italicize** slants the text to the right. **Underline** draws a rule (a line) under the text. These features are used to emphasize text. **Strike through** draws a rule through the center of the text, which normally indicates that text is or will be deleted. **Shadow** draws a copy of the character in another color to one or more sides—usually to the right and down, as if the character were casting a shadow. The copy is drawn to the opposite side of the light source. **Outline** draws the character with only the outside of the lines showing. The inside is either transparent or of another color. **Emboss** gives the character a three-dimensional appearance, as if the character is being pressed outward from the paper. **Engrave** is basically the same as emboss, with the exception that the character looks as if it is being pressed inward on the paper.

These enhancements are normally not used for the text of the body of a project as they make the text harder to read. **Subscript** places the reduced-size character lower than the normal text and **superscript** places the reduced-size character higher than the normal text. These are used for reference characters, mathematical equations, and other special applications.

Horizontal Spacing

Kerning, Tracking, and Horizontal Scaling

Kerning, tracking, and horizontal scaling are similar in that they vary the horizontal spacing or size of characters. **Kerning** is normally used with bit mapped fonts and refers to the bringing of one letter closer to another letter by using the white space within one letter to place another letter, such as the letters *TA*. Kerning will place the *A* closer to the *T* so that the *A* is actually taking up part of the space of the *T*. **Tracking** will bring all letters closer or farther apart by increasing or decreasing the normal space between the characters. See Figure 4.6. **Horizontal scaling** modifies the size of all characters hori-

Boldface	~~Strike Through~~	Engrave
Italicized	Shadow	Subscript $_{\text{Subscript}}$
Underlined	Emboss	Superscript ^{Superscript}

Figure 4.5 Character Enhancements

This is an example of Tracking:
Normal Tracking
Very Loose Tracking
Very Tight Tracking

This is an example of Horizontal Scaling:
100% Scaling example (Normal)
80% Scaling example
120% Scaling example

Figure 4.6 Examples of Tracking and Horizontal Scaling

zontally without increasing the point size. Kerning, tracking, and horizontal scaling are used to fill a column or a page or increase the aesthetics of a page, for example.

Fonts Types

Text Fonts, Display Fonts

There are hundreds of fonts available to use. Fonts have two basic uses: text that is in paragraph form, called *body text,* and text that is used for display such as headings, subheadings, advertisements, and titles. We will call these two categories of fonts **text fonts** and **display fonts.** Text fonts may be used as display fonts; however, for the most part, display fonts should not be used as text fonts because of readability problems when the display font size is too small. See Figure 4.7 for some common fonts.

Serif versus Sans Serif

Serif and Sans Serif Fonts

Fonts are categorized into **serif fonts** and **sans serif fonts.** The serif fonts have extra projections at the top and bottom of the letters, whereas sans serif fonts do not. Refer again to Figure 4.7. Are you able to identify the serif fonts and the sans serif fonts? Times New Roman is a serif font. Note that the bottoms and tops of the letters have extra lines. Arial is a sans serif font. Notice there are no extra projections on the letters. Most serif fonts are classified as traditional fonts. The serif was first used to finish characters when engraving in stone. The chisels that craftmen used left the ends of the lines jagged and therefore the added serif finished the character. Sans serif fonts are classified as modern or transitional fonts and are used as display fonts and informal text fonts.

Font Uses

Symbol Fonts

Font Uses

Symbol fonts have no letters or numbers. These are sometimes called PI fonts. They are entirely made up of special symbols. You may want to use symbol fonts for bullets, mathematical symbols, and so forth. They have very specialized use.

Because of the large number of different type designs available to the user, the choice of which one to use in a given situation is sometimes a problem. You will find that most fonts are attractive, fun, and look great in a given situation; however, some of your favorite fonts may not be appropriate for the function of the project. The inappropriate use of some fonts may detract from the readability of the project and therefore its message. Investigate the fonts on your computer and categorize them into text fonts and display fonts. Which would you use in formal projects? Which would you use in informal projects? Which would you use in a serious project? Which would you use in a fun proj-

This is an example of Times New Roman.
This is an example of Arial.
This is an example of Bookman Old Style.
This is an example of Century Schoolbook.
THIS IS AN EXAMPLE OF COMIC SANS MS.
This is an example of Courier New.
This is an example of Helvetica.
This is an example of Impact.
This is an example of Lucida Handwriting.

Figure 4.7 Examples of Some Common Fonts

ect? Many software packages do not show how each font looks. It is helpful to make a chart as shown in Figure 4.7 with the fonts on your computer. This resource will help you to remember how each font appears in hard copy. In the following section of this chapter you will find guidelines for font usage.

Guidelines for Well-Designed Projects

The design guidelines presented here should increase the aesthetics of your project, increase the communication and retention of the message presented in the project, and hopefully decrease your frustrations in project planning. They are guidelines only. Any of these guidelines may be changed if you have special reasons. Table 4.2 shows a list of the following guidelines.

Guidelines for the General Layout of a Project

Layout Guidelines

The **layout** of a project is the placement of project elements on the page. The elements include such items as the text, page guidelines, artwork, color, white space, lines, and so forth. A well-designed project—whether it is a report, a letter, a spreadsheet, an advertising flyer, a business card, or a user interface on the computer—should be a carefully planned combination of project elements. The following guidelines are for the general layout of a project.

1. *Do not lose sight of the message* that your project is intended to communicate. Try to enhance the message.
2. *Be creative.* Layouts should not be the same all the time. Try something new and different.
3. *Align the elements of your project: the text, graphics, lines, and so on.* If you want to misalign the elements, be sure the misalignment is obvious. See Figure 4.8. Which one looks better?
4. *Plan where you want the eye to start on the page.* When the reader's eye is attracted to the upper left-hand corner, it will follow a Z pattern while scanning the page; however, the eye tends to go to the upper right-hand corner or to the middle of a blank page. Take a blank piece of paper, close your eyes, open them, and then take note of where your eyes immediately focus. Find out from others where their eyes focus on a page. Most people's eyes are either attracted to the upper right-hand corner of the page or to the left-hand side of the bottom of the middle section. Therefore, you should add something to the layout of the page that makes the eye travel to the place on the page that you want the viewer to start. This may be artwork, borders, or lines.
5. *Keep your project layout simple.* Simple does not mean boring. A simple, well-designed project can communicate the message very well. A general guideline is to limit the number of font designs to two and the number of font sizes to four. The number of colors and artwork used on a project should enhance the message. Too many colors and too many graphics may decrease the communication of the message. It is easy to get caught up in the volumes of fonts, artwork, and colors while designing a project such that the end result becomes cluttered, unattractive, and loses the message to be communicated.
6. *Unify the design of your layout.* The elements of your design must work together. Try to unify the elements by being consistent with fonts and borders,

Table 4.2 Guidelines for a Well-Designed Project

Guidelines for the General Layout of a Project
1. Don't lose sight of the message. 2. Be creative. 3. Align the elements of your project: the text, graphics, lines, and so on. 4. Plan where you want the eye to start on the page. 5. Keep your project layout simple. 6. Unify the design of your layout. 7. Use white space: *Don't crowd your elements.* 8. Use rules or lines sparingly. 9. Use borders to unify and separate. 10. Align columns. 11. Keep the most important elements foremost in your mind and on paper.
Guidelines for Text
1. Limit the number of typeface designs. 2. Base your selection of fonts on the character of the project. 3. Choose serif fonts vs. sans serif fonts. 4. Treat margins as frames for your text. 5. Use font sizes for text to be used in columns that will print 1.25 to 2.5 lowercase alphabets on one line. 6. Do not use ragged-left or center alignments for body text. 7. Always hyphenate justified text.
Guidelines for Adding Graphics
1. Art should serve a purpose. 2. Aim artwork toward the intended direction of eye flow. 3. Use artwork that is appropriate for the purpose of the project.
Guidelines for Adding Color
1. Coordinate the colors to be used on the project. 2. Limit the number of colors. 3. Use gray tones if the project is to be inexpensively duplicated.
General Guidelines
1. Learn when to stop tweaking. 2. Be consistent, but aim for variety. 3. Ask for advice. 4. Don't be afraid to try something new and different.
Guidelines for Interface Design
1. Decrease file size of the objects on your web page. 2. Focus on consistency in navigation. 3. Think about your audience.

and consistent with color combinations, lines, and so on. The message is communicated better if the elements are united.

7. *Use white space: Do not crowd your elements.* **White space** is the negative space, the space where there is nothing displayed. This space may be blue, green, pink, or any other color but it is still called white space. It is not the left-over space of page design. White space is just as important an element as the text or artwork. There should be enough white space to give the other elements

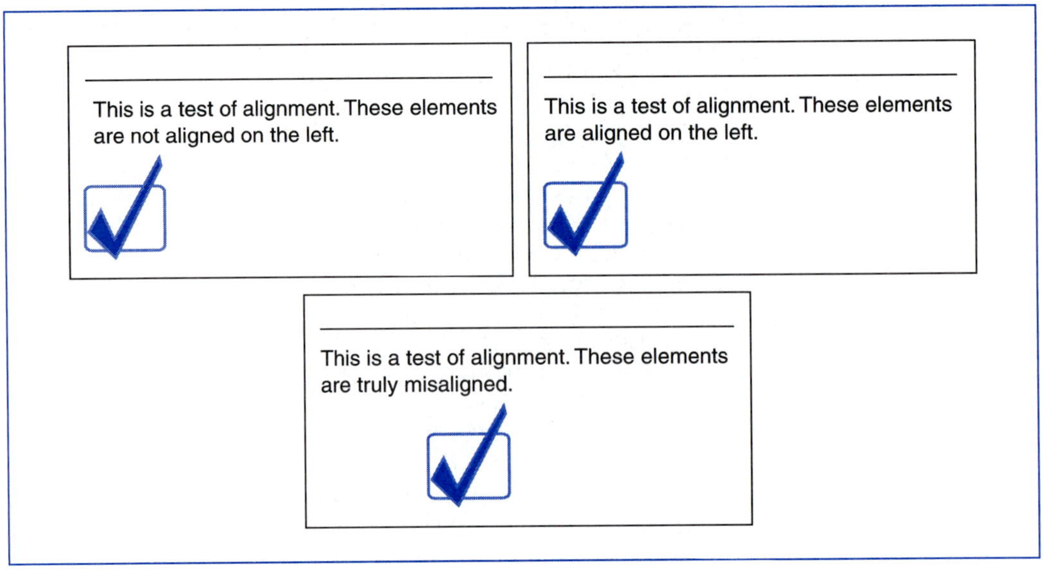

Figure 4.8 Alignment of Elements

"breathing room," but not so much that areas look empty. Then readers will think that something is missing. When you plan your page layout, take time to incorporate the white space among all of the other elements.

8. *Use rules or lines sparingly.* Rules and lines can add relief to plain pages or they can support other elements of the page. Use a line width that provides unity on the page and does not overwhelm the design. Lines should be unobtrusive and add elegance to the project.
9. *Use borders to unify and separate.* Borders isolate the contained elements. You should use them to focus on an element; separate text or art; give finishing touches to figures, tables, and artwork; and emphasize parts of the message. Do not overdo the boxes. Too many boxes give a cluttered look to the project. Try to avoid clutter.
10. *Use columns.* When using columns on a page, always align the bottoms of the columns on same page and on adjacent pages. Added artwork is best to use to align or misalign columns at the top and bottom. You also may add a small amount of leading to complete the alignment. Too much leading will give the columns a look of misalignment.
11. *Keep the most important elements foremost in your mind and on paper.* Establish a "hook" to entice the reader to read the project. Decide which elements have to be there and which could be eliminated. When the project becomes cluttered, eliminate the less important elements.

Guidelines for Text

Text Guidelines

Text is one of the most important elements of a project. People expect to have some text on most projects. The use of appropriate fonts, sizes, and enhancements is very important to the communication of the message. The following are some guidelines for the use of text.

1. *Limit the number of typeface designs.* Too many typeface designs tend to give a cluttered appearance to the project, so try to limit the number to two. When deciding on the typeface designs or fonts, be sure they have a unity to them. For example, do not mix serif fonts with sans serif fonts unless there is good reason.
2. *Base your selection of fonts on the character of the project.* Think about such things as function, formality, the reader, and the message of the project; and match the available fonts to achieve the look you desire for the project.
3. *Choose serif fonts versus sans serif fonts.* Serif fonts are normally used for formal, long body text because the serifs help the eye connect one character to the next and eliminate some white space between characters. This provides for easier reading. Sans serif fonts are normally used for headlines, display text, small sizes, and modern informal style, long body text.
4. *Treat margins as frames for your text.* Margins are the frames for your text. They provide the white space needed to emphasize your text on the page.
5. *Use font sizes for text to be used in columns that will print 1.25 to 2.5 lowercase alphabets on one line.* Any more or less characters makes the text hard to read. Using a large font in a column creates too much white space and not enough text per line. Too small a font size creates insufficient white space and thus too much text per line for easy readability in columns. Remember that columns add extra elements to a page.
6. *Do not use ragged-left or center alignments for body text.* People are not accustomed to anything but left-aligned copy for long body text.
7. *Hyphenate justified text.* Eliminate as much of the white space as possible in justified text. Hyphenation will help with this. Study the software package you are using to determine how hyphenation is accomplished. Some software packages do not do a good job of hyphenation.

Guidelines for Adding Graphics

Artwork Guidelines

Use of artwork in your project can increase the communication and retention of the message, but it needs to be appropriate, limited, and well placed. Artwork can be in the form of scanned images (**photo art**), **clipart,** or computer-drawn art. When using scanned images and clipart, be sure to check the copyrights. Chapter 5 discusses copyright issues. Many clipart and photo packages are not royalty free. Preapproved image usage will be printed on the package. Scanned images from magazines and other sources including the internet are usually copyrighted. To use these images you must get permission from the owner of the image.

Artwork is important to add to the text of a project. If used correctly, it should almost double the reader's retention rate of the material. The following guidelines are for the addition of artwork to a project.

1. *Art should serve a purpose.* Justifying why a graphic element is added to a project helps to make appropriate artwork choices to enhance the message of the project.
2. *Aim artwork toward the intended direction of eye flow.* Most artwork faces or points a specific direction. This may help the reader's eye flow to the information on the page or it may direct the eye off the page. See Figure 4.9. Which example is easier to read? Which one helps the eye to stay on the page? Most times correct placement of artwork can increase communication and retention of the information with very little effort.

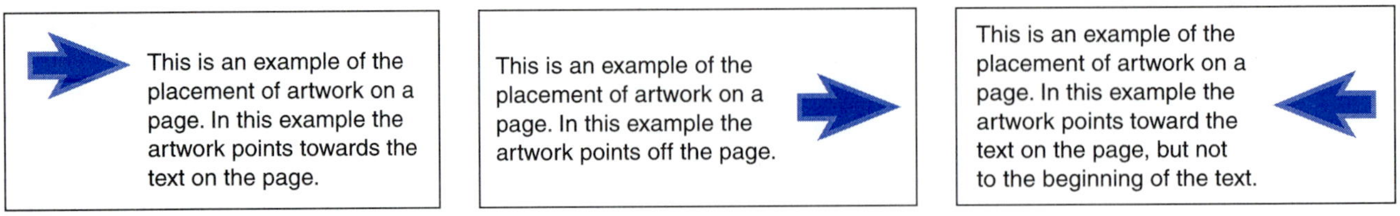

Figure 4.9 Artwork Placement

3. *Use artwork that is appropriate for the purpose of the project.* It is better to use no artwork than inappropriate artwork. For example, you would not use a picture of a football player to advertise a tennis match or a picture of penguins at the South Pole to advertise a trip to the tropics.

Guidelines for Adding Color

Color Guidelines

Color is used to enhance the message and add to the aesthetics of your project. Using too much color, too many colors, or colors that do not blend, however, may detract from the message. The following are some guidelines for the use of color in a project.

1. *Coordinate the colors to be used on the project.* Use colors that blend with each other. For example, red on blue or blue on red is hard to read because the eye has a difficult time perceiving both colors at the same time. Use colors that enhance the function of the project.
2. *Limit the number of colors.* You have 16 million different color choices on the computer, but avoid using them all in one project. Use only the number of colors that will enhance the project, typically four or five coordinated colors. Ask yourself why color would be important in this place. For example, do not make each character in a word a different color unless you have a good reason, such as with the word *rainbow.*
3. *Use gray tones if the project is to be inexpensively duplicated.* If the project will be duplicated in black and white, then create it in gray tones. Because some colors do not duplicate well, it is better not to use color. Since there are 16 million shades of gray, many people prefer to use just gray tones instead of color, even if they have the option to use color to create a project. You can do some great things using gray tones.

General Guidelines

General Guidelines

Following are some general guidelines to use when creating your projects.

1. *Learn when to stop tweaking.* There is always one more change you can make to a project. You need to know when to say, "This is it, no more changes."
2. *Be consistent, but aim for variety.* Consistency is an important design concept. For example, in a slide show, use the same background and the same fonts in most of the slides. In a report, use the same font for the body text, the same one for headlines, the same one for captions, and the same number of columns for all pages. In so doing, however, avoid creating boring projects: Add vari-

ety in the form of artwork, placement of the artwork, placement of text, by making a different first page or first slide, and in the selection of colors.

3. *Ask for advice.* Do not hesitate to ask for someone's opinion of the project. Listen to the advice and follow it, if you desire.
4. *Do not be afraid to try something new and different.* Be creative. Try right justification on letterheads, mastheads on newsletters, and on flyers. Experiment to see what looks good. Remember when you are planning a project, it is only the starting place. You can make modifications at any time on the computer.

Web Page Guidelines

Guidelines for interface design are included in Chapter 19. These guidelines will help you design Web pages. Good interface design is important to the success of a Web page. In addition to the above guidelines and those in Chapter 19, other things to consider in web page design include the following:

1. *Decrease file size of the objects on your web page.* These objects should be as small as possible because of the download time. You can include some wonderful graphics or animations, but if they take too long to download then the user may not want to wait.
2. *Focus on consistency in navigation.* Include a control panel on all pages in the same place on every page and with the same buttons. Include buttons that go to the home page, to the previous page, and to the next page. The navigation should be user friendly.
3. *Think about your audience.* Design your Web page around the computers that your audience might have. If they are low-end, slow computers, then you do not want to have a Web page that takes a long time to download to their computers. If you can assume your audience will have high-end, fast computers with fast internet connections, then you can add wonderful animations, sound, and video to your Web page.

These guidelines are developed to help you create a well-designed project. They are guidelines, not rules. Guidelines may be broken when there is good reason. Trust your eye and your friend's eye as to what looks the best.

Summary

Computer typography is the art of using electronic fonts and their enhancements in the layout of text on a page. A font is a set of characters with a common design. The size of a font is measured from the top of one line to the top of the next line of type. Size is usually measured in points. One point equals 1/72 of an inch. Leading is extra space between lines. Alignment of text refers to where the text is aligned on a page: left side, right side, center, or both right and left, called justified. There are many character enhancements found on the computer including boldface, italics, underline, shadow, emboss, engrave, strike through, subscripts, and superscripts. Tracking and horizontal scaling increase the amount of horizontal spacing and the horizontal size of the characters. There are many categories of fonts including text fonts and display fonts, serif and sans serif fonts, and symbol fonts.

It is important to follow guidelines to create a well-designed project. The categories of guidelines presented in this chapter include those for layouts, text use, adding artwork, adding color, Web page design, and general guidelines.

Key Words

- Alignment
- Bit mapped fonts
- Clipart
- Display fonts
- Enhancements
  - Boldface
  - Emboss
  - Engrave
  - Italics
  - Outline
  - Shadow
  - Strike through
  - Subscript
  - Superscript
  - Underline
- Font
- Horizontal scaling
- Kerning
- Layout
- Leading
- Letter width
- Lowercase letters
- Photo art
- Pixelation
- Sans serif fonts
- Scalable fonts
- Serif fonts
- Size
- Symbol fonts
- Text fonts
- Tracking
- Typography
- Typeface
- Uppercase letters
- White space

Exercises

1. Define typography.
2. What is a font?
3. How is the size of a font determined?
4. Define a point.
5. What is the size in inches of the following point sizes:
   a. 10 points
   b. 12 points
   c. 18 points
   d. 48 points
   e. 72 points
6. What is a scalable font?
7. Why is a scalable font preferred?
8. Define leading, and tracking.
9. Name and explain the nine character enhancements defined in this chapter. In your explanation, name a possible use for each enhancement.
10. What is the difference between a serif font and a sans serif font?
11. Pick four guidelines and explain how they will help you create a well-designed project.

Problems

1. Make a project that contains examples of all the fonts on your computer.
2. Select an advertising flyer and evaluate the design of the flyer in terms of the design guidelines found in this chapter.
3. Select a business card and evaluate the design of the business card in terms of the design guidelines found in this chapter.
4. Select a brochure and evaluate the design of the brochure in terms of the design guidelines found in this chapter.

Chapter 5

Graphics Concepts and Tools

Overview

File Management
Copyright Issues
Clipart and Photo Clips
Paint and Draw Software
Scanned Graphics
Digital Photography
Graphics Tools
- **Pointer Tool**
- **Line and Shape Tools**
- **Fill Tool**
- **Group and Ungroup**
- **Selection Tool in a Paint Software Package**
- **Eraser Tool**
- **Painting Tools**
- **Eye Dropper Tool**
- **Character Tools**
- **Stacking and Layering**
- **Manipulating Graphics**
- **Distributing and Aligning**
- **Sizing versus Cropping**

Graphics Use

Objectives

When you have finished this chapter, you should be able to:

1. Develop good file organization for your graphic files.
2. Choose graphics with copyright issues in mind.
3. Understand the difference between paint and draw graphics software.
4. Choose appropriate software from multiple sources including clipart, scanned graphics, photo clips, digital photography, and computer art.
5. Understand the use of various graphics tools and techniques including the pointer tool, line and shape tools, fill tool, group and ungroup, selecting

graphics, painting tools, character tools, stacking graphics, layering graphics, manipulating graphics, distributing and aligning graphics, sizing graphics, and cropping graphics.

Retention of information is increased by as much as 100% through the addition of appropriate graphics to text. Graphics add interest to a project and provide graphical representation to the printed word. When computers were first developed, it was difficult to incorporate graphics into projects due to the lack of graphic capabilities, memory limitations, and computer speed limitations. Today, however, new technologies in software and hardware allow ways to include graphics. Graphic design is an important consideration when planning a project. Remember, even though use of graphics increases the retention rate, the text is still the most important element of the project, because text communicates the most information. Graphics should always enhance the text, not overwhelm it.

Graphics include artwork, lines, borders, frames, and other elements that are not considered text. Graphics originate from a variety of sources including clipart, computer-drawn art, scanned art, photo clips, digital photos, and the internet. You do not have to know how to draw to include graphics in your projects.

File Management

Graphic File Organization

Good file management is important for the efficient use of graphics. By organizing graphics files into categories, it is easier to find the perfect graphics for a project, and it saves considerable time. You may end up with hundreds if not thousands of graphics files. These may be on any storage device such as your hard drive, a CD-ROM, or a zip cartridge.

When you purchase new graphics, take time to sort through them, select your favorites, and then copy the graphics to an appropriate category folder on a specific storage device. Plan the categories you would like to use and make a folder for each category, for example, holidays, with subcategories such as Valentine's Day, Fourth of July, and Thanksgiving. Other categories may include Months, Office, School, Home, Vacation, and Seasons. Include the categories that you would use most; they should be individualized to fit your taste. Next, copy each file into the appropriate category folder or subfolder. You may not want to include all files. There may be clipart or photo clip files that you do not like or know you will never use. Leave these on the original disk. You can always go back and retrieve them. As you are copying the graphics files, change any names that do not indicate what those files depict. Copy only the files that you like and will use. If one graphic fits into more than one category, copy it into all related folders. If there are too many graphics files in one folder, subcategorize them into folders within the main category folder. You may want to separate the file types such as bit mapped, TIFF, and so forth. Organization may take a little time; however, it is time well spent.

Copyright Issues

Copyrights

Copyright infringement is an issue in graphics. Try to determine whether the graphic you are planning to use is copyrighted. If it is, you must obtain a release to use it unless its use is permitted under the **fair use policy. Copyright** is the right of the owner to control the following:

1. *Right to reproduce:* You may not reproduce the copyrighted work in hard copy or soft copy without the written consent of the owner.
2. *Right to modification:* You may not modify the copyrighted work in any way without the written consent of the owner.
3. *Right to distribute:* You may not distribute copies of the copyrighted work to the public by sale; by transfer of ownership; by rental, lease, or lending without the consent of the owner.
4. *Right to perform:* You may not perform the copyrighted work publicly. In the case of literary, musical, dramatic, and choreographic works, pantomimes, and motion pictures and other audiovisual works, you may not perform the copyrighted material without the consent of the owner. In the case of sound recordings, you may not use sound recordings to perform the copyrighted work publicly through the use of any type of audio transmission.
5. *Right to display the copyrighted work publicly:* You may not display the copyrighted work publicly in the case of literary, musical, dramatic, and choreographic works, pantomimes, and pictorial, graphic, or sculptural works, including the individual images of a motion picture or other audiovisual work, without the consent of the owner.

Fair Use Policy of Copyrighted Work

There is a loophole for some users in the fair use policy, which states that you may use a small portion of the copyrighted work under the following circumstances:

1. *Use of the copy.* The copy must be used for noncommercial educational, study, or research use.
2. *Nature of the copyrighted work.* The less artistic the copy is, the more copying is allowed.
3. *The amount copied.* Only a small percentage of the work may be used.
4. *Economics.* Use of the copyrighted work may not significantly impact the potential market value of the original copyrighted work.

If you use copyrighted work under any other circumstances, then you must have a copyright release.

You may purchase your graphics files, download them from the internet, copy them from a friend, or obtain them from within a software package. Wherever you obtain your graphics, you should determine their copyright restrictions. Before you purchase any graphics, determine usability in terms of copyright infringement. Information is usually provided on the label and in the licensing agreement about copyright terms. Graphics may be royalty free; they may be royalty free for nonprofit projects; or you may have to pay royalties on them. Sometimes inexpensive graphics are not so inexpensive in the long run if you have to pay royalties on their use.

Clipart and Photo Clips

Clipart and Photo Clips

Clipart is available with some software or may be purchased on CD-ROMs. See Figure 5.1 for examples of clipart. **Clipart** is predrawn artwork that is usually small in memory size and oftentimes small in physical size. Clipart comes in black and white or in color. Many times the same clipart will come in both color and black-and-white images. Most clipart collections contain a large number of files. You should take the time to sort these files into your graphics folders.

Figure 5.1 Examples of Clipart

Photo clips are purchased, electronic photographs usually on a CD-ROM, and usually consist of some very nice photos. Be sure to investigate the copyright agreement before you purchase either clipart or photo clips. You may have to pay royalties.

The internet is a great and easy way to obtain clipart and photo clips, but again, there is the problem of copyrights. Be sure the artwork you have downloaded is copyright free. Accompanying information should state whether the artwork is copyright free or royalty free.

Paint and Draw Software

Computer-drawn art may vary from lines and shapes to beautiful pictures created with the use of computer software programs. Lines and shapes are used for borders, text frames, arrows, tables, and so on. These take little time to generate and are easy to use. Creating beautiful pictures on the computer, however, takes time and talent. It takes as much time to create a beautiful drawing on the computer as it would on canvas. Just as most people require the talent and training to create an artistically drawn picture on canvas, they should have the same talent and training to create one on the computer. In a sense, the computer is another art medium.

Paint and Draw Software

The two basic types of graphics software used to create pictures are a draw package and a paint package. It is important to know the difference between these two packages in order to understand their uses. **Draw software** works with groups of pixels (screen dots); **paint software** works with individual pixels.

Vector Graphics

Draw-type software is called **vector graphics** because each group of pixels is drawn by executing a set of drawing commands in a vectorlike manner using lines, circles, arcs, and directions. When you use a draw package to render a rectangle, the software will treat the rectangle as a group of pixels called an object. You may move the object individually, put other objects on top of it and still move each object separately, and change the color of the lines and the fill color. You may not color each side of the rectangle a different color, however, because all sides are treated as one group.

Bit Mapped Graphics

When you use a paint package to draw a rectangle, the software will treat the rectangle as individual pixels. Paint-type software is called **bit mapped graphics** because the software addresses or keeps track of each pixel in a picture. You may erase part of the rectangle, color every pixel a different color, and paint other shapes over the top. However, you may not move the rectangle individually, recolor the lines except pixel by pixel, or fill the entire rectangle if other shapes are on top of it.

Think about a draw package as you would a bulletin board. You can build a picture of a house from various shapes. You can put in a fence and flowers in front of the house with other shapes. You still can move the house without moving the fence and the flowers by moving each individual shape in the house. A paint package, on the other hand, is more like painting on a canvas. Once you have painted the house, fence, and flowers, you cannot move the house without moving the fence and flowers with it.

Scanned Graphics

Scanned Graphics

Scanned graphics are printed artwork transferred into an electronic format. The process creates a bit mapped image of the picture by dividing it into dots according to the resolution directions you give to the scanner such as 300 **dots per inch (dpi).** The **resolution** on a computer refers to the number of pixels or dots per inch. The higher the resolution, the better the graphics will be defined. Scanned art can produce very large files. If you have a 5 × 8 inch picture to scan into the computer at 300 dpi, you will have a file that is 5 inches times 300 dots on one side and 8 inches times 300 dots on the other side, for a total area of 3.6 million dots. If the picture is in color you may have as many as three computer bytes per dot for the color and therefore your file will be 10.8 megabytes (million bytes). If the file is too large, try lowering the dpi until just before a noticeable difference in the image takes place. You want to keep your files as small as possible. A good rule of thumb on dots per inch is 100 dpi for electronic computer screen image use and 300 to 600 for good hard copy printing use. If you are using your scanned artwork for the computer screen only, remember that your screen is probably only 96 dpi. There is no need to use graphics that have a higher resolution since the graphic cannot be defined any better than the maximum resolution of the monitor.

Digital Photography

Digital Photography

Digital photography involves using a digital camera to take photos. These photos are royalty free for your own use because you own the copyrights. Digital cameras produce electronic photos that are later downloaded into your computer. This is a great way to obtain pictures of the employee of the month, a reunion, a picnic, or people working. If you are taking pictures of people, make sure you have permission to use their pictures. Again this is a copyright issue, and therefore you may need model releases. If you are taking photos of objects or places that include copyrighted artwork, logos, or signs, make sure you have a copyright release from the owners of these items.

Graphics Tools

Most software packages come equipped with **graphics tools.** These tools allow you to import, draw, and modify graphics. They are similar in every graphics package. Following are common tools found within most paint and/or draw packages or draw/paint features within other types of software. Table 5.1 lists the graphics tools described below.

Pointer Tool

Pointer Tool

The **pointer tool** allows you to select objects in a draw package. You will not find the pointer tool in paint packages. To select an object, aim the pointer tool at the object and click the mouse button. Eight small squares, called handles, will appear on the perimeter of the object, indicating that it has been selected. The pointer tool must be selected in order to use other operations in a draw type of software package such as moving, sizing, and coloring. The cursor usually looks like an arrow when this tool is selected.

Line and Shape Tools

Line and Shape Tools

Line and shape tools are sometimes called rubber band tools. These tools are found in both draw and paint packages. To create a line or a shape, designate one end or one corner of the desired object by pressing down on the mouse button and then dragging the cursor to the other end or opposite corner before releasing the mouse button. You may draw lines, arrows, ellipses, rectangles, polygons, plus many more shapes and lines. You

Table 5.1 Graphics Tools

Tool	Description
Align	Aligns the centers, tops, bottoms, right side, or left side of selected objects.
Character tools	Selects tools to enhance, color, and twist characters.
Cropping graphics	Selects a portion of a graphic to use.
Distribute	Places objects evenly in either a vertical or horizontal direction on a page.
Eraser	Eliminates color in a paint package.
Eye dropper	Selects a specified color on a graphic.
Fill	Places a color within a specified area.
Group	Makes multiple objects into one object.
Layering graphics	Allows the user to work on sections of graphics as if on multiple transparencies.
Line and shape tools	Rubber band tools include lines, rectangles, ellipses, and polygons.
Painting tools	Shows pencils and brushes available in a paint package.
Pointer	The selection tool in a draw package.
Select	Used in a paint package, selects parts of the image.
Sizing graphics	Changes the width and/or height of an image.
Stacking graphics	Puts one object on top of another object.
Ungroup	Makes multiple objects out of one object.

may create right polygons such as circles and squares by pressing the shift key while dragging the cursor.

You may designate the color of the lines and the color of the fill, but the method differs depending on whether you are using a draw or a paint package. If using a draw package, you may change the color of these before or after you draw the shape or line. If using a paint package, you must specify the color before you draw the line or shape.

Fill Tool

Fill Tool

The **fill** tool allows you to specify or change the content of the center of a shape. Depending on the graphics software, you may choose from as many as 16 million different colors, gradient colors, textures, patterns, and pictures. When working in a paint package, you may fill a contained area. If the contained area has an opening in the edge, the color may fill up the whole page. Just like a bucket of water with a hole in it, the water leaks out. It is best to save before you fill when using a paint type of package. Of course, you may use the undo feature if needed. The fill tool is available in a paint package. In a draw package, you can change the fill color of a shape by selecting the object and then selecting the fill color. In a draw package you can fill the entire shape even if another shape is on top of the one you are filling.

Group and Ungroup

Group and Ungroup

The options to group, ungroup, and regroup objects are available only in draw packages. They allow you to change multiple objects into one object or one object back into multiple objects if the object had been grouped before. The **group** option is like gluing the parts of the house together such as in the previous bulletin board example. After grouping parts together, they will act as one object similar to the glued house. To make them separate objects, simply ungroup them. The **ungroup** option is like ungluing the pieces of the house. It often takes a lot of time to put objects in just the right place, so you do not want to change the positioning when you move the objects together or leave an object behind as you move them. Therefore, you would group the objects before you move them. To group objects, first select all of the objects in either of two ways. One, press the shift key while you click on each of the objects; or two, use the marquis feature. Using the pointer tool, press the mouse button and drag around all of the objects you wish to select. You will see a dotted rectangle appear. When you release the mouse button, the dotted line will disappear and everything that was completely within the dotted rectangle will be selected. Make sure that the rectangle surrounds all objects that need to be selected. If any part of any object lies outside the rectangle, then it will not be selected. Learning the art of grouping and ungrouping helps to decrease frustrations and time spent in repositioning objects.

Selection Tool in a Paint Software Package

Selection Tool in a Paint Software Package

Selecting a section of a picture while using a paint package requires a different tool than in a draw package. In a paint package, the selection is completed with the **selection tool.** When the selection tool is used, all pixels within the dotted lines will be selected. When you move this section, all pixels will move just as if you could cut out part of the painted canvas and paste it on top of another section of the canvas. The only thing that will be left behind is the color of the canvas. You may choose between a free form selection tool, a rigid shaped selection tool (usually a rectangle), or a lasso tool.

Eraser Tool

Eraser Tool

The **eraser** tool is used in paint-type software packages to remove anything that has been drawn. You may erase at any level including the pixel level, thus erasing pixel by pixel. The eraser works just like a pencil eraser. However, remember that the eraser removes everything in an area. Some packages have a color eraser that will erase only a designated color.

Painting Tools

Painting Tools

A paint package includes many different **painting tools.** These tools are not available in draw packages. The pencil tool draws a thin line. The brush tool acts like a paintbrush. You may designate the brush tip design from a point to a line and from narrow to wide. The spray can and airbrush tools are available on many paint packages. These tools allow the artist to have similar tools as a spray paint can and an airbrush. You may designate the size of the nozzle and the color of these two tools. Some packages have a rainbow or variegated color effect. Choose from the available options to create the desired effect in your graphic.

Eye Dropper Tool

Eye Dropper Tool

The **eye dropper** tool is available in paint packages only. It allows you to select a color from your painting and use it in a different area. Many times you cannot remember how a certain color was mixed or someone else may have mixed it. The eye dropper picks up a color, after which you may use that color as a fill color or as a line color in a new shape.

Character Tools

Character Tools

Characters in paint packages, both text and graphics, are treated as bit mapped graphics. They may become pixelated when resized. When a graphic is pixelated, the computer creates a stairstep effect within the graphic. A pixelated graphic is less pleasing to the eye and has less definition. Once you have finished entering text, the text cannot be edited again because the characters are no longer text—they are bit mapped graphics. Text in a draw-type software package is treated as if it were in a word processor, because the characters are drawn with a set of commands just as with other graphics. Text can be colored. The color may be changed at any time if you are using a draw package; but it must be preset if using a paint package. Text art is the manipulation of text into shapes such as twisting and slanting. See Figure 5.2 for an example of text art.

Stacking and Layering

Stacking Graphics

Stacking is available in both paint and draw packages. Graphics may be stacked one on top of the other or they may be layered. When you stack graphics in a paint package, they become permanently placed just as if you were painting on a canvas. When you place objects one on top of the other in a draw package, each remains as a separate object that may be moved at any time. As these objects are introduced on the page in a draw package, they are drawn at different object levels in the order of introduction. For example, if you have 10 objects on the page, you have 10 object levels with the most recent in front. These objects may be sent forward one object level, sent backward one object level, sent to the back level, or to the front level. When objects are stacked, the top object covers the lower objects unless you have designated the objects as transparent or translucent when these options are available.

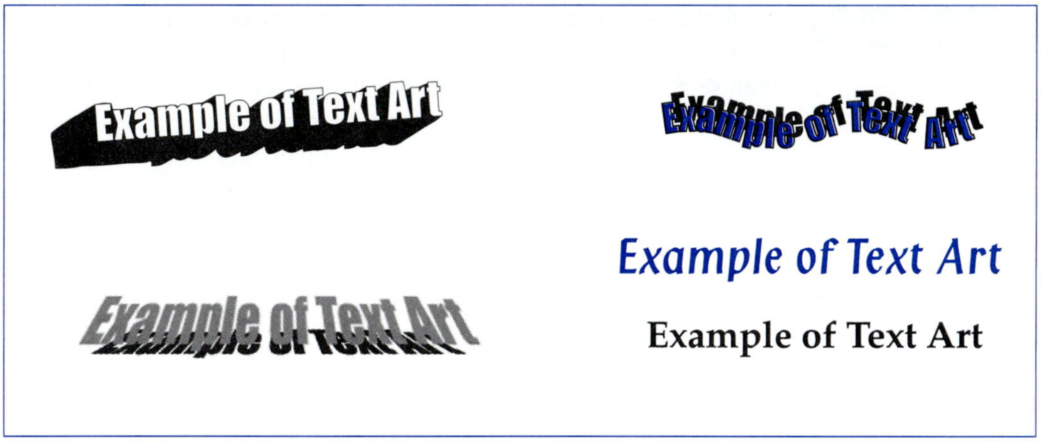

Figure 5.2 Examples of Text Art

Layering Graphics

Layering is available in more sophisticated paint and draw packages, and is especially helpful in paint packages. Layering is like working on different sheets of transparencies. You may work on one layer without affecting the other layers. This solves the problem in paint packages of wanting to move the house without moving the fence and flowers. This option allows you to put the background on one layer, the house on the next layer, the fence on the third layer, and the flowers on the fourth layer; you may move the house without affecting the background, the fence, or the flowers on the other layers. You may use an unlimited number of layers. When you are finished with your graphic, save it with the layers in place and then save it again with the layers combined into one layer and saved in a compatible format. Most file formats that involve layers are not compatible formats with other software packages.

Manipulating Graphics

Graphics may be altered in many ways. They may be slanted, stretched, rotated, and flipped. They may be sent through filters to change the effect, such as the look of charcoal, a stained glass window, or a swirl. These are the common ways graphics may be altered. Investigate your graphics packages to find other ways and experiment. Save projects with each of the different effects to help you at a later date remember how the effect alters the picture.

Aligning and Distributing

To **align** objects in a draw software package, you have the choice of two different methods. One is using the snap to guides or snap to grids feature. When you use this feature and move

TIP

Keep a notebook of key information about the packages in which you are working. Place in the notebook such things as fonts, graphic filter effects, special formulas, and other key information you would like to have at your fingertips. This notebook may be electronic or hard copy. If electronic, then be sure to designate a single folder in which you keep this information.

Align and Distribute

an object close to a guideline or a gridline, the object jumps to the line. The second method is to use the align feature. When using this feature, you select all objects to be aligned, and then select the align command and the objects will snap into alignment. You may choose right, left, or center alignment. Objects may be aligned vertically or horizontally.

Sometimes you may want your objects to be evenly spaced either vertically or horizontally. In this case, you would use the **distribute** command in the same way as you would the align command.

Sizing versus Cropping

Sizing an Object

Cropping an Object

Sizing and cropping are only available in draw packages. **Sizing** refers to changing the size of the object by either making it smaller or larger or changing its proportion. **Cropping** refers to selecting and using a portion of the object.

To size an object, first select the object with the pointer tool. Then point to one of the handles on the selected object, press the mouse button, and drag the cursor to the desired size. If you wish to keep the relationship between the height and the width the same, press the shift key as you drag the cursor.

To crop a picture, select the cropping tool, select the graphic to be cropped, and drag the cursor to enclose the part of the object you want to use. You are not actually cutting away the graphic. Think about the cropping lines as a frame around the picture where the picture is behind the frame. As you crop the graphic, you are only changing the inside size of the frame. You may come back at a later time and enlarge the size of the frame as the picture is still behind the frame. In some graphics packages, you may position the picture behind the frame by pointing the cursor to the middle of the picture and dragging the picture around.

Graphics Use

Chapter 4 listed guidelines for adding graphics to a project. You may want to review those guidelines. As discussed, graphics should always enhance the text message. They should communicate the message in graphical form. If you want to use a graphic to fill in white space, then be sure it still enhances the message.

The type of graphic you use depends on the quality of the project, the function of the project, the audience, and the amount of time, energy, and talent you have to complete the project. If the project is a high-cost brochure, it is worth the time and energy to create high-quality graphics even if you have to hire a graphic artist to create them. If the project is an in-house newsletter that is produced every week and you have very little time to complete it, then clipart is best to use. Part of project planning will include the type of graphics you want to use and why.

Summary

Graphics are important elements used to enhance text in a project. Their use can increase retention by as much as 100% over text alone. Graphics include lines, borders, frames, clipart, computer-drawn art, scanned artwork, and photo clips.

File organization of graphic files can save time and frustrations in finding the appropriate graphics for the project. Graphics files should be organized into folders named for various categories of graphics.

Copyright infringement is always an issue in graphics. Copyright is the right of the owner to control the following:

1. right to reproduce,
2. right to modification,
3. right to distribute,
4. right to perform, and
5. right to display copyrighted work publicly.

Fair use policy allows small amounts of copyrighted material to be used under the following circumstances:

1. use of the copy,
2. nature of the copyrighted work,
3. the amount copied, and
4. the impact on the market.

Paint and draw software differs in the way the computer addresses the parts of the graphic. Paint software addresses individual pixels whereas draw software addresses groups of pixels. Paint software produces bit mapped graphics and draw software produces vector graphics.

Graphic tools used in most paint and/or draw software include the pointer tool, line and shape tools, fill, group and ungroup, selection tools, eraser tool, painting tool, eye dropper tool, character tools, stacking graphics, layering graphics, distributing graphics, aligning graphics, sizing graphics, and cropping graphics.

Most importantly, graphics should always enhance the text message. A project is only successful in communicating its message if it has well-written text and appropriate graphics.

Key Words

- Bit mapped graphics
- Clipart
- Copyright
- Digital photography
- Dots per inch (dpi)
- Draw software
- Fair use policy
- Graphics tools
  - Align
  - Character tools
  - Cropping
  - Distribute
  - Eraser
  - Eye dropper
  - Fill
  - Group
  - Layering
  - Line and shape tools
  - Painting tools
  - Pointer tool
  - Selection tool
  - Sizing
  - Stacking
  - Ungroup
- Paint software
- Photo clips
- Resolution
- Scanned graphics
- Vector graphics

Exercises

1. Why do you think the use of graphics increases the retention of information?
2. Name some examples of graphics.
3. Why is it important to organize your graphic files?
4. What five rights does the owner have in terms of copyrights?
5. What constitutes fair use of copyrighted material?
6. What are the basic differences between paint and draw software?
7. What can you do in a paint software package that you cannot do in a draw software package?
8. What can you do in a draw software package that you cannot do in a paint software package?
9. How many bytes will be used to scan in a 3×5 inch picture using a resolution of 300 dpi and 3 bytes per pixel for color?
10. Name and explain five graphic tools used in a draw software package.
11. Name and explain five graphic tools used in a paint software package.
12. What is the difference between stacking graphics and layering graphics?
13. What is the difference between sizing a graphic and cropping a graphic?

Problems

1. Using Figure 3.1, create a file structure for your graphics files.
2. Review clipart and photo clip CD-ROMs advertised in a computer software catalog. Indicate types of clipart and photo clips, any copyright limitations, number of files included, and any other given information. Which one(s) would you purchase? Why?
3. What type of graphics would you use for the following types of projects:
   a. memo
   b. letter
   c. report on computer hardware
   d. sales report for a lumber company
   e. newsletter for a high school alumni association

Chapter 6

Presentation Graphics

Overview

Objectives

When you have finished this chapter, you should be able to:

1. Understand the different uses of an electronic slide show.
2. Understand the elements of a slide show.
3. Develop a plan to create a slide show.
4. Understand the precautions to take to ensure a successful presentation.

Presentation graphics is computer software for producing an **electronic slide show,** a multimedia presentation using text, graphics, charts, video, sound, animation, and interactivity to either help a user communicate, or to independently communicate, a message. In a traditional noncomputer slide show, individual slides are photographed, developed, and placed in a slide holder for showing. If the slide show requires modification, slides must be physically rearranged; or if incorrect, slides that require changing must be removed, another one photographed, developed, and replaced. Presentation graphics have taken the traditional slide show concept and made it electronic. Electronic slides replace the traditional slides, and the computer and projection system replace the slide projector.

Presentation graphics software has become an important element for people who give presentations, lectures, speeches, and training sessions. Visual aids increase the retention of information presented to an audience. These visual aids have traditionally been in the form of transparencies, slide shows, flip charts, and chalkboards. With the increase of graphics capabilities on computers, people are replacing the traditional visual aids with electronic slide shows. Presentation graphics, therefore, has become an important software package for presenters to learn whether they are teachers, business people, scientists, or any number of other occupations.

Electronic slide shows are used for many types of presentations. One of the most common uses is to enhance a speaker's presentation such as in the classroom, in a boardroom, at a dinner, or at a conference. Another use of an electronic slide show is as a medium for one-on-one training when there is no instructor present. Continuously running slide shows are also used to present information at fairs and expositions. In this case, people view the slide show as they walk by an exhibit. Typically there is someone at the exhibition booth to answer questions but not necessarily to present the message. In all cases, slide shows should be designed so that the message is best communicated to the audience. It is easy to get overexuberant when developing a slide show and create a glitzy presentation that loses the message due to excess graphics and text. A good slide show can be created and edited in a short time with minimal planning and use of software tools featured in a presentation graphics package.

Elements of a Slide Show

Elements of a Slide Show

Slide shows are considered multimedia presentations because they have all the elements of multimedia: text, graphics, video, animation, sound, and interactivity. Text is found on most slides and generally communicates the message. Graphics may be placed on a slide in the form of clipart, photographs, charts, or computer art to increase the retention of the message. Video clips may be added to communicate part of the message in video form. Sound may be added to the slide for narration, music, and other effects to also help increase retention rate. Elements on the slide may be animated to add interest and improve communication. A slide show may be interactive, enabling users to have control of or otherwise be involved in the presentation. Interactivity may include proceeding to the next slide, the previous slide, the beginning slide, the ending slide, or temporarily go to another program or on the internet. Presentation graphics have added new dimensions to the traditional slide show through the use of multimedia elements.

Using presentation graphics software may seem complicated, but this is not true. Because of predesigned elements and features built into a presentation graphics program, it is one of the easier software packages to learn. Slide shows are now fun to develop.

Predesigned Backgrounds

Predesigned elements include backgrounds. The **background** is a design that appears on every slide. It is placed on the lowest level of each slide to provide consistency in the slide show. See Figure 6.1. On top of the background are predesigned layouts for text, graphics, video, and sound.

Predesigned Layouts

The **predesigned layouts** are holders for preformatted text, graphics, video, and sound. Part of the layout involves placement of the elements. Next on the slide is the sequenced entering of additional data in proper places. Predesigned buttons may be added for interactivity. Next, the developer may select animations for various elements on the slide and transitions for the advancement of the slide onto the screen. These slide options make it relatively easy to create a well-designed slide show in a relatively short amount of time.

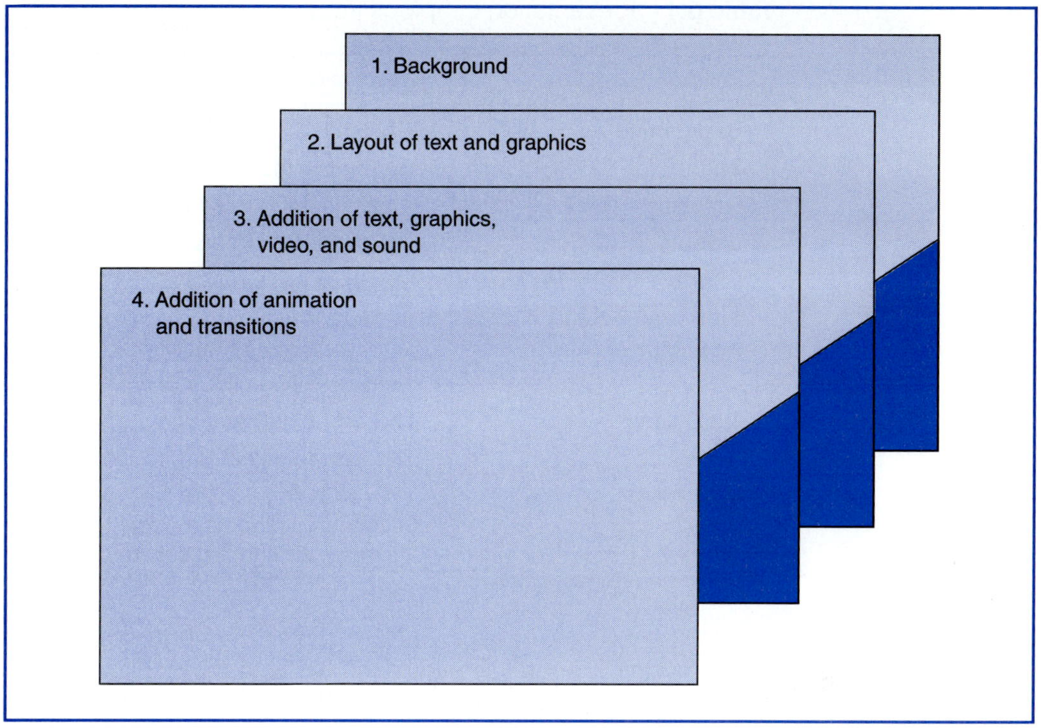

Figure 6.1 Anatomy of a Slide

Speaker Notes and Handouts

After the slide show is completed, the user may elect to create **speaker notes** that contain a reproduction of the slide and additional word-processed information on each page which can then be printed. **Audience handouts** may also be electronically prepared and then printed. They may contain multiple slide reproductions on one or more pages.

Predesigned elements and features are included, making a presentation graphics software package easy to learn and use to develop a well-designed slide show. Preplanning can speed slide show development and decrease frustrations that often occur when developing most anything on the computer.

Basic Features of a Presentation Graphics Program

A presentation graphics program is easy to learn and use as a result of the basic features designed into the software such as backgrounds, layouts, charts, and transitions. It was designed with the speed of slide show creation in mind. Table 6.1 presents these features.

Use of predesigned features is optional. You may create your own backgrounds and layouts for the slides. Finished product design depends on your time available and the quality desired for the created slide show. Basic features can be an asset when time is limited and high quality is not desired.

Background

Backgrounds

One of the first things you will want to think about is the background design for the slides. You may choose a predesigned background or create your own.

Table 6.1 Presentation Graphics Features

Feature	Description
Background	The bottom layer of a slide
Text	Text blocks that are added to a slide
Graphics	Graphics that are added to a slide
Layouts	The placement of elements on a slide
Charts	Ability to create bar, column, line, and pie charts
Video and Sound	Addition of video and sound clips
Slide Sorter	Ability to see multiple slides on the screen and rearrange them directly on the monitor
Transitions	The way a slide is introduced on the screen
Animation	The way an object is introduced on a slide
Interactivity	The ability to add user control to a slide show by adding buttons or hot spots to jump to another slide, activate a data file, open an internet site, or activate sound or video clips

Your background should be attractive to the eye and enhance the text. Slide shows should have consistency throughout all slides, which can be achieved by using the same background on all or most of your slides. The background should be relevant to the message of the slide show. A seascape may be relevant to a presentation on sea life but not relevant to a presentation on the desert. You may want a plain background with a border on one side or a relevant graphic that blends into a background color. Be careful when choosing a graphic to be placed on the entire slide as a background. The text must be clearly visible on top of all parts of the graphic, so choose a graphic that has a limited number of colors and has mostly dark colors or light colors. If there is a combination of light and dark colors, it is hard to find a text color that is visible over the entire graphic. You will find many nice predesigned backgrounds in your presentation graphics software program. You may find it helpful to make a slide show with each design on a different slide and print them as handouts, six to a page, for your reference notebook.

Text

Text on a Slide

Text in presentation graphics is placed in text blocks. The blocks become objects with handles for resizing or moving. The block is the container for the text; when the block is resized, only the container changes size not the text. In the slide design, the amount of text and size of the font will vary depending on the purpose of the slide show and the audience. In all slide shows, the font size will be larger than in most other software packages. Very seldom should there be a font size of less than 18 points. The further away the intended audience, the larger you will want to make the font size. Normally font sizes vary from 24 to 44. A larger audience generally requires less text of increased font size on each slide.

If the slide show is to accompany a speech, the text should be topical and not in paragraph form. Remember the speaker is delivering the message. One problem that people have when designing slide shows is how to limit the text to the fewest number of words. We are taught to use complete sentences. Slide shows are one place where complete sentences place too much text on a slide and take too much time for the viewer to read. The slide show's only purpose is to enhance communications. If the slide show is developed for a one-on-one training session or is used for an exhibit, more text of smaller font size is needed to explain the message because the slide show must deliver the message. Even here, words should be kept at a premium, thus eliminating all unnecessary text.

A one-on-one training session using a slide show should be as detailed as necessary. The detail of an exhibit slide show depends on the subject content, size of the display screen, and distance from the audience. The audience must be able to read all text. It is better to divide text between several slides than to crowd it all on one slide.

Do not be afraid to move the text around on the slide. You may want graphics on the left side of the slide and text on the right side. You may want to split the text into several text blocks and place the text in different places on the slide especially if you have a graphic associated with different lines of text. Be creative and try different layouts.

Graphics

Graphics on a Slide

Graphics help to enhance the message and increase interest of a slide. They also help to intersperse some levity into a presentation. Graphics should always be relevant and appropriate. If your time is limited, clipart is readily available to add dynamics to your slide show. You do not want your presentation to be boring. Text alone tends to be boring even if the background is interesting. Be sure your choice of graphics keeps the viewers' interest. Flip your graphic or move it to the other side if it points off the slide. Careful choice and placement of graphics to enhance the text can make your slide show one that the audience will enjoy watching.

Layouts

Layouts

The layout of a slide is the placement of slide elements on the slide. There are many predesigned slide layouts from which to choose such as a title slide or a bulleted list. The layout of a title slide consists of text blocks in the center of the slide. A bulleted list layout has a text box at the top to introduce the slide topic and another text box for the bulleted list of subtopics. Other predesigned layouts include charts and text, double bulleted lists, video and text, and slide topic only. Investigate your software to find the types of predesigned layouts available to you. These predesigned layouts are only a starting point. Graphics and other text blocks may be added to any layout, or any element on a layout may be deleted.

Charts

Charts on a Slide

Slides shows were originally developed to help analyze spreadsheet data through the use of electronic **charts.** Figure 6.2 shows the three chart types that are most widely used.

The column chart is used to compare data such as how much wheat was produced in succeeding years by two or more states. Bar charts are similar to column charts with the exception that bar charts are horizontal whereas column charts are vertical. In some software packages bar charts are synonymous with column charts. Line charts are used to show progression over a period of time such as how much profit per month was made during the last year. A pie chart is used to show the percentage of the whole such as what is the percentage of each item of the whole budget.

It is important to choose the correct type of chart to represent the analysis of the data being presented. It is also important to present the data in a manner that does not misrepresent the information. You should compare equivalent values such as inches to

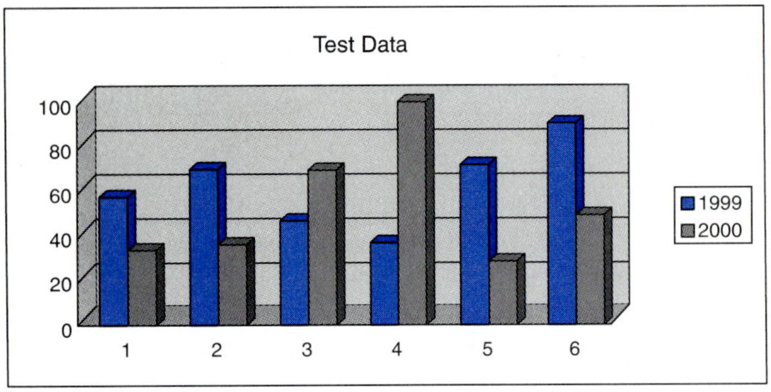

Column Chart

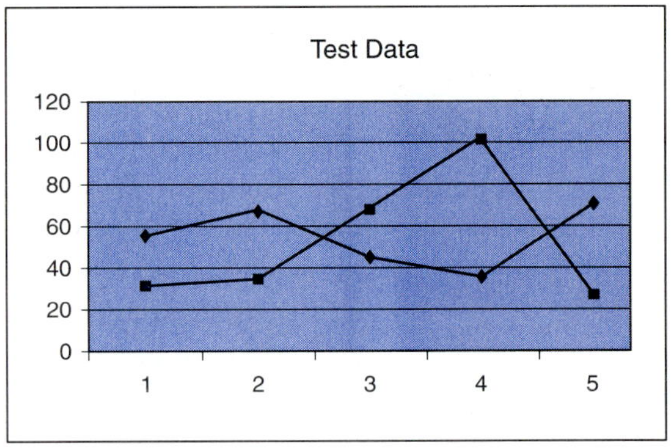

Line Chart

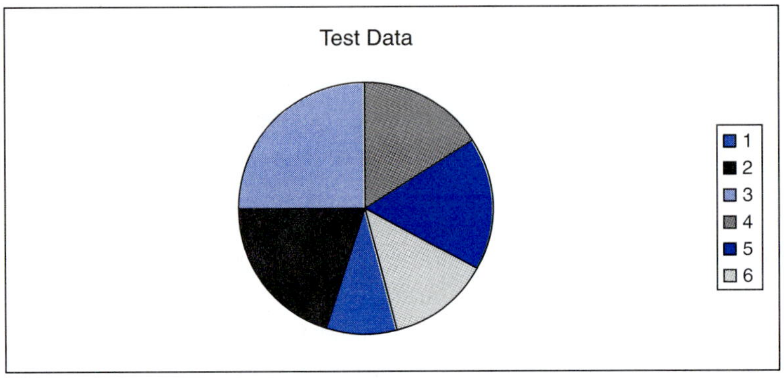

Pie Chart

Figure 6.2 Examples of Charts

inches instead of inches to feet. People usually prefer to see a chart for quick analysis of data rather than a table of numbers. See Chapter 13 for more detailed information about charts.

Video and Sound

Video and Sound on a Slide

Video and sound may be added to your slide show. Be sure your computer for the slide show has the multimedia capabilities to play video and sound. Some video and sound clips come with your software, or you may also purchase these clips. You may want to capture video from videotape, or sound from an audiotape, CD, or real voice. To capture media is to digitize this video or sound and save it to a file so that it may be imported into a project or slide show at a later time. You would then use these imports as a way to add video, audio, or narration to the slide show. You may control when the video and sound starts and stops. Sound may also be used in transitions and in animation of elements. Sound can be distracting so be careful of its use. Avoid repeating sounds often and playing sounds when the speaker is talking.

Slide Sorter

Slide Sorter

The **slide sorter** is like a light table for slides. It shows slides side by side and allows you to move slides around and to easily designate transitions.

Transitions

Transitions between Slides

Transitions are added to each slide to tell the computer how it will be presented on the screen. A slide may enter from the right, left, top, bottom, or diagonally. It may come in like a puzzle with individual pieces being added to the screen to make up the slide. There are many transitions.

You may also designate a sound or music to accompany the slide transition; but take care to use short transitions so the speaker does not have to talk over the sound or wait for the sound to finish. Use a sound that is relevant to the slide; for example, use the sound of water running when showing a waterfall rather than a loud sound that does not fit the slide.

A good time to add music is at the beginning when people are just settling down for the presentation. Soft, soothing music can quiet people and get them ready for the speaker to start. Music should be relevant to the slide show and the audience. For example, if the audience is mostly teenagers, then the intro music should be something they will enjoy. Likewise, if the audience is mostly adults then the music should be chosen with their likes in mind. Always be aware of the copyright issue when choosing music for your slide show.

Transitions add interest to your slide show and should enhance it. Table 6.2 lists some transitions you might find in your presentation graphics software. Investigate all transitions in your software and make note of your favorites in your resource notebook.

A slide show may advance manually through the use of the mouse or automatically through designated time settings for each slide. For most uses, a manual advance is preferred. A speaker does not know exactly how long a speech will take during a slide. People require different time periods per slide in a training session. **Interactivity** designates that the user controls the advancement of slides. Automatic advancement is used for slide shows that should be continuous such as during an exhibit.

Animation

Animations on a Slide

You may animate any element on the slide. Depending on the software, there are many different ways to animate an element. You may have the element fly in from any direction, crawl in, or have a spiral effect. Text may be added to the slide one letter at a time, one word at a time, one line at a time, or all at once. As one line is added to the slide, the previous line may be dimmed so only what the speaker is talking about is highlighted. You may add sound with any of these animations. Be cautious, however, in adding sounds to animation because they detract from the speaker and become an annoyance to the audience. Table 6.3 lists some animations that you might find in your presentation graphics software. Investigate the animations in your software to discover your favorites.

Interactivity

Interactivity

A slide show may be made interactive through the addition of electronic buttons on a slide. Slides may be hidden and therefore skipped when normally viewing the slide show. They may be shown through the use of a button to jump to a specific slide or a group of slides. Buttons may also be used to return to the beginning of the slide show, to the slide where the button was activated, or to the end of the slide show.

Buttons may be used to open a data file in other programs, thus activating another program. When you exit the activated program, the execution will revert back to the slide

Table 6.2 Transitions

Transition	Description
Blinds Horizontal	Horizontal strips that change to new slide
Blinds Vertical	Vertical strips that change to new slide
Box In	Changes to new slide from outside to the middle
Box Out	Changes to new slide from middle to the outside
Checkerboard Across	Small square changes from right to left
Checkerboard Down	Small square changes from top to bottom
Cover Down	Slide covers the old one from the top
Cover Left	Slide covers the old one from the right
Cover Left Down	Slide covers the old one from the top right
Cover Left Up	Slide covers the old one from the bottom right
Cover Right	Slide covers the old one from the left
Cover Right Down	Slide covers the old one from the left top
Cover Right Up	Slide covers the old one from the left bottom
Cover Up	Slide covers the old one from the bottom
Dissolve	Old one disappears in pieces as new one appears
Uncover Down	Old slide uncovers the new slide from top
Uncover Left	Old slide uncovers the new slide from right
Uncover Left Down	Old slide uncovers the new slide from right top
Uncover Left Up	Old slide uncovers the new slide from right bottom
Uncover Right	Old slide uncovers the new slide from left
Uncover Right Down	Old slide uncovers the new slide from left top
Uncover Right Up	Old slide uncovers the new slide from left bottom
Uncover Up	Old slide uncovers the new slide from bottom

Table 6.3 Animations

Animation	Description
Appear	Appears without animation
Flash Once	Appears and then immediately disappears
Fly In from Bottom	Element comes in from bottom
Fly In from Left Bottom	Element comes in from left bottom
Fly In from Left Top	Element comes in from left top
Fly In from Left	Element comes in from left
Fly In from Right Bottom	Element comes in from right bottom
Fly In from Right Top	Element comes in from right top
Fly In from Right	Element comes in from right
Fly In from Top	Element comes in from top
Spiral	Appears and spirals in place
Wipe Down	Appears on slide from top of element to bottom
Wipe Left	Appears on slide from right of element to left
Wipe Right	Appears on slide from left of element to right
Wipe Up	Appears on slide from bottom of element to top

where the program was activated. You may access the internet through the use of a button that is linked to an internet site, and also activate a sound or a video clip through the use of a button.

Hot objects may be created that will do the same thing as a button when clicked. For example, you may want to click on a photo to view a video clip or click on a clipart exit sign to stop the slide show. You may also activate something by using the mouse to roll over an object, called a rollover, instead of clicking on the object. These buttons and hot objects can add flexibility to your slide show. If you include interactivity, then, you must view the slide show on manual control.

To add a button to a slide, designate the location on the slide and the shape of the button. Then select what action the button is to complete by selecting a slide to go to and indicating a data file to open, a sound or video to be activated, or an internet site to go to. Also designate whether the action is on a click of the mouse or on a rollover. Hot objects are similar with the exception that instead of using a button you use an object to activate an action.

Design Considerations

Design Considerations

Many things should be considered when designing an electronic slide show. They include the purpose of the presentation, the audience, the environment, the message, and the time you have to design and create the slide show. These design considerations will assist you in the choice of text and graphics when planning your show.

Purpose of the Slide Show

Knowing the purpose of the presentation is important because it governs the text, the graphics, and the overall design of the slide show. For example, the purpose might be to design a slide show as a one-on-one session to train employees on a new piece of equipment. The text would be complete instructions on the use of the equipment. The terminology should correspond to the knowledge base of the employees. The graphics should pertain to the new equipment. You might consider narration and interactivity to add more information and to allow the user as much time as needed to view a slide. Interactivity would also allow the user to go back to previous slides. If the training content is extensive enough to require several sessions, then interactivity may be added to include one of the first slides as a menu to select the session.

If the purpose of the slide show is to enhance a speaker's lecture, then the text should be topical and limited to few words. The speaker would like the audience to listen to the speech and not have their attention diverted to trying to read a lot of text on a slide show. The graphics should be relevant to the topic with some funny ones every so often. The terminology should be geared to the audience. Interactivity would probably be limited to going forward and backward. Transitions should be without sound. Animation should probably be limited to line-by-line text. Study the purpose of the intended slide show before you begin to plan it.

Whatever the purpose of the slide show, text should be kept at a minimum. For a speaker, the text should be kept to the topics at hand. For the most part, eliminate complete sentences. For a one-on-one training session, keep the text to as few words as possible while still conveying the message. Rework your text to reduce excess words. Too many words on a slide can confuse the viewer and obstruct the intent of the message. It is better to divide the topic into more slides if more text is required. Review the design guidelines on white space in Chapter 4.

The Audience

The audience dictates the graphics and the terminology. Age and knowledge base of the audience should be considered when creating text and graphics. For example, it makes a difference in the graphics selection if the audience is 12 to 16 year olds versus 30 to 60 years of age. It also makes a difference if the knowledge base of the audience is nontechnical and uneducated about the subject, or if the audience is knowledgeable of the content and the terminology. You want your audience to understand the slide show but not be insulted by the lack of appropriate terminology.

Environment

The environment makes a big difference in how you will design your slide show. If the room is large, then the amount of data on each slide should be limited. If the audience is small, then each slide may contain more information. A large room requires selection of larger text size. The person in the last row should be able to read the text and see the graphics clearly.

Communicate the Message

The slide show message should be easily communicated through the use of proper terminology, amount of text, and choice of graphics. The communication of the message is most important. If the message is lost, the presentation is a failure.

Development Time

The time you have to design and create the slide show dictates what type of background and graphics you will use. If you have little time, then select a predesigned background, add the proper amount of text, and add relevant clipart to the message. If the slide show will be used often, then it is worth your time to design the presentation with care. You could take the time to design a custom background using digital pictures or graphics created by a graphic artist. Keep in mind changes that may need to take place at a later date. Even if you have very little time, a well-designed slide show that communicates the message can be developed rather quickly if you do proper preplanning.

Problems with Using an Electronic Slide Show

Inherent Problems

As popular as electronic slide shows have become, there are inherent problems connected with using them. If you are aware of the potential problems, then you will be able to take measures to ensure a successful presentation. Make a checklist of things to bring and things to do before the presentation to avoid forgetting something. Figure 6.3 shows a possible checklist. You may add or delete items from this list.

Compatibility of Hardware and Software

One of the biggest problems with using computerized visual aids is compatibility with hardware and software. Each computer system tends to be a little different, so if possible, bring your own equipment. A notebook computer and a small but powerful projector system are easy to carry and will assure you compatible hardware and software. These tend to be expensive, however, the reduction in compatibility problems will be worth the expense to yourself and your company. If you are to use equipment from another source, be sure to inquire about the hardware system and adjust your slide show to the available equipment. A laser pen and a remote mouse are helpful during a presentation.

Software compatibility is another problem. If you do not bring your own hardware and software, be sure to inquire as to the version of the presentation graphics software that is available. Save your slide show presentation in that version. Once you are sure that there will be no last-minute changes in the slide show, you may want to produce an executable file of your show. With this file you will not need the presentation graphics software to use the slide show. If there will be last-minute changes, then it is wise to save the slide show in several version formats; thus, you will be sure to have a compatible file with as many features as possible in your slide show. Each newer version of the software adds new features. Bring extra backups of your slide show as insurance in case your original files become corrupted.

Figure 6.3 Checklist for Presentation

1. Equipment
________ Computer/storage device(s)/keyboard/mouse
________ Projector
________ Cables
________ Extension cord and plug bar
________ Extra bulbs for the projector
________ Tool kit (survival kit)

2. Software
________ Presentation on computer
________ Backup on storage cartridge
________ Software on computer

3. Notes
________ Audience handouts
________ Speaker notes

4. Other items
________ Glass for water
________ Pen/pencil
________ Pad of paper
________ Business cards
________ Watch

5. Before presentation
________ Check on room arrangements
________ Set up equipment
________ Test software and equipment
________ Set glass of water beside podium
________ Get audience handouts ready
________ Set speaker notes on podium

Survival Kit

Because things can go wrong with a presentation that have nothing to do with the hardware and software, it is wise to pack a "survival kit." This kit would include extra extension cords and plug bars, extra bulbs for your projector system, a small tool kit used to install equipment onsite, and a small flashlight.

Environment

The presentation environment is also a factor. You will want to inquire about such items as room size, availability of a podium and tables for your equipment, and use of a screen. If you need internet connections, make sure the site manager is informed. Inquire about the type of communication lines into the site. This may make a difference especially if you are presenting at a busy time of the day. If you need other equipment, be sure to ask for it in advance to be at the site or bring your own. Do not assume that equipment will be there for your use.

Audience Handouts

If you have handouts for your audience, inquire about how many people to expect at your session. Have extra handouts in case there are more people than expected or some people want more than one handout. It is better to have a few handouts left over than not enough.

Speaker's Needs

Do not forget the speaker's needs. A glass of water at the side of the podium is nice if the session is long. Speaker notes should be in a notebook or on a second computer. A copy of the handouts should be on the podium along with the speaker notes. The speaker needs to feel at ease as much as possible.

Slide Show Run-Through

A few precautions can change a possible disaster into a successful presentation. It is best to get the equipment set up and tested before the audience arrives. If time allows, do a complete run-through of the slide show in the environment where the presentation will take place. Ask some friends to position themselves at different places in the room including at different distances and angles to be sure all slides can be readily seen. Even the most careful planning may have glitches in the new environment. Last-minute changes may take care of these problems.

If the presentation is long and important, it is nice to have a second person to field problems such as to change a light bulb, pass out handouts to latecomers, and to get another glass of water. You will want to do as much as possible to make the presentation run smoothly.

Slide Show Planning Guide

Slide shows should be well planned before starting on the computer. Figure 6.4 is a slide show planning guide. This guide should help you in planning your slide show by following the six steps in problem solving.

The first step identifies the problem through the use of a problem statement. This one to two paragraph narrative should describe the problem in general terms but include such things as what the slide show is about, who will be giving it, where it will be shown, and why it is to be given. You may want to use the problem analysis chart introduced in Chapter 1 to sort out needed information for this and the next step.

Step two helps to understand the problem. Included here are a description of the audience, required outcomes of the slide show, required knowledge base of the developer and the audience, and environment of the presentation. The required outcomes lists what the slide show should accomplish. The required knowledge of the developer lists what the developer needs to know to create the slide show. If the developer does not know any of these items, the method of acquiring the knowledge should be included. The expected knowledge base of the audience lists what the audience should know to be able to understand the presentation. The developer should know this information in order to have a knowledge base on which to build the slide show. A description of the environment is also helpful.

Step three lists alternative methods of developing the slide show. Step four lists the selected method from the alternatives in step three. There may be several items to consider, such as graphics, transitions, animation, video, sound, narration, and interactivity. Part of step four should include a brief overview of what will be on each of the slides.

Step five presents the general plan of the slide show, in accordance with the previous steps. The first part of step five indicates such items as the background, files to be imported, materials required to present the slide show, printing instructions for the handouts and the speaker's notes, and the contents of the header and footer. Step five also includes space to sketch the interactivity between the slides. The interactivity chart shows the possible progressions from one slide to another along with activating data files, internet sites, and sound or video clips. It shows the actions of buttons and hot objects. Other pages are the storyboards for the slide show. Storyboards are thumbnail sketches

Figure 6.4 Slide Show Planning Guide

SLIDE SHOW PLANNING GUIDE

Name of Document: ______________________________ Date: ______________

Location of Electronic File: ______________________________

Name: ______________________________

Name of Client: ______________________________

Step 1: Identify the Problem by Writing the Problem Statement.

Step 2: Understand the Problem.

Audience:

Required Outcomes of the Slide Show:

Required Knowledge of the Problem to Develop the Slide Show:

Expected Knowledge of the Audience:

Environment of Presentation:

Step 3: Identify Valid Alternative Methods to Solve the Problem.

Step 4: Select the Best Method to Solve the Problem from the List of Alternative Solutions.

Slide Show Overview:

(continued)

Figure 6.4 Slide Show Planning Guide

Step 5: Plan Your Solution.

Software to be used: Presentation graphics

Background:

__________ Premade Background Name: ______________________________

__________ Own Background Description:

Files to be imported:

File	Description	Use	Location

Slide Size: __________

Paper Color for Handouts: __________ No. of Slides Per Page: __________

Print in Color/B&W: Handouts: __________ Speaker's Notes: __________

Header Contents:

Footer Contents:

Materials Needed:

Hardware: ______________________________

Software: ______________________________

Projector/Screen: ______________________________

Handouts: __________ Number: __________

Speaker's Notes: __________ Notebook/Computer: __________

Other: ______________________________

____

____

Figure 6.4 (continued)

Step 5: Plan Your Solution (con't)

Interactivity Chart:

Storyboards: Indicate animation on the diagram of the slide:

Transition: ______________________

Layout: ______________________

Comments: ______________________

____

____

Transition: ______________________

Layout: ______________________

Comments: ______________________

____

____

(continued)

Figure 6.4 Slide Show Planning Guide

Step 5: Plan Your Solution (con't)

Transition: ____________________

Layout: ____________________

Comments: ____________________

____

____

Transition: ____________________

Layout: ____________________

Comments: ____________________

____

____

Step 6: Evaluate the Solution. List the criteria for evaluating the completed document.

of each slide. One page contains four slides. On each slide you will want to indicate where graphics are going to be placed along with the text. You should also include object rotation, specification of special text enhancements, and anything else needed to be able to easily create the project on the computer. On lines beside the storyboard, you should indicate the transition used to initiate the slide and the predesigned layout if one is used. Also, add any comments about the slide that you want to remember.

Step 6 lists the criteria for evaluation of the slide show. Since the slide show cannot be tested until it is on the computer, it is best to determine if the presentation reflects the problem statement. The criteria should refer to the requirements in steps one and two.

Example Slide Show

The following exercise is developed as an example of planning a slide show:

> You are taking a computer class. As part of the semester's requirements, you are to give a five-minute oral report on one type of computer hardware. You have chosen printers. As part of the report you are to have a slide show of at least seven slides. The first requirement of the report is to turn in a slide show planning guide.

Figure 6.5 shows the planning guide for this problem. Step one gives a narrative of the problem statement. Step two helps to understand the problem with an analysis of the audience, the required outcomes, the expected knowledge of the developer and the audience, and a description of the environment which includes room size, required equipment and software, the audience description, and time of presentation.

Step three lists alternatives of developing the slide show. These include information about the type of interactivity, background, images, and topics to be presented. Step four lists the best alternatives from each of the items in step three and a slide overview, which gives a list of the slides and the topic of each.

The next few pages are step 5, the plan. Included are the plan for the background, files to be used, the slide size, information on printing handout and speaker notes, header and footer contents, and materials required. Also included in the plan are the interactivity chart and the storyboards. The interactivity chart shows the previous and the next slide for each slide, including the jumps to other slides. This slide show is linear, which means the flow of the slides goes from one slide to the next. No buttons are used, so there are no jumps to previous slides or to skip slides. The storyboards are thumbnail sketches of each slide with transition option, layout information, and comments at the side of the sketch. A thumbnail sketch should show roughly where the text and graphics will be placed and animation of each element, but should not be detailed. Step 6 lists the criteria for evaluation of the slide show. When this planning guide is completed, the creation time of the slide show on the computer should be fast. There should be few design corrections and developer frustrations should be low. If there are many corrections, then the planning guide was not well thought out or was not complete.

Figure 6.5 Slide Show Planning Guide

SLIDE SHOW PLANNING GUIDE

Name of Document: Computer Report Date: 4/22/2002

Location of Electronic File: c:\my data\school\computer\

Name: Tom Williams

Name of Client: for Computer Literacy Class

Step 1: Identify the Problem by Writing the Problem Statement.

The term report in my computer class is to include a 5-minute oral report with an accompanying slide show of 7 or more slides. My report will be on printers.

Step 2: Understand the Problem.

Audience:

The audience will be my instructor and my class.

Required Outcomes of the Slide Show:

1. Communicate information about printers to our class.
2. Get a good grade.

Required Knowledge of the Problem to Develop the Slide Show:

1. Knowledge of printers
2. Knowledge of computer hardware systems
3. Knowledge of basic computer terminology
4. Research information on the internet, our textbook, and computer magazines

Expected Knowledge of the Audience:

1. Knowledge of basic computer terminology

Environment of Presentation:

1. Classroom for 50 people
2. Computer and screen in classroom
3. Software installed on computer
4. College students ages 18 through 65
5. Computer literacy class
6. Report presentation to be given at the end of the semester

Step 3: Identify Valid Alternative Methods to Solve the Problem.

1. Interactive with a menu to choose types of printers or linear slide show
2. Make own background or use a predesigned background
3. Use scanned images, electronic clips, or digital photographs
4. What to report about each printer?
   Type of printer
   Cost per page (special paper required, ink cartridges, toner cartridges, etc.)
   Initial cost
   Max. paper size
   Other????

Figure 6.5 (continued)

Step 4: Select the Best Method to Solve the Problem from the List of Alternative Solutions.

1. Linear slide show since it will go with oral report
2. Use a predesigned background
3. Use scanned images from magazines, catalogs, and the internet. No copyright problems because of being a school report.
4. Use the following for table of comparisons:
   Type of printer
   Cost per page
   Initial cost
   Max. paper size
5. Put definitions of printers with pictures on slides and comparisons in table on second to last slide.

Slide Show Overview:

Slide 1: Introduction

Slide 2: Ink Jet Printer

Slide 3: Laser B&W Printer

Slide 4: Laser Color Printer

Slide 5: Thermal Printer

Slide 6: Dye Sublimation Printer

Slide 7: Table of Comparisons

Slide 8: The End

Step 5: Plan Your Solution.

Software to be used: Presentation graphics

Background:

X Premade Background Name: Notebook

________ Own Background Description:

Files to be imported:

File	Description	Use	Location
Printer	Clipart	Slide 1	c:\graphics\clipart\
Ink Jet Printer	Scanned	Slide 2	c:\my data\school\computer\report\
Laser Printer	Scanned	Slide 3	c:\my data\school\computer\report\
Color Laser	Internet	Slide 4	c:\my data\school\computer\report\
Thermal	Internet	Slide 5	c:\my data\school\computer\report\
Dye Sub	Scanned	Slide 6	c:\my data\school\computer\report\
Cartoon	Clipart	Slide 8	c:\graphics\clipart\

(continued)

Figure 6.5 Slide Show Planning Guide

Step 5: Plan Your Solution (con't)

Slide Size: 10 x 7½

Paper Color for Handouts: Light Blue No. of Slides Per Page: 3

Print in Color/B&W: Handouts: B&W Speaker's Notes: Color

Header Contents: None

Footer Contents:

Date		Slide X

Materials Needed:

Hardware: Computer in classroom

Software: Software on computer

Projector/Screen: Screen in classroom

Handouts: Yes Number: 35

Speaker's Notes: Yes Notebook/Computer: Notebook

Other: Magazines with information on printers

Interactivity Chart:

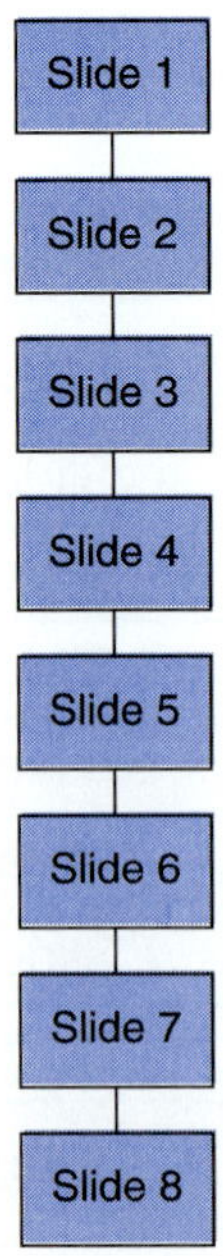

Figure 6.5 (continued)

Step 5: Plan Your Solution (con't)

Storyboards: Indicate animation on the diagram of the slide:

Transition: Dissolve

Layout: Title

Comments: Slide 1

Introduction

Transition: Cover Right

Layout: Bulleted List

Comments: Slide 2

Ink Jet Printer

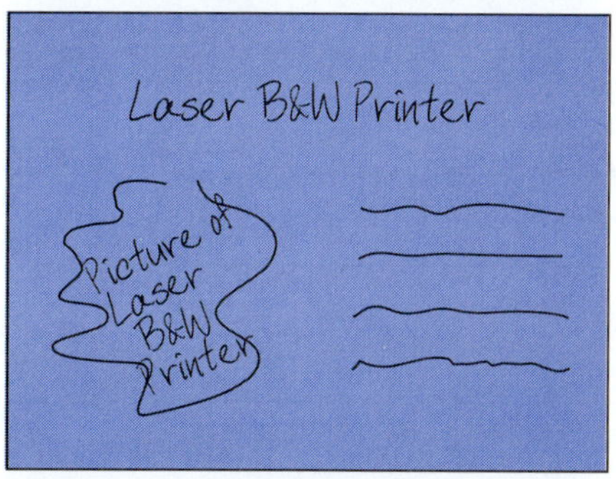

Transition: Cover Right

Layout: Bulleted List

Comments: Slide 3

Laser B&W Printed

Transition: Cover Right

Layout: Bulleted List

Comments: Slide 4

Laser Color Printer

(continued)

Figure 6.5 Slide Show Planning Guide

Step 5: Plan Your Solution (con't)

Transition: Cover Right

Layout: Bulleted List

Comments: Slide 5

Thermal Printer

Transition: Cover Right

Layout: Bulleted List

Comments: Slide 6

Dye Sublimation Printer

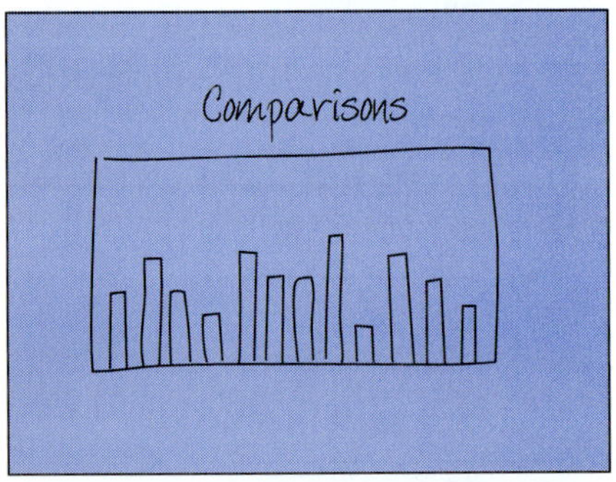

Transition: Cover Right

Layout: Bulleted List

Comments: Slide 7

Table of Comparisons

Transition: Dissolve

Layout: Title

Comments: Slide 8

Ending

Figure 6.5 (continued)

Step 6: **Evaluate the Solution. List the criteria for evaluating the completed document.**

1. Did the class understand the information presented?
2. Did the graphics help to add interest to the slides?
3. Did the graphics keep the viewer's attention?
4. Was there too much information for students to read on the slides? Was there enough?
5. Was the information on each printer complete?
6. Was the table easy to read?
7. Was there a beginning and an end?
8. Did I like it?

Summary

Presentation graphics software programs help to produce multimedia slide shows that include text, graphics, animation, sound, video, and interactivity. Slide shows are used as visual aids for speeches, one-on-one training sessions, and exhibits.

Features in a presentation graphics programs include predesigned backgrounds; predesigned layouts of text, graphics, video, and sound; predesigned buttons for interactivity, transitions between slides, animation of elements on a slide, plus many more features. Design considerations include the purpose of the slide show, the audience, text considerations, the environment, the message, and time for development.

Some problem areas of using electronic slide shows include hardware and software compatibility, lack of proper support equipment, and lack of rehearsal time before the presentation.

Preplanning helps decrease the time required to develop the slide show. The slide show planning guide is a tool used for planning a slide show before you go to the computer.

Key Words

Audience handouts
Background of a slide
Chart
Electronic slide show
Interactivity
Presentation graphics
Slide predesigned layouts
Slide sorter
Speaker notes
Transitions

Exercises

1. What is an electronic slide show?
2. Name the seven elements that can be part of a slide show.
3. What is the purpose of electronic slide shows?
4. Name and describe four features of presentation graphics software.

5. What type of chart would you use to present the following information? Explain why you would use that type.
   a. your budget
   b. cost of hotels, transportation, and meals for three different vacations
   c. cost of food and utilities over the last year
   d. amount of snow at four ski resorts
   e. projected car costs over the next year
6. Name and explain three design considerations in developing a slide show.
7. Name and explain three problems that you might have when giving a presentation using an electronic slide show.
8. Why would you provide handouts of your slide show to the audience?
9. Why would you want speaker notes?

Problems

1. Create your own checklist for a presentation that you might make.
2. You are in competition for a scholarship given by a local service organization. One requirement for getting the scholarship is to give a 15-minute presentation on why you are going to college. You want to create an electronic slide show to accompany your speech. Develop a slide show planning guide for this speech.
3. Develop a planning guide for an electronics slide show to accompany a speech that you have to give in one of your classes.
4. Your instructor has asked you to give a presentation to the Computer Advisory Committee on this class. Include the class objectives, the topics, and what you like about the class. Develop a planning guide for an electronics slide show to accompany this presentation.
5. You have been asked by your PE instructor to give a presentation on your favorite sport. Develop a planning guide for an electronics slide show to accompany this presentation.

Chapter 7

Presentation Graphics Case Studies

Overview

Case Study 1: Speaker's Presentation
Case Study 2: Training Session
Case Study 3: Exhibit

Objectives

When you have finished this chapter, you should be able to:

1. Problem solve and develop plans to create slide shows for a speaker's presentation, a training session, and an exhibit.
2. Use the slide show planning guide and the six problem-solving steps to develop a slide show that will be created using a presentation graphics software program.

Chapter 7 presents three presentation graphics case studies. The six steps in problem solving and the slide show planning guide are used to develop a solution for each of these case studies. Study how each solution was determined and use the same methodology for the problems at the end of the chapter.

Case Study 1: Speaker's Presentation

Case Study 1: DTP Class Oral Report

You are taking a class in desktop publishing. One requirement for the class is to report on a type of design guideline as presented in Chapter 4. You have your choice of the following guideline types:

1. Guidelines for layouts
2. Guidelines for text use
3. Guidelines for adding artwork
4. Guidelines for adding color
5. General guidelines

The report is to be written and orally presented with a slide show to accompany the oral presentation. For each guideline in your chosen topic, include the following:

1. Statement of the guideline
2. Explanation of the guideline
3. Reasons why you should follow the guideline

Create the presentation using a menu design, with each guideline in the set of guidelines as a menu item. Each slide must include the options to go to the next slide, the previous slide, the menu slide, or the ending slide. Figure 7.1 presents the slide show planning guide for this case study.

Figure 7.1 Slide Show Planning Guide for Case Study 1.

SLIDE SHOW PLANNING GUIDE

Name of Document: DTP Report Slide Show Date: 10/20/2002

Location of Electronic File: c:\my data\school\DTP\

Name: John Brown

Name of Client: DTP Class

Step 1: Identify the Problem by Writing the Problem Statement.

A requirement of my DTP class is to present a report on one set of guidelines as described in Chapter 4 in our book. The choices are:

1. Guidelines for layouts
2. Guidelines for text use
3. Guidelines for adding artwork
4. Guidelines for adding color
5. General guidelines

The report will be written and oral with a slide show to accompany the oral presentation. For each guideline the following will be included:

1. Statement of the guideline
2. Explanation of the guideline
3. Demonstration of why you should follow the guideline

The presentation will be created using a menu to select each guideline. Each slide will have interactive buttons to go to the next slide, the previous slide, the menu slide, or the ending slide.

Step 2: Understand the Problem.

Audience:

The audience will be the DTP class. There are 35 graphics majors in the class. Two others are non-majors but have a good knowledge of graphics.

Required Outcomes of the Slide Show:

1. Communicate a set of graphics guidelines to classmates.
2. Design a menu-driven, well-designed slide show.
3. Communicate these guidelines to classmates that were not in class.

Required Knowledge of the Problem to Develop the Slide Show:
The guidelines in the chosen guideline type

Expected Knowledge of the Audience:
Basic knowledge of graphics and design

Environment of Presentation:

1. Classroom with computer/projector/screen and software
2. Room seats up to 50 people.

Figure 7.1 (continued)

Step 3: Identify Valid Alternative Methods to Solve the Problem.

1. Choice sets of guidelines:
   a. Guidelines for layouts
   b. Guidelines for text use
   c. Guidelines for adding artwork
   d. Guidelines for adding color
   e. General guidelines
2. Background: Choose a predesigned background or make my own.
3. Layouts of each slide
4. Graphics for each slide
5. Slide sequence
6. Buttons on background or on individual slides
7. Sound or no sound
8. Transition choice
9. Animation, if any

Step 4: Select the Best Method to Solve the Problem from the List of Alternative Solutions.

1. Choice of guideline types: Guidelines for adding artwork:
   a. *Art should serve a purpose.* It is important to justify why a graphic element is to be added to a document. This serves to help you add appropriate artwork to enhance the message of the document.
   b. Aim artwork toward the intended direction of eye flow. Most artwork is facing or pointing a specific direction. This may help the viewer's eye flow to the information on the page or it may direct the eye off the page. Which one is easier to read? Which one helps the eye to stay on the page? It often takes little effort to increase communication and retention of the information by placing the artwork correctly on your designed page.
   c. Use artwork that is appropriate for the purpose of the document. It is better to use no artwork than inappropriate artwork. For example, you would not use a picture of a snowmobile in a slide show about scuba diving or a map of Asia in a slide show about Brazil.
2. Background: Use a predesigned background: Notebook design.
3. Layouts of each slide: Use the title layout for the first and last slides and the bulleted list layout for other slides.
4. Graphics for each slide: Use clipart to demonstrate each guideline.
5. Slide sequence. See below.
6. Buttons on background or on individual slides. Buttons on the background of all slides except the intro slide and the ending slide will include the EXIT button that jumps to last slide, the MENU button that jumps to the menu slide, the NEXT button that goes to the next slide, and the PREVIOUS button that goes to the previous slide. Those slides using the title layout will have no buttons. The menu slide will have buttons that jump to each set of slides that are about each guideline. No slides will be hidden; thus, the slide show may be viewed continuously or through the use of the menu.
7. Sound or no sound: No sound will be included since this will accompany a speech.
8. Transition choice: Transitions will be used. The storyboards will designate the transition for each slide.
9. Any animation: Text will be animated to come in one line at a time with the previous line dimmed to a lighter shade of the same color.

(continued)

Figure 7.1 Slide Show Planning Guide for Case Study 1.

Step 4: Select the Best Method to Solve the Problem from the List of Alternative Solutions. (con't)

Slide Show Overview:

Slide 1: Intro slide
Slide 2: Menu slide
Slide 3: First guideline: Statement of guideline 1
Slide 4: Explanation of guideline 1
Slide 5: Good Example
Slide 6: Bad Example
Slide 7: Second guideline: Statement of guideline 2
Slide 8: Explanation of guideline 2
Slide 9: Good Example
Slide 10: Bad Example
Slide 11: Third guideline: Statement of guideline 3
Slide 12: Explanation of guideline 3
Slide 13: Good Example
Slide 14: Bad Example
Slide 15: Ending Slide

Step 5: Plan Your Solution.

Software to be used: ___Presentation graphics___

Background:

___X___ Premade Background Name: ___Notebook___

______ Own Background Description:

Files to be imported:

File	Description	Use	Location
Clipart files to demonstrate good and bad and to add variety to other slides.			c:\my data\graphics/clipart

Slide Size: ___10 x 7½___

Paper Color for Handouts: ___White___ No. of Slides Per Page: ___6___

Print in Color/B&W: Handouts: ___B&W___ Speaker's Notes: ___Color___

Figure 7.1 (continued)

Header Contents: None

Footer Contents:

Date	Student Name and Class	Slide XX

Materials Needed:

Hardware: In classroom

Software: On classroom computer

Projector/Screen: In classroom

Handouts: Yes Number: 40

Speaker's Notes: Yes Notebook/Computer: Notebook

Other: ______

Interactivity Chart:

Slides 2 through 14 have buttons going to slide 15.

Slides 3 through 14 have buttons going to slide 2.

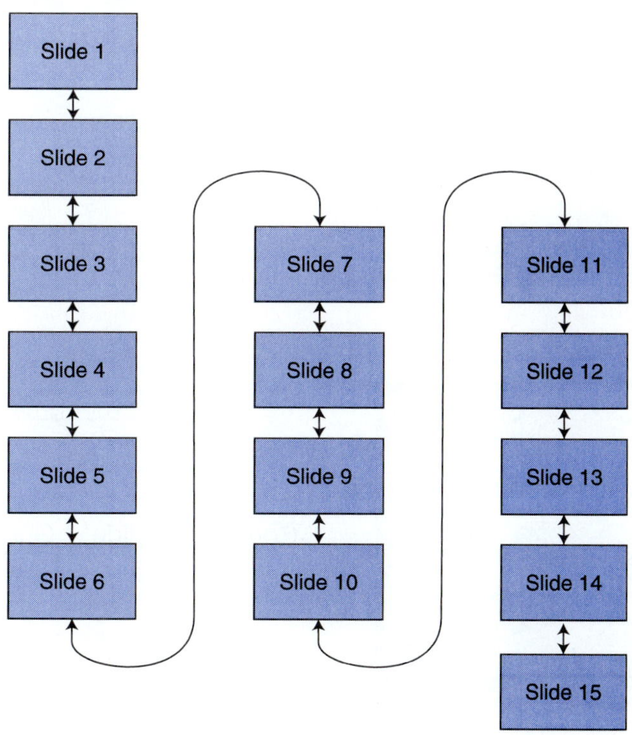

(continued)

Figure 7.1 Slide Show Planning Guide for Case Study 1.

Step 5: Plan Your Solution. (con't)

Storyboards: Indicate animation on the diagram of the slide:

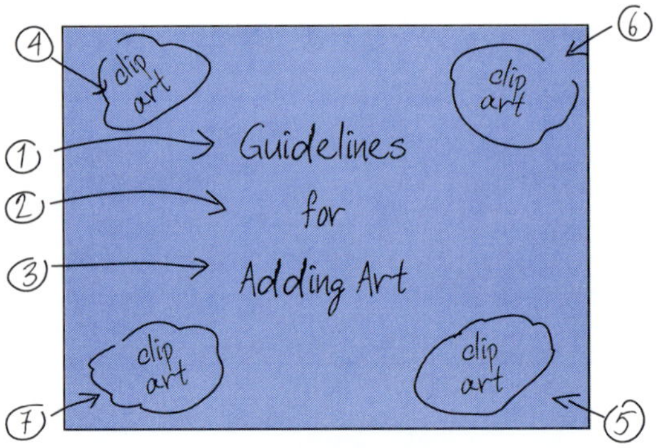

Transition: Cover right

Layout: Title

Comments: Slide 1: Intro Slide

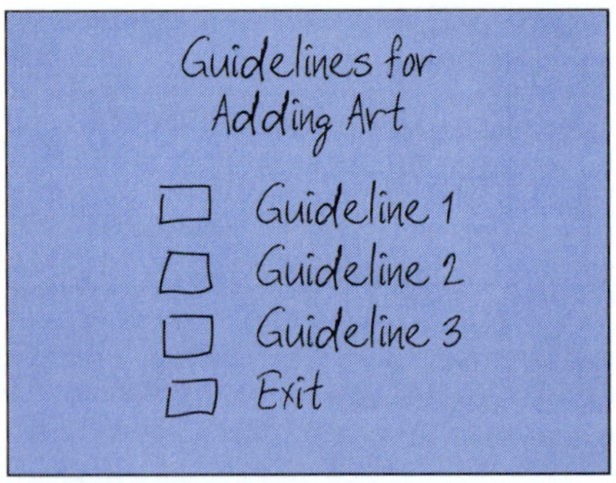

Transition: Cover right top

Layout: Bulleted List

Comments: Slide 2: Menu

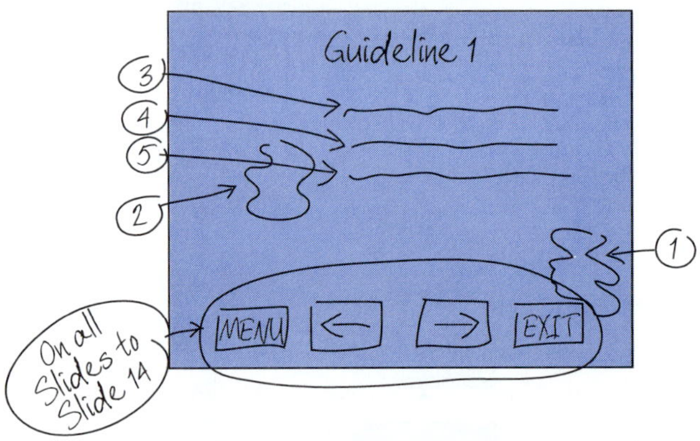

Transition: Cover right top

Layout: Bulleted List

Comments: Slide 3: Guideline 1:

Art should serve a purpose.

Statement of the guideline

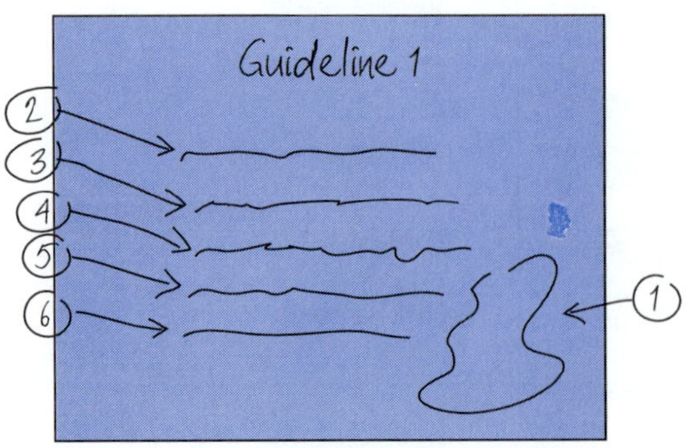

Transition: Cover right top

Layout: Bulleted List

Comments: Slide 4: Guideline 1

Explanation of Guideline

Figure 7.1 (continued)

Storyboards: Indicate animation on the diagram of the slide:

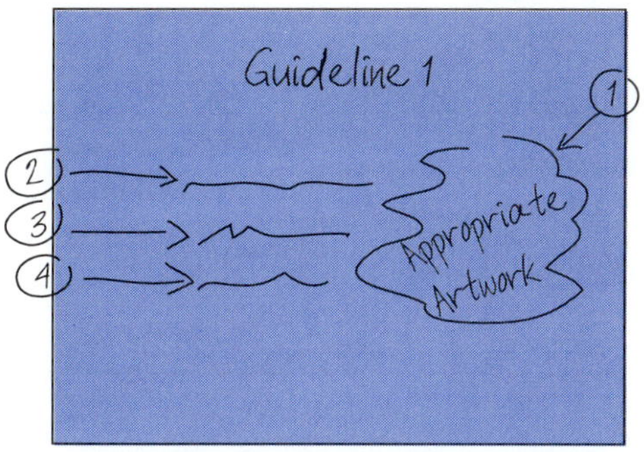

Transition: Cover right top

Layout: Bulleted List

Comments: Slide 5: Guideline 1

Good Example

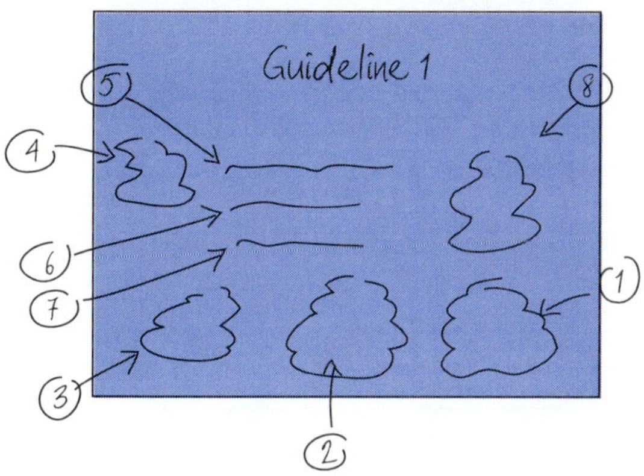

Transition: Cover right top

Layout: Bulleted List

Comments: Slide 6: Guideline 1

Bad Example

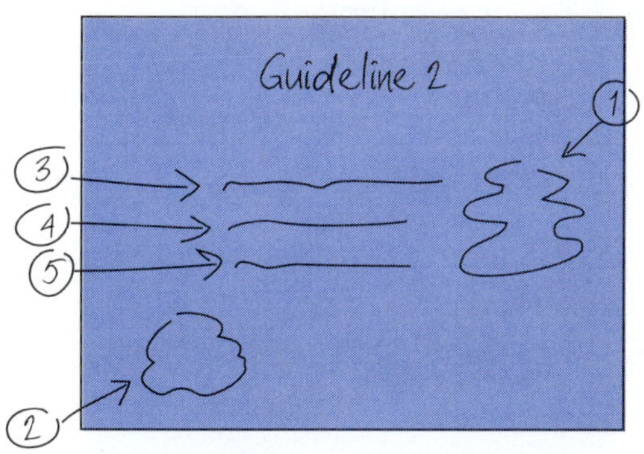

Transition: Cover left top

Layout: Bulleted List

Comments: Slide 7: Guideline 2:

Aim artwork toward the intended direction of eye flow. Statement of the guideline

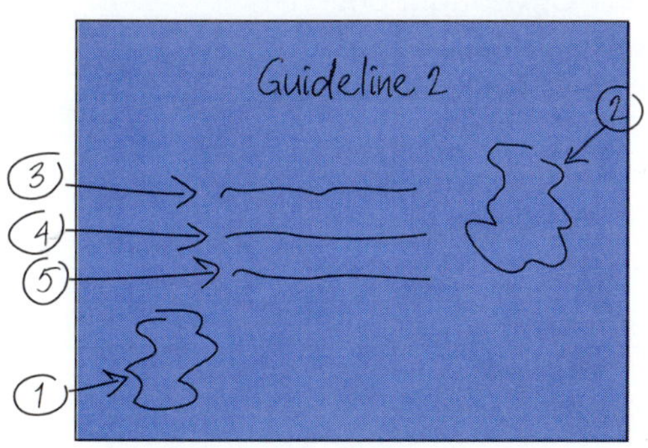

Transition: Cover left top

Layout: Bulleted List

Comments: Slide 8: Guideline 2

Explanation of Guideline

(continued)

Figure 7.1 Slide Show Planning Guide for Case Study 1.

Step 5: Plan Your Solution. (con't)

Storyboards: Indicate animation on the diagram of the slide:

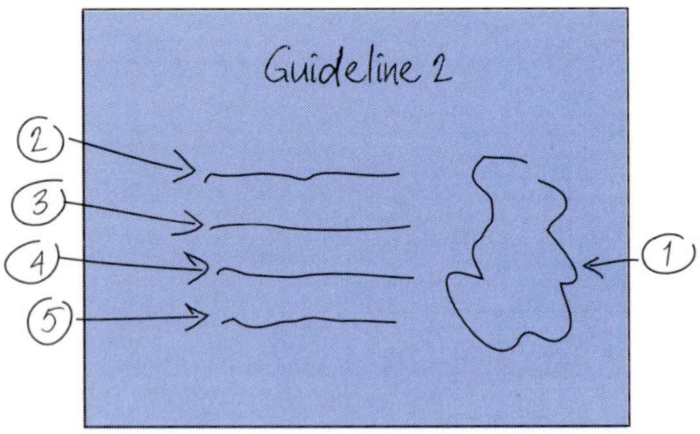

Transition: Cover left top

Layout: Bulleted List

Comments: Slide 9: Guideline 2

Good Example

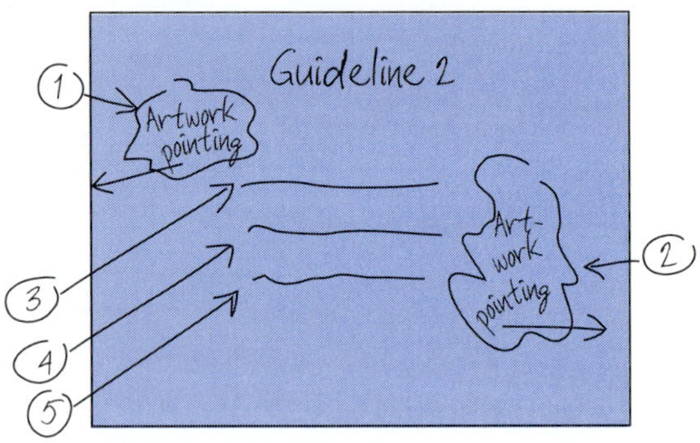

Transition: Cover left top

Layout: Bulleted List

Comments: Slide 8: Guideline 1

Bad Example

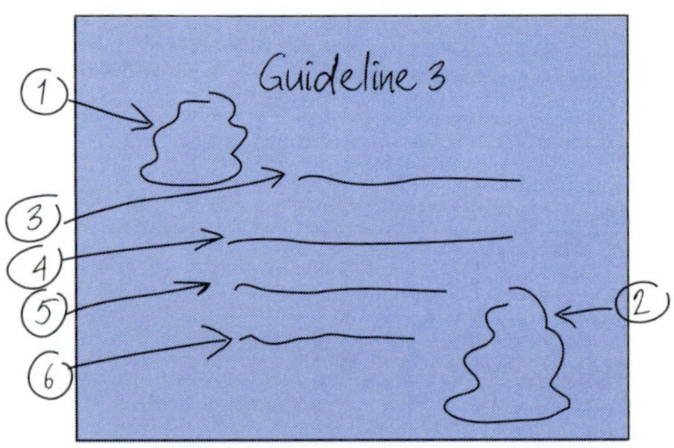

Transition: Cover right bottom

Layout: Bulleted List

Comments: Slide 11: Guideline 3:

Use artwork that is appropriate for the purpose of the document. Statement of the guideline

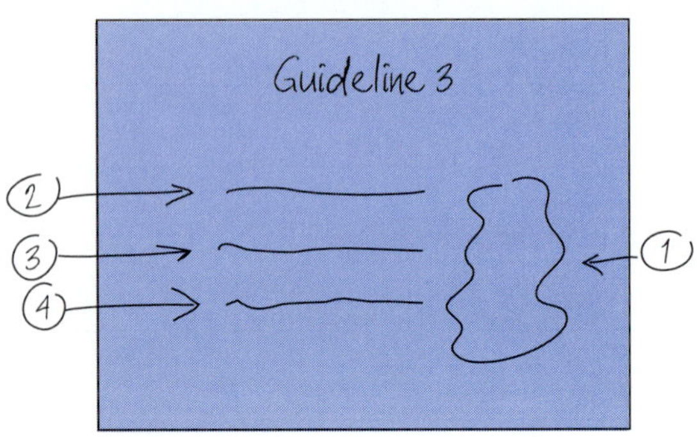

Transition: Cover right bottom

Layout: Bulleted List

Comments: Slide 12: Guideline 3

Explanation of Guideline

Figure 7.1 (continued)

Storyboards: Indicate animation on the diagram of the slide:

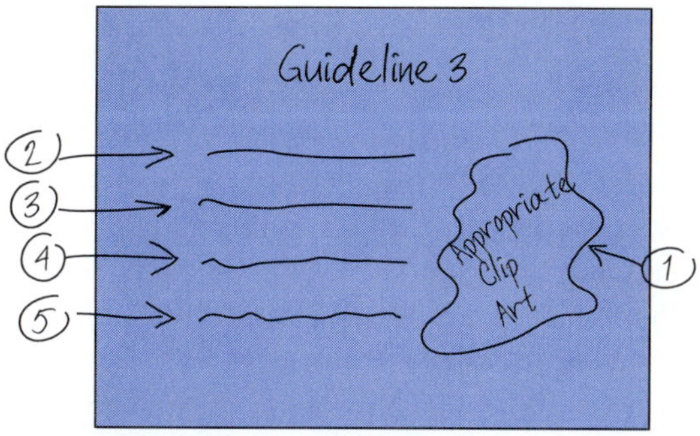

Transition: Cover right bottom

Layout: Bulleted List

Comments: Slide 13: Guideline 3

Good Example

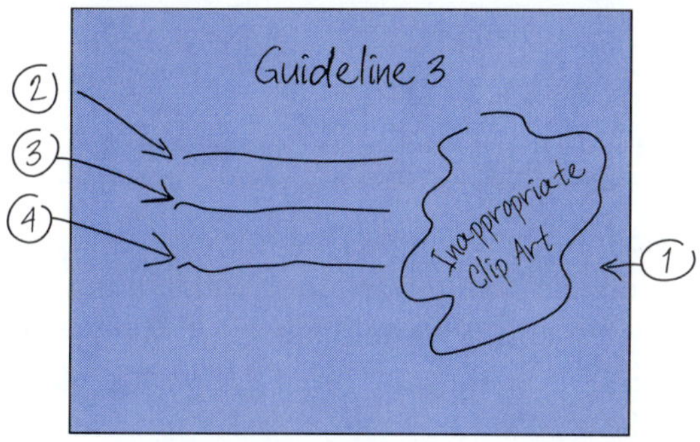

Transition: Cover right bottom

Layout: Bulleted List

Comments: Slide 14: Guideline 3

Bad Example

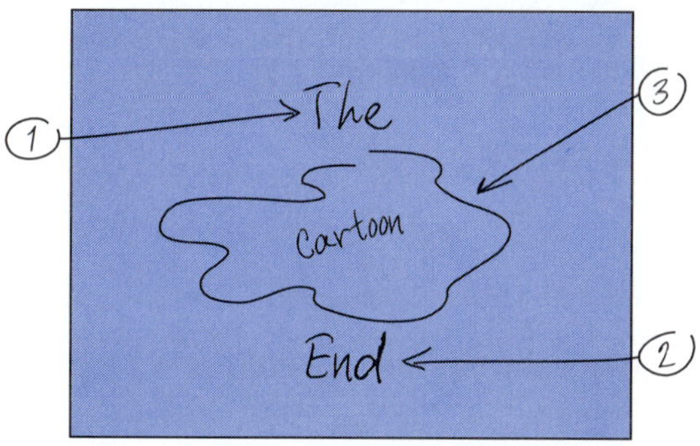

Transition: Dissolve

Layout: Title

Comments: Slide 15: Ending

Step 6: Evaluate the Solution. List the criteria for evaluating the completed document.

Criteria for evaluation of the slide show:

1. Did the slide show communicate information about the guidelines?
2. Were the graphics appropriate?
3. Was the spelling correct?
4. Did the interactivity work correctly?
5. Could you easily read the slides from the back of the room?
6. Were any of the slides cluttered?
7. Were any of the slides too empty?

This is an example of a presentation that would be given in a classroom situation by a student. The slide show consists of six parts:

1. Introduction
2. Menu
3. First guideline information
4. Second guideline information
5. Third guideline information
6. Ending

Slide shows should have an introduction section, an information section, and an ending or summary section. You want to introduce what the slide show is about, present the information, and end with a summary of what was presented. You want your audience to know when the slide show is completed. Provide consistency throughout the slide show in the form of background, transitions, and text formats. Some variety in the form of graphics and/or animations must be incorporated.

Case Study 2: Training Session

Case Study 2: A Lab Assistant Training Session

You have been working as a student assistant in the computer lab for over one year. The lab instructor is impressed by your knowledge of lab procedures, which are a required part of the lab assistant's duties, and with your ability to help students. The lab instructor needs a slide show to train new lab assistants as they are hired. He would like you to create this presentation. The sections that he would like to have in the slide show are as follows:

1. Opening procedures
2. Closing procedures
3. Hardware failure procedures
4. Software failure procedures
5. Material checkout procedures
6. Student help procedures

The lab instructor has taken pictures of activities in the lab including:

Location of keys
Student opening doors
Student locking doors
Hardware failure notice
Software failure notice
Student checking out a book
Right way to help another student
Wrong way to help another student
Students working in the lab
Student lab assistants
Lab technician

The lab instructor would like you to incorporate these pictures into the slide show. He would like the slide show to be menu driven for each of the above topics. Each slide should have the option to go to the next slide, the previous slide, the menu slide, and the ending slide. You will need to include instructions on how to use the slide show and a printed page as to how to start the show. Figure 7.2 presents the slide show planning guide for this case study.

Figure 7.2 Slide Show Planning Guide for Case Study 2.

SLIDE SHOW PLANNING GUIDE

Name of Document: Lab Training Slide Show Date: 1/20/2002

Location of Electronic File: m:\lab assistants\

Name: William Ernest

Name of Client: Mr. Computerman, Lab Instructor

Step 1: Identify the Problem by Writing the Problem Statement.

A slide show is needed to train new lab assistants as they are hired in the computer lab. The sections that will be included in the slide show are as follows:

1. Opening procedures
2. Closing procedures
3. Hardware failure procedures
4. Software failure procedures
5. Material checkout procedures
6. Student help procedures

The lab instructor has taken digital pictures of activities in the lab including:

Location of keys
Student opening doors
Student locking doors
Hardware failure notice
Software failure notice
Student checking out a book
Right way to help another student
Wrong way to help another student
Students working in the lab
Student lab assistants
Lab technician

These pictures are to be incorporated into the slide show. The slide show must be menu driven for each of the above topics. Each slide must have the option to go to the next slide, the previous slide, the menu slide, and the ending slide. Instructions as to how to use the slide show will be included on one slide. After the slide show is completed, a printed page as to how to start the show will be created. There will be a six-question quiz at the end of the slide show with one question on each topic.

(continued)

Figure 7.2 Slide Show Planning Guide for Case Study 2.

Step 2: Understand the Problem.

Audience:

Newly hired lab assistants.

Required Outcomes of the Slide Show:

1. To train new lab assistants on six of their duties.
2. To communicate how to complete tasks in these areas.
3. To design an interesting slide show.

Required Knowledge of the Problem to Develop the Slide Show:

Knowledge of the lab, duties of the lab assistants, and how to properly help students on the computer.

Expected Knowledge of the Audience:

Computer experience, computer literate, and working knowledge of the lab from a student's point of view.

Environment of Presentation:

The slide show will be a one-on-one presentation. The lab assistant will use a computer in the lab to go through the training. The slide show and other needed software will be located on the lab server.

Step 3: Identify Valid Alternative Methods to Solve the Problem.

1. Background: Choose a predesigned background or make my own.
2. Layouts of each slide
3. Graphics for each slide
4. Slide sequence
5. Buttons on background or on individual slides
6. Sound or no sound
7. Transition choice
8. Animation, if any

Step 4: Select the Best Method to Solve the Problem from the List of Alternative Solutions.

1. Background: Make my own.
2. The intro slide, the intro slide to each section, and the ending slide will use title layouts. Other slides will use text and graphics layouts.
3. Graphics will consist of digital pictures and clip art.
4. Slide sequence. See below.
5. The next, previous, menu, and ending buttons will be placed on the background for all but the title layout slides. The menu slide will have buttons to go to each section. All section slides will be hidden.
6. No sound.
7. Transition choice. See storyboards.
8. Any animation? Each line should come in separately with the previous line dimmed.
9. Text should be short and technical.

Figure 7.2 (continued)

Slide Show Overview:

Slide 1: Intro slide
Slide 2: Instructions for use
Slide 3: Menu
Slide 4: Intro to Opening Procedures
Slide 5–8: Information about Opening Procedures
Slide 9: End of Opening Procedures
Slide 10: Intro to Closing Procedures
Slide 11–14: Information about Closing Procedures
Slide 15: End of Closing Procedures
Slide 16: Intro to Hardware Failure Procedures
Slide 17–20: Information about Hardware Failure Procedures
Slide 21: End of Hardware Failure Procedures
Slide 22: Intro to Software Failure Procedures
Slide 23–26: Information about Software Failure Procedures
Slide 27: End of Software Failure Procedures
Slide 28: Intro to Material Checkout Procedures
Slide 29–32: Information about Material Checkout Procedures
Slide 33: End of Material Checkout Procedures
Slide 34: Intro to Student Help Procedures
Slide 35–38: Information about Student Help Procedures
Slide 39: End of Student Help Procedures
Slide 40–45: Six Questions
Slide 46: Wrong Slide
Slide 47–48: Ending Slides with Credits

Step 5: Plan Your Solution.

Software to be used: ______Presentation graphics______

Background:

__________ Premade Background Name: ______________________________

_____X_____ Own Background Description:

The background will be light blue with a photograph of the lab in the upper left corner. Coming off the right bottom of this photograph will be one of a computer cable.

(continued)

Figure 7.2 Slide Show Planning Guide for Case Study 2.

Step 5: Plan Your Solution. (con't)

Files to be imported:

File	Description	Use	Location
Students in Lab	Students working in the lab	Slide 1	m:\lab assistants\train\
Key Location	Location of keys	Slide 2	m:\lab assistants\train\
Open Doors	Student opening doors	Slide 3	m:\lab assistants\train\
Lock Doors	Student locking doors	Slide 11	m:\lab assistants\train\
Hardware Failure	Hardware failure notice	Slide 17	m:\lab assistants\train\
Software Failure	Software failure notice	Slide 23	m:\lab assistants\train\
Book Checkout	Student checking out book	Slide 29	m:\lab assistants\train\
Student Help Okay	Right way to help student	Slide 35	m:\lab assistants\train\
Student Help Not	Wrong way to help student	Slide 36	m:\lab assistants\train\
Lab Assistants	Student lab assistants	Slide 47	m:\lab assistants\train\
Lab Tech	Lab technician	Slide 47	m:\lab assistants\train\

Slide Size: 10 x 7½

Paper Color for Handouts: White No. of Slides Per Page: 6

Print in Color/B&W: Handouts: B&W Speaker's Notes: ____________

Header Contents: None

Footer Contents:

Date	Student Name and Class	Slide XX

Materials Needed:

Hardware: Use lab computers

Software: On lab computers

Projector/Screen: Use computer monitor

Handouts: Yes Number: 20

Speaker's Notes: No Notebook/Computer: ____________

Other: Printed page for execution instructions

Figure 7.2 (continued)

Interactivity Chart:

Note:
Slides 4–46 are hidden.
Slides 2–46 have a button to slide 3.
Slides 4–38 have a button to slide 40.
Slides 2–38 have a Next button and a Previous button.
On slides 4, 10, 16, 22, 28, and 34 the Previous button returns to slide 3. On slides 9, 15, 21, 27, and 38 the Next button returns to slide 3.

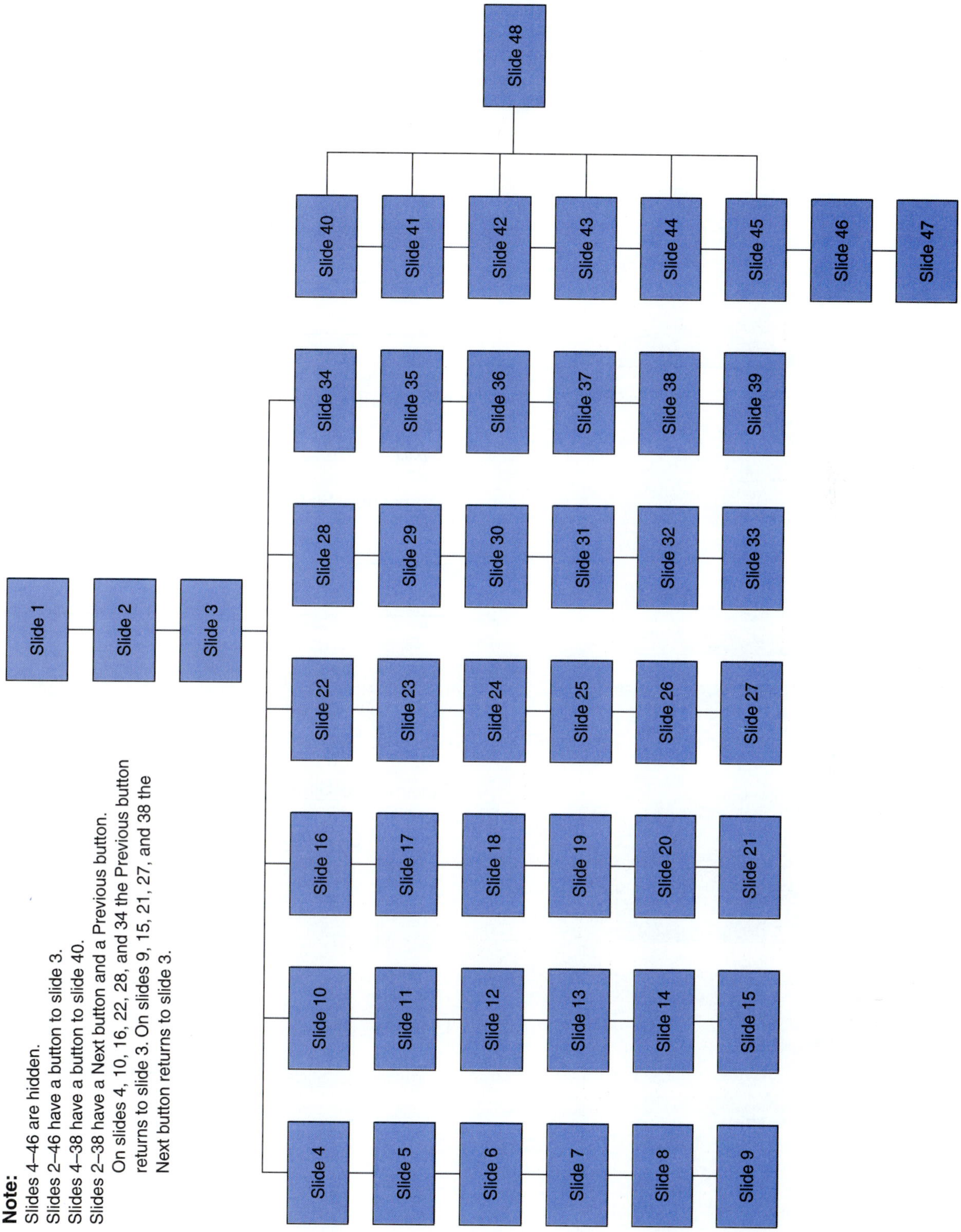

(continued)

Figure 7.2 Slide Show Planning Guide for Case Study 2.

***Step 5:* Plan Your Solution. (con't)**

Storyboards: Indicate animation on the diagram of the slide:

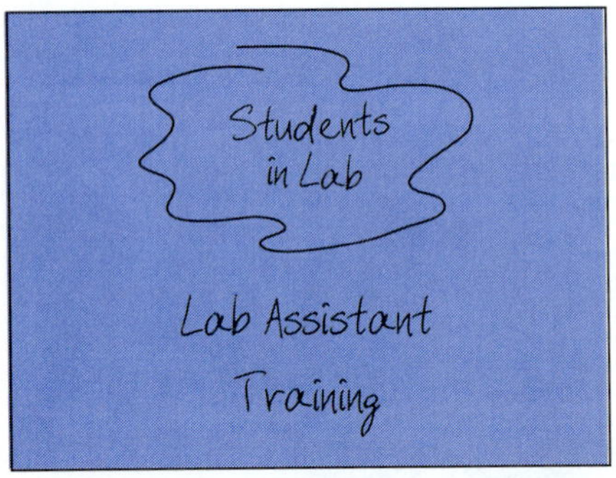

Transition: Box In

Layout: Title

Comments: Slide 1: Intro

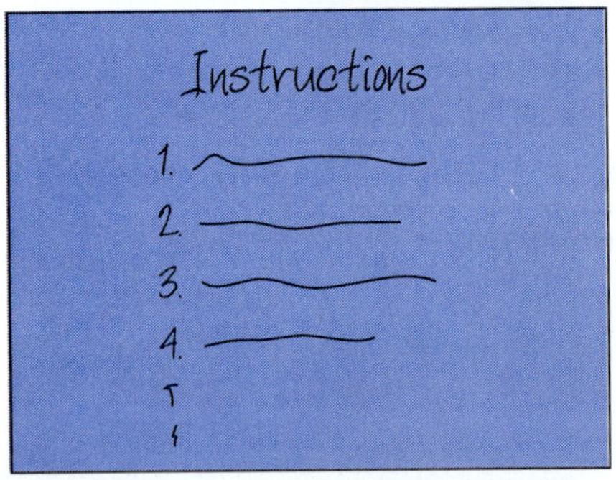

Transition: Box Out

Layout: Text

Comments: Slide 2: Instructions

Transition: Checkerboard Across

Layout: Bulleted List

Comments: Slide 3: Menu
6 buttons for sections

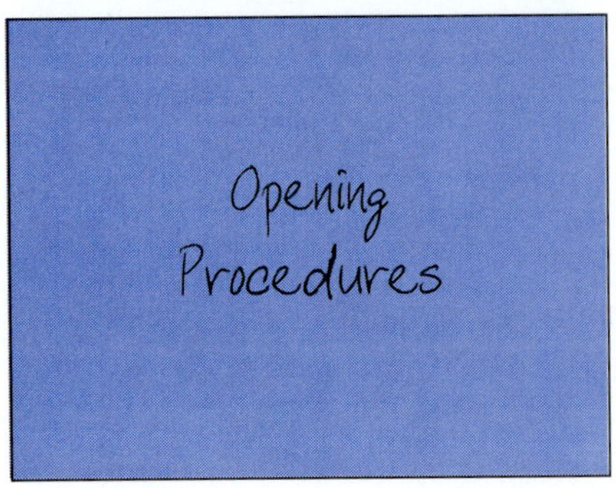

Transition: Uncover right

Layout: Title

Comments: Slide 4: Intro to Section
Opening Procedures

Figure 7.2 (continued)

Storyboards: Indicate animation on the diagram of the slide:

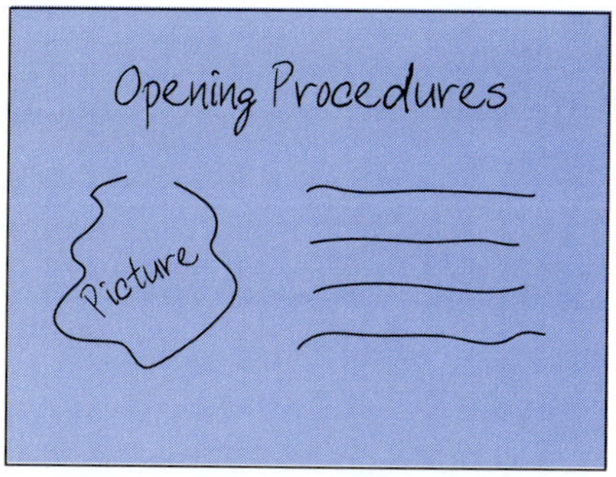

Transition: Uncover Right

Layout: Text and Graphics

Comments: Slides 5–8: Information on Opening Procedures—Same Layout

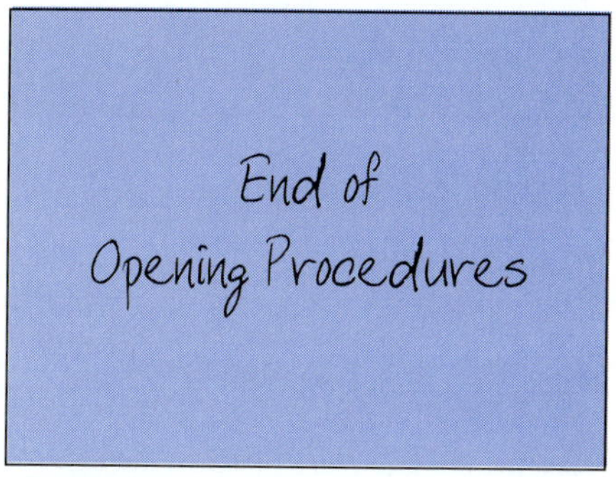

Transition: Uncover Right

Layout: Title

Comments: Slide 9

End Opening Procedures Section

Transition: Uncover Right Top

Layout: Same as Opening Procedures

Comments: Slides 10–15

Closing Procedures section

Same format as Opening Procedures

Transition: Uncover Left Top

Layout: Same as Opening Procedures

Comments: Slides 16–21

Hardware Failure Procedures section

Same format as Opening Procedures

(continued)

Figure 7.2 Slide Show Planning Guide for Case Study 2.

Step 5: Plan Your Solution. (con't)

Storyboards: Indicate animation on the diagram of the slide:

Transition: Uncover Right Bottom

Layout: Same as Opening Procedures

Comments: Slides 22–27

Software Failure Procedures section

Same format as Opening Procedures

Transition: Uncover Left Bottom

Layout: Same as Opening Procedures

Comments: Slides 28–33

Material Checkout Procedures section

Same format as Opening Procedures

Transition: Uncover Top

Layout: Sames as Opening Procedures

Comments: Slides 33–39

Student Help Procedures section

Same format as Opening Procedures

Transition: Dissolve

Layout: Text

Comments: Slides 40–45

Questions

True and False Buttons

Figure 7.2 (continued)

Storyboards: Indicate animation on the diagram of the slide:

Transition: Dissolve

Layout: Text

Comments: Slide 46

Wrong answer

Hot spot to go back to question

Transition: Blinds Vertical

Layout: Bulleted List

Comments: Slide 47

Credit Lines

Transition: Blinds Vertical

Layout: Title

Comments: Slide 48

Ending slide

Step 6: **Evaluate the Solution. List the criteria for evaluating the completed document.**

1. Does the slide show communicate the information to the new lab assistants?
2. Can the new lab assistant answer the questions?
3. Does the slide show hold the interest of the trainee?
4. Are the graphics appropriate to each slide?
5. Are the words spelled correctly?
6. Do I like the slide show?
7. Does Mr. Computerman like the slide show?

In this case the slide show is made of eight parts:

1. Introduction
2. Opening procedures
3. Closing procedures
4. Hardware failure procedures
5. Software failure procedures
6. Material checkout procedures
7. Student help procedures
8. Ending

The introduction includes instructions as to how to use the slide show. The ending has a quiz with one question about each of the six sections of information. The answers are buttons linked to a slide that says if the answer is right or wrong. If the answer is correct it goes to the next slide, if wrong it goes back to the question. The last slide is the ending slide with credits as to who developed the slide show.

Case Study 3: Exhibit

Case Study 3: A Computer Club Exhibit

Your school has a showcase that is used to highlight various clubs. The computer club has the showcase for the month of March. The club has decided to put a computer in the showcase and pictures of club activities. The computer will have a continuous running slide show of the club's activities. You have been put in charge of creating this slide show. Another club member is in charge of pictures for use in the presentation and in the exhibit. The items the club would like to highlight are meetings, fun activities, fund-raising activities, and service activities for the school and the community. Figure 7.3 presents the slide show planning guide for this case study.

Figure 7.3 Slide Show Planning Guide for Case Study 3

SLIDE SHOW PLANNING GUIDE

Name of Document: Club Exhibit Slide Show Date: 9/7/2002

Location of Electronic File: c:\my data\school\club\exhibit\

Name: James Poly

Name of Client: Computer Club

Step 1: Identify the Problem by Writing the Problem Statement.

The computer club at school is planning a continuous running slide show on computer club activities during an exhibit in the student showcase. The slide show will highlight meetings, fun activities, fund-raising activities, and service activities for the school and the community.

Step 2: Understand the Problem.

Audience:

The audience will be the school community including students, faculty, staff, and visitors to the campus.

Figure 7.3 (continued)

Required Outcomes of the Slide Show:

1. Communicate to others as to what the computer club activities include.
2. Demonstrate the abilities of computer students through a well-designed slide show.
3. Advertise the club activities to prospective members.

Required Knowledge of the Problem to Develop the Slide Show:
The computer club's activities.

Expected Knowledge of the Audience:
None.

Environment of Presentation:
Student showcase in the main hall of the administration building.

Step 3: Identify Valid Alternative Methods to Solve the Problem.

1. Background: Choose a predesigned background or make our own.
2. Layouts of each slide
3. Graphics for each slide
4. Slide sequence
5. Transition choice
6. Animation, if any

Step 4: Select the Best Method to Solve the Problem from the List of Alternative Solutions.

1. Design our own background with the computer club logo and name on each slide.
2. Use title layouts for the intro and ending slides for each section. All other slides will use bulleted list layout.
3. Julie is taking digital photographs of each activity.
4. Slide sequence. See below.
5. Transitions will be specified on the storyboards
6. Text should be animated one line at a time.

Slide Show Overview:

Slide 1: Intro to Meetings section
Slides 2–5: Photographs and text on meetings
Slide 6: Ending to Meetings section
Slide 7: Intro to Fun Activities section
Slide 8–11: Photographs and text on fun activities
Slide 12: Ending to Fun Activities section
Slide 13: Intro to Fund-raising Activities section
Slide 14–17: Photographs and text on fund-raising activities
Slide 18: Ending to Fund-raising Activities section
Slide 19: Intro to Service Activities for the School and the Community section
Slides 20–23: Photographs and text on service activities for the school and the community
Slide 24: Ending to Service Activities for the School and the Community Section

Execute as a continuous running slide show.

(continued)

Figure 7.3 Slide Show Planning Guide for Case Study 3

Step 5: Plan Your Solution.

Software to be used: Presentation graphics

Background:

_____ Premade Background Name: _____

X Own Background Description:

The background will be light green with the computer club log, club name, and contact person.

Files to be imported:

File	Description	Use	Location
Meetings Off	Meetings Officers	Slide 2	c:\my data\school\club\exhibit
Meetings Mem	Meetings Members	Slide 3	c:\my data\school\club\exhibit
Meetings Chat	Meetings Social Hour	Slide 4	c:\my data\school\club\exhibit
Meetings Vote	Meetings Voting	Slide 5	c:\my data\school\club\exhibit
Fun Act Picnic	Picnic	Slide 8	c:\my data\school\club\exhibit
Fun Act Bowl	Bowling	Slide 9	c:\my data\school\club\exhibit
Fun Act Party	Party	Slide 10	c:\my data\school\club\exhibit
Fun Act Expo	Exposition	Slide 11	c:\my data\school\club\exhibit
Money Coffee	Coffee Stand	Slide 14	c:\my data\school\club\exhibit
Money Disks	Selling Supplies	Slide 15	c:\my data\school\club\exhibit
Money Art Fair	Food at Art Fair	Slide 16	c:\my data\school\club\exhibit
Money Car	Car Wash	Slide 17	c:\my data\school\club\exhibit
Service Clean	Clean up campus	Slide 20	c:\my data\school\club\exhibit
Service Help	Help students	Slide 21	c:\my data\school\club\exhibit
Service Tutor	Tutor students	Slide 22	c:\my data\school\club\exhibit
Service Bowl	Bowl-a-thon	Slide 23	c:\my data\school\club\exhibit

Slide Size: 10 x 7½

Paper Color for Handouts: None No. of Slides Per Page: _____

Print in Color/B&W: Handouts: None Speaker's Notes: _____

Figure 7.3 (continued)

Header Contents: None

Footer Contents:

Date	Developer Name	Slide XX

Materials Needed:

Hardware: Computer/monitor in showcase

Software: On computer

Projector/Screen: None

Handouts: None Number: ______

Speaker's Notes: None Notebook/Computer: ______

Other: ______

Interactivity Chart:

The interactivity chart for this case is linear. The slide show starts with slide 1 and continues automatically through the last slide. The slide show then returns automatically to slide 1.

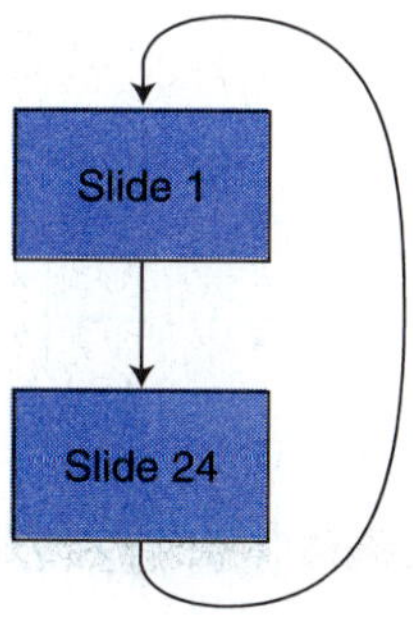

(continued)

Figure 7.3 Slide Show Planning Guide for Case Study 3

Step 5: **Plan Your Solution. (con't)**

Storyboards: Indicate animation on the diagram of the slide:

Transition: Dissolve

Layout: Title

Comments: Slide 1: Intro to Meetings

Transition: Cover Right

Layout: Bulleted List

Comments: Slides 2–5

Slides will have photograph of meeting

and text explaining activity

Transition: Cover Right Top

Layout: Title

Comments: Slide 6

End of Meetings section

Transition: Dissolve

Layout: Title

Comments: Slide 7: Intro to Fun activities section

Figure 7.3 (continued)

Storyboards: Indicate animation on the diagram of the slide:

Transition: Cover Right

Layout: Bulleted List

Comments: Slides 8–11

Slides will have photograph of fun activites and text explaining activity

Transition: Cover Right Top

Layout: Title

Comments: Slide 12

End of Fun Activities section

Transition: Dissolve

Layout: Title

Comments: Slide 13: Intro to Fund-Raising

Activities section

Transition: Cover Right

Layout: Bulleted List

Comments: Slides 14–17

Slides will have photograph of fund-raising activities and text explaining each activity

(continued)

Figure 7.3 Slide Show Planning Guide for Case Study 3

Step 5: **Plan Your Solution. (con't)**

Storyboards: Indicate animation on the diagram of the slide:

Transition: Cover Right Top

Layout: Title

Comments: Slide 18

End of Fund-Raising Activities section

Transition: Dissolve

Layout: Title

Comments: Slide 19: Intro to School and

Community Service Activities section

Transition: Cover Right

Layout: Bulleted List

Comments: Slides 20–23

Slides will have photograph of school and

comm. serv. act and text explaining activity

Transition: Cover Right Top

Layout: Title

Comments: Slide 24

End of School and Community Service

Activities section

Figure 7.3 Slide Show Planning Guide for Case Study 3

Step 6: **Evaluate the Solution. List the criteria for evaluating the completed document.**
1. Does the slide show communicate the club's activities? **2.** After seeing the slide show, would a prospective member want to join? **3.** Does the slide show communicate to faculty, staff, and visitors the purpose of the club? **4.** Are the graphics appropriate to the information on the slides? **5.** Does the club like the slide show? **6.** Does the slide show communicate to others the abilities of computer students?

Because this slide show is meant to be continuous, there is no one introduction slide or ending slide. In this type of a slide show each section should have an introduction slide and an ending slide so people know when the section begins and ends. The slide show has four sections:

1. Meetings
2. Fun activities
3. Fund-raising activities
4. Service activities for the school and the community

Information on each section is complete. It is divided between several slides since the slide show will be viewed on a computer screen and from at least four feet away. The audience could be anyone, but normally will be students. Part of the background is the club name and logo so they are visible to whomever is viewing any slide. The slide show is linear since it is continuous.

Summary

This chapter presents three case studies to be completed using a presentation graphics program. Case Study 1 is a speaker presentation, Case Study 2 is a training session, and Case Study 3 is a presentation for an exhibit. Each case study presents its own completed slide show planning guide.

Problems

1. Develop a slide show planning guide for an interactive slide show on fonts to accompany a speech on fonts. Each slide must have a way to go to the previous slide, the next slide, the ending slide, and skip to the next topic.
2. Develop a slide show planning guide for an interactive slide show on your favorite animal. Include where the animal originates, what it eats, its habitat, and why you like this creature. Each slide must have a way to go to the next slide, the next slide, get more information on the topic, the ending slide, and skip to the next topic.
3. Develop a slide show planning guide for an interactive slide show on your favorite type of vehicle such as sports car, SUV, or sedan. Include in your slide show the type of vehicle, a description of the vehicle, accessories, special features, and why you

like this type of vehicle. Each slide must have a way to go to the next slide, the next slide, get more information on the topic, the ending slide, and skip to the next topic.

4. Develop a slide show planning guide on a trip you would like to take. Include in the slide show options for transportation, lodging, meals, and activities. The slide show must be menu driven by each of the topics. Include a comparison of two selections for a trip such as car transportation, camping, cooking own meals, and fishing; or compare car transportation, hotels, eating out, amusement parks, and museums. Each slide must have a way to go to the previous slide, the next slide, get more information on the topic, the ending slide, and skip to the next topic.
5. Develop a slide show planning guide for a slide show of your choice.

UNIT THREE

WORD PROCESSING AND DESKTOP PUBLISHING

Chapter 8

Word-Processing Concepts and Tools

Overview

Features of a Word Processor

Entering Text

Formatting Text

Editing Text

Printing Text

Planning a Word-Processed Document

Document Planning Guide

Common Documents

Letters on Letterhead

Memos

Reports

Templates

Objectives

When you have finished this chapter, you should be able to:

1. Understand when you would select and use a word processor.
2. Understand functions and features of a word processor.
3. Plan for entering information into a word processor.
4. Know how to edit text in a word processor.
5. Know how to format text in a word processor.
6. Develop text styles.
7. Plan the printing options for a document.
8. Create the plan for developing a document using the document planning guide.

Other than the internet and games, the majority of work created on personal computers at home and in the office is completed through the use of a word processor. Word processing is electronic text editing. In the last 15 years, the word processor has essentially replaced the typewriter. Only a few forms still require a typewriter to complete. Most people who own a computer do not even own a typewriter and if they do it has been stored away in the attic, basement, or garage for posterity.

The basic functions of a word processor are to enter, format, edit, and print text electronically. Other functions include importing files, adding graphics, and completing some spreadsheet and database functions, such as adding formulas to tables and sorting data. This chapter discusses the features of a word processor and explains how to plan a word-processed document.

Features of a Word Processor

The features of a word processor are divided into the basic functions of entering text, formatting text, editing text, and printing text. When you think about completing a document using a word processor, think about these basic functions. For example, ask yourself the following: How will I enter the text? How will I format the text? How will I edit the text? What graphics will I add? How will I print the text? The possible answers to these questions will be presented in this section. Table 8.1 presents the features of a word processor and some examples.

Entering Text

Entering Text

Most text is entered into a word processor through the use of a keyboard. Keyboarding skills are necessary to efficiently use a word processor, just as they were when you used a typewriter. If you will be doing a lot of keyboard entry of text, it is worth your time and money to invest in a keyboarding class or use keyboarding software that will help you increase these skills.

Scanning Text Using OCR Software

If the text is already in typed form or printed hard copy form, with no compatible electronic equivalent, then it may be scanned into the computer using **optical character recognition (OCR)** software. OCR software is very good, as it looks at groups of dots and interprets them as specific characters; however, keep in mind that OCR software interprets text one character at a time, line by line. If your hard copy document is in columns, you will want to scan one column at a time, as it is difficult to separate the columns when they are read in as one line instead of two column lines. Scanned text is not perfect, so after you have scanned in your text, send it through the spell checker to catch any obvious spelling errors. Then take time to proofread the document. Scanning text from hard copy saves time in rekeying the text.

File Compatibility

If you have an electronic file of the text from a different source, then you may import the text assuming it is compatible with your word processor. If it is not compatible, you may have to save the original text file as a rich text format (RTF) or an ASCII (American Standard Code for Information Interchange) format file. If you do not have a way to make the text compatible electronically with your present software and you do not have a hard copy, then the file is considered lost. Text that you plan to archive for possible future use should be saved in both the original software format and in RTF or ASCII format. In this way you should be able to import it into whatever software you will be using in the future.

Tables and Table Functions

Text, including numbers that will be entered into tables, should be planned carefully, with specialized spacing and positioning. See Table 8.2 for an example of a table developed in a word processor. Column four contains the formula to sum the numbers to the left (SUM(LEFT)). A word processor contains many functions for tables. Table 8.3 lists some common functions. To efficiently enter data in a table, preplan the number of rows and columns you will need and the contents for each of the table cells such as numbers,

Table 8.1 Word-Processing Features

Feature	Description
Entering Text	
OCR scanning of text	
Tables	Allows the user to enter data in tabular form. See Table 8.2 for an example. Functions used in tables are listed in Table 8.3.
Columns	Allows the user to enter data in column form; for example: This is data in one column as an example of columns. — This is another column of data in the example of columns.
Auto correct feature	Allows the user to set up certain corrections to words for the computer to automatically complete the correction.
Formatting Text	
Character formatting	Specifies how the characters are to look, as discussed in Chapter 4.
Paragraph formatting	Includes alignment, indentation, numbering, bullets, leading, tabs, line control, and page break control. Alignment is discussed in Chapter 3; leading is discussed in Chapter 5. See Figure 8.1 for an example of tabs. Line and page break control allow the user to control where the line and page break occur. Indentation includes left, right, and first-line indents on a paragraph. An example of numbering and bullets include: 1. Norm √ Norm 2. Maureen √ Maureen 3. Sarah √ Sarah
Leading	Indicates the space between paragraphs. Specified either as before or after the paragraph.
Hyphenation	Allows the computer to hyphenate a word that does not fit on a line.
Drop cap	A single character at the beginning of a paragraph that is larger in size and dropped below the line. See Figure 8.2 for an example of a drop cap.
Margin	Includes the space between the edges of the paper and the text area. Header and footer margins are located in the top and bottom margins. The printer margin is the area in which the printer does not print.
Gutter	The area between columns or between the inside margins of facing pages.
Page orientation	The direction of the paper. Landscape makes the width greater than the height; portrait makes the width less than the height.
Editing Text	
Spell check, Grammar check, and Thesaurus	These tools help in spelling, grammar, and choosing alternative words.
Sorting	Arranges the paragraphs in alphabetical or numerical order.
Case change	Allows the user to change to all uppercase, all lowercase, sentence case, title case, or to toggle the case.
Style	Allows the user to set up the formatting for characters and paragraphs as a style. This style is kept with the document. Any paragraph can be designated with a specific style.
Printing Text	Allows the user to specify how the document is to be printed in hard copy form.

Table 8.2 Example of a Table Created in a Word Processor

Sprankle	4.5	3.6	8.1
Jones	3.9	4.0	7.9

Table 8.3 Functions for Use in a Word-Processing Table

Function	Description
ABS(x)	Returns the positive value of a number.
AND(x,y)	Returns the logical resultant of *x* AND *y*.
AVERAGE()	Returns the average of a list of numbers.
COUNT()	Counts the values in a list.
IF(x,y,z)	Returns the value of *y* when *x* is true, and the value of *z* when *x* is false.
INT(x)	Returns the whole part of the number *x*. Does not round.
MIN()	Returns the smallest value in a list.
MAX()	Returns the largest value in a list.
MOD(x,y)	Returns the resultant of *x* MOD *y*.
NOT(x)	Returns the resultant of NOT *x*.
OR(x,y)	Returns the resultant of *x* OR *y*.
PRODUCT()	Returns the product of a list.
ROUND(x,y)	Returns the rounded value of *x* to the *y* decimal places.
SUM()	Returns the sum of a list of numbers.

text, or formulas. Tables may be developed in a word processor or imported from a spreadsheet. A table with many formulas is more efficiently completed in a spreadsheet and then imported into the word-processed document. A simple table may be efficiently completed in the word processor.

Columns

Magazine articles, newsletters, and other types of documents may require columns for text. Columns should be planned carefully as to their width, type and size of font, graphics, and so forth. Due to font differences, font size for columns should be chosen according to font width not point size. Given the same font size, the same sentence may use more or less horizontal space when using different fonts. Font size should be between 1.25 and 2.5 lowercase alphabets in width per column. Columns should be aligned at the bottom and at the top. Any extra space should be taken up with leading or appropriate graphics.

Auto correct

Some word-processing programs have an auto correct function. This function allows you to have the computer correct certain words, capitalization, and certain formatting as you key the text into the computer. This is a wonderful feature especially if you have certain words you are always misspelling in the same way. However, at times you may want to turn off this feature, for example, if you are typing in many acronyms. You do not want the computer to auto correct *th* and replace it with *the* all the time when you really want *th*.

Formatting Text

Formatting Text

When formatting a document, you tell the computer how you want the document to look. Formatting includes character, paragraph, and page formatting. Careful planning of each of these items before you start on the computer should save time in editing at a later date,

Word, Sentence, Line, and Paragraph

especially in the use of preset styles. Some basic definitions need to be clarified here. A **word** is from one space to the next space. A **sentence** is from one period to another period. A **line** is from one cursor return to the next—either a hard cursor return (one that you enter by pushing the enter key) or a soft cursor return (one that the computer inserts). A **paragraph** is from one hard cursor return to the next hard cursor return.

Character Enhancement

Characters may be enhanced in many ways, as described in Chapter 4. Most word-processing software includes character enhancements such as **bold,** *italicized,* underline, ~~strike through~~, double ~~strike through~~, shadow, outline, emboss, engrave, superscript^{superscript}, and subscript$_{\text{subscript}}$. Other character formatting includes font type, font size, character color, and spacing. Chapter 4 discusses fonts and their uses. Knowing the fonts on your computer will help in selecting the appropriate character formatting, which should improve readability, understanding, and retention of information.

Formatting a Paragraph

Formatting a paragraph includes such things as alignment, indentation, numbering, bullets, leading, tabs, widow and orphan control, line control, and page break control. Alignment includes left, right, center, and justified as discussed in Chapter 4.

Indentation

Indentation includes first-line, left, right, and hanging indentations. First-line indentation automatically indents the first line of a paragraph by the selected amount, usually specified in inches. A left or a right indentation indents the entire paragraph by the selected amount on the selected side. **Hanging indentation** indents the second plus lines of a paragraph more than the first line. This is accomplished by using a left indentation of the entire paragraph of a specified amount, such as 0.25 inch, and then specifying the first-line indentation as an equal but negative amount, such as –0.25 inch. The first-line indentation is an additional indentation from the left indentation. Therefore, by indenting the first line by the negative amount of the rest of the paragraph, the first line should be at the margin and the rest of the paragraph "hanging" the specified amount.

Paragraph Numbering and Bullets

You may number your paragraphs in a list form or outline form. The numbering may be single leveled as in a list, or multileveled as in an outline. By using this feature, your paragraphs will automatically be numbered. When using multileveled numbering, use the tab key to indent to the next level and the backspace key or the shift/tab keys to return to a previous level. You may use letters, Arabic numerals, Roman numerals, or any combination in your lists and outlines. Bullets may be used instead of numbers or letters. You may choose any style of bullet. This is the time to explore the symbol fonts to find great bullet characters such as checks, flowers, circles, hearts, and trees. Always remember to use appropriate bullets to enhance the document you are creating.

Leading

Leading is the space either between the lines of the paragraph, before the paragraph, or after the paragraph. You may specify any of these amounts. It is better to specify the leading rather than specifying double or triple spacing. It is easier to modify leading up or down to fit the text in a specified space than it is to adjust the spacing with 1½, double, or triple spacing, unless the required spacing throughout the entire document is double or triple spacing.

Tabs

There are four different types of **tabs:** left, right, center, and decimal tabs. See Figure 8.1 for examples of each. Notice that all tabs are specified from the tab line. In this example, the tab line is at 2 inches. The left tab will **left align** to the **right of the tab line. This is the tab with which most people are familiar. The right tab will right align to the left of the tab line.** The center tab will **center align around the tab line**. The decimal tab will **center align the decimal point on the tab line**. These functions are important to know since whole numbers should use the right tab, decimal numbers should use the decimal tab, and text should use the left or the center tab. The tab leader may be used with any of these tabs. A **tab leader** is the variable-length line between the last character before the tab and the first character after the tab. Figure 8.1 shows examples of a

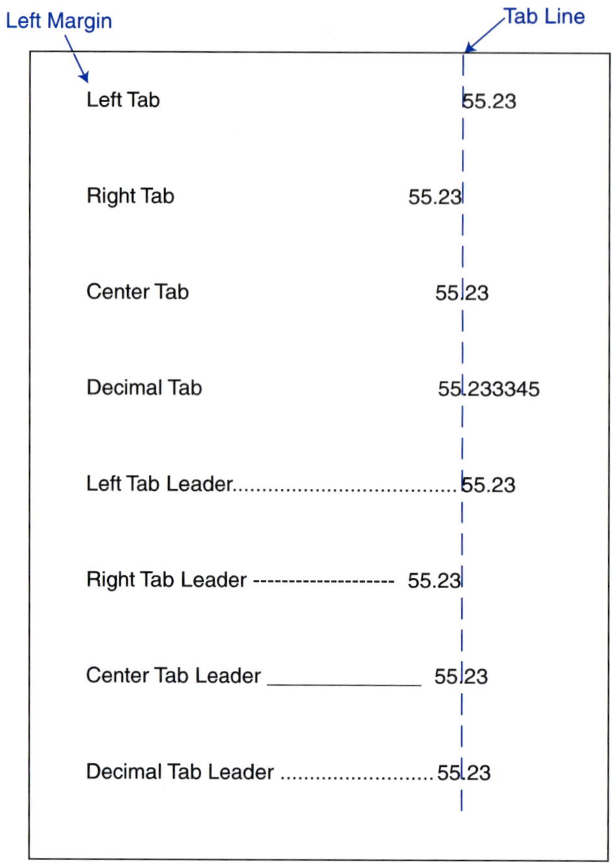

Figure 8.1 Examples of Tabs and Tab Leaders

tab leader with each of the tabs. You may use a variety of lines for the tab leader. Figure 8.1 shows three different line types. These lines are so called because the line "leads," or comes before, the characters typed after the tab key was pressed. Leaders are used in tables of contents, menus, lists of figures, and so forth.

Line Control

Line control includes widow and orphan control, line control, and page break control linked to a paragraph. Widows and orphans are single lines of text at the top or bottom of a page. In most contexts, it is better to avoid an isolated single line. You may specify that at least two lines of text are at the top and bottom of a page. You may also specify the number of lines that are kept together, or specify that the designated paragraph is to be kept on the same page as the next paragraph. You may specify that a page break is linked to a paragraph so that one is inserted before the designated paragraph. These are all options that you should think about when planning and creating a well-designed document.

Hyphenation

Hyphenation is designated as part of the paragraph formatting. You may turn hyphenation on or off, depending on your specifications. When hyphenation is turned on, the computer will soft-hyphenate a word at the end of a line according to the hyphenation rules of the word-processing software. These rules may include hyphenation as designated in the dictionary or a set of rules to follow as to where the hyphen should be placed. The later is not as good as the former; however, it takes more time to look up each word. Use hyphenation if using justified alignment. It is best to turn hyphenation off if you are not pleased with the way your software hyphenates words.

> Drop caps are sometimes used at the beginning of a document. A drop cap is designated to the first letter of the first word in a paragraph, usually the first paragraph of the document. It is enlarged to three lines of text and dropped down to set beside the first three lines of text either in the margin or within the paragraph on the left side.

Figure 8.2 Example of a Drop Cap

Drop Caps

Drop caps are sometimes used at the beginning of a document. A **drop cap** is designated to the first letter of the first word in a paragraph, usually the first paragraph of the document. It is enlarged to three lines of text and dropped down to set beside the first three lines of text either in the margin or within the paragraph on the left side. See Figure 8.2 for an example of a drop cap.

Page Layout

Formatting the way the page should look is called the page layout. Page layout includes how the page looks with text and specified graphics. Page setup is part of the page layout. Page setup designates text margins, header and footer margins, gutter size, paper size, and paper orientation. Page layout includes the page setup items, header contents, footer contents, columns, borders, graphics, and anything else that specifies how the page will look. Page layout is important in the planning of a document. You can save time by sketching the page layout before you go to the computer.

Margins

There are two and sometimes three sets of margins on a page—the text margins, the header and footer margins, and the printer margins. The text margins designate the container for the required text of the document. The footer margin specifies how far from the bottom edge of the paper the footer will be placed. The header margin specifies how far from the top edge of the paper the header will be placed. The printer margin is the distance in from the edge of the paper where the printer does not print.

There are two critical things to remember about margins. First, the header and footer margins must be less than the top and bottom text margins or the header or footer will be printed on top of the text. Second, these margins must be within the printable area. Some printers do print to the edge of the page, but, most printers have a printer margin of 0.25 to 0.5 inch where no printing takes place. Check your printer as to its allowable margin. It is quite disillusioning to finish printing a 15-page report only to find that the page number is half printed on each page.

TIP

To find out your printer's minimum margin, follow these directions:

1. Select a new document.
2. Zoom to view the full page.
3. Draw a 6-point horizontal line from the left to the right edge of the paper.
4. Draw a 6-point vertical line from the top to the bottom edge of the paper.
5. Print the page.
6. Measure the distance where the line begins to the edge of the paper on each of the top, bottom, left, and right sides to find the printer margins.

You will then see how close to the edge of the paper your printer will print. If any of your margins are less than the corresponding amount, your text will not print.

Gutters

The **gutter** is the amount of space between facing pages or between columns. Page gutters are specified by the inside margins of your facing pages. Column gutters are specified when you create your columns. You want enough space between the columns to allow easy readability of the text.

Paper size and Orientation

Most documents are standard letter size; however, you may choose whatever paper size you need. You may need larger paper for a brochure or smaller paper for a specialized document. Be sure your printer will support the paper size you choose. Paper orientation is either portrait (tall) or landscape (wide). **Portrait page orientation,** depending on your operating system, displays the page as taller than it is wide. **Landscape page orientation** displays the page as wider than it is tall. Usually the page orientation defaults to portrait (tall). Use the appropriate orientation for the data being presented on the page. If the data are too wide for portrait, it is better to change to landscape than to decrease the font or graphic size.

Headers and Footers

The header is one or more lines of text printed in the top margin of every page. A footer is one or more lines of text printed in the bottom margin of every page. Typical items in a header or footer are the page number, the date, the time, and other desired text such as the document title or chapter name. Most headers and footers are divided into three areas—the left one-third, the center third, and the right third. You may specify the page number in many different ways and places. You may print the page number by itself in any of the sections of the header or footer, or as, for example, page 13 of 26. If you are printing facing pages, called a spread, the page number may be printed on the outside third of both pages. Think about where and how you want the page numbers printed. During the creation of the document, it is helpful to have the time and date printed in either the header or the footer in order to have a record of when updates were made on the document. You will find that during the creation of a document, there are many edited versions. By printing the time and date, you have control over the versions.

Columns, Borders, and Graphics

Other items for consideration on a page layout includes columns, borders, and graphics. Columns are used to contain text in a smaller area. They are used when part of the page needs to have other information such as a list of people or places, information on a company, or other short articles. Columns break up a page. You may want to consider separating the columns by framing them, or placing a vertical line in the column gutter between. Borders, text boxes, or frames are used to emphasize and/or separate, but use them wisely and sparingly. You may want to shade or color the background inside the border to add extra emphasis.

Editing Text

Editing Text

Once the text has been entered it usually needs editing. Spell check and grammar checks are important to use (see Chapter 3). Other editing may also be required, some of which can be accomplished using cut/copy/paste, deletions, insertions, and type-overs. Other editing tools include sorting, case change, and use of styles.

Thesaurus

The thesaurus allows you to choose synonyms for a selected word. Use this tool when you overuse a word or need a different word to increase readability of the text.

Sorting

Sorting arranges selected paragraphs in ascending or descending order. You may want to use this feature on a list of vocabulary words or key words, for example. This function saves time in alphabetizing a list.

Case Changes

Case change allows you to change the case to all lowercase, all uppercase, title case, sentence case, and toggle case. Changing to lowercase makes all characters lowercase, including proper names. Uppercase makes all characters uppercase. Title case refers to the style of a title where all but small words (a, an, the) start with an uppercase character. Sentence case makes all but the first character in the sentence lowercase. All words that are designated as proper names (first character is uppercase) are not changed even though it may not be a proper name.

Paragraph Styles

A major time-saver is in the use of styles. **Styles** allow you to predefine how you want your text to look before you start. It takes a little time to set up styles, but it saves time in the long run. You need to predetermine how you want the text in each section of your document to look. You may have three or four or more different sets of styles, for example, one style for your body text, one for your headings, another for the subheadings, another for captions, and another for lists. You may select a style to use as you are entering your text or you may select a style for a paragraph or a word at a later time. After you have selected a style for a paragraph, that style is linked to that paragraph or word. At a later date you may decide that you want to use a different font for the captions. Instead of trying to find all of the different captions to change the font, you simply change the font in the caption style. When you do, it will change all paragraphs or words that have been designated with the caption style. You may save any of the styles you like and build a library of styles so you will not have to re-create them. Figure 8.3 shows a style sheet to track your favorite styles and help you create new styles.

Printing Text

Print Options

Printing your document includes such choices as number of copies, reverse printing order, page collation, select printing, color options, plus many more items that differ among software programs and printers. If you change printers, your print window may change. Explore the print window to see what is there. Associated with the print window are page setup and print preview. These options will show you exactly how your pages will look when printed and, thus, save both time and materials.

Planning a Word-Processed Document

Before you start to create a document on the computer, it is best to problem solve as to how to complete the document. Figure 8.4 shows the word-processing planning guide, a six-step problem-solving tool to help you achieve the best document in the least amount of time. A little preplanning can save time in the creation process on the computer. This is the thinking time.

Document Planning Guide

Word-Processing Planning Guide

The word-processing planning guide follows the six steps of problem solving. The first step identifies the problem through the use of a problem statement. The problem statement is a one- or two-paragraph narrative that describes the problem.

Step two helps to understand the problem. Included in this step are the description of the audience, required outcomes of the document, and the required knowledge base of the developer and the audience. A description of the audience is important because it dictates the graphics and terminology. The terminology will differ depending on the age and the knowledge base of the audience. The graphics to be used will also differ especially with age. You probably would not use children's graphics for an audience of 40 year olds who have an in-depth knowledge base of the subject. If the audience has such a knowledge base of the information, buzzwords can be frequently used. On the other hand, if the

Style Sheet

					Enhancements					Indentation		
	Style Name	Style Based On	Font Name	Size	Bold	Underline	Italics	Other	Alignment	Left	Right	First Line
1												
2												
3												
4												
5												
6												
7												
8												
9												
10												
11												
12												
13												
14												
15												
16												
17												
18												
19												
20												
21												
22												
23												
24												
25												
26												
27												
28												

Figure 8.3 Style Sheet

Style Sheet

		Paragraph Leading					Line Controls						
	Style Name	Lines	After	Before	Tabs	Hyphenation	Widows	Orphans	Page Break	Numbering	Bullets	Borders	Other
1													
2													
3													
4													
5													
6													
7													
8													
9													
10													
11													
12													
13													
14													
15													
16													
17													
18													
19													
20													
21													
22													
23													
24													
25													
26													
27													
28													

Figure 8.3 Style Sheet

Figure 8.4 Word-Processing Planning Guide

WORD-PROCESSING PLANNING GUIDE

Name of Document: ______________________________ Date: ______________

Location of Electronic File: ______________________________

Name: ______________________________

Name of Client: ______________________________

Step 1: Identify the Problem by Writing the Problem Statement.

Step 2: Understand the Problem.

Audience:

Required Outcomes of the Document:

Required Knowledge of the Problem to Develop the Document:

Required Knowledge of the Audience:

Step 3: Identify Valid Alternative Methods to Solve the Problem.

Figure 8.4 (continued)

Step 4: Select the Best Method to Solve the Problem from the List of Alternative Solutions.

Step 5: Plan Your Solution.

Software to be used: ____________________

Margins:

Top: ____________________ Top Printer: ____________________
Bottom: ____________________ Bottom Printer: ____________________
Left/Inside:__________Binder:__________ Left Printer: ____________________
Right: ____________________ Right Printer:____________________
Header: ____________________ Top Printer: ____________________
Footer: ____________________ Bottom Printer: ____________________

Tabs:

Files to be imported:

File	Description	Use	Location

Paper Size: ____________________ Paper Color:____________________
Orientation: ____________________ Color/B&W: ____________________
Number of Columns: ____________________ Gutter: ____________________
Header Contents:

Footer Contents:

(continued)

Figure 8.4 Word-Processing Planning Guide

Step 5: **Plan Your Solution. (con't)** Estimated Number of Pages:____________________ Sketch(s) of Individual Page Layout(s) ***Step 6:*** **Evaluate the Solution. List the criteria for evaluating the completed document.**

knowledge base is shallow, then buzzwords should be defined or eliminated. The required outcomes are what you expect the document to accomplish. The required knowledge of the developer is what the developer needs to know to complete the document. If the developer has limited knowledge of these items, then the method of acquiring the knowledge should be included. The expected knowledge base of the audience is what the audience should know to be able to use the document. The developer should know this information in order to have a knowledge base upon which to build the document.

Step three lists alternative methods of developing the document. Step four lists the selected method from the alternatives in step three. There may be several items to consider such as columns or no columns, page orientation, and type of document.

Step five presents the general plan of the document including the margins, tabs, other files needed to complete the document, paper size, orientation, columns, and header, and footer contents. These are in accordance with the previous section. Part of step five includes an area to sketch the page layout. Indicate here where graphics and text will be placed and how the text will be wrapped around the graphics. Also include any object rotation, specification of text styles, and anything else necessary to easily create the document on the computer.

Step six presents a list of criteria for evaluating the document. Since the document is not completed, step six should list how the document will be evaluated. Each section of this list should be in question form, for example:

Is the message communicated?

Do the fonts fit the style of the document?

Are the graphics appropriate?

Do the graphics improve the communication of the message?

Am I pleased with the document?

Is the client pleased with the document?

When the document is completed on the computer, these questions should be revisited and answered during the testing of the document.

You may think that this is a lot of planning work for a memo or a letter, which it is. Although you probably would not put all of this information on paper, you should think about these items. As you start to use word processing efficiently, fill out the document planning guide for most projects. If you learn to complete the guide on easy documents, then problem solving on longer and more complicated documents will not be as stressful.

Common Documents

The following are some examples of common types of documents that are best created using a word processor. For the most part, these are not complicated documents to create. Chapter 9 presents the development of three case studies with more complex projects that are best suited for a word processor. Start with the projects in this chapter and then continue with those in Chapter 9. You may use all of the pages in the document planning guide or only a few. In the first two examples, you will only need step five. Information in steps one through four and in step six is not needed to create letters. In the second example you will use only the page layout for step five since it is a memo. The third example is a report and requires steps one through six.

Letters on Letterhead

Example 1: Letters

When beginning a document, the first thing you should create is the style sheet. Figure 8.5 shows the style sheet for the examples in this chapter. After the style sheet is developed, then proceed with the word-processing planning guide.

One of the most common documents people create is letters. The planning of your letter document should include how the letterhead is printed on the paper you will be using. If the printed letterhead is on the left edge of the page, then your left margin should be increased by the size of the letterhead. See Figure 8.6 for examples of letterhead layouts. If the letterhead is on the top and/or bottom, those margins should be increased to reflect the amount of area required by the letterhead. Figure 8.7 shows step five of the word-processing planning guide for our letter example. Steps one through four and six have been omitted, as mentioned. If the letterhead is in electronic form or you are creating it as you create the letter, then include these in the sketch in your word-processing planning guide. Use your style sheet to note the various styles utilized in a letter.

Step five presents basic information about the document including the margins, tabs, paper size, color, orientation, headers, and footers. Notice the left margin is 2 inches. This space will allow the letterhead to be placed on the left side of the paper. The margins are all greater than the printer margins. There is no header or footer. Notice in the page layout that the circled style number beside the paragraph indicates the style. Figure 8.8 presents other layouts of a letter with a letterhead.

Memos

Example 2: Memo

Memos are also common documents which involve simple and informal in-house communications. When creating memos, use styles that increase readability and thus allow the recipients to quickly understand the contents. See Figure 8.9 for the page layouts from step five of the word-processing planning guide which show two sketches of a memo. We will use the style sheet developed in the first example. Circled numbers indicate the styles on the layout. You may want to include a graphic that reflects the company logo or image. Any graphic image that is used should be appropriate to the memo and the company. Printed memos are being replaced today by e-mail messages and electronic memos.

Style Sheet

					Enhancements					Indentation		
	Style Name	Style Based On	Font Name	Size	Bold	Underline	Italics	Other	Alignment	Left	Right	First Line
1	Body Text	None	Arial	12					Left			0.25
2	Body Text 2	Body Text	Arial	12					Left			
3	Headings	Body Text	Arial	24	X				Center			
4	Subheadings	Headings	Arial	18	X				Center			
5	Small Headings	Subheadings	Arial	14					Center			
6	Captions	Body Text	Arial	10			X		Left			
7	Hanging Indent	Body Text	Arial	12					Left	0.25		-0.25
8	Table of Contents	Body Text	Arial	12					Left			
9	Numbered list	Hanging Indent	Arial	12					Left			
10												
11												
12												
13												
14												
15												
16												
17												
18												
19												
20												
21												
22												
23												
24												
25												
26												
27												
28												

Figure 8.5 Style Sheet for Examples

Style Sheet

		Paragraph Leading					Line Controls						
	Style Name	**Lines**	**After**	**Before**	**Tabs**	**Hyphenation**	**Widows**	**Orphans**	**Page Break**	**Numbering**	**Bullets**	**Borders**	**Other**
1	Body Text				Every 0.5 inch	Off	X	X					
2	Body Text 2		0.25		Every 0.5 inch	Off	X	X					
3	Headings		0.25		Every 0.5 inch	Off							
4	Subheadings		0.25		Every 0.5 inch	Off							
5	Small Headings		0.25		Every 0.5 inch	Off							
6	Captions				Every 0.5 inch	Off							
7	Hanging Indent				Every 0.5 inch	Off	X	X					
8	Table of Contents		0.25		rt at 6, tab leader	Off							
9	Numbered list		0.25		Every 0.5 inch	Off				X			
10													
11													
12													
13													
14													
15													
16													
17													
18													
19													
20													
21													
22													
23													
24													
25													
26													
27													
28													

Figure 8.5 Style Sheet for Examples

Figure 8.6 Letterhead Placement Examples

Reports

Example 3: Report

Reports are longer and more complicated documents. Some elements of a report include a title page, table of contents, and the body of the report with appropriate graphics, charts, and so forth. A report may also include footnotes or endnotes, appendices, and a bibliography. Your style sheet for a report should reflect body text, headings, small headings, subheadings, footnotes, hanging indent, captions, and bibliography. Figure 8.10 presents a word-processing planning guide for a term report on computer hardware that is required in a computer literacy class. Note the four different page layouts—one for the title page, one for the body of the report, another for the tables page, and a last one for the bibliography.

Follow problem-solving steps one through six as you view Figure 8.10. Step one involves writing the problem statement. It should be one to two paragraphs on what the problem is all about. Step 2 helps you to understand the problem by defining the audience,

Step 5: Plan Your Solution.

Software to be used: Word Processor

Margins:

Top:	1.0	Top Printer:	0.25
Bottom:	1.0	Bottom Printer:	0.5
Left:	2.0	Left Printer:	0.25
Right:	1.0	Right Printer:	0.25
Header:	1.0	Top Printer:	0.25
Footer:	none	Bottom Printer:	0.5

***Tabs:* every 0.5 inch**

Files to be imported:

File	Description	Use	Location

Paper Size: 8½ × 11 Paper Color: White

Orientation: Portrait Color/B&W: Color

Number of Columns: one Gutter:

Header Contents: None

Footer Contents: None

Sketch of Individual Page Layout

Estimated Number of Pages: 1

(continued)

Figure 8.7 Step Five of the Word-Processing Planning Guide for Example 1

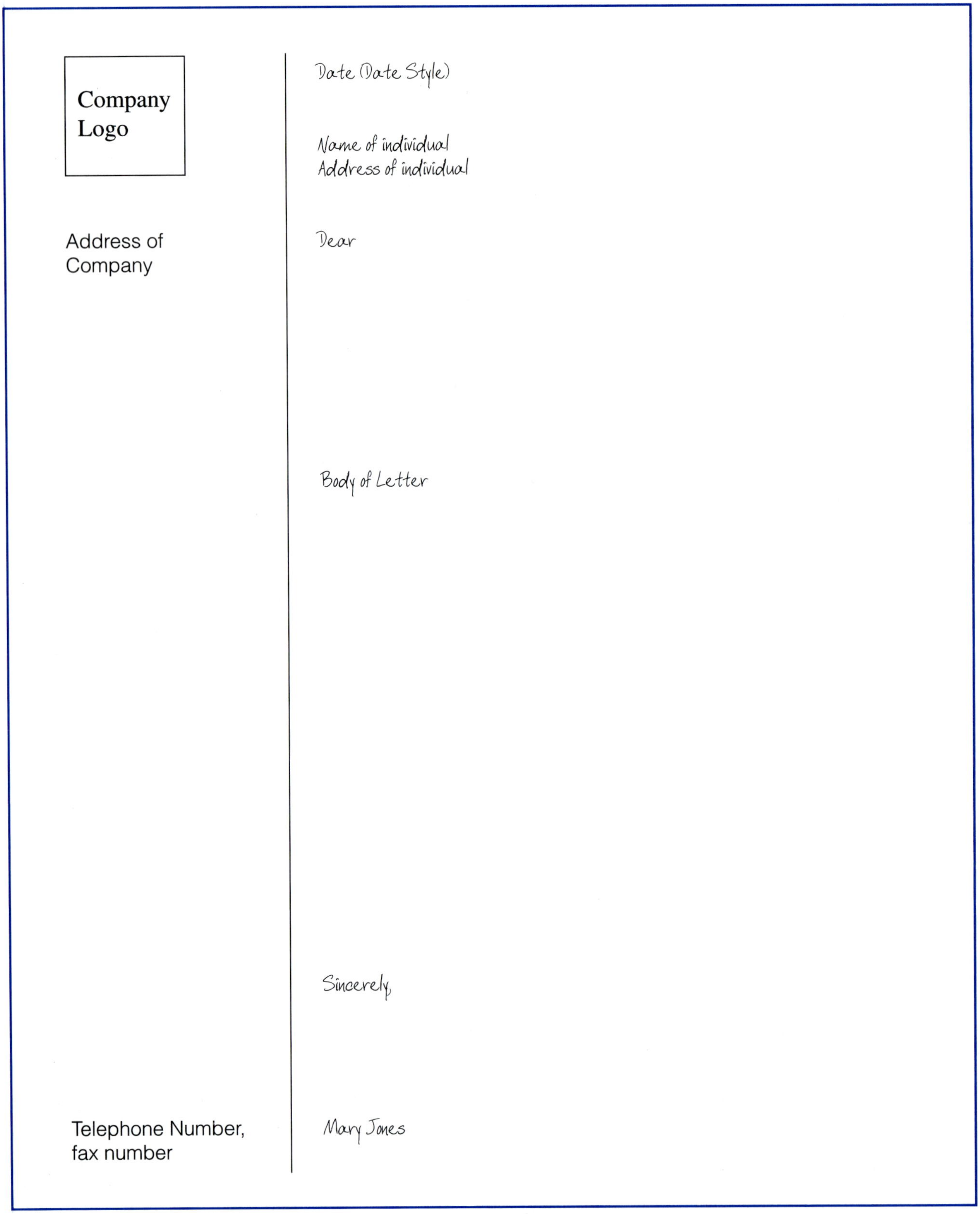
Company Logo

Address of Company

Telephone Number, fax number

Date (Date Style)

Name of individual
Address of individual

Dear

Body of Letter

Sincerely,

Mary Jones

Figure 8.7 Step Five of the Word-Processing Planning Guide for Example 1

Figure 8.8 Other Letter layouts for Example 1

the outcomes, your knowledge requirements, and the knowledge requirements of the audience. The required knowledge of the developer should indicate how you would obtain the knowledge if you do not already have it. Step 3 is a list of alternatives from which to choose your final report document method. Step 4 is a list of the selected items in the project including topic of report (printers), the format of the report, information in the tables, the number of tables, and items to be researched. Step five presents the planning information on the report itself such as the layout, margins, and tabs. Step 6 lists the criteria for evaluation when the report is completed.

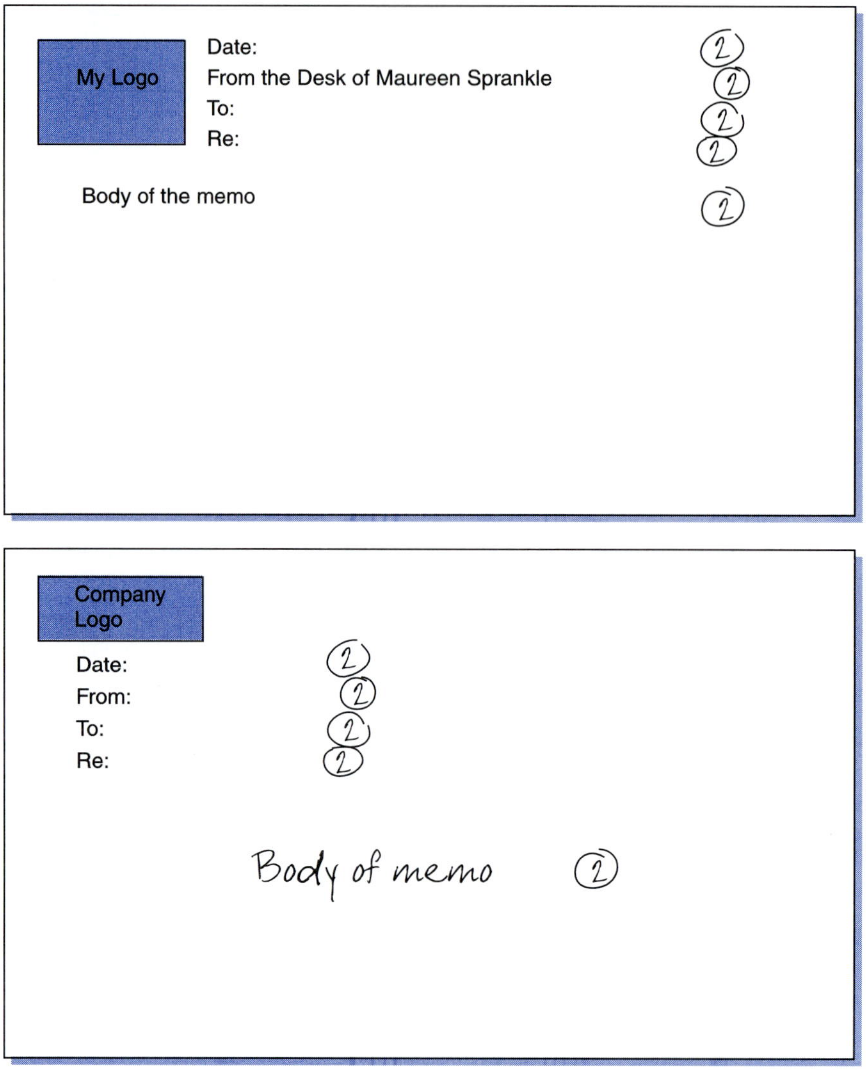

Figure 8.9 Page Layouts for Memo of Step Five of the Word-Processing Planning Guide

Templates

Templates

There are many types of documents that you will create that are similar such as letters, memos, and forms. To save time, you may want to develop a preformatted template. A **template** is a master document that has all of the key elements that are common to that type of a document. For example, a letter would have the same margins and letterhead, use the same styles, and so forth. It takes a little time to develop the template, but this time is saved for each new letter you create. Some word processors have predesigned templates. Explore these templates and either use them or modify them to serve your needs. Figure 8.11 shows sketches of letter and memo templates.

Figure 8.10 Word-Processing Planning Guide for Example 3

WORD-PROCESSING PLANNING GUIDE

Name of Document: Computer Literacy Report Date: 4/24/2002

Location of Electronic File: C:\my documents\school\computer literacy

Name: Mary Jones

Name of Client: Report on Computer Hardware for Computer Literacy Class

Step 1: Identify the Problem by Writing the Problem Statement.

A report is due in Computer Literacy at the end of the semester on a hardware component. The report is to be 4 to 5 pages long and have a title page and a bibliography. Internet research is to be part of the basic research for the report. At least one table is to be included in the report.

Step 2: Understand the problem.

Audience:
The report would be directed to an audience of students who have little or no knowledge of computers. The instructor will also read the report; however, the level of the report should be directed to the students.

Required Outcomes of the Document:
The report should explain one component thoroughly enough that a novice can understand what it is, how it works, how much it costs, and the rankings of the brands.

Required Knowledge of the Problem to Develop the Document:
Through my research, I must come to know enough about one hardware computer component to explain it to a novice in computers. I will gain this knowledge through research on the internet and from computer magazines in the library and in the lab.

Required Knowledge of the Audience:
People in the audience are computer novices.

Step 3: Identify Valid Alternative Methods to Solve the Problem.

a. The report may be on one of the following topics:
  1. monitors
  2. printers
  3. keyboards
  4. storage devices
  5. scanners
  6. sound input and output
  7. video input and output

b. I can import a spreadsheet on the hardware or use the table function in a word processor.

c. I can use one column or two columns.

(continued)

Figure 8.10 Word-Processing Planning Guide for Example 3

Step 4: Select the Best Method to Solve the Problem from the List of Alternative Solutions.

My best solution is:

a. Write my report about printers because I need a new printer and have to complete the research before I buy one.

b. I will use a traditional report format, no columns, a title page, footnotes, and a bibliography.

c. I will create three tables in my word processor, one for inkjet printers, another for laser printers, and the third for thermal printers.

d. I will research printers on the internet and in magazines in the library and in the computer lab. I will need at least five references.

e. I will research five to six different brands of each of the following:

1. inkjet printer
2. laser printer
3. thermal printer

f. The tables will contain six columns, one for each of the following: brand name, color or black and white, cost, cost of cartridge or toner replacements, pages per cartridge or toner, and cost per page.

Step 5: Plan Your Solution.

Software to be used: Word Processor

Margins:

Top:	0.75	Top Printer:	0.25
Bottom:	0.75	Bottom Printer:	0.5
Left:	0.75	Left Printer:	0.25
Right:	0.75	Right Printer:	0.25
Header:	0.5	Top Printer:	0.25
Footer:	0.5	Bottom Printer:	0.5

***Tabs:* Every 0.5 inch**

Files to be imported:

File	Description	Use	Location
Printer1	Picture	On title page	Clipart
Printer2	Picture	On page one	Clipart
Printer scan	Scanned Art	On page with table	Graphics/Hardware

Paper Size: 8½ × 11 Paper Color: White

Orientation: Portrait Color/B&W: Color

Number of Columns: one Gutter: ______

Figure 8.10 (continued)

Header Contents: None

Footer Contents:

	Page xx	

Estimated Number of Pages: 7 pages

Sketchs of Individual Page Layouts

A. Title page

B. Body of text

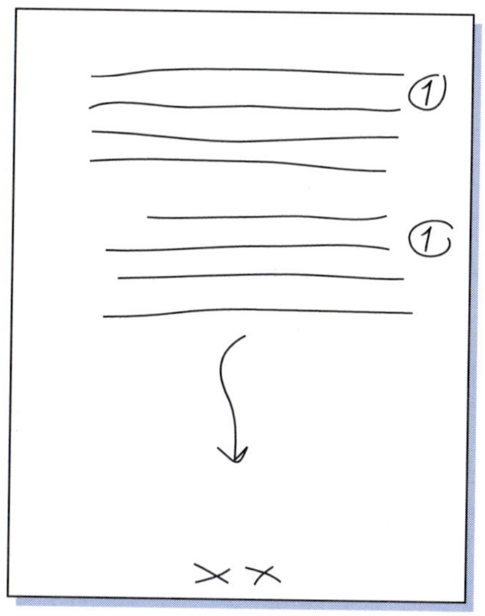

C. Page with table

D. Bibliography

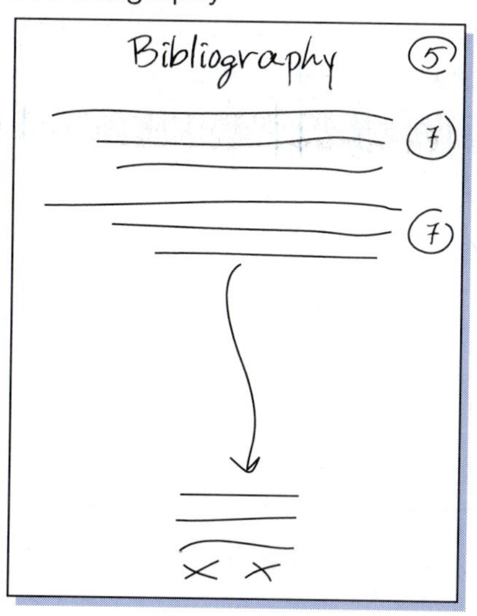

(continued)

Figure 8.10 Word-Processing Planning Guide for Example 3

Step 6: Evaluate the Solution.

Criteria for evaluation:

a. Is the terminology appropriate for the novice computer user?
b. Is my research thorough?
c. Is the report easily read?
d. Is the report well organized?
e. Is the information in the table easily understood?
f. Is the correct information on the title page?
g. Are all of the references included in the bibliography?

My Logo

Date:

From the Desk of Maureen Sprankle

To:

Re:

Company Logo

Date:

From:

To:

Re:

Figure 8.11a Page Layouts for Memo Template

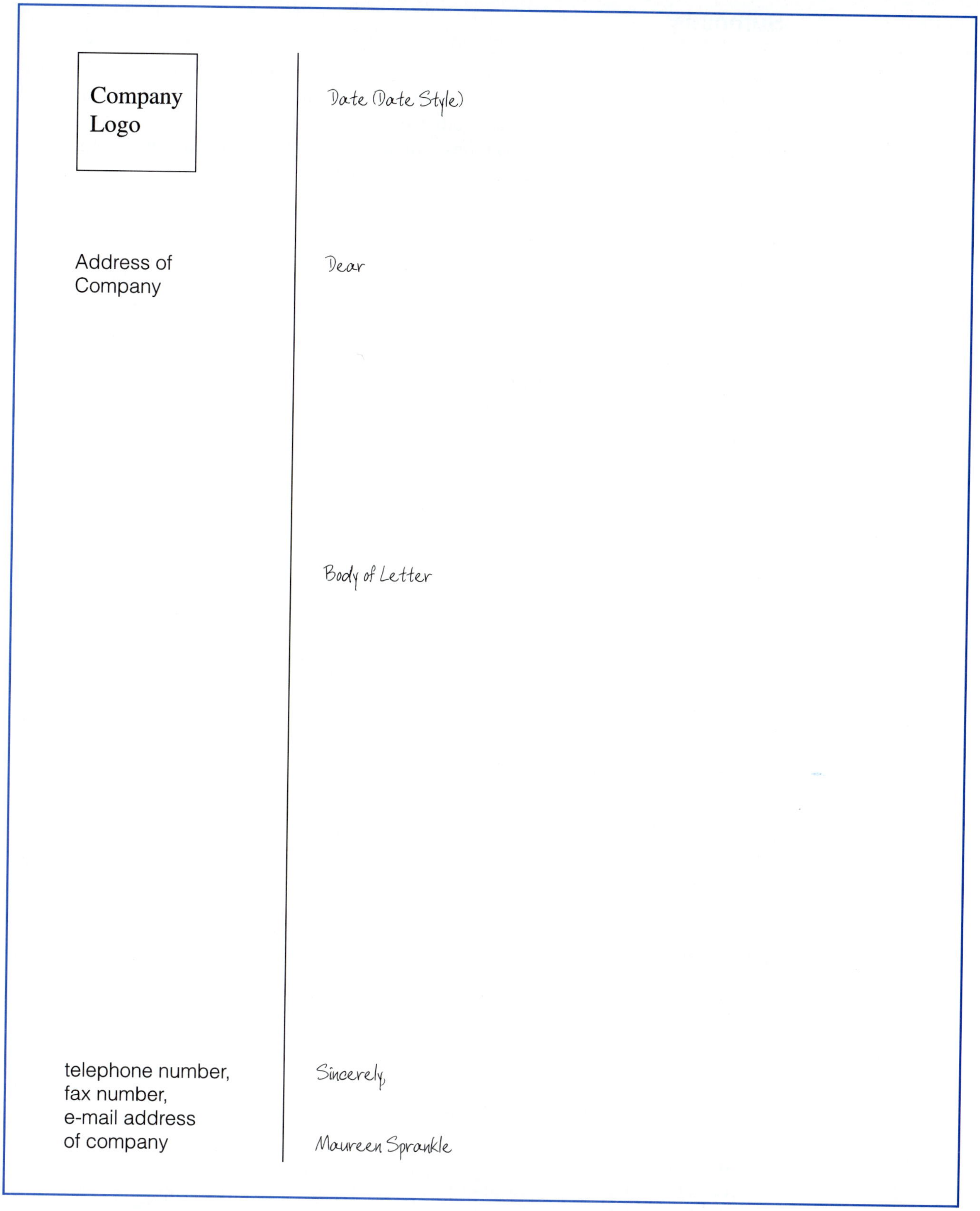

Figure 8.11b Page Layout for Letter with Letterhead Template

Summary

Word processing is one of the first software packages that people learn to use. The basic functions of a word processor are entering text, editing text, formatting text, and printing text. Word processors also have other functions such as importing text, creating tables with formulas, and using columns. You may want to import text from another electronic file or scan it into the computer using optical character recognition software. Formatting text includes such functions as alignment, indentation, numbering, bullets, tabs, line control, character enhancements, leading, tabs, and drop caps. The page layout is used to designate how the page will look when it is completed. This includes where text and graphics are placed, the margins, and footers and headers. The use of precreated styles for text is a great time-saver because you can set up how the text will look for a specific type of text such as body text, captions, and headings, and then you may choose the style for a certain set of characters.

The document planning guide helps you to preplan how your document will be created. A little preplanning can save many hours on the computer. Some common documents presented in this chapter include letters, memos, and reports.

Key Words

- Drop cap
- Gutter
- Hanging indentation
- Landscape page orientation
- Line
- Line control
- Optical character recognition (OCR)
- Paragraph
- Portrait page orientation
- Sentence
- Styles
- Tabs
  - Center
  - Decimal
  - Left
  - Right
  - Tab leader
- Template
- Word

Exercises

1. What are the four basic features of a word processor?
2. What is an OCR?
3. What is RTF?
4. Evaluate the following functions:
   a. AND(T,F)
   b. OR(T,F)
   c. IF(5 < 9, 8, 10)
   d. IF(5 > 9, 8, 10)
   e. IF(5 <= 9, 8, 10)
   f. INT(5.6875)

g. MOD(23, 5)
h. AVERAGE(3, 6, 8, 2, 10)
i. MIN(43, 34, 65, 22, 36)
j. MAX(43, 34, 65, 22, 36)

5. How do you determine the font size for columns?
6. How would you create a hanging indent of 0.25 inch?
7. Name and explain the four types of tabs.
8. What are widows and orphans?
9. What is a drop cap?
10. What is a page layout?
11. What is a page gutter?
12. What is a style?
13. Why is the use of styles a real time-saver?

Problems

1. Using the word-processing planning guide, create a plan for the computerization of your lecture notes for one of your classes.
2. Using the word-processing planning guide, create a plan to word-process a report due in one of your classes.
3. Sketch a plan for a memo to tell your teacher that you will be absent from class during the next two sessions. Include your logo.
4. Sketch a plan to develop a study guide for a test in this class.
5. Using the word-processing planning guide, create a plan for the development of your resume.
6. You are taking a U.S. history class. Your final assignment in this class is to report on the presidents of the United States. You will need to include a table of all presidents, their years in office, what state they were from, and the party they ran under. Using the word-processing planning guide, create a plan as to how you will create this report.

Chapter 9

Case Studies for a Word Processor

Overview

The Style Sheet
Case Study 1: Training Manual
Case Study 2: Mail Merge
Case Study 3: Report with Tables and Columns

Objectives

When you have finished this chapter, you should be able to:

1. Develop style sheets for documents.
2. Problem solve and develop plans to create complex documents using mail merge, columns, and tables with formulas, and to create a training manual.
3. Use the document planning guide and the six problem-solving steps to develop a solution for a document that could be created with a word processor.

Chapter 9 presents three word-processing case studies. The six steps in problem solving in the word-processing planning guide are used to develop a solution for each of the three case studies. Study how each solution is determined, and use the same methodology for the problems at the end of the chapter.

The Style Sheet

Style Sheet

To start your library of styles, develop a style sheet for all of your documents. Figure 9.1 shows the style sheet for the case studies presented in this chapter. More styles will be added in the following chapters. Be sure to investigate the style library that comes with your word processor to find styles that are already defined and add these to your style sheet. Your style sheet will grow as you develop different types of documents.

There are nine styles defined for the three case studies in this chapter. These styles are as follows:

1. *Body text:* Used for normal paragraphs of text. It should be easy to read. Body text style uses Arial font, size 12, no character enhancements, left aligned, first line is indented, no paragraph leading, tabs are every 0.5 inch, hyphenation is off, and there is widow and orphan control.
2. *Body text 2:* Based on body text style. The difference is body text 2 style is used for letters. There is no first-line indent and there is additional leading after the paragraph.

Style Sheet

					Enhancements					Indentation		
	Style Name	Style Based On	Font Name	Size	Bold	Underline	Italics	Other	Alignment	Left	Right	First Line
1	Body Text	None	Arial	12					Left			0.25
2	Body Text 2	Body Text	Arial	12					Left			
3	Headings	Body Text	Arial	24	X				Center			
4	Subheadings	Headings	Arial	18	X				Center			
5	Small Headings	Subheadings	Arial	14					Center			
6	Captions	Body Text	Arial	10			X		Left			
7	Hanging Indent	Body Text	Arial	12					Left	0.25		–0.25
8	Table of Contents	Body Text	Arial	12					Left			
9	Numbered List	Hanging Indent	Arial	12					Left			
10												
11												
12												
13												
14												
15												
16												
17												
18												
19												
20												
21												
22												
23												
24												
25												
26												
27												
28												

Figure 9.1 Style Sheet.

Style Sheet

		Paragraph Leading					Line Controls						
	Style Name	Lines	After	Before	Tabs	Hyphenation	Widows	Orphans	Page Break	Numbering	Bullets	Borders	Other
1	Body Text				Every 0.5 inch	Off	X	X					
2	Body Text 2		0.25		Every 0.5 inch	Off	X	X					
3	Headings		0.25		Every 0.5 inch	Off							
4	Subheadings		0.25		Every 0.5 inch	Off							
5	Small Headings		0.25		Every 0.5 inch	Off							
6	Captions				Every 0.5 inch	Off							
7	Hanging Indent				Every 0.5 inch	Off	X	X					
8	Table of Contents		0.25		rt at 6, tab leader	Off							
9	Numbered List		0.25		Every 0.5 inch	Off				X			
10													
11													
12													
13													
14													
15													
16													
17													
18													
19													
20													
21													
22													
23													
24													
25													
26													
27													
28													

Figure 9.1 Style Sheet.

3. *Headings:* Based on body text style. Heading style is used for large headings that are centered on the page, such as on a title page or cover page. The size has been increased to 24 points, characters are boldfaced, center aligned, leading after the paragraph, and no widow and orphan control.
4. *Subheadings:* Based on the headings style. Subheadings are the same as headings except the size is 18 instead of 24 points. They are used under text defined with headings style such as an explanation of a report placed under the major report name.
5. *Small headings:* Based on the subheadings style. Small headings are 14 points and are not boldface. They are used on the cover and title page for the name of the report author, date, class, etc.
6. *Captions:* Based on body text style. Captions are italicized, with no first-line indent, decreased font size, and no widow and orphan control. Caption style is used for text associated with graphics.
7. *Hanging indent:* Based on body text style. Hanging indent has a left indent with a first-line indent equal to a negative left indent value. Hanging indent is used for lists or other places where the second plus lines of a paragraph have a greater indent than the first line.
8. *Table of contents:* Based on body text style. The changes include no first-line indent, tabs to right tab at 6-inch mark with tab leader, and no widow or orphan control.
9. *Numbered list:* Based on hanging indent style. The only change is the paragraphs are numbered.

The preceding list explains some basic styles; however, you may want other styles for your documents. By using styles, you do not have to continually reset the definitions for your paragraphs.

Case Study 1: Training Manual

Case Study 1: Telephone System Training Manual

You have been given the task of learning how to use a new computerized telephone system at your work. Since the manual that comes with the telephone system is hard to read and difficult to locate information in, you have also been given the task of developing a training manual to help others learn how to use it. The training manual should include a section for answers to most frequently asked questions. The computerized telephone system has voice mail, transfer calls, forward calls, group calls, voice mail to other people, voice mail to groups of people, recall of 20 often-called numbers, and a memory to put up to five calls on hold.

Figure 9.2 presents the document planning guide for this case study. In step one you identify the problem with a problem statement. This should be one or two paragraphs describing the problem in narrative form.

In step two you describe the audience, the required outcomes of the document, and the knowledge base of the author and the audience. Step two should assist in understanding the problem. Describing the audience helps to define the terminology and types of graphics to be used; in this case, the audience is the people who will be using the new telephone system. Listing the desired outcomes of the document helps to understand what needs to be communicated to the audience. If you understand what knowledge is required to create the document, you will be better able to communicate the required information to the audience. If you do not have some of the knowledge, then you need to

Figure 9.2 Word-Processing Planning Guide for Case Study 1

WORD-PROCESSING PLANNING GUIDE

Name of Document: Telephone Manual Date: 4/8/2002

Location of Electronic File: S:\Manuals\

Name: Mary Jones

Name of Client: Mr. John Manager

Step 1: Identify the Problem by Writing the Problem Statement.

The problem is to develop a training manual to help others learn how to use the new computerized telephone system. The manual should include a section for answers to frequently asked questions. The telephone system has voice mail, transfer calls, forward calls, group calls, voice mail to other people, voice mail to groups of people, recall of 20 often-called numbers, and a memory to place up to 5 calls on hold.

Step 2: Under the Problem.

Audience:
People at work who will be using the telephone system.

Required Outcome of the Document:
An employee of the company can learn to use the computerized telephone system through the use of this training manual.

Required Knowledge of the Problem to Develop the Document:
In-depth knowledge of the computerized telephone system. Training will be provided by the telephone installation company.

Required Knowledge of the Audience:
How to use a telephone.

Step 3: Identify Valid Alternative Methods to Solve the Problem.

- **a.** Notebook form, booklet form, or bound book form
- **b.** Standard report form or individual pages for instructions
- **c.** Step-by-step instructions or narrative instructions
- **d.** Key words: italics, margins, underlined, listed at end of section, and/or in glossary
- **e.** Graphics: included or not
- **f.** Color or black and white
- **g.** Publish online

Step 4: Select the Best Method to Solve the Problem from the List of Alternative Solutions.

- **a.** Loose-leaf notebook with extra pages at end for notes
- **b.** Standard format:
  1. Title page
  2. Table of contents
  3. Introduction
  4. Instruction page for each function using numbered step-by-step instructions
  5. FAQ page: Numbered questions with answers
  6. Summary

(continued)

Figure 9.2 Word-Processing Planning Guide for Case Study 1

Step 4: Select the Best Method to Solve the Problem from the List of Alternative Solutions. (con't)

7. Glossary
8. Blank note pages

c. Key words: italicized and in glossary
d. Graphics: Scanned graphics, digital photographs, and clipart
e. Color printing

Step 5: Plan Your Solution.

Software to be used: Word Processor

Margins:

Top: 1.0		Top Printer: 0.25
Bottom: 1.0		Bottom Printer: 0.5
Inside: 1.5	Binder 0.5	Left Printer: 0.25
Outside: 1.5		Right Printer: 0.25
Header: 0.5		Top Printer: 0.25
Footer: 0.6		Bottom Printer: 0.5

Tabs: Use defaults

Files to be imported:

File	Description	Use	Location
Telephone	Digital Photo	On cover, title page	c:\manuals\graphics
Keypad	Digital Photo	Instruction pages	c:\manuals\graphics
Telecartoon	Clipart Cartoon	Introduction	c:\manuals\graphics

Paper Size: 8½ × 11 Paper Color: White, Cover Blue

Orientation: Portrait Color/B&W: Color

Number of Columns: None Gutters:

Header Contents:

Telephone Training Manual		

Footer Contents: Page number

	XX	

Figure 9.2 (continued)

16 pages

Estimated Number of Pages:__________________________

Sketchs of Individual Page Layouts

a. Cover page (1 page):

b. Title page (1 page):

c. Table of contents (1 page):

d. Text pages (11 pages):

1. Introduction (1 page)

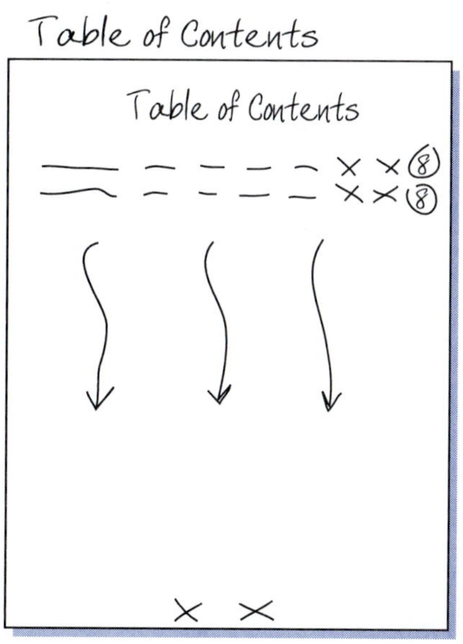

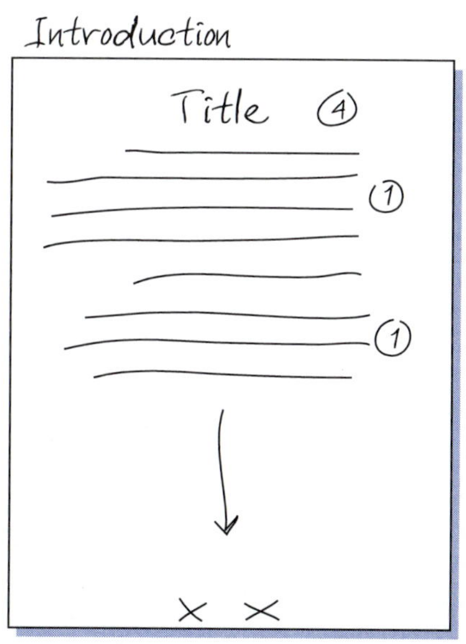

(continued)

Figure 9.2 Word-Processing Planning Guide for Case Study 1

***Step 5:* Plan Your Solution. (con't)**

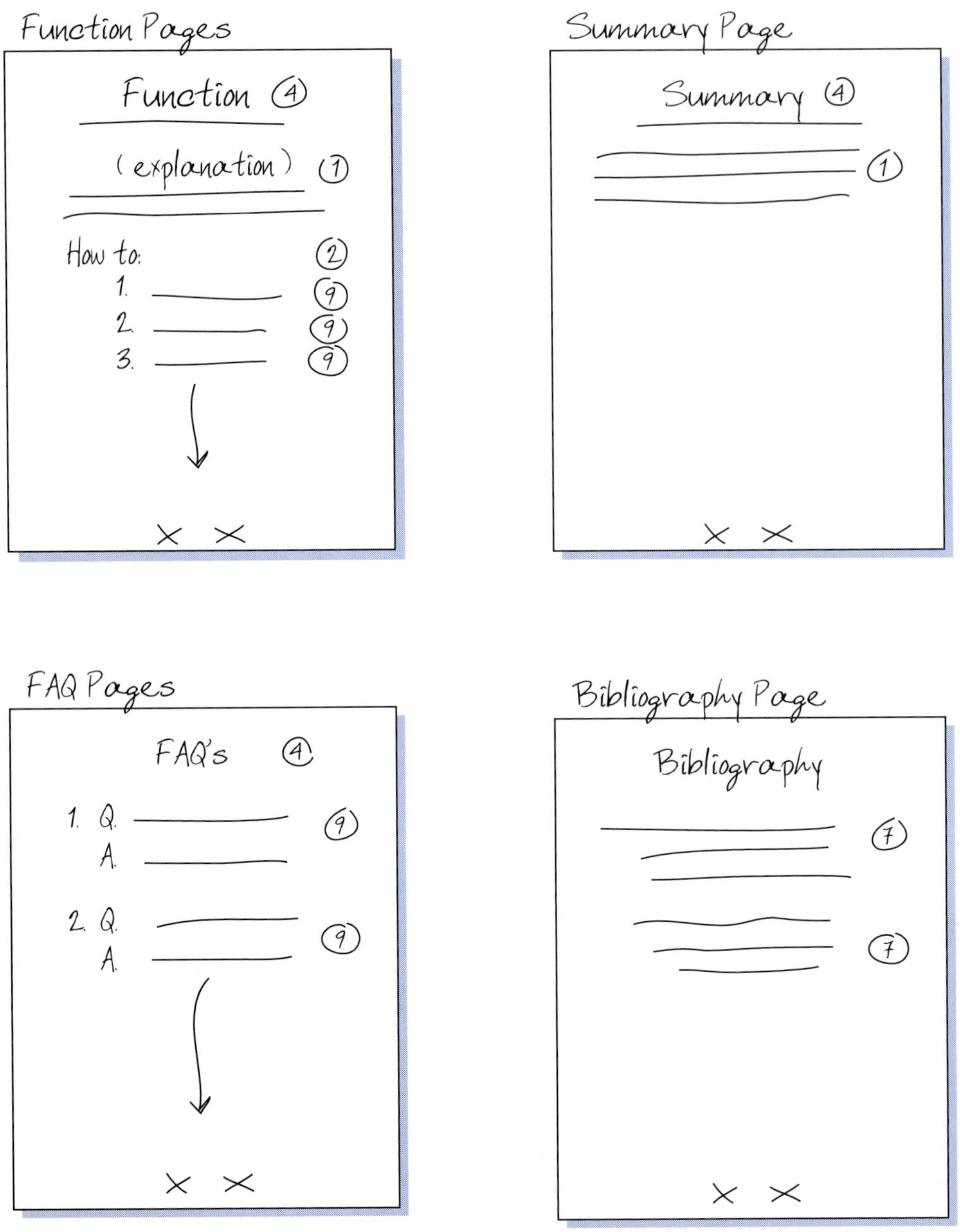

Figure 9.2 (continued)

2. One page for each function (8 pages)
3. Summary (1 page)
4. FAQs (1 page)

e. Bibliography (1 page):
f. Back cover (1 page):

Step 6: **Evaluate the Solution.**

explain how you will obtain it. The last section is the expected knowledge of the audience. This further defines the vocabulary to be used and the starting place of explanations. It defines what is assumed.

In step three you list alternative methods. This list is a choice of options, such as: Are you going to develop this document to be put into a notebook? Will it be bound? Will you publish it online? Will it be in a booklet form? Can you think of other alternatives than what are listed?

In step four you list your choices from the alternatives in step three that you will be using in the document. You may also add other important items here. This is the thinking stage.

In step five you actually define how the document will look. This is the draft document you will take to the computer. You define general information about the document, page layout information, and the actual page layouts. Note the circled numbers on the page layout. These numbers indicate the style for the corresponding text. When you have completed this step, be sure to recheck the numbers and the layout.

In step six you list the criteria for evaluation when the document is completed. After you have the criteria established, review the document in step five to see if it meets the criteria.

By going through these six steps of problem solving, your task on the computer will be much simpler and less time consuming. Remember this is only the starting place. You will more than likely make changes as you actually enter the document into the computer. These changes should be minimal. If you make major changes when you get to the computer, then you probably have not put enough thought into the word-processing planning guide.

Case Study 2: Mail Merge

Case Study 2: Computer Club Mail Merge

You are secretary of the computer club at school. The club would like you to send out a letter to all members reminding them of upcoming events including the next meeting, the next fun activity, and the next fund-raiser. You also need to alert each member about the amount of money he or she needs to turn in to the club from the previous fund-raiser. A database has been set up with the information you need to use. This database could have been set up in the word processor or in a database program, but for this case study, the database has been set up previously for the mail merge. The following information is in the database:

Information	Data Name
Last name	last
First name	first
Street address	address
City	city
State	state
Zip code	zipcode
Telephone number	telephone
Money owed	money_owed
Member since	year

Figure 9.3 presents the word-processing planning guide for this case study. There are no new text styles for the style sheet related to this case study. The case study itself is ideal for a mail merge using a word processor. The **mail merge** allows the end user to print multiple documents with different information through the use of one document and a database file of information. The end user develops a main document, such as a letter, which contains variable data to be inserted as the individualized letters are printed. The database contains the data that will change within each letter. Each printed letter will use one related record from the database.

In this case study, the database has been set up for the end user. Chapter 19 presents a case study of setting up a database and a document for a mail merge. You may be familiar with mail-merged documents that you receive in your mail. They may be advertisements, magazines, or some other type of document that has your name, address, and other information about you printed throughout the document. You may receive a letter that is obviously a form letter that not only has data on you inserted in the letter but also is signed in ink. You know that one person did not sign thousands of letters. There are machines that sign letters for the sender.

The information about the database is included in the problem statement in step one. Step two identifies the audience, the required outcomes, and the required knowledge of the club secretary and the club members. In steps three and four you identify alternatives and select the best method to complete the letters to the members. Mail merge is

Figure 9.3 Word-Processing Planning Guide for Case Study 2

WORD-PROCESSING PLANNING GUIDE

Name of Document: Letter April 3 Date: 4/2/2002

Location of Electronic File: c:\Computer Club\letters\,

Database: c:\Computer Club\Member Information\, File Name: Members

Name: Mary Smith

Name of Client: Computer Club

Step 1: Identify the Problem by Writing the Problem Statement.

A letter needs to be sent to each member of the computer club. The letter must include information about:

a. the next meeting
b. a Club party
c. the next fund-raiser
d. money to be turned in from the last fund-raiser

These letters require the club's logo and return address information on the letterhead. Envelopes will need to be printed. A database has already been set up with information about each member. Information in the database includes:

Information	Data Name
Last name	last
First name	first
Street address	address
City	city
State	state
Zip code	zipcode
Telephone number	telephone
Money owed	money_owed
Member since	year

Step 2: Understand the Problem.

Audience:
Computer club members

Required Outcomes of the Document:
Information communicated to members

Required Knowledge of the Problem to Develop the Document:
Information about events, and members

(continued)

Figure 9.3 Word-Processing Planning Guide for Case Study 2

Step 2: Understand the Problem. (con't)

Required Knowledge of the Audience:
Knowledge about the computer club

Step 3: Identify Valid Alternative Methods to Solve the Problem.

a. Individual letters versus mail merge
b. Use letterhead or print letterhead
c. Print individual envelopes or use mail merge
d. Standard letter format or use a flyer-type document

Step 4: Select the Best Method to Solve the Problem from the List of Alternative Solutions.

a. Use mail merge.
b. Use standard letter format.
c. Print envelopes using mail merge.
d. Print letterhead with letter.
e. Computer club logo will be included on letterhead and envelopes.

Step 5: Plan Your Solution.

Software to be used: Word Processor

Margins:

Top: 1.0	Top Printer: 0.25
Bottom: 1.0	Bottom Printer: 0.5
Left: 2.0	Left Printer: 0.25
Right: 1.0	Right Printer: 0.25
Header: none	Top Printer: 0.25
Footer: none	Bottom Printer: 0.5

***Tabs:* every 0.5 inch**

Files to be imported:

File	Description	Use	Location
Club Logo	Graphics Logo	In letterhead	c:\computer club\graphics
Members	Database	Letters, Envel	c:\computer club\member Information

Figure 9.3 (continued)

Paper Size: 8½ × 11 Paper Color: White

Orientation: Portrait Color/B&W: Color

Number of Columns: One Gutters:

Header Contents: None

Footer Contents: None

Estimated Number of Pages: 1 letter, 78 prints

Sketch(s) of Individual Page Layout(s)

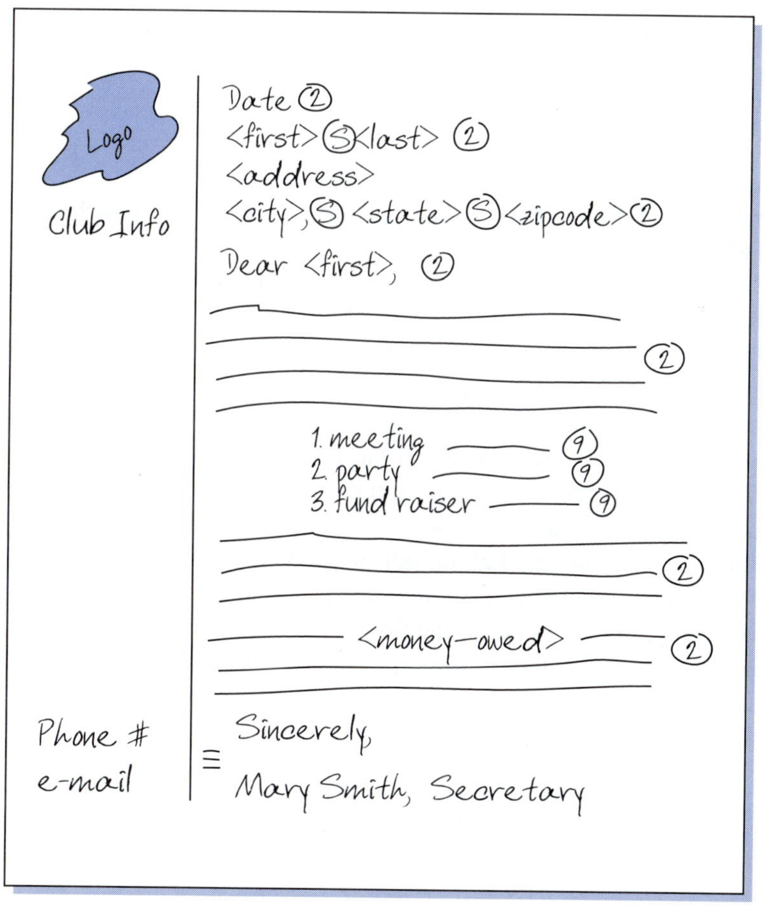

(continued)

Figure 9.3 Word-Processing Planning Guide for Case Study 2

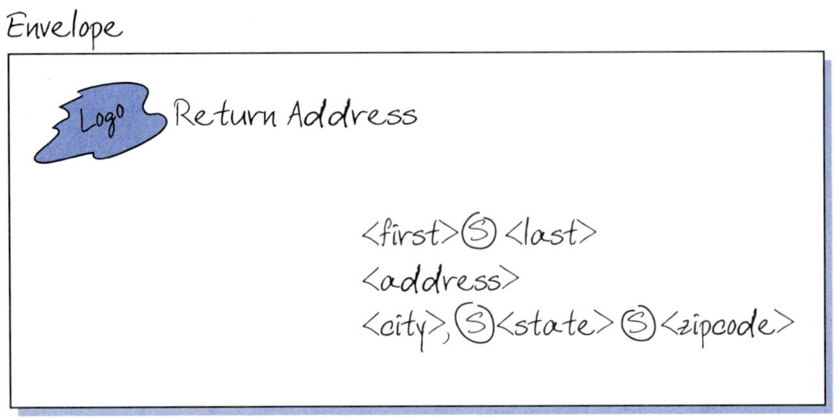

Step 6: Evaluate the Solution.

Criteria for evaluation:

- **a.** Does the letter contain all needed information including times, dates, and locations?
- **b.** Are all members included?
- **c.** Is the letter easy to read?

the best alternative. The letter will be developed using a standard letter format with the letterhead printed as the letters are printed. Envelopes will also be printed using mail merge. The club's logo will be printed as part of the letterhead and as part of the return address on the envelopes.

Step five is the plan for developing the documents. The letterhead will be printed in the left 1.75 inches of the paper, therefore the left margin of the letter will be 2 inches. The letter will be printed in color since the logo is in color. In the layout of the letter and the envelopes, the data are presented as field names in the database. Each piece of data is defined as follows: <field name>, for example: <last> or <first> or <city>. Notice the space inserted between the first and last names and indicated by a circled *s*. If more than one space is required, then the number of spaces is inserted before the *s* in the circle. Also, a comma followed by a space has been placed after the city and before the state. Any characters that are not in the database must be added to the letter.

When you actually begin to create the mail-merged documents, complete the database first in order to know the field names. Next develop the main document, then complete the steps for the mail merge. In most word processors today, these steps are fairly simple as long as you understand the concepts of mail merge.

Case Study 3: Report with Tables and Columns

Case Study 3: Sales Report

You are a sales manager of a large corporation that develops computer games. The company specializes in five different types of games. You have been asked to produce the annual sales report that is mailed to the board of directors. Comparisons of data should include regions, types of computer games, and number of clients over the last five years.

The current year's data should be highlighted. The text in this report is traditionally done with two columns per page. Tables of information should include the following:

1. Sales of computer games per region for the last five years
2. Total sales of computer games for the last five years
3. Sales of the five different types of computer games per region for this year
4. Total sales of the five different types of computer games
5. Number of clients per region
6. Total number of clients

This information may be taken from an existing database sales analysis report. The board of directors meeting is on July 30. The report must be mailed to members by July 20.

Figure 9.4 presents the word-processing planning guide for this case. Step one identifies the problem through a narrative problem statement. Notice all information about requirements is included. Step two defines the problem further to include an understanding of the audience, the outcomes, and the knowledge base of the developer and the audience. Steps three and four identify alternative methods and define the best method. In this case, the tables could be imported from a spreadsheet or created in the word processor. The chosen method is to develop the tables in the word processor, which means that the number of rows and columns of the table and any formulas should be developed in the planning guide. The charts will be imported from a chart program.

Figure 9.4 Word-Processing Planning Guide for Case Study 3

WORD-PROCESSING PLANNING GUIDE

Name of Document: Sales Report Date: July 15, 2002

Location of Electronic File: c:\my documents\work\sales report

Name: Joe Small

Name of Client: James Big

Step 1: Identify the Problem by Writing the Problem Statement.

As sales manager, my job is to develop the computer games sales report for the board of directors this year. This report should be completed with all information on the sales of computer games since July 1 of last year. Information to be included is as follows:

a. Sales of computer games per region for the last five years
b. Total sales of computer games for the last five years
c. Sales of the five different types of computer games per region for this year
d. Total sales of the five different types of computer games
e. Number of clients per region
f. Total number of clients

The report must be sent to the members of the board by July 20 for the board meeting on July 30. The related database already exists.

(continued)

Figure 9.4 Word-Processing Planning Guide for Case Study 3

Step 2: Understand the Problem.

Audience:

The members of the board of directors are the audience. Each has some knowledge of the company and of computer games, but otherwise no related in-depth knowledge. Most members are over 45 years of age. All members are businesspeople who have an in-depth knowledge of business.

Required Outcomes of the Document:

The outcome of the report is to communicate to the board how the sales of computer games have done in the last year compared with the previous five years. Data must be easy to comprehend because the members are extremely busy people.

Required Knowledge of the Problem to Develop the Document:

a. In-depth knowledge of the present and past sales of computer games
b. Knowledge of the company
c. Knowledge of computer games and their market
d. Knowledge of the sales personnel
e. Knowledge of people on the board of directors

Required Knowledge of the Audience:

a. Knowledge of the company
b. Knowledge of computer games
c. Knowledge of business, especially sales

Step 3: Identify Valid Alternative Methods to Solve the Problem.

a. Notebook, bound report
b. Back to back or one sided
c. Columns or none
d. Tables from spreadsheet or developed in the word processor
e. Paper color, cover color

Step 4: Select the Best Method to Solve the Problem from the List of Alternative Solutions.

a. Bound report, back-to-back facing pages
b. Two columns
c. Tables developed in the word processor
d. Charts imported from a spreadsheet
e. Graphics: Digital picture of computer game, and company logo

Step 5: Plan Your Solution:

Software to be used: Word Processor

Margins:

Top: 1.0 Top Printer: 0.25
Bottom: 1.0 Bottom Printer: 0.5
Outside: 1.0 Left Printer: 0.25
Inside: 1.5 Right Printer: 0.25 Binding: 0.5
Header: 0.6 Top Printer: 0.25
Footer: 0.6 Bottom Printer: 0.5

Figure 9.4 (continued)

Tabs:

Files to be imported:

File	Description	Use	Location
Computer game	Digital Photograph	Cover, and inside	s:\reports\graphics\
Logo	Company Logo	Cover and title page	s:\reports\graphics\
This year chart	Excel chart	In body of text	s:\reports\sales 02\
Five year chart	Excel chart	In body of text	s:\reports\sales 02\

Paper Size: 8½ × 11 Paper Color: White

Orientation: Portrait Color/B&W: Color

Number of Columns: 2 Gutters: 0.4

Back to back of single sided: Back-to-back pages

Header Contents:

Computer Games Sales Reprot 2002		July 30,2002

Footer Contents: Page number

	XX	

Estimated Number of Pages: 20 pages

Sketchs of Individual Page Layouts

- **a.** Cover
- **b.** Title page
- **c.** Table of contents
- **d.** Body of text
    - **1.** text pages
    - **2.** chart pages
    - **3.** table pages
- **e.** Back cover

(continued)

Figure 9.4 Word-Processing Planning Guide for Case Study 3

Step 5: Plan Your Solution. (con't)

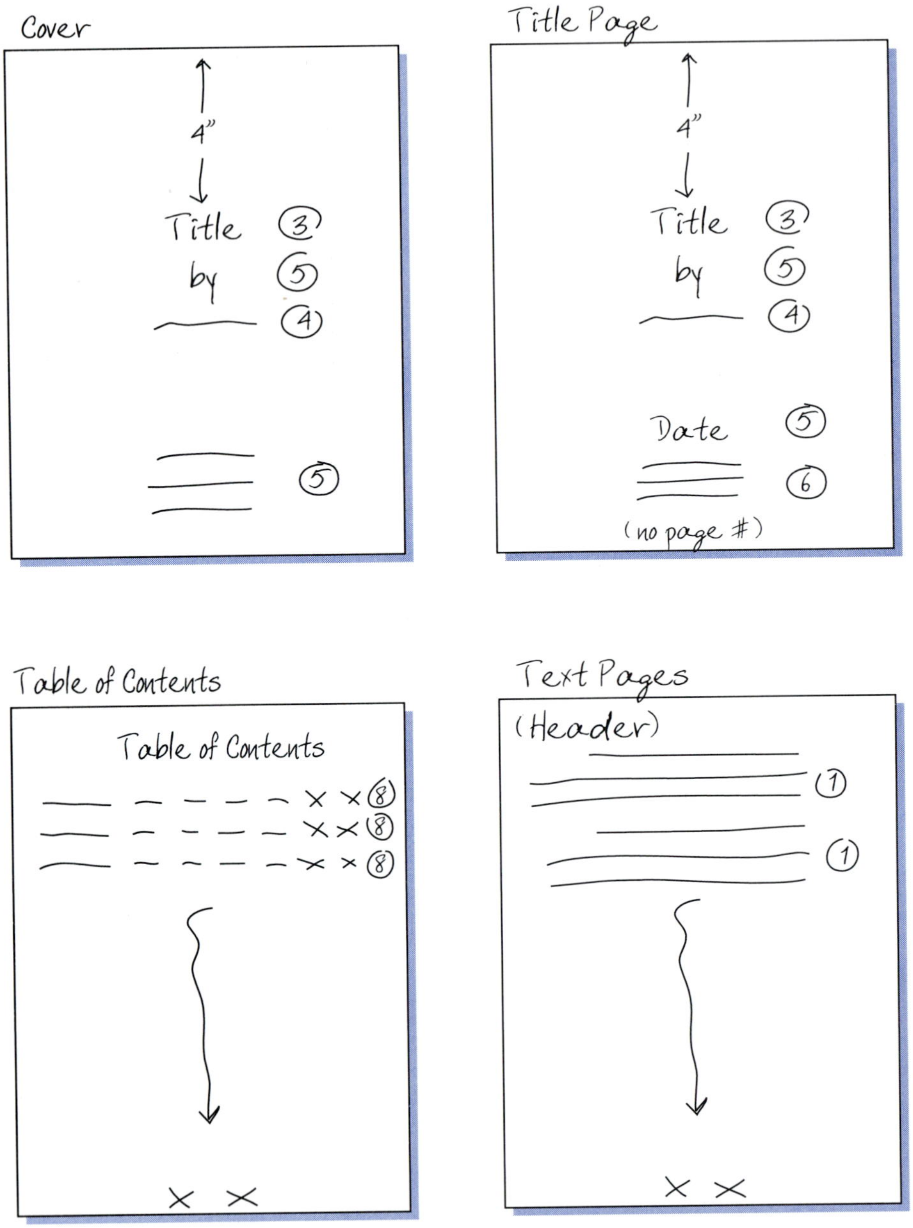

Figure 9.4 (continued)

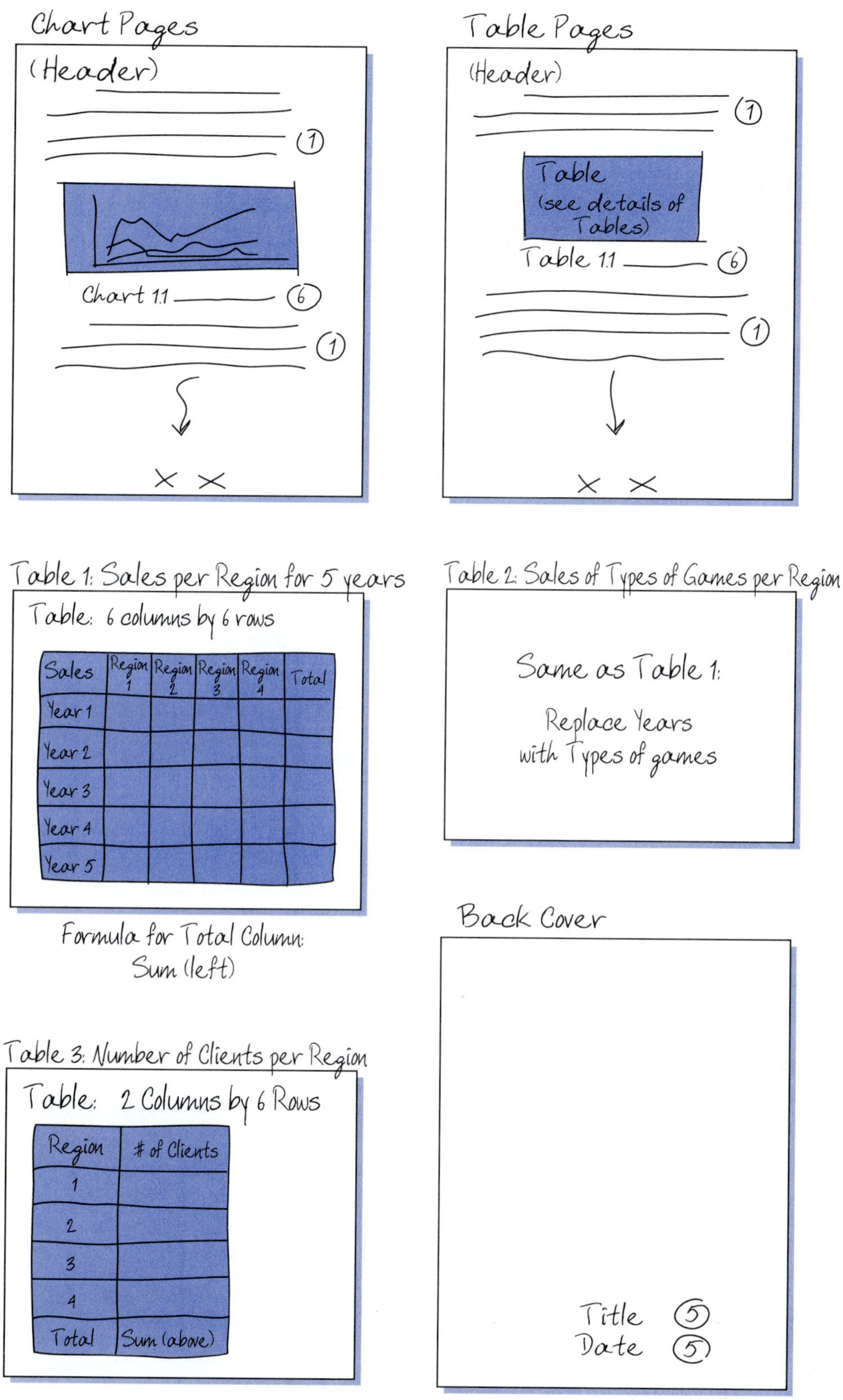

(continued)

Figure 9.4 Word-Processing Planning Guide for Case Study 3

Step 6: **Evaluate the Solution.**

Criteria for Evaluation:

- **a.** Communicates information about the sales of computer games, past and present.
- **b.** Text is easy to read.
- **c.** Report is easy to understand.
- **d.** Material is concise.
- **e.** Summarizes important information in tables and charts.

In step five you define the plan to develop the solution. The report will be double sided with facing pages. Therefore, define the side margins in terms of inside and outside margins instead of left and right margins, because the left margin is on the inside on one side and on the outside on the other side. The report will be bound and therefore the inside margin must be larger by the amount of paper the binding will take, in this case 0.5 inch. Your printing service can tell you this amount.

Charts have been developed in a chart program and will be imported into the report. Chapter 17 presents a problem in which a spreadsheet will be developed and imported into a word-processed document. In this case study, however, the tables will be developed in the word processor and the charts are already completed. The layout sketches include the layout for the front and back covers, the title page, the table of contents, the text pages, the chart pages, and the table pages. Step six lists the criteria to be used to evaluate the finished report.

A report such as this must look professional. It should be in color since there are charts, and only a few copies need to be printed. Once your planning guide is complete, you are ready to finish the report on the computer. Remember you may have changes as you enter the data into the computer. If you were careful with your planning, though, these changes should be minimal.

Summary

This chapter presents three case studies to be completed with a word processor. The style sheet was developed first. Case study 1 is a telephone system manual, case study 2 is a mail merge letter, and case study 3 is a formal report with tables and columns. The completed word-processing planning guide for each case is presented.

Key Word

Mail merge

Problems

1. Create the beginning of your style sheet for use in this class. Enter the styles you will use for the assignment(s) from your instructor as given to you. You will add to the style sheet as you progress through the semester.

2. Develop the word-processing planning guide for the following problem:

You work for a shoe outlet. Your boss would like a letter sent to advertise a private sale to preferred customers only. Preferred customers are those who have signed a list to have sale information sent to them. Each customer has specified a type and brand of shoe that they prefer. This type and brand of shoe preferred by the customer should be included in the letter. There are 1,500 customers on this list. Envelopes will need to be printed. The company has letterhead paper with the letterhead on the top 2 inches of the paper, and envelopes preprinted with the return address. The existing database is as follows:

Date Description	Field Name
Last Name	last
First Name	first
Street address	street
City	city
State	state
Zip code	zipcode
Brand preference	brand
Shoe type preference	type
Date of last purchase	last purchase

3. You are a computer lab assistant and you have been assigned the job of designing a lab manual for students. The lab manual should contain information about lab usage such as hours open, people on duty, policies, how to use the computers, and how to report problems. As a student, what other items would you like to have in a lab manual? How would you design this lab manual to:
   a. entice students to read it?
   b. communicate the messages?
   c. emphasize changes from semester to semester?
4. In your computer literacy course you are asked to analyze and evaluate two computer hardware systems. You are to take advertisements of a computer hardware system from two computer catalogs and complete the following:
   a. Define the terms.
   b. Define criteria for evaluation.
   c. Compare the entire system, component by component.
   d. Compare the prices.
   e. Recommend one system and explain why.

   You will need to research terminology and equipment and write an interesting report. How will you:
   a. Make the report interesting enough for a fellow student to want to read it?
   b. Present your data?

   Your report should include columns and tables, and be in report form with a title page and bibliography.

Chapter 10

Desktop Publishing Concepts and Tools

Overview

Objects
Guide
Text Threading
Master Pages
Other Desktop Publishing Tools
Desktop Publishing Planning Guide
Common Desktop Publishing Documents
- **Business Cards**
- **Letterhead**
- **Flyers**
- **Signs**
- **Schedule**

Objectives

When you have finished this chapter, you should be able to:

1. Differentiate between documents that should be completed on a word processor and those that should be completed on a desktop publisher.
2. Understand the concept of an object and use it in the development of a document.
3. Use the three types of guidelines to plan and develop a document.
4. Understand and use the concept of threading text from one text box to another in the development and creation of documents.
5. Understand and use the concept of master pages.
6. Use the desktop publishing planning guide to plan and create a document.

A **desktop publisher** is a composition software program that easily combines text and graphics on a page. It differs from a word processor in several ways. Desktop publishers are not word processors, and word processors are not desktop publishers. Word processors have desktop publishing capabilities, but lack the ease of working with text and graphics as you have in a desktop publisher. Desktop publishers have word-processing capabilities, but lack many of the features of a word processor. Desktop publishers have tools to ease the process of combining text and graphics on a page. They treat text as a

Table 10.1 Desktop Publishing Features

Feature	Description
Autoflow	Continuous flow of text onto pages when imported.
Facing Pages	Adjustment of margins and view of pages that are facing each other.
Group and Ungroup	Make one object from many or many from one object.
Guides	Guidelines for measuring and placing objects on a page. The three types of guides are column, margin, and ruler guides.
Layers	Working on parts of a document on different transparencies.
Master Pages	Template of a page. Contains objects and guides required on all pages.
Objects	One element of a page—image, text block, or text frame.
Page Sorter	Allows the user to exchange page positions.
Text Blocks	The holder of text.
Text Frames	The holder of text that includes a border.
Text Threading	The connection between text blocks or frames to allow the text to flow from one text block to another when the top block is changed in size.
Text Wrap	The way text is designated to flow around an image.

group of characters in a box instead of individual characters as in a word processor. Desktop publishers look at the page as a document with margins and column guides that are moveable or that may be ignored. Desktop publishers have many of the features that graphic artists have on a composition table such as the pasteboard and blue lines. These concepts will be explained further in this chapter. Electronic desktop publishers emulate and make easy the job of the manual composition graphic artist.

You may not have the availability of a desktop publisher on your computer. If not, you will need to use the limited desktop publishing capabilities of your word processor or purchase desktop publishing software. The ideal solution for the creation of many documents is to first complete the entering and the preliminary editing of text in a word processor; then, import this text into the desktop publisher to be formatted and combined with graphics. If there are few or no graphics required of the document, then a word processor is probably the best tool. See Table 10.1 for desktop publishing features.

Objects

Objects

An **object** is a group of characters and/or graphics that are treated as one group. Figure 10.1 shows examples of objects. Objects may be resized, moved, rotated, or grouped with other objects. Vector graphic images are objects or grouped objects that may be resized, moved, rotated, or grouped with other objects. Each graphic is an object.

Notice that text is considered an object and does not have to stay within the margins, because the container in which it is housed can be sized due to the fact that margins are guidelines in desktop publishers. Desktop publishers place text in a text box (block) or a text frame. Both are containers for text. These containers may be sized, moved, or grouped with other objects. When the container is resized, the text adjusts to

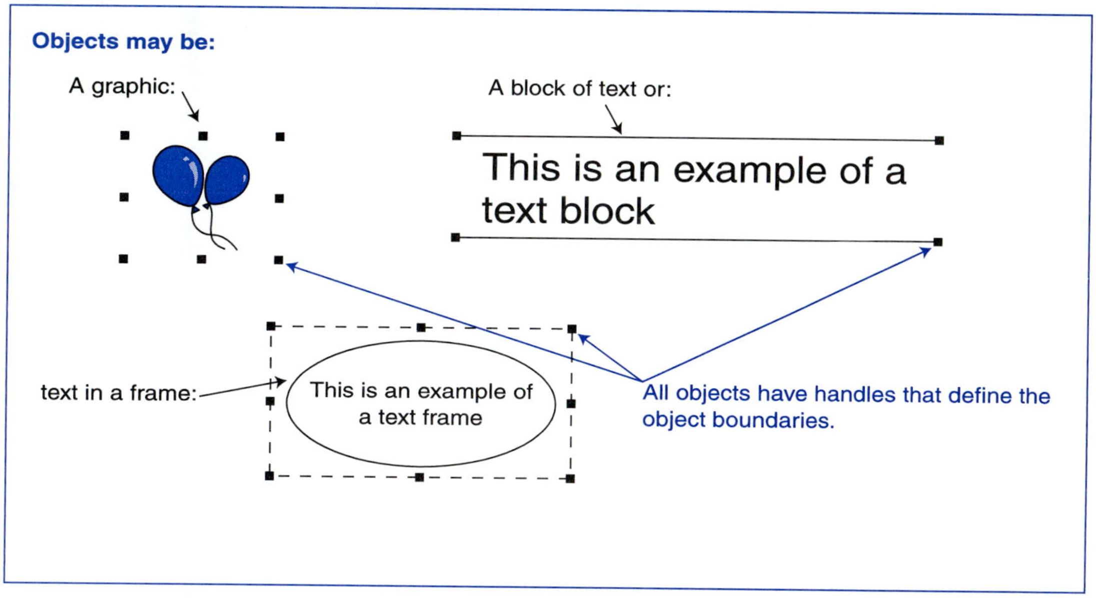

Figure 10.1 Examples of Objects

Text Blocks and Frames

the size of the container using the word wrap feature. If the text does not fit, the remaining text is not shown in the container. The remaining text will wait to be placed at a different time either in another container or when the container is enlarged. A **text block** simply holds the text in a rectangular form. A **text frame** holds the text in a chosen shape such as a circle, rectangle, polygon, or star. The text frame allows you to have a colored border and background as well as a different shape. The text box or text frame is then treated as an object that can be resized, moved, rotated, or grouped with other text boxes, text frames, and/or graphics.

Guides

Margin, Column, and Ruler Guides

There are three types of guides used in desktop publishers: **margin guides, column guides,** and **ruler guides.** See Figure 10.2. These guides may be easily changed on the page through a click-and-drag process. Margins are set the same as they are in a word processor. Columns are designated as to the number of columns and the gutter width. You may then modify the column width any time by dragging the column guides to any other point on the page. Ruler guides are sometimes called blue lines, because in the manual process a blue pencil was used to create **guidelines** for the placement of objects. The blue lines do not copy and therefore serve as guidelines that are visible in the creation process but not in the printing process. All of these lines are only guidelines.

If text blocks are not predetermined in size, then the software will make the box fit within the margins or the column lines. However, the text blocks may be resized and moved away from the margin lines or column lines or even into the margins. You may place text in all areas on the page, which may not be possible using a word processor. Figures 10.1 and 10.3 show text in text blocks and frames.

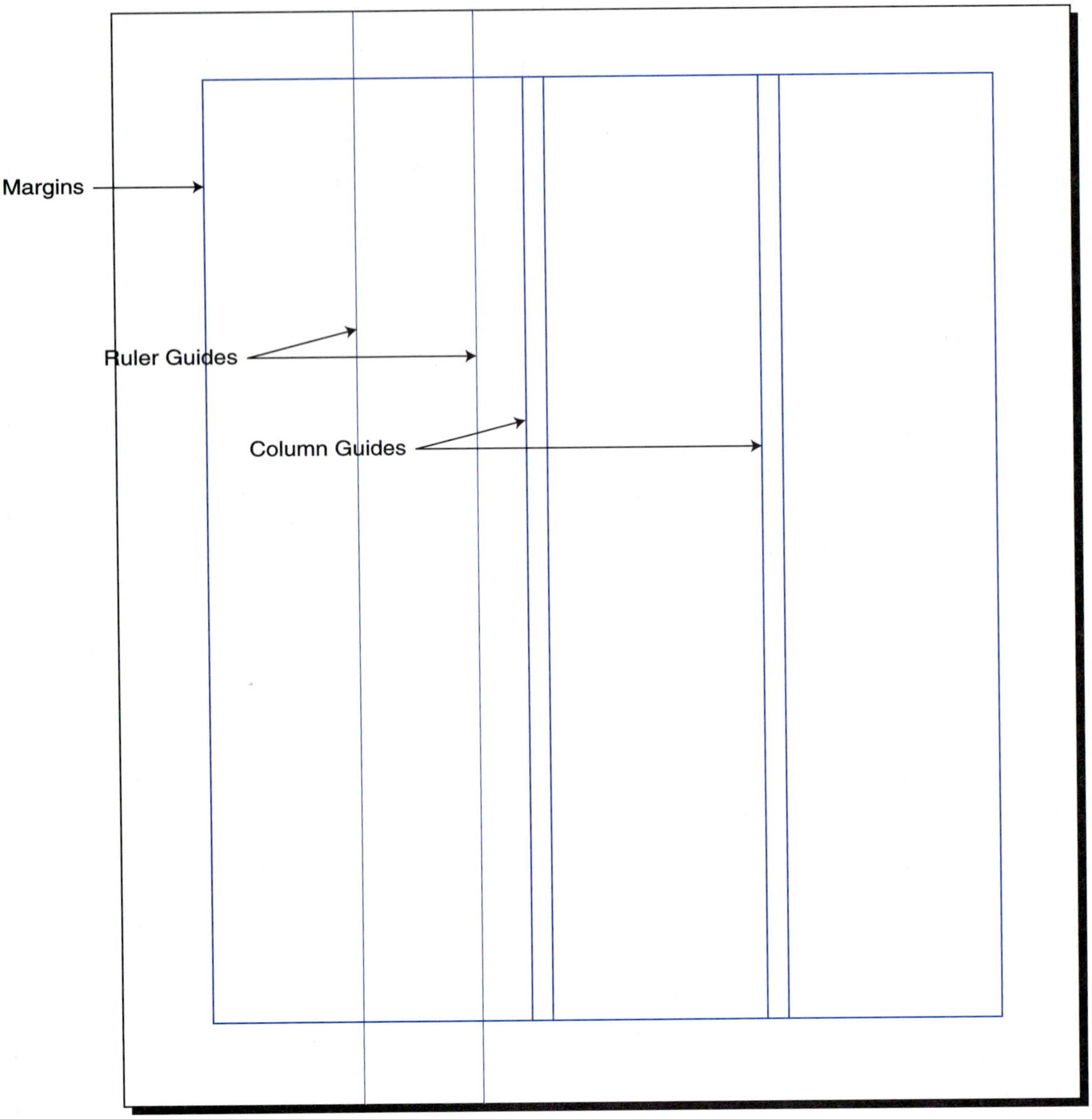

Figure 10.2 Guideline Examples

Text Threading

Text Threading

When text is placed in a text box or text frame, it fills the size of the box. If you want to fill the box with the remaining text, the box needs to be resized to increase the space in the box or the text needs to be reformatted to a smaller size and/or a narrower font width. The remaining text may be connected to another text box, called **text threading.** When this happens, an invisible thread connects the two boxes. See Figure 10.3 for an example of threading.

When a text box or frame is resized, only the container of the text is changed—not the text. If the first box is decreased in size, the extra characters will spill down the thread into the second box. If the first box is increased in size, the needed characters are siphoned up the thread into the first box. There is no limit as to the number of text boxes that hold all of the text. At the end of a page, the text box for that page is full. If more text exists, the text is then threaded to the next page. In this way, whenever the text is

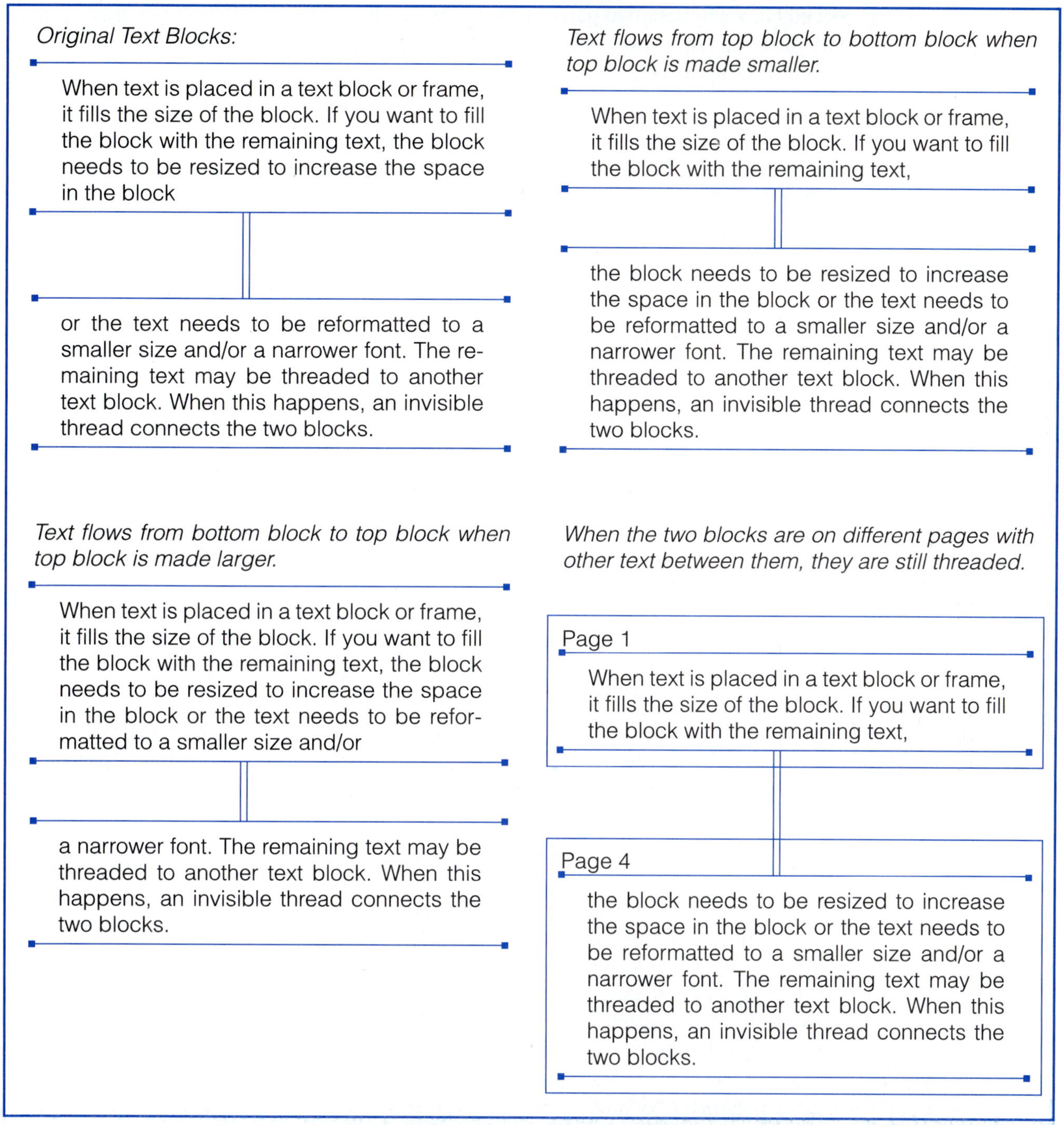

Figure 10.3 Example of Threading Text

modified, it will flow back and forth as necessary between pages during the editing process.

The threaded text boxes do not need to be on the same page or even consecutive pages. There may be a second set of threaded text boxes intermixed with the first set. For example, when developing a newsletter, a feature front-page article may not all fit on the first page and thus needs to be continued on the fourth page. The remainder of the article will be threaded to a second text box on the fourth page. Other articles can then be placed between these two parts. If there are changes in the feature article, the threading will allow the text to flow back and forth between the first threaded text box and its connected second text box.

Master Pages

Master Page

Master pages are page templates for items that you want printed on every page. Master pages do not specify styles to be used on the page; they only contain the items to be viewed and/or printed on each page. These might include guides, images, and text. You may have more than one master page with each individual page assigned to a specific master page. You may not change the master page items on the individual pages.

There are two reasons to use master pages. First, master pages are used to create the same items on all pages so you do not have to re-create them for each individual page. These items include the page number, the headers and footers, guidelines, columns, borders, and so forth. This saves time, energy, and computer storage space. Second, master pages are useful in creating templates for such things as newsletters, forms, or calendars. These are similar documents that are created over and over with some information that remains constant and other information that is changed from time to time. For example, a newsletter would have the same masthead, same setup for each page, and the same editorial information. The articles and some of the graphics will change. The masthead, the setup for each page, and the editorial information would be put on the master pages. As each new newsletter is created, all objects on the document pages will be deleted and replaced with new articles and graphics. When you delete the objects on the individual pages, the items on the master pages that show on the document pages will not be deleted, because master page items may not be changed on the document pages. The same is true for schedules or calendars.

Other Desktop Publishing Tools

Text styles are just as valuable in desktop publishing as in word processing. You may use the same style sheet planning guide as you did in word processing. You may want to add to the style sheet created in Chapter 9. Styles are used in the same manner in desktop publishing as in word processing.

Layers

Many desktop publishers allow you to work in layers. You may put different parts of your document on different layers. You may only change the data on the layer on which you are working. As you plan your document, indicate what content will be placed on each layer. You may have a detailed graphic that you want to remain fixed on the document, or you may have data that need to be changed often. In either of these cases, you would place this information on separate layers. Remember you may delete everything on one layer without destroying anything on other layers.

Text Wrap

Most word-processing software allows text wrap in rectangles or diamonds. Desktop publishers take this one step further to allow a custom text wrap. You have complete control over the shape. For example, you may have a graphic of a butterfly and want the text to wrap around the graphic in the shape of the butterfly. As you are planning your document, specify the shape for the text wrap.

Facing Pages/Double Sided

Desktop publishing software provides easy creation of double-sided or facing pages in a document. You may create both left and right master pages, so that you can easily see how two pages look side by side as you create them. When creating a document that involves double-sided or facing pages, you will have inside and outside margins instead of left and right margins, because the margin size will change from right to left depending on the front and back side of the page. Remember that the inside margins must be larger than the outside margins to leave room for binding. As you plan your document, ask the people who will be doing the reproduction work how much space the binding will take. The inside margins will need to be this amount larger than the outside margins. For example, if your margins are 0.75 inch and the binding margin is 0.5 inch, the inside margin should be 1.25 inches and the outside margin should be 0.75 inch. Booklets, books, and some reports are usually reproduced using double-sided or facing pages. You may have a single page that is double sided. In this case, your margins would be left and right and should be equal unless the page will be inserted in a three-ring binder, wherein it should be treated as a bound document.

Page Sorter

Sometimes after you have created a document with separate information on each page, you may want to change the order of the pages. In a desktop publisher you would be able to sort, or rearrange, the pages by a drag-and-drop procedure similar to the slide sorter in presentation graphics. The threading will not change. For example, if you have two text boxes threaded from page 2 to page 3 before sorting, but then you changed page 3 to page 5, the boxes then would be threaded from page 2 to page 5. If you changed page 2 to page 5, then page 3 would become page 2 and the pages would be threaded from page 5 to page 2. The desktop publisher appropriately modifies the inside and outside margins.

Autoflow

When importing text, you may allow the text to flow into the designated text box or frame, which leaves any text that does not fit into the space to be placed at a later time or you may use the autoflow function. Autoflow allows all of the text to be placed on a page. If there are not enough pages to place all of the text, the software will add more pages to the document.

Group and Ungroup

The group and ungroup functions allow you to combine multiple objects into one object. That object can then be moved as one without disturbing the placement of any of the individual parts. This feature is invaluable when using the cut/copy/paste options or moving the objects. If you want to change the grouping, simply ungroup the combined object to have the individual objects again.

Desktop Publishing Planning Guide

Desktop Publishing Planning Guide

The desktop publishing planning guide in Figure 10.4 is similar to the word-processing planning guide. On the layout pages you will find a different page for the master page(s) and for the individual pages. You will also find a ruler to help in the placement of the guidelines. It is important to plan the layout of the guidelines during the planning of your documents. Steps one through four are optional for small or simple documents, but they are important for large or complex documents. Steps five and six are important for all documents.

The layout of the ruler guides or blue lines should be completed before you go to the computer. These are additions to the layouts created in Chapters 7 and 8. The text wrap around the graphics should also be indicated on the layout. Study how the following projects use columns, ruler guides, and text wrap.

Figure 10.4 Desktop Publishing Planning Guide

DESKTOP PUBLISHING PLANNING GUIDE

Name of Document: ______________________________ Date: ______________

Location of Electronic File: ______________________________

Name: ______________________________

Name of Client: ______________________________

Step 1: Identify the Problem by Writing the Problem Statement.

Step 2: Understand the Problem.

Audience:

Required Outcomes of the Document:

Required Knowledge of the Problem to Develop the Document:

Required Knowledge of the Audience:

Step 3: Identify Valid Alternative Methods to Solve the Problem.

Step 4: Select the Best Method to Solve the Problem from the List of Alternative Solutions.

Figure 10.4 (continued)

Step 5: Plan Your Solution.

Software to be used: Desktop Publisher

Margins:

Top: ____________ Top Printer: ____________

Bottom: ____________ Bottom Printer: ____________

Left/Inside: ________ Binding: ______ Left Printer: ________

Right/Outside: ____________ Right Printer: ____________

Header: ____________ Top Printer: ____________

Footer: ____________ Bottom Printer: ____________

Tabs:

Files to be imported:

File	Description	Use	Location

Paper Size: ____________ Paper Color: ____________

Orientation: ____________ Color/B&W: ____________

Number of Columns: ____________ Gutters: ____________

Header Contents:

Footer Contents:

(continued)

Figure 10.4 Desktop Publishing Planning Guide

Step 5: Plan Your Solution. (con't)

Estimated Number of Master Pages:____________________________
Sketch(s) of Master Page Layouts:

	1	2	3	4	5	6	7
1							
2							
3							
4							
5							
6							
7							
8							
9							

Figure 10.4 (continued)

Estimated Number of Individual Pages:____________________________

Sketch(s) of Individual Page Layouts:

	1	2	3	4	5	6	7
1							
2							
3							
4							
5							
6							
7							
8							
9							

(continued)

Figure 10.4 Desktop Publishing Planning Guide

Step 6: **Evaluate the Solution.**

Common Desktop Publishing Documents

Following are some examples of common types of documents that are best created using a desktop publisher. For the most part, these are not complicated documents. Chapter 11 presents the development of three case studies with projects that are also best suited to be completed on a desktop publisher. Start with the easy projects in this chapter and continue with those in the next chapter.

Business Cards

Business Cards

Business cards are easy to make using a desktop publisher. You can make them look professional by using nice card stock paper. The blue line layout is important in the design process to be sure the cards look good and are a standard size (2 × 3 1/2 inches). Look at the layout of business cards produced by others. What do you like? Why do you like the layout? Figure 10.5 shows the blue line layout for a page of 10 business cards. To create this page, follow these steps:

1. Create the document setup using the printer margin for the page margins. The edge of the card should not be closer to the edge than the printer margin.
2. Complete the blue line layout on the master page. If you use the master page for the layout, you may then make other cards on other pages without recreating the blue line layout. The zero marker is placed on the upper left margin corner. Blue lines are then added to designate the card edges. The card requires a margin also, usually no greater than 3/8 inch. Blue lines are added to the upper left card for these margins.
3. Design one card in the upper left card area on the individual page, not on the master page.
4. When the design is exactly as you want it to be for the first card, group all objects on the card.
5. Go to the master page and place blue lines indicating the top and left margins of the rest of the cards. Go back to the individual page.

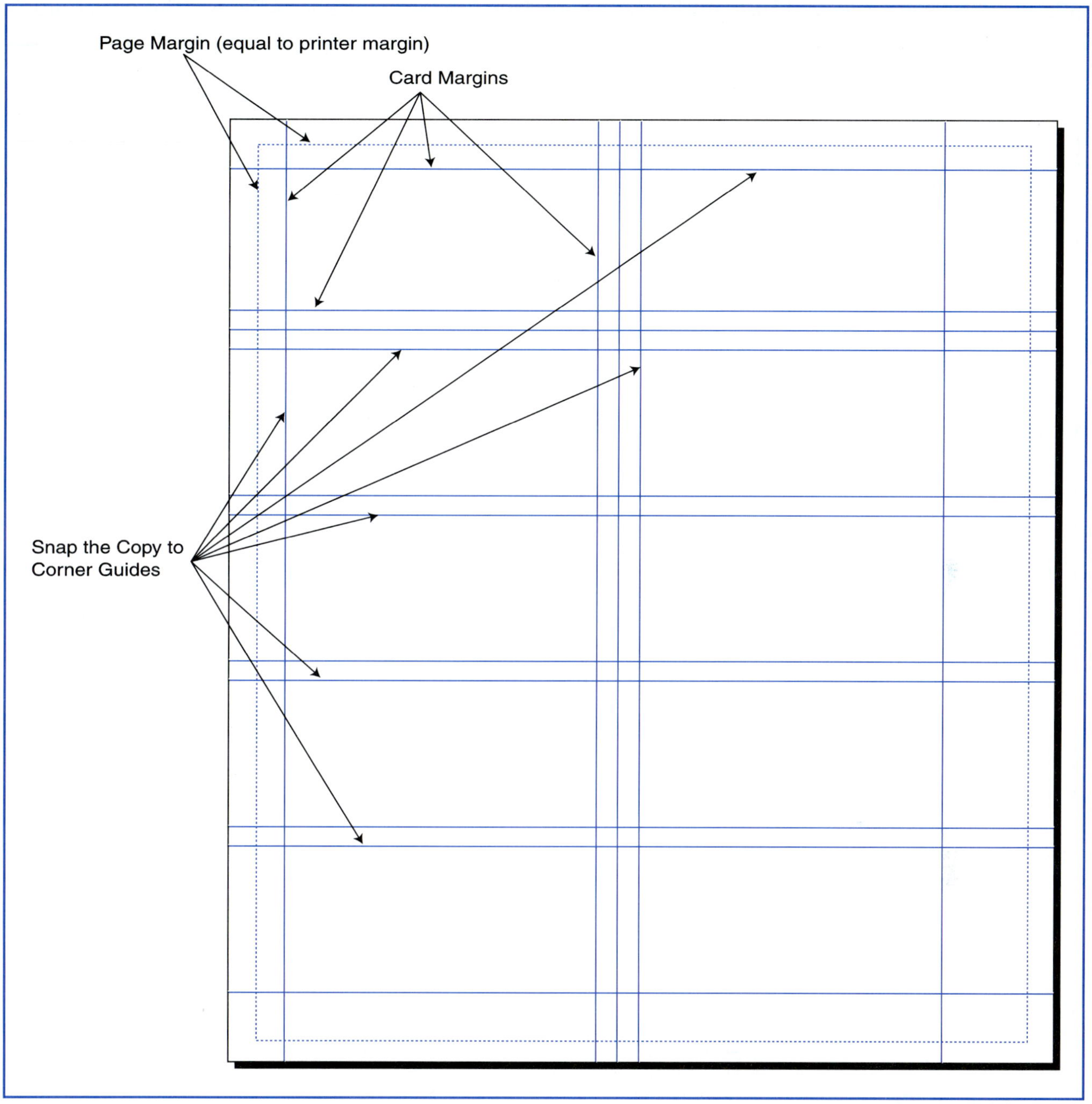

Figure 10.5 Business Card Layout

6. Copy the grouped objects of the first card and paste it such that the grouped objects snap to the top and left margin lines of each of the remaining cards. Save your file.
7. Reproduce professionally or print the sheet on card stock paper and have professional reproducers cut the cards to size. It will require nine cuts. This will produce 10 cards per page.

Figure 10.6 presents steps five and six in the desktop publishing planning guide. Note there is both a page layout and a card layout. It is important to be able to see both.

Figure 10.6 Steps Five and Six of the Desktop Publishing Planning Guide for a Page of Business Cards

Step 5: Plan Your Solution.

Software to be used: Desktop Publisher

Margins:

Top: 0.25 Top Printer: 0.25

Bottom: 0.25 Bottom Printer: 0.5

Left: 0.25 Binding: ______ Left Printer: 0.25

Right: 0.25 Right Printer: 0.25

Header: None Top Printer: ______

Footer: None Bottom Printer: ______

***Tabs:* Default**

Files to be imported:

File	Description	Use	Location
Logo	Graphic	on card	c:\my documents\graphics

Paper Size: 8½ × 11 Paper Color: Blue

Orientation: Portrait Color/B&W: Color

Number of Columns: N/A Gutters: ______

Header Contents: None

Footer Contents: None

Figure 10.6 (continued)

Sketch(s) of Individual Page Layout(s)

(continued)

Figure 10.6 Steps Five and Six of the Desktop Publishing Planning Guide for a Page of Business Cards

Step 5: Plan Your Solution. (con't)

Estimated Number of Pages: 1

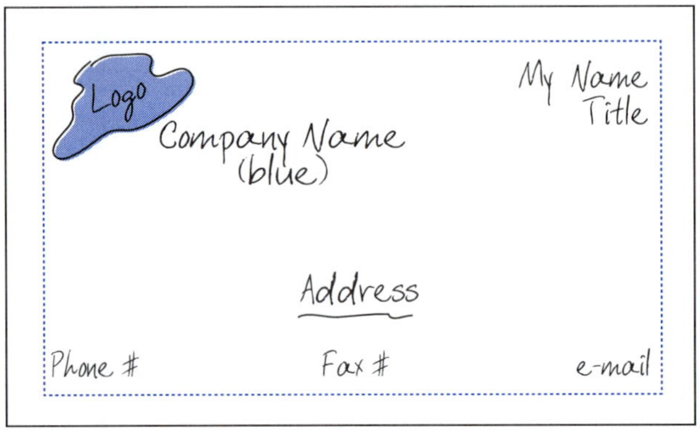

Step 6: Evaluate the Solution.

Criteria for Evaluation:

- **a.** Are all the data on the card?
- **b.** Is the card attractive?
- **c.** Is the white space appropriate? (Not too much or too little?)
- **d.** Are the data easy to read?
- **e.** Does the name stand out as the first thing that is read?
- **f.** Do you like it?
- **g.** Is the logo well placed and appropriate?

Letterhead

Letterhead

Letterhead is also easy to create on a desktop publisher. A letterhead needs to be well designed and incorporate data about the company on the page. Lines work very well to separate the letterhead information from the letter. Figure 10.7 shows several letterhead designs. Look at letterheads designed by others and discover what type of design you like best and why.

Flyers

Flyers

Advertising flyers are commonly developed in-house. Even though a flyer is usually inexpensively done, it can be very effective if it is well designed. Review some of the design guidelines in Chapter 4. Some of the most important considerations for a flyer are as follows:

1. The flyer must have a hook. Most people will spend only a fraction of a minute first looking at a flyer. If the flyer has something of interest to hook the reader, then the reader will look further. This hook may be text or a graphic. The flyer must convey the message with a single glance from the reader; otherwise, it may have lost a potential customer.
2. There must be a center of attention. All graphics and text must work toward this center, and be positioned so the eye will follow to this area. Text must flow around graphics without distraction.

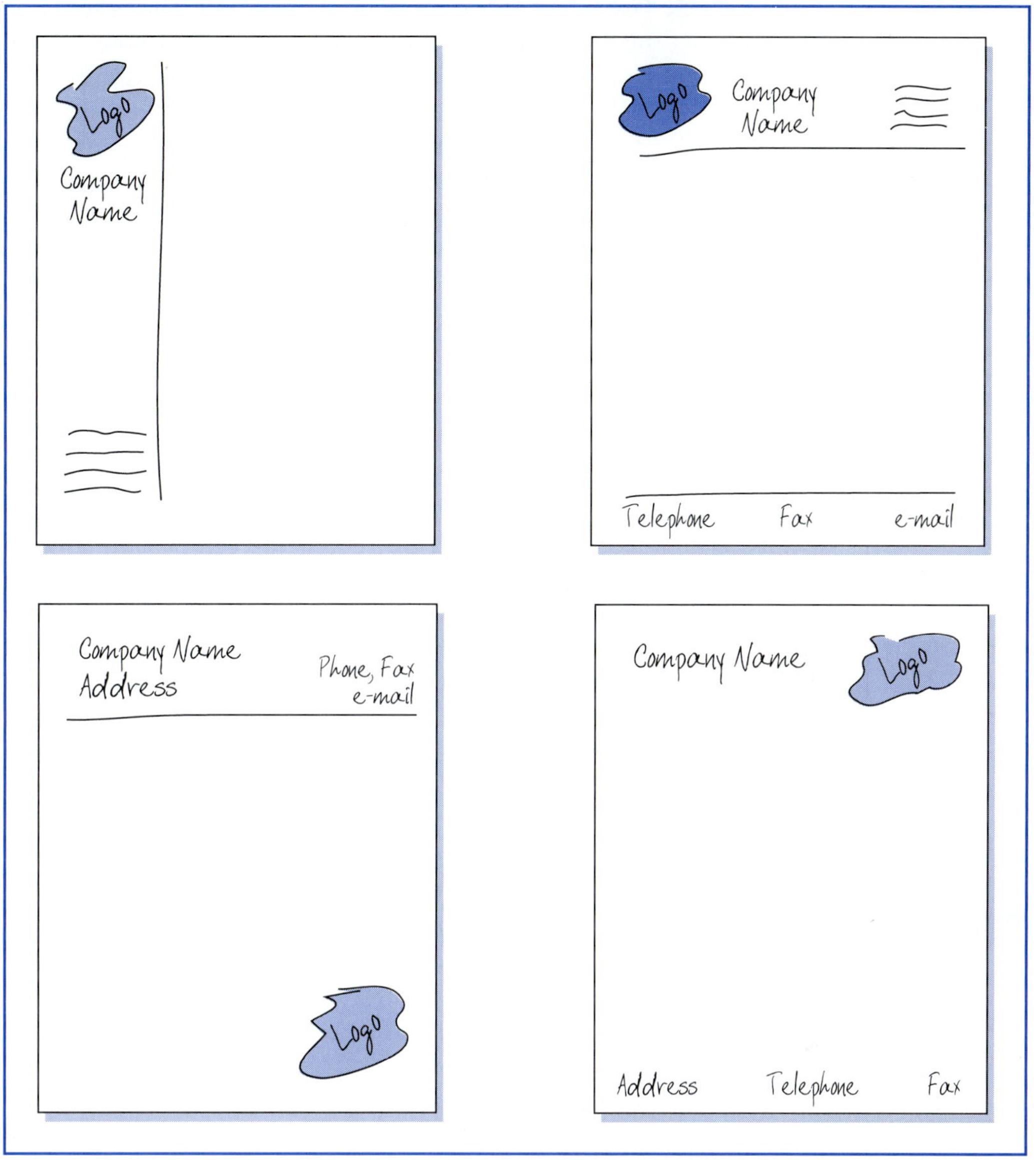

Figure 10.7 Letterhead Layouts

3. Pertinent information should be in larger type size, such as the nature of the event and important items about the event. Other information should be in smaller type and in a less conspicuous place. If you have hooked the reader and the reader is interested, he or she will find the other information about the event such as date, time, or place. All text should be in topical form, with no complete sentences. People are not interested in reading a lot of material. If you are advertising a garage sale, for example, you will want to list the main items for sale and not describe each item in detail.
4. Avoid clutter. Use your white space carefully. Make sure there is enough white space for the eye to read the text and to view the graphics. Also, make sure there are no large, open spaces that look as if something is missing. There is a fine line between these two rules, but a well-designed flyer will illustrate that line.

5. Use boxes, circles, and borders wisely. They should be used to contain information, so use them only if they have a purpose. You want the elements of the flyer to complement each other and not be isolated.
6. Avoid centering everything. Centering all elements creates a boring layout for the reader. Try to right align some of the objects or have the objects cascade down the page at an angle or in a sideways V shape.
7. Align objects that should be aligned. Make sure the objects that are left, right, or center aligned are done so at the same place. Often graphics are not aligned with other graphics and the text. This tends to throw the eye off and make the flyer look as if there is something wrong. If the objects are not aligned intentionally, then make sure there is enough difference in the alignment so the reader knows they are not supposed to be aligned.

Figure 10.8 shows steps five and six of the planning guide for a flyer to advertise a coffee bar that is a fund-raiser for the computer club. It will be used only on campus. It will be posted in many of the classrooms around campus and will have the students as an audience. Notice the coffee cup is the center of attention. The text on top of the flyer and the coffee cup are the hooks. Pertinent information about where and when are in smaller text and near the bottom of the page. Notice the graphics lead to the bottom information and not off the page. The color of the paper is important. Rarely is white paper a good choice. Colored paper costs a little more but can be more effective. Choose a light color that will complement the message. A flyer that is well designed can be effective in sending the message to the audience. A flyer that is boring will tend to go unnoticed.

Signs

Signs

Signs are always needed for any business. They might include an open/closed sign, a time open sign, a list of policies and guidelines, and so on. Many signs use pictographs, or line drawings that depict an object or an event without using text, such as the question mark for the information booth, the airplane for an airport, and the woman and man for restrooms. Many pictographs are internationally accepted.

Your intent is for people to read the sign. You do not want the sign to appear boring. It is best to use some graphics to hook the people into reading the sign. People may ignore signs that have only text. Many times pictographs alone will do the job; however, a combination of graphics and text is usually best. Do not use complete sentences, and try to use as few words as possible to still communicate the message. For the most part, people will not stop to read lengthy text on a sign.

Figure 10.9 shows the layouts for three signs for a coffeehouse that sells bakery goods and coffee. One is the open/closed sign, another is the time open sign, and the third is a reminder sign for a door to ensure that customers have all of their personal belongings.

Schedule

Schedules

Schedules are types of forms. You may want to develop a schedule for your week or a work schedule for people you manage. Any form can be developed on a desktop publisher. Some of the key items to think about are as follows:

1. What data do you want to collect or manage?
2. In what order do you want to have the data entered?

Figure 10.8 Steps Five and Six of the Desktop Publishing Planning Guide for a Flyer

Step 5: Plan Your Solution.

Software to be used: Desktop Publisher

Margins:

Top: 0.75	Top Printer: 0.25
Bottom: 0.75	Bottom Printer: 0.5
Left: 0.75 Binding: ______	Left Printer: 0.25
Right: 0.75	Right Printer: 0.25
Header: None	Top Printer: 0.25
Footer: None	Bottom Printer: 0.25

***Tabs:* Use Defaults**

Files to be imported:

File	Description	Use	Location
Coffee Cup	Clipart	Middle of page	c:\graphics\clipart\

Paper Size: 8½ × 11 Paper Color: Bright Yellow

Orientation: Portrait Color/B&W: B&W

Number of Columns: N/A Gutters: N/A

Header Contents: None

Footer Contents:

C:\my data\school\club\Coffee Flyer		Date

(continued)

Figure 10.8 Steps Five and Six of the Desktop Publishing Planning Guide for a Flyer

Step 5: **Plan Your Solution. (con't)**

Sketch(s) of Individual Page Layout(s)

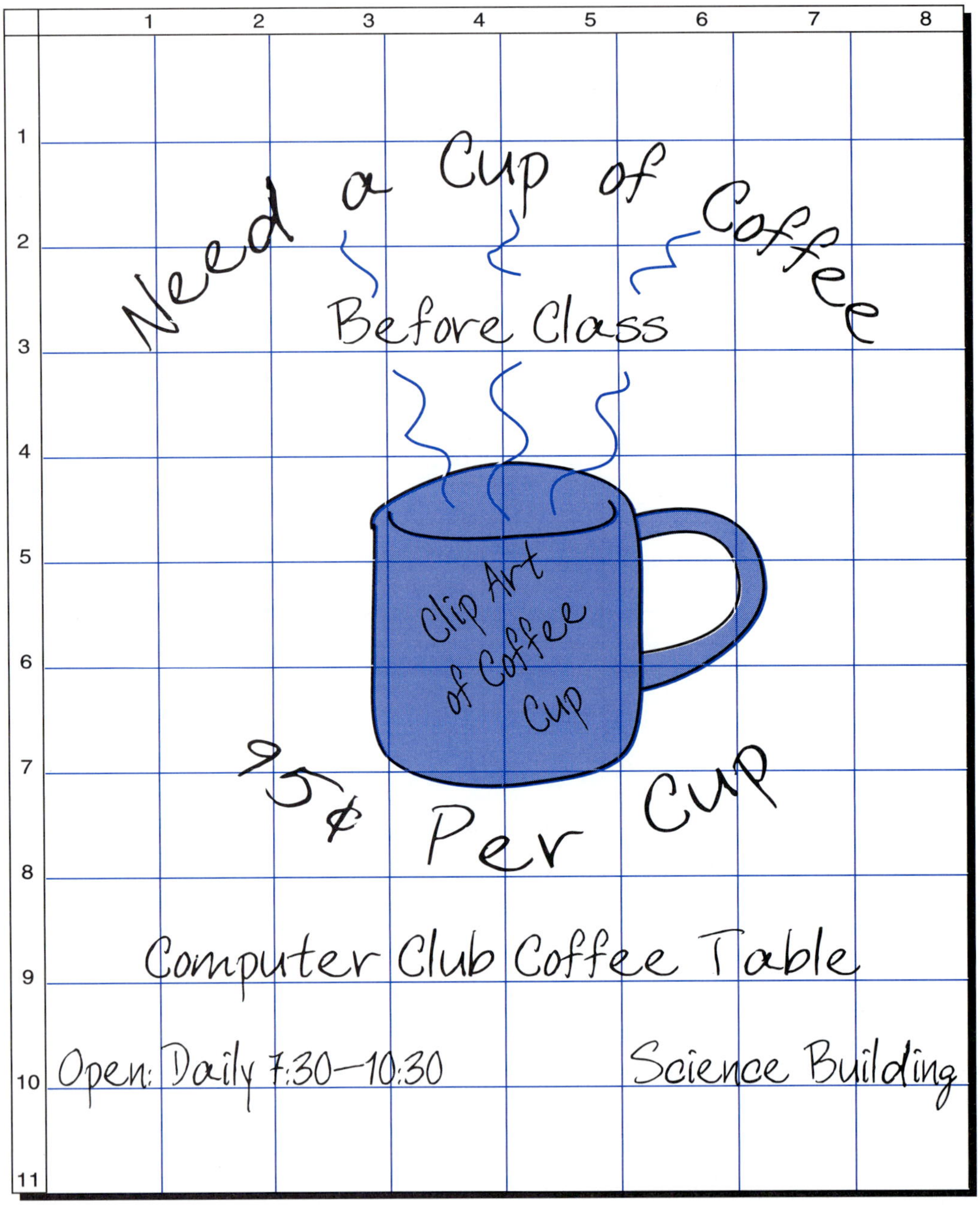

Figure 10.8 (continued)

Step 6: Evaluate the Solution.

The criteria for evaluation is:

a. Does the flyer have a hook?
b. Does the eye stay on the page?
c. Is the primary message apparent at first glance?
d. Is the flyer pleasing to the eye?
e. Are appropriate graphics used?
f. Are the fonts appropriate for the message of the flyer?
g. Do you like it?

3. Is this form an internal or external form? An internal form is used only within the company. People outside the company would use a more formal external document. An example of an internal form is a time card; an example of an external form is an employment application or a sales receipt. An internal form requires as much company information as an external form, whereas an external form may require more explanation than an internal form.
4. Does the form require a control number? This number is to control forms after they have been completed in order to further process data such as a sales receipt.

Figure 10.10 shows steps five and six of the desktop publishing planning guide for a personal weekly schedule. The template form is created on the master page and the weekly data are entered on the individual page. Following are the steps to completing a schedule.

1. Create the document setup using equal margins all around.
2. Create columns for each set of data—in this case eight columns, one for the time row headings and seven columns for the days of the week.
3. Complete the blue line layout on the master page. The zero marker is placed on the upper left margin corner. It is usually easier to measure from the margins than from the corner of the paper. Add blue lines to designate each of the time rows. Remember the top row is for the weekday headings of the columns.
4. Place the document heading at the top of the page, the time in the row headings, and the days of the week in the column headings.
5. Draw a rectangle on the perimeter of the form.
6. Draw the inside black horizontal and vertical lines on the ruler guides and the column guides within the perimeter of the rectangle.
7. Zoom to 200% and lengthen or shorten any lines that fall outside or inside the rectangle. You may have to hide the guidelines to do this. Lines that do not align make your form look sloppy and unprofessional. This will complete the master page.
8. On the individual page, place the events of the week.
9. When you change to the next week, return to the individual page, and select and delete all objects. This can be done using Select All from the edit menu and then using the delete key. You will delete all events from last week, but leave the basic form since the form is on the master page.

Figure 10.9 Layouts for coffeehouse signs

Forms can be completed easily in a desktop publisher. If done correctly, they can save much time. Notice in Figure 10.10 that the date and the file name are contained in the footer. This is a way to know where the file is located, the name of the file, and also the last date that it was modified. If the date is added to the footer, people using the form will know what forms are out of date and which ones they should be using.

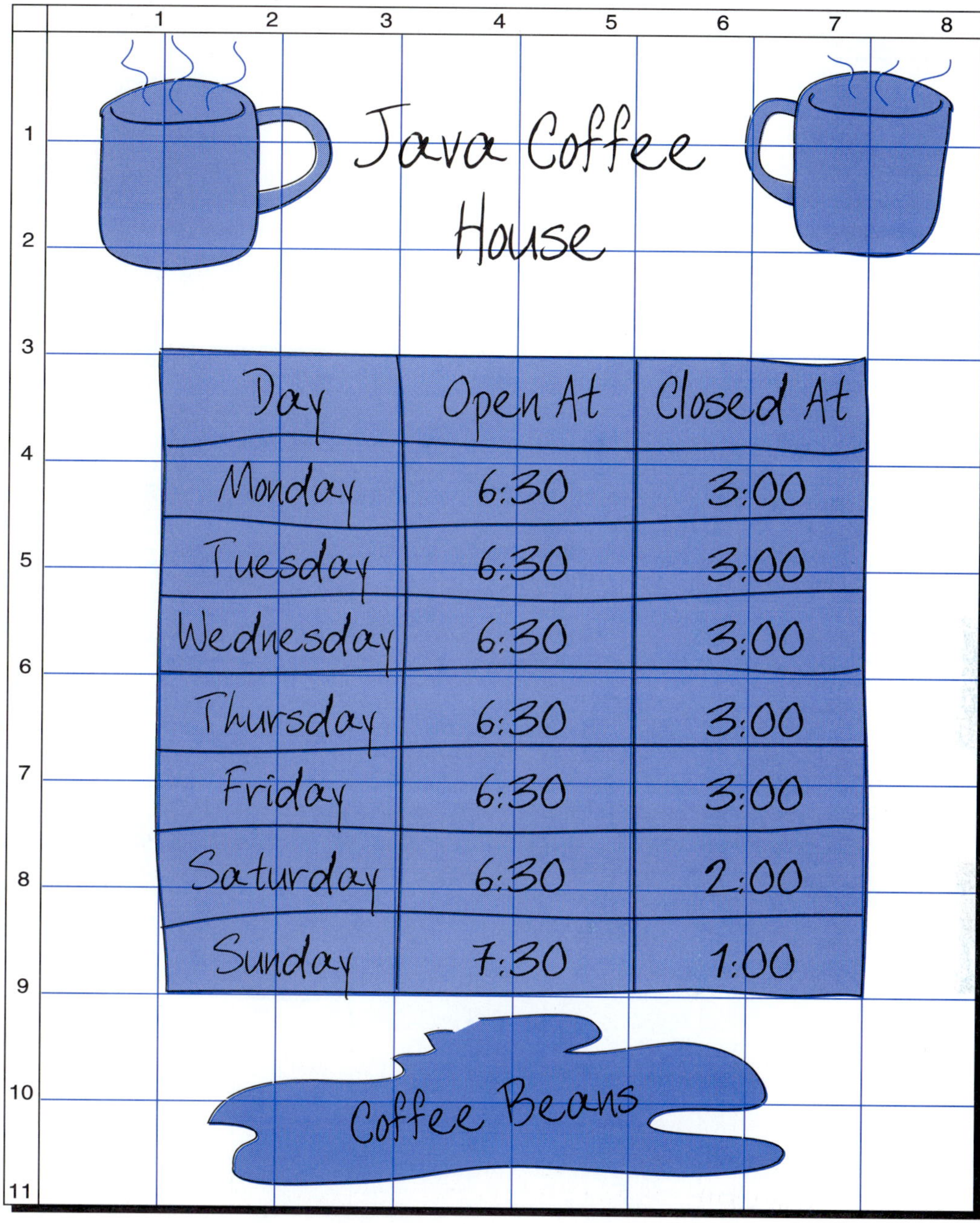

Figure 10.9 Layouts for coffeehouse signs

There are many other documents that can be easily completed on a desktop publisher such as buttons, memo pads, CD covers, labels for storage media, placemats, programs, menus, and class assignments. You can make an ordinary event into a special one by using additional niceties such as personalized placemats, easy table decorations, buttons, and awards—it only takes a little imagination, a desktop publisher, and some great graphics.

Figure 10.9 Layouts for coffeehouse signs

Figure 10.10 Steps Five and Six of the Desktop Publishing Planning Guide for a Schedule

Step 5: Plan Your Solution.

Software to be used: Desktop Publisher

Margins:

Top: 0.75 Top Printer: 0.25
Bottom: 0.75 Bottom Printer: 0.25
Left: 0.75 Binding: N/A Left Printer: 0.25
Right: 0.75 Right Printer: 0.25
Header: None Top Printer: 0.25
Footer: None Bottom Printer: 0.25

***Tabs:* Use Defaults**

***Files to be imported:* None**

File	Description	Use	Location

Paper Size: 8½ × 11 Paper Color: Light Green
Orientation: Portrait Color/B&W: B&W
Number of Columns: N/A Gutters: N/A
Header Contents: None

Footer Contents:

C:\my data\personal\schedule 2002		Date

(continued)

Figure 10.10 Steps Five and Six of the Desktop Publishing Planning Guide for a Schedule

Step 5: Plan Your Solution. (con't)

Master Page Layout of Guidelines before Black Lines Were Added

Maureen's Schedule

Time	Mon.	Tues.	Wed.	Thurs.	Fri.	Sat.	Sun.
8:00							
9:00							
10:00							
11:00							
12:00							
1:00							
2:00							
3:00							
4:00							
5:00							
6:00							
7:00							
8:00							
9:00							

Figure 10.10 (continued)

Master Page Layout of Guidelines after Black Lines Were Added

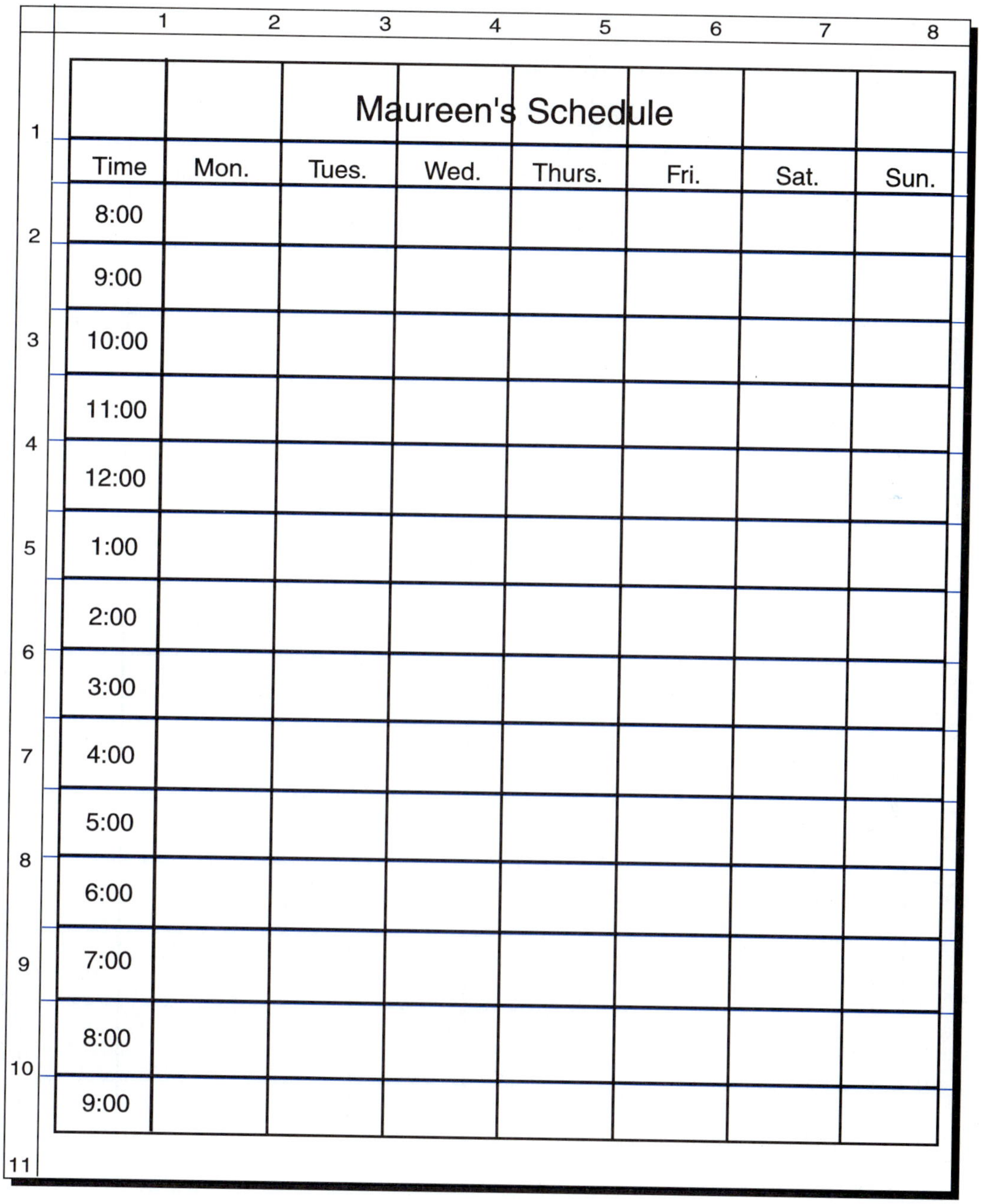

(continued)

Figure 10.10 Steps Five and Six of the Desktop Publishing Planning Guide for a Schedule

Step 5: Plan Your Solution. (con't)

Individual Page Layout with Events Added

Maureen's Schedule							
Time	Mon.	Tues.	Wed.	Thurs.	Fri.	Sat.	Sun.
8:00		CIS 100		CIS 100			
9:00			Lab				
10:00			Lab				
11:00		Biol 2		Biol 2			
12:00							
1:00							
2:00							
3:00							
4:00							
5:00					Work		
6:00					Work		
7:00							
8:00							
9:00							

Step 6: Evaluate the Solution.

The criteria for evaluation is:

a. Is the schedule easy to read?
b. Can you clearly enter the event of the week?
c. Is the schedule in a form that you will use?
d. Do you like it?
e. Is the schedule easy to change?

Summary

A desktop publisher is a composition software program that allows for easy placement of text and graphics. Even though word processors have some desktop publishing capabilities, they do not have many of the features of a desktop publisher.

Desktop publishers work with objects that may be moved, resized, cropped, grouped, and ungrouped. This includes text as it is contained in a text block or text frame. Text can be threaded from one text block to another, even if other text or other pages separate them.

Desktop publishers work with three types of guidelines: margin guides, column guides, and ruler guides. These are not absolute in that text does not have to reside within the guidelines.

Desktop publishers have other features that word processors may not have such as multiple master pages, layers, irregular text wrap around graphics, and easy creation of booklets and books.

The desktop publishing planning guide helps to plan how the document will be set up on the computer. Some common documents include business cards, letterhead, flyers, and forms.

Key Words

Desktop publisher
Guidelines:
- Column guides
- Margin guides
- Ruler guides

Master pages
Object
Text block
Text frame
Text threading

Exercises

1. What is a desktop publisher?
2. How does a desktop publisher differ from a word processor?
3. What is an object?
4. What can you do with an object?
5. What happens to a graphic when it is resized?
6. What happens to the text when a text box is resized?
7. What is the difference between cropping and resizing?
8. What are the three types of guidelines and how are they used?
9. What is text threading?
10. What is a master page?
11. How and why would you use a master page?

Problems

1. You have just finished taking a class in which you developed an educational multimedia presentation to teach third-grade mathematics. Using the desktop publishing

planning guide, create a design for the CD-ROM cover. What are the items that should be placed on a CD-ROM?

2. Sketch a label design for your floppy disk or an insert label for your zip cartridges.
3. The computer lab needs a sign to place on the door to remind students to be sure they have their storage media: floppy disks or zip cartridges. Sketch a design for this sign.
4. A good friend of yours, Grennin Thum, has just started a florist business called The Last Rose. He would like you to create the following for his business.
   a. business cards
   b. letterhead
   c. client form
   d. open/closed sign
   e. advertising flyer for the grand opening
   f. memo pads and buttons for the grand opening

   The address of the store is 123 Floral Lane, Greenest Country, CA 99222. The telephone number is 567-768-5555. Using the desktop publishing planning guide, decide how you will create these documents.
5. A local restaurant called The Ginger Root would like you to design a menu and placemat. Using the desktop publishing planning guide, decide how you will create these documents.
6. The Ginger Root in question 5 makes a very special barbecue sauce. The owner would like you to create a label for the bottle. Using the desktop publishing planning guide, decide how you will create this project.
7. Choose a favorite poem. Sketch a plan of how you would create a document using text and graphics to depict this poem for display in an 8 1/2 × 11 photo frame. Indicate the type of graphics you would use.

Chapter 11

Case Studies for a Desktop Publisher

Overview

Style Sheet
Case Study 1: Newsletter
Case Study 2: Brochure
Case Study 3: Booklet

Objectives

When you have finished this chapter, you should be able to:

1. Develop more styles for the style sheet.
2. Problem solve and develop a plan to create complex desktop publishing documents such as a newsletter, a brochure and a booklet.
3. Use the desktop publishing planning guide and the six problem-solving steps to develop a solution to a document that should be created in a desktop publisher.

Chapter 11 presents three desktop publishing case studies using the six steps in problem solving and the desktop publishing planning guide. Study how each solution was determined and use the same methodology for the problems at the end of the chapter.

Style Sheet

There are several styles to be added to the style sheet. See Figure 11.1 for the updates, including:

1. *Text right:* Text right is based on the body text 2 style. The difference is that text right is right aligned.
2. *Big text:* Big text is based on body text 2 style. The only change is that the size is 18 points.
3. *Big text right:* Big text right is based on big text style. The only change is that it is right aligned.
4. *Text center:* Text center is based on the body text 2 style. The difference is that text center is center aligned.
5. *Big text center:* Big text center is based on big text style. The only change is that it is center aligned.

Style Sheet

					Enhancements					Indentation		
	Style Name	**Style Based On**	**Font Name**	**Size**	**Bold**	**Underline**	**Italics**	**Other**	**Alignment**	**Left**	**Right**	**First Line**
1	Body Text	None	Arial	12					Left			0.25
2	Body Text 2	Body Text	Arial	12					Left			
3	Headings	Body Text	Arial	24	X				Center			
4	Subheadings	Headings	Arial	18	X				Center			
5	Small Headings	Subheadings	Arial	14					Center			
6	Captions	Body Text	Arial	10			X		Left			
7	Hanging Indent	Body Text	Arial	12					Left	0.25		t-0.25
8	Table of Contents	Body Text	Arial	12					Left			
9	Numbered list	Hanging Indent	Arial	12					Left			
10	Text right	Body Text	Arial	12					Right			
11	Big text	Body Text	Arial	18					Left			
12	Big text right	Big Text	Arial	18					Right			
13	Text center	Body Text	Arial	12					Center			
14	Big text center	Big Text	Arial	18					Center			
15												
16												
17												
18												
19												
20												
21												
22												
23												
24												
25												
26												
27												
28												

Figure 11.1 Style Sheet

Style Sheet

		Paragraph Leading					Line Controls						
	Style Name	Lines	After	Before	Tabs	Hyphenation	Widows	Orphans	Page Break	Numbering	Bullets	Borders	Other
1	Body Text				Every 0.5 inch	Off	X	X					
2	Body Text 2		0.25		Every 0.5 inch	Off	X	X					
3	Headings		0.25		Every 0.5 inch	Off							
4	Subheadings		0.25		Every 0.5 inch	Off							
5	Small Headings		0.25		Every 0.5 inch	Off							
6	Captions				Every 0.5 inch	Off							
7	Hanging Indent				Every 0.5 inch	Off	X	X					
8	Table of Contents		0.25		rt at 6, tab leader	Off							
9	Numbered list		0.25		Every 0.5 inch	Off				X			
10	Text right		0.25		Every 0.5 inch	Off	X	X					
11	Big text		0.25		Every 0.5 inch	Off	X	X					
12	Big text right				Every 0.5 inch								
13	Text center		0.25			Off	X	X					
14	Big text center												
15													
16													
17													
18													
19													
20													
21													
22													
23													
24													
25													
26													
27													
28													

Figure 11.1 Style Sheet

Case Study 1: Newsletter

Newsletter

You work for the Do-It-Right Cleaning Company and the owners would like to publish a two-page employee **newsletter** each month. You have been selected to design and publish the newsletter. The owners would like the following to be included:

1. Spotlight of an employee of the month
2. Letter from one of the owners
3. Monthly events
4. Birthdays for the month
5. Special outside distinctions of any of the employees

You have been given release time of eight hours a month to publish this newsletter.

Newsletter text is usually set in columns. The columns may be offset so that the left column is wider or narrower than the right column. The larger column usually has more important information than the narrower column, which makes the newsletter look different. The bottoms of the columns should be aligned. The masthead sides should be aligned with the sides of the columns of text or with the borders if they are used. Use graphics to add interest to the text articles. You may want to wrap the text around the graphic. You may want a graphic in the middle of the page so the text from both columns wraps around the graphic. Since you are only allowed eight hours to complete the newsletter each month, you will not have time to create a lot of graphics. Therefore, digital photographs and clipart are your best choices of graphics. Try new ideas on layouts. You do not want the newsletter to become boring. You want people to look forward to seeing what changes you have made from month to month. See Figure 11.2 for the desktop publishing planning guide for this case study.

A newsletter should have two master pages. These are used as templates to start the newsletter each month. Master page 1 is the front page and should contain the borders and the masthead without the date and volume number. Master page 2 is the back page and should contain the borders and the boxed information about the newsletter. Anything else that will not change also goes on the master pages. The new monthly data will then be placed on the individual pages.

A newsletter is a great way to improve communication in an organization. Designing and publishing a newsletter can be fun. If it is set up right in the beginning, the newsletter should take little time to assemble each month after you have received the current articles. Getting the information for the newsletter is usually the main problem. People are great procrastinators about writing such articles.

Case Study 2: Brochure

Brochure

Since you did such a good job on the first newsletter, the owners of the Do-It-Right Cleaning Company would like you to develop a **brochure** for their organization. The brochure should be a trifold design, printed on 8½ × 11 inch paper. The owners have photographs of the company building, of the employees at work, and of themselves. These will need to be scanned into the computer.

A brochure can be tricky to design in many ways. First, you must think about how you want to put the brochure together, and what type of information you want on each page. With a trifold brochure, you have six panels, three on a page of a double-sided sheet. Take a piece of paper, turn it in the landscape mode, and fold it in thirds. You

Figure 11.2 Desktop Publishing Planning Guide for Case Study 1: Newsletter

DESKTOP PUBLISHING PLANNING GUIDE

Name of Document: Newsletter—May 2002 Date: 4/20/2002

Location of Electronic File: c:\my data\work\newsletter

Name: Jill Jack

Name of Client: Owners

Step 1: Identify the Problem by Writing the Problem Statement.

The owners of the Do-It-Right Cleaning Company have elected to put out a two-page employee newsletter each month. The following should be included:

- **a.** Spotlight of an employee of the month
- **b.** Letter from one of the owners
- **c.** Monthly events
- **d.** Birthdays for the month
- **e.** Special outside distinctions of any of the employees

The newsletter has to be completed in eight hours each month.

Step 2: Understand the Problem.

Audience:

The audience will be the employees of the Do-It-Right Cleaning Company. They are all ages and have been working for the company for between 6 months and 16 years. The employees hold a variety of jobs.

Required Outcomes of the Document:

- **a.** A newsletter that communicates to the employees of the company the following:
  - **1.** Spotlight of an employee of the month
  - **2.** Letter from one of the owners
  - **3.** Monthly events
  - **4.** Birthdays for the month
  - **5.** Special outside distinctions of any of the employees
- **b.** To improve management–employee communication.

Required Knowledge of the Problem to Develop the Document:

- **a.** Employee of the month
- **b.** Letter from one of the owners
- **c.** Monthly events
- **d.** List of birthdays
- **e.** Communication of outside distinctions
- **f.** Use of clipart—limited time to produce the newsletter
- **g.** Name of the newsletter
- **h.** Photographs of company activities

Required Knowledge of the Audience:

Knowledge of the company and some of the other employees.

Step 3: Identify Valid Alternative Methods to Solve the Problem.

- **a.** Two- or four-page newsletter
- **b.** All pages the same or first page with masthead

(continued)

Figure 11.2 Desktop Publishing Planning Guide for Case Study 1: Newsletter

Step 3: Identify Valid Alternative Methods to Solve the Problem. (con't)

- **c.** Color of paper, same color each month or change color each month
- **d.** Columns: 2 or 3
- **e.** Borders: yes or no

Step 4: Select the Best Method to Solve the Problem from the List of Alternative Solutions.

- **a.** Two-page newsletter
- **b.** Masthead on the front page with the following information:
  1. Company logo
  2. Date
  3. Volume and number
  4. Newsletter name
  5. Dividers between masthead and newsletters
- **c.** Change color of paper each month
- **d.** Two columns
- **e.** Borders around the text and a line between the columns
- **f.** Boxed section with publishing information—editor, helpers, company name and address, etc.
- **g.** Owner's letter on left side of front page

Step 5: Plan Your Solution.

Software to be used: Desktop Publisher

Margins:

Top: 0.5 — Top Printer: 0.25

Bottom: 0.5 — Bottom Printer: 0.25

Left/Inside: 0.5 — Binding: none — Left Printer: 0.25

Right/Outside: ______ — Right Printer: 0.25

Header: none — Top Printer: 0.25

Footer: none — Bottom Printer: 0.25

***Tabs:* default**

Files to be imported:

File	Description	Use	Location
Masthead	Graphics with Name	Masthead	c:\graphics\newsletter
Employee	Digital Photo	Article on Employee	c:\graphics\newsletter
Appropriate clipart	Clipart	Various places	c:\graphics\newsletter
Company	Digital Photos	With owner's message	c:\graphics\newsletter

Figure 11.2 (continued)

Paper Size: 8½ × 11 Paper Color: Different color each month

Orientation: Portrait Color/B&W: Color

Number of Columns: 2 Gutter: 0.167

Header Contents: None

Footer Contents: None

Estimated Number of Master Pages: 1 of 2

Sketch(s) of Master Page Layouts:

(continued)

Figure 11.2 Desktop Publishing Planning Guide for Case Study 1: Newsletter

Step 5: Plan Your Solution. (con't)

Estimated Number of Master Pages: 2 of 2

Sketch(s) of Master Page Layouts:

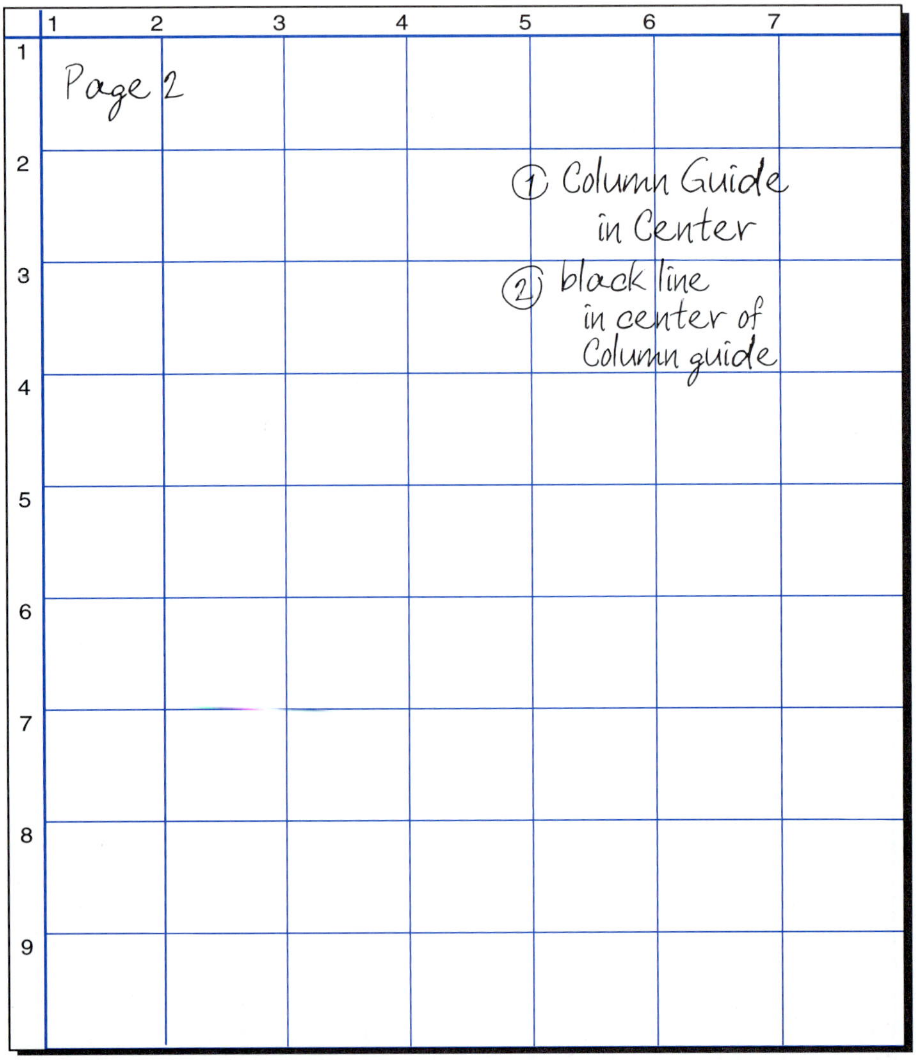

Figure 11.2 (continued)

Estimated Number of Individual Pages: 1 of 2

Sketch(s) of Individual Page Layouts: Master Page 1

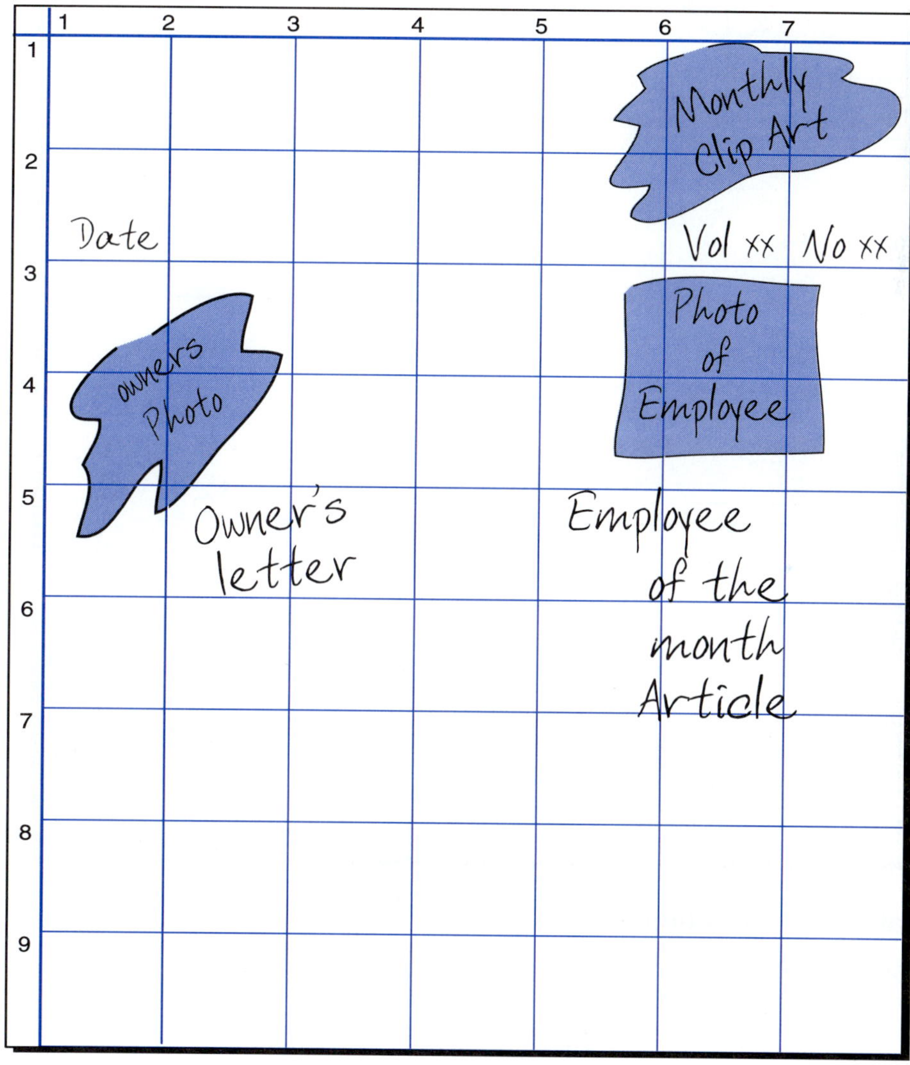

(continued)

Figure 11.2 Desktop Publishing Planning Guide for Case Study 1: Newsletter

Step 5: **Plan Your Solution. (con't)**

Estimated Number of Individual Pages: 2 of 2

Sketch(s) of Individual Page Layouts: Master Page 2

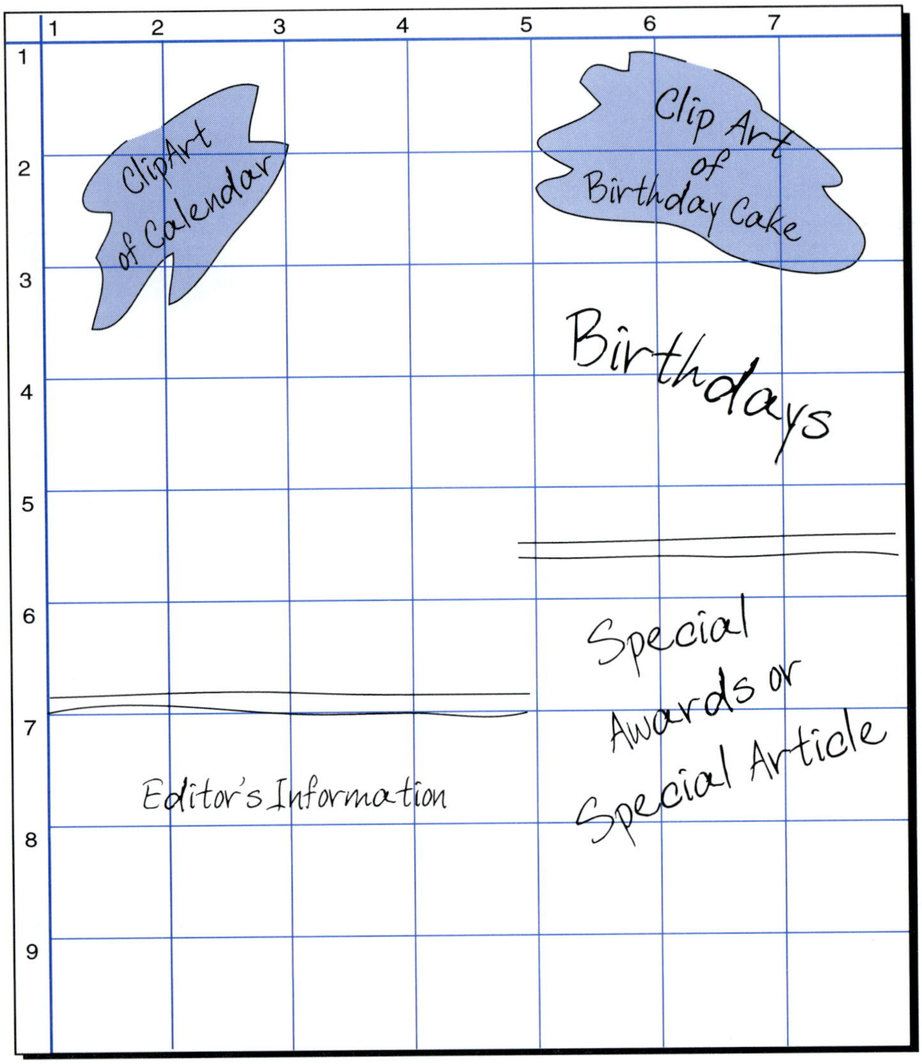

Step 6: **Evaluate the Solution.**

Criteria for evaluation:

- **a.** Is the newsletter pleasing to the eye?
- **b.** Does it have data that the employees will want to read?
- **c.** Is it easy to read?
- **d.** Is the spelling correct?
- **e.** Is it aligned correctly?
- **f.** Are the bottoms of the columns aligned?
- **g.** Is there enough white space? Too much white space?
- **h.** Do you like it?
- **i.** Do the owners like it?

should end up with six panels that are 3 2/3 × by 8 1/2 inches. The folded brochure should have the front opening on the right. See Figure 11.3.

After you have folded the paper, label each of the panels to help you visualize their placement as they are located on the two 8 1/2 × 11 pages. You will create two desktop publisher pages and then print them back to back. When you open the brochure you will turn the front page to the left. You will now have the left inside panel to your left and the left outside panel to your right. See Figure 11.3 again. These two pages must correspond as to content and alignment. Avoid placing content that is totally unrelated on these two panels. When you open the brochure fully, the three inside pages are in view, left to right. These three panels also should relate to each other. The middle outside panel is usually the address panel. The logo and the return address are rotated 90 degrees on this panel to match the proper placement of the computer-generated address labels.

Figure 11.4 shows the desktop publishing planning guide for case study 2. Notice in step five the placement of the information on the panels. The margins are the printer margins. Each of the two pages is set up with three columns, with the gutter value twice the margin value. This will set the inside margins for the three panels. It is important to

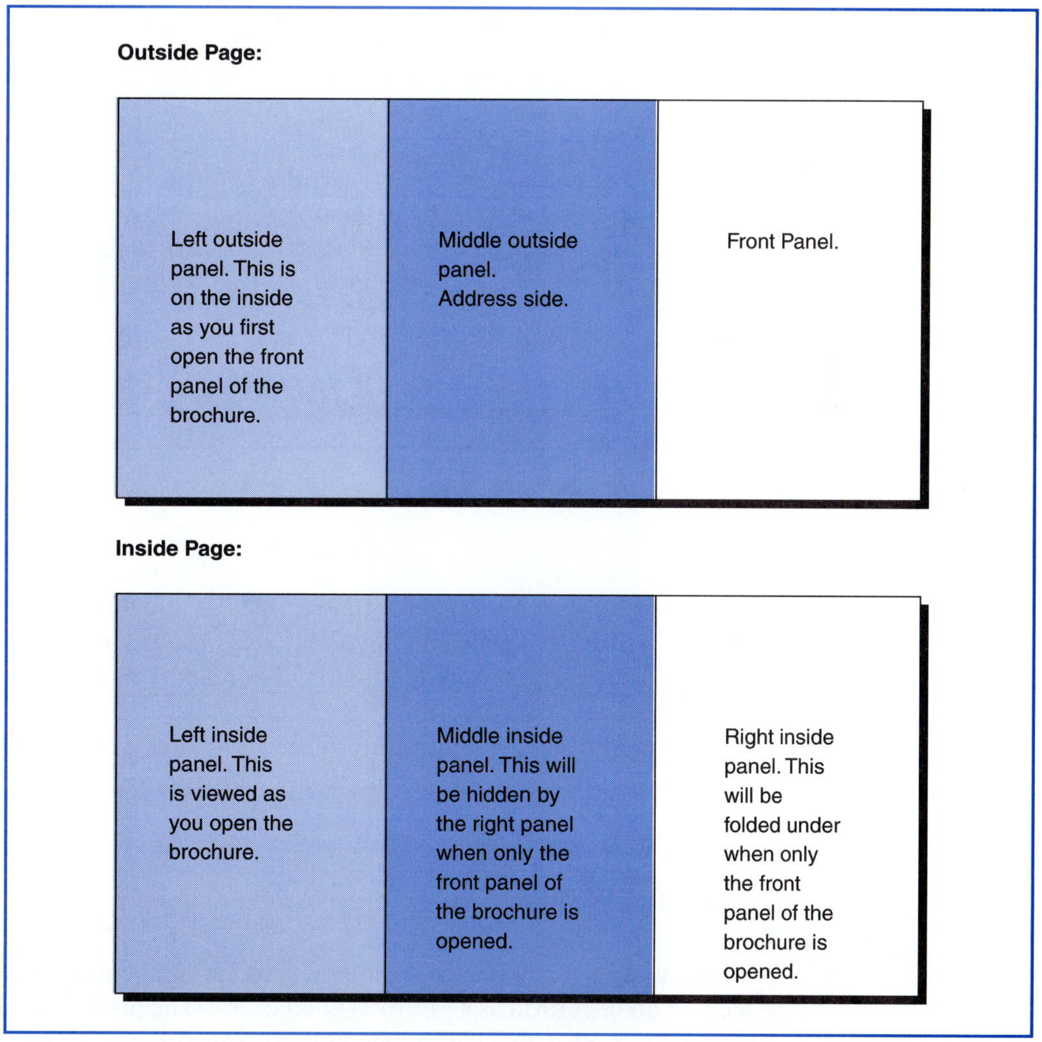

Figure 11.3 Folding the Brochure

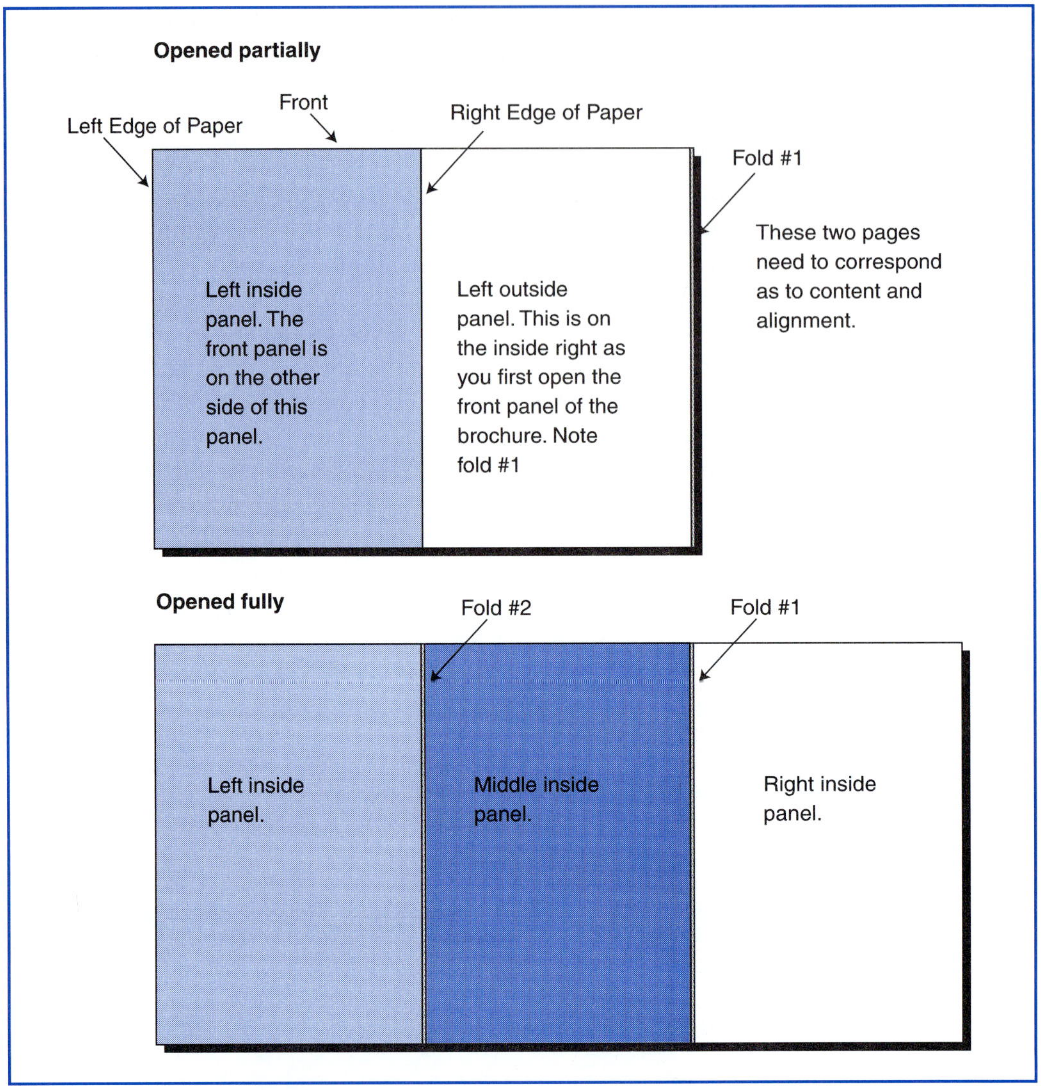

Figure 11.3 Folding the Brochure

set your margins and column guides correctly to ensure that when the brochure is folded, the panels will have equal margins on all sides. Since it is hard to print and fold the brochure exactly right, it is better not to use borders. You may use boxes so long as they are not centered on the page.

Be patient when creating your project. Brochures can be frustrating, but if you follow the above directions, you should have minimal design or publishing problems.

Case Study 3: Booklet

You have written many poems during the past several years and you desire to print nine of them in booklet form as a gift for a good friend. The poems must fit on a 5½ × 8½ inch paper (an 8½ × 11 inch paper folded in half). You also have some digital photographs to accompany the poems.

Figure 11.4 Desktop Publishing Planning Guide for Case Study 2: Brochure

DESKTOP PUBLISHING PLANNING GUIDE

Name of Document: Brochure Date: 5/22/2002

Location of Electronic File: c:\my data\work\

Name: Jill Jack

Name of Client: Owners

Step 1: Identify the Problem by Writing the Problem Statement.

Create a trifold brochure for the Do-It-Right Cleaning Company.

Step 2: Understand the Problem.

Audience:

- **a.** Potential customers
- **b.** General public

Required Outcomes of the Document:

- **a.** Increase customer base
- **b.** Well-designed trifold brochure

Required Knowledge of the Problem to Develop the Document:

- **a.** Information about the company
- **b.** Pictures of the owners, the company, and the employees
- **c.** Services provided by the company

Required Knowledge of the Audience:

Knowledge of the type of services provided by the company.

Step 3: Identify Valid Alternative Methods to Solve the Problem.

- **a.** 8½ × 11 or 8½ × 14 paper size
- **b.** Color of paper—blue, tan, or green (selected by owners)
- **c.** Pictures to be used:
    - **1.** employees at work
    - **2.** owners
    - **3.** building
- **d.** Color or black and white
- **e.** Address side or none
- **f.** Orientation: landscape or portrait

Step 4: Select the Best Method to Solve the Problem from the List of Alternative Solutions.

- **a.** 8½ × 11 paper size as it is readily available
- **b.** Color of paper—tan as it is a neutral color
- **c.** Pictures to be used:
    - **1.** employees at work
    - **2.** owners
    - **3.** building
- **d.** Black and white because of cost and reproducibility

(continued)

Figure 11.4 Desktop Publishing Planning Guide for Case Study 2: Brochure

Step 4: Select the Best Method to Solve the Problem from the List of Alternative Solutions. (con't)

e. Address panel because this brochure may be sent to potential customers
f. Orientation: portrait orientation for panel design because the objects fit better, but the three-panel pages have landscape orientation

Step 5: Plan Your Solution.

Software to be used: Desktop Publisher

Margins:

Top: 0.25 Top Printer: 0.25
Bottom: 0.25 Bottom Printer: 0.25
Left: 0.25 Binding: none Left Printer: 0.25
Right: 0.25 Right Printer: 0.25
Header: None Top Printer: 0.25
Footer: None Bottom Printer: 0.25

***Tabs:* every 0.25 inch**

Files to be imported:

File	Description	Use	Location
Building	Scanned Image	On front page	All on:
Employees 1	Scanned Image	On inside right page	c:\my data\
Employees 2	Scanned Image	On inside middle page	work\
Owners	Scanned Image	On outside left page	brochure\
Logo	Graphics Image	On outside middle page	
Employees 3	Scanned Image	On inside left page	

Paper Size: 8½ × 11 Paper Color: Tan
Orientation: Paper: Landscape; Brochure: Portrait Color/B&W: B&W
Number of Columns: 3 Gutter: 0.5
Header Contents: None

Footer Contents: None

Figure 11.4 (continued)

(continued)

Figure 11.4 Desktop Publishing Planning Guide for Case Study 2: Brochure

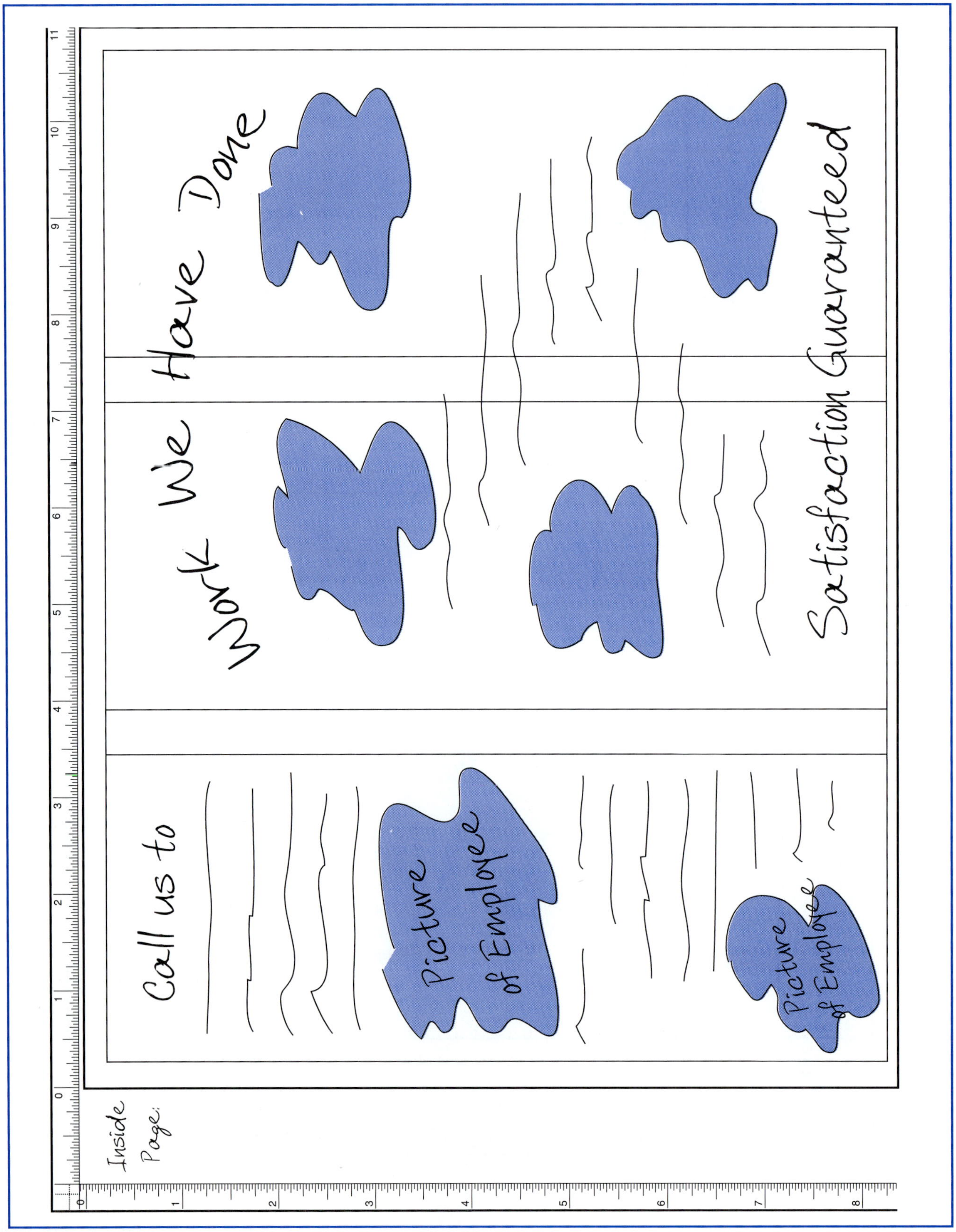

Figure 11.4 (continued)

Step 6: Evaluate the Solution.

The criteria for evaluation is as follows:

a. Is the brochure easy to read?
b. Does the front panel have a "hook"?
c. As you open the brochure is the information relevant on the facing panels?
d. Are the graphics relevant?
e. Are the owners happy with the brochure?
f. Do you like it?
g. Is the information centered on each panel?

Booklet

A **booklet** is a group of individual desktop-published electronic pages that are printed two to a page and then folded together and stapled at the fold. For a booklet, you will have two different files. One file is for the individual pages, as in a book, that we are calling the original pages. These original pages are then copied to a second file where they are reordered, two to a page, to be printed in booklet form. The pages of this new file we are calling the print pages. If there are eight original pages, then there will be four print pages since two original pages are placed on one print page. To visualize a booklet, take two pieces of paper and put one on top of the other. Turn the pages in the landscape orientation. Fold these pages in half so that the fold is parallel to the 8½-inch edge. Now turn this booklet so the fold is on your left. Number the individual booklet pages on both sides starting with 1 for original page 1 and ending with 8. Each of these eight individual pages represents the original pages. Now separate the two pieces of paper and examine which original pages would be printed together on a printed page. See Figure 11.5. Notice that the original pages are in a different order when placed on the print pages than they are in the original page file. These two files are not linked in any way. Therefore, if the original page is modified, the print page must be updated also.

After the print pages are output from the printer, they are machine copied or computer printed back to back such that when finished, four original pages make one finished double-sided page. Therefore, the number of original pages in a booklet must be a multiple of four such as 4, 8, 12, or 16. The original page size is half of the print page size. In this case, the booklet will be printed on 8½ × 11 paper in landscape mode, so the original page size is 5½ × 8½ inches and created in portrait orientation. Since the print pages are output in landscape mode, the width of the printed page becomes the height of the original page. If you were to print on 8½ × 14 inch paper, the original page size would be 7 × 8½ inches. The original pages should be created as facing or back-to-back pages. See Figure 11.5.

After you have finished creating the original pages, go through the process of making the print pages. Check your desktop publisher as to how to do this. The booklet feature is ideal. If your desktop publisher does not have a booklet feature, then you will need to create print pages in a new file and copy the original pages to the correct place on the print pages in the new file.

Figure 11.6 presents the desktop publishing planning guide for this case. Notice that pages 8 and 9 have graphics that go over the inside edges of the page. This causes no trouble in the printing stage as these original pages are placed on the same printed page. In the case study there are 16 original pages that will produce a total of 8 print pages. These 8 print pages will be printed back to back to produce four finished 8½ × 11 inch sheets of paper per booklet. When collated, folded, and bound, the booklet will have 16 pages.

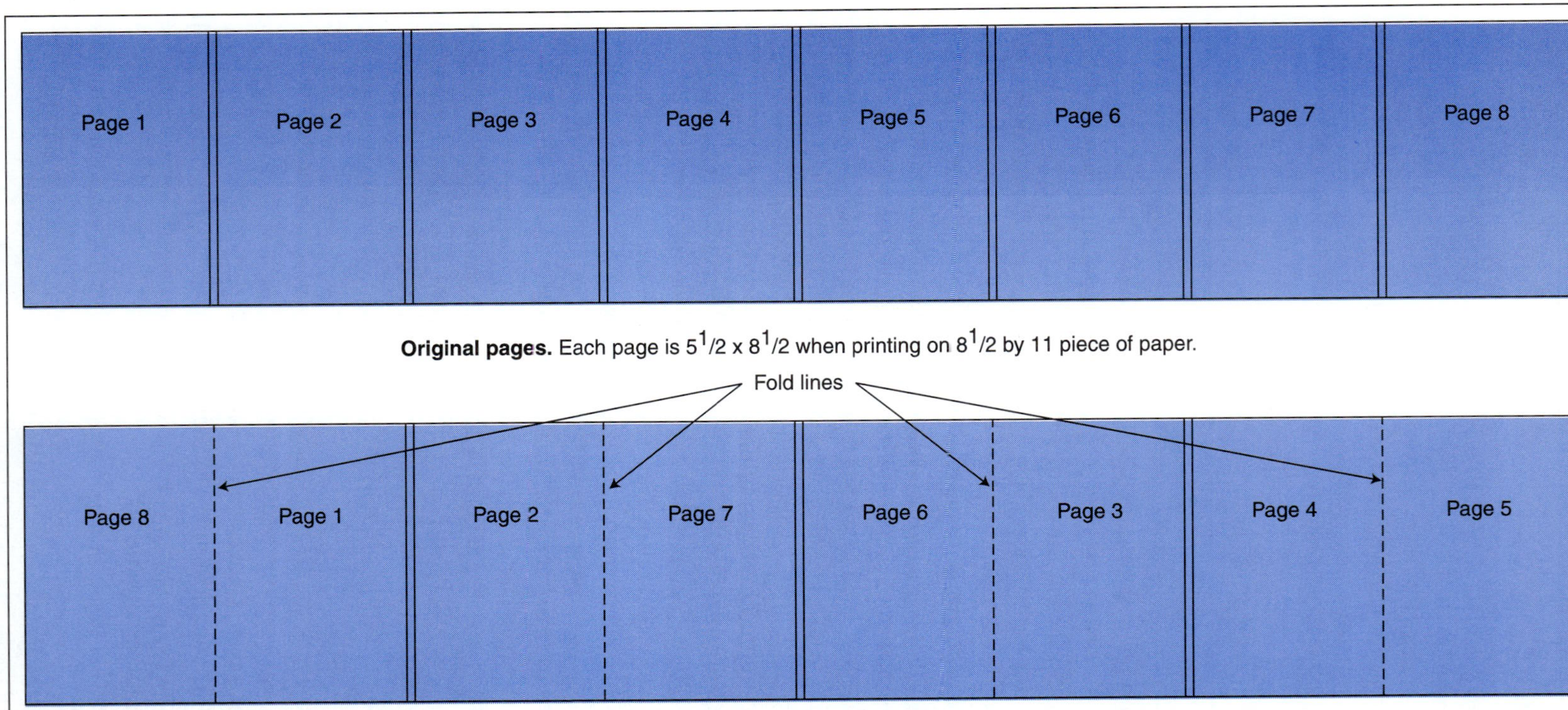

Print pages. After the eight original pages are created, they are copied into a second file for printing. In this file, two original pages are placed on one print page that is $8^1/2$ by 11-inch paper. When the print pages are printed back to back and folded together, the original pages will be in sequential order. Original pages 2 and 7 will be printed on the back of pages 8 and 1, pages 4 and 5 on the back of pages 6 and 3. Original pages 4 and 5 will be the center pages.

Figure 11.5 Original and Print Pages

Figure 11.6 Desktop Publishing Planning Guide for Case Study 3: Booklet

DESKTOP PUBLISHING PLANNING GUIDE

Name of Document: Book of Poems Date: 2/10/2002

Location of Electronic File: c:\my data\personal\poems\

Name: John Pomes

Name of Client: None

Step 1: Identify the Problem by Writing the Problem Statement.

Create a booklet to publish nine of my poems as a gift to my good friend.

Step 2: Understand the Problem.

Audience:

Created for a good friend who has read and likes my poetry.

Required Outcomes of the Document:

Have my friend enjoy the poems.

Have the booklet look professional.

Required Knowledge of the Problem to Develop the Document:

Know the poems that go into the booklet.

Required Knowledge of the audience:

Knowledge of the poems' contents.

Step 3: Identify Valid Alternative Methods to Solve the Problem.

- **a.** 5½ × 8½, 8½ × 11, or 8½ × 14 paper size
- **b.** Color of paper—blue, tan, or green (my favorites)
- **c.** Pictures to be used: Photographs that I took that will go with each poem
- **d.** Color or black and white
- **e.** Booklet or book form
- **f.** Binding: spiral, fastback, or staple along edge (saddle stitch)
- **g.** Orientation: landscape or portrait

Step 4: Select the Best Method to Solve the Problem from the List of Alternative Solutions.

- **a.** 5½ × 8½ because one poem will fit nicely on this size paper
- **b.** Color of paper—light blue with darker blue cover (my favorites)
- **c.** Pictures to be used: Photographs that I took that will go with each poem. These are already in digital form. They are all pictures of landscapes around our area.
- **d.** Color
- **e.** Booklet form, middle page will have one poem on both pages.
- **f.** Binding: staple along edge (saddle stitch). This would be best for a booklet.
- **g.** Orientation: Page portrait for creating and landscape for two-page printing back to back
- **h.** Pages:

(continued)

Figure 11.6 Desktop Publishing Planning Guide for Case Study 3: Booklet

Step 4: Select the Best Method to Solve the Problem from the List of Alternative Solutions. (con't)

Page 1: Cover—no page number

Page 2: Back of cover—no page number, nothing on this page

Page 3: Title page—no page number

Page 4: Back of title page—dedication

Pages 5–14: Poems—on middle pages (pages 8 and 9) the poem will be on both pages.

Page 15: Inside of back cover—no page number, nothing on this page

Page 16: Back cover—no page number, date and title at bottom

Step 5: Plan Your Solution.

Software to be used: Desktop Publisher

Margins:

Top: 0.5 Top Printer: 0.25

Bottom: 0.5 Bottom Printer: 0.25

Inside: 0.5 Binding: 0 Left Printer: 0.25

Outside: 0.5 Right Printer: 0.25

Header: none Top Printer: 0.25

Footer: none Bottom Printer: 0.25

***Tabs:* Every 0.25 inch**

Files to be imported:

File	Description	Use	Location
10 pictures	Digital Images	One for each poem	c:\graphics\digital\
of local		and one for cover	
landscapes			

Paper Size: Printing: 8½ × 11; page size: 5½ × 8½ Paper Color: Blue

Orientation: Printing: landscape; Pages: Portrait Color/B&W: Color

Number of Columns: 0 Gutter: 0

Header Contents: None

Footer Contents: None

Figure 11.6 (continued)

Page 1: Cover

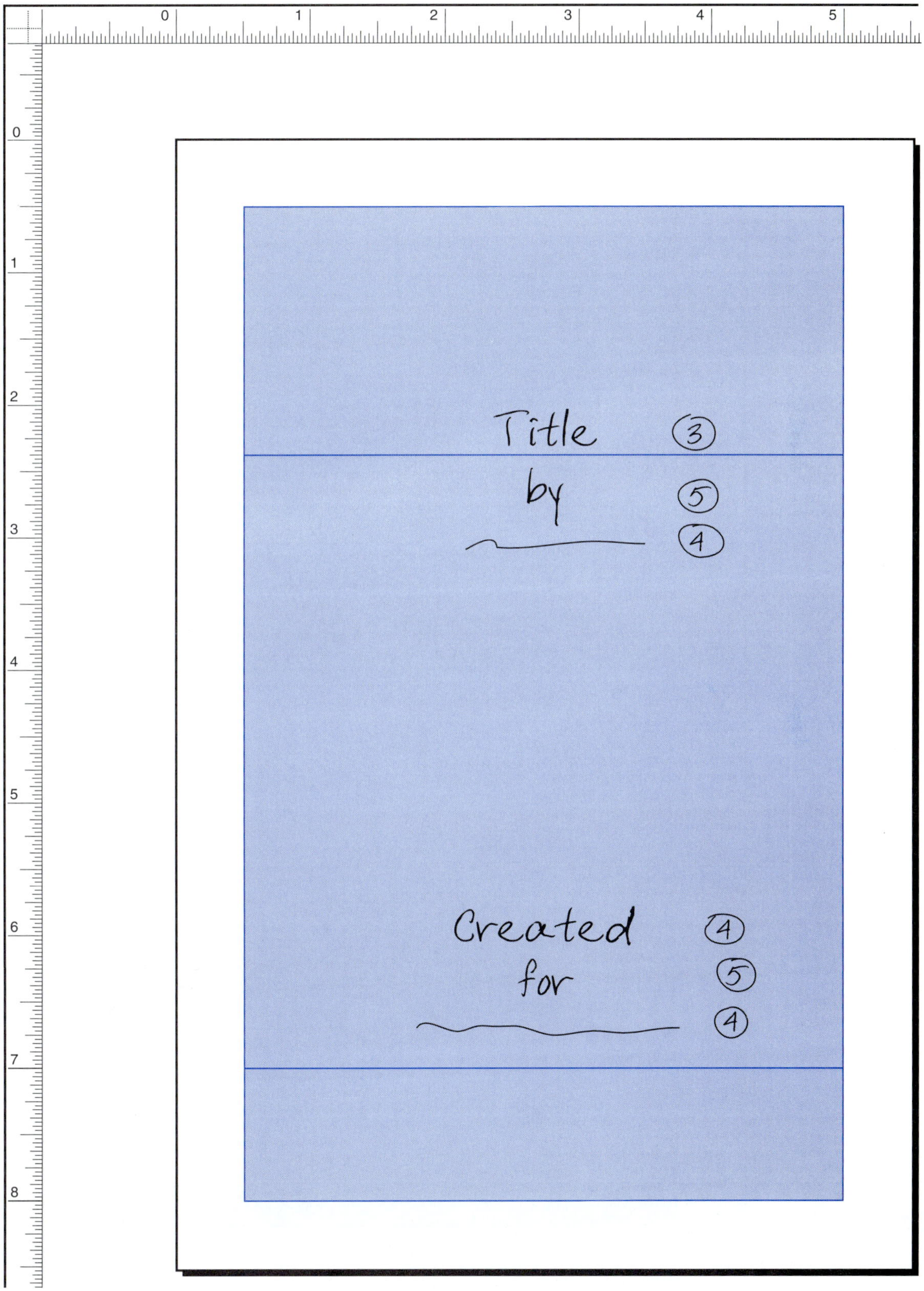

(continued)

Figure 11.6 Desktop Publishing Planning Guide for Case Study 3: Booklet

Step 5: Plan Your Solution. (con't)

Page 2 and 15: Inside front cover and inside back cover

Figure 11.6 (continued)

Page 3: Title page

(continued)

Figure 11.6 Desktop Publishing Planning Guide for Case Study 3: Booklet

Step 5: Plan Your Solution. (con't)

Page 4: Dedication page

Figure 11.6 (continued)

Pages 5–7 and 10–14: One poem per page

(continued)

Figure 11.6 Desktop Publishing Planning Guide for Case Study 3: Booklet

Step 5: Plan Your Solution. (con't)

Pages 8 and 9: Center poem

Step 6: Evaluate the Solution.

The criteria for evaluation is as follows:

- **a.** Are the poems easy to read?
- **b.** Is the spelling correct?
- **c.** Does the front page have an artistic look?
- **d.** Are the graphics relevant?
- **e.** Do the graphics match the poems?
- **f.** Do you like it?
- **g.** Are the poems in the correct order?

Figure 11.6 (continued)

Page 16: Back cover

Summary

This chapter presents three case studies to be completed with a desktop publisher. Case study 1 is a newsletter, case study 2 is a brochure, and case study 3 is a booklet. Each case study presents a corresponding, completed document planning guide.

Key Words

Newsletter

Brochure

Booklet

Problems

1. Add at least six new styles to your style sheet.
2. You are the secretary of the local swim club. The club has decided to publish a newsletter once a month to inform all club members of the following:
   a. upcoming events
   b. results of swim meets
   c. birthdays
   d. article about one of the members
   e. list of new members
   f. note from the president

   As secretary, it will be your job to publish and mail this newsletter. Create a desktop publishing planning guide for this newsletter. Include how you will send it to the members.
3. A friend of yours is opening a new section to her nursery and flower shop, called Native Plantings. She would like you to develop a brochure to be sent to prospective customers to inform them of the new section. All plants in this new section are native to the area. Other sections of the nursery include cut flowers, garden tools, plants, and trees. She would like you to include something about these also. Create a desktop publishing planning guide for this brochure.
4. Your boss has asked you to create a booklet on how to use the features of the desktop publisher installed on the computers at your workplace. Create a desktop publishing planning guide for this booklet. There will be 16 original pages in this booklet.
5. Create a desktop publishing planning guide for a newsletter of your choice.
6. Create a desktop publishing planning guide for a brochure of your choice.
7. Create a desktop publishing planning guide for a booklet of your choice.

UNIT FOUR

SPREADSHEETS

Chapter 12

Mathematical Concepts and Functions for Spreadsheets

Overview

Objectives

When you have finished this chapter, you should be able to:

1. Recognize a simple spreadsheet that includes labels, values, and formulas.
2. Differentiate between the basic data types and data formats.
3. Develop and evaluate formulas using values, functions, operators, and the hierarchy of operations.

When the solution to a problem involves many calculations, a spreadsheet is the application of choice. Spreadsheets are basically sophisticated, electronic calculators. Most problems that use spreadsheets in the solution consist of only two types, computational and logical. Computational problems involve some kind of mathematical processing such as calculation net profit for a company. Logical problems involve relational or logical processing used in decision making on the computer such as choosing between two values. Spreadsheets use text, numbers, and formulas to find a solution to a problem. Spreadsheet software involves more mathematics than most other horizontal software packages because of the creation of formulas that are mathematical expressions.

This chapter presents fundamentals of spreadsheets, mathematical concepts required to develop formulas, and functions used in formulas. Also included in this chapter are examples of methods to develop and evaluate formulas for use in a spreadsheet. These concepts are important for the end user in order to create a well-designed, correct spreadsheet as a solution to a problem.

Formulas are the focal point of spreadsheets. If you do not require many formulas to reach your solution, then other types of horizontal software packages will probably be better suited for your problem solving. The development of formulas is the key topic of this chapter. Two of the most basic mathematical concepts presented are the constant and the variable. Constants and variables are the building blocks of formulas. They will be defined later in this chapter.

Other concepts that are essential to the development of formulas are operators and functions. Operators are symbols that show relationships between constants and variables in formulas. You will also need to know the order, or hierarchy, in which operators are processed. Functions are sets of common instructions that are incorporated into the software package for you to use, such as calculating the square root, finding a maximum value, or finding the sum of a group of numbers.

Incorrect formulas may lead to disasters for a company. For example, incorrect formulas in the costing of a project may lead to a bid that is too high or too low. If the bid is too high then you may not get the contract; if it is too low, then you may get the contract but have less profit or you may lose money. Therefore, it is important to know how to set up formulas and how to test them. The last part of this chapter will demonstrate the development and the testing of formulas.

These concepts are key to the development of formulas. End users will have an easier time developing the formulas needed for a well-designed spreadsheet if they (1) have an understanding of how the computer uses and defines data; (2) know about constants, variables, functions, and operators; and (3) know how to use these concepts to construct and test formulas.

Spreadsheet Fundamentals

Row and Columns

Before mathematical concepts are presented, some basic fundamentals of spreadsheets need to be explored. A spreadsheet program helps the end user to create a two- or three-dimensional table of values. The work area of the spreadsheet program contains rows and columns. See Figure 12.1. Columns in a spreadsheet are labeled in alphabetical order, starting with A. After Z the labeling is AA to AZ, then BA to BZ, and so on. The rows are incrementally labeled with numbers starting with 1. This will produce a two-dimensional spreadsheet. Many spreadsheet programs also have additional pages called sheets. The default labels for the pages are labels of sheet 1, sheet 2, and so forth. You may rename the labels for the sheets. This creates a three-dimensional spreadsheet.

Cells

The intersection of a row and a column creates a rectangular box called a **cell.** The cell is named starting with the column letter followed by the row number; for example, A4 is the intersection of column A and row 4, and D2 is the intersection of column D and row 2. These are default names. You may rename the cells. This will be discussed further in Chapter 13.

Contents of a Cell

A cell may contain one of three things: a label, a value, or a formula. A label is text that consists of letters, numbers, and special symbols. Labels are used to define rows or columns and to add text information such as names, addresses, or social security numbers. A value is a number such as 3.5,–75.00, and 2,365. Values are used to add numerical information to be analyzed or to be used in formulas. A formula is a mathematical expression, such as =A1+B1. Formulas are used to complete mathematical computations.

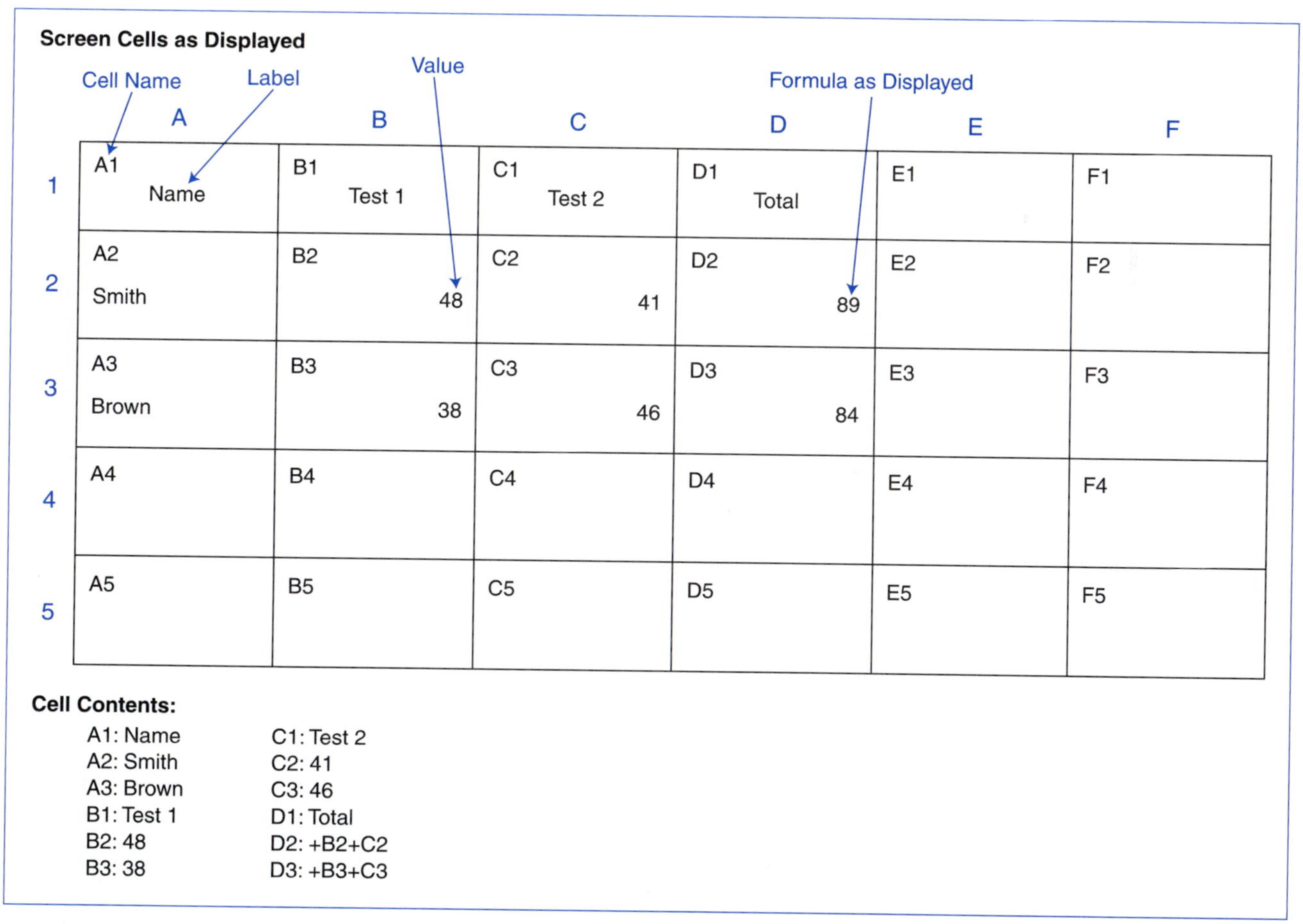

Figure 12.1 Spreadsheet Example

Cell Contents and Cells as Displayed

Spreadsheet cells have two parts. First, the data and formulas that you type into the cells are kept in the computer's memory. Here, we call this part of the cell the *cell contents.* See Figure 12.1. The second part is the way the computer displays the cell contents on the screen. Here again, we call this part *cell as displayed.* The computer's memory holds the cell contents, or the data that you have entered. The monitor displays text that fits into a cell, and formatted values and formatted results of the formula.

Entering Labels

When you enter text into a cell, all of this text will stay in the cell contents. If the cell contents is greater than the width of the cells as displayed on the monitor, the text will be visible in the *empty* adjoining cells until information has been entered there. When the adjoining cell(s) contains information, the text will be truncated to the cell-as-displayed size. This will not affect the cell contents. If the column is widened sufficiently, all text in the cell contents will be displayed.

Entering Values

Values are entered into a cell with a required starting character, as an equal sign, a plus sign, or a negative sign. In many spreadsheet packages the equal sign and the plus sign are optional. The computer will assume that an entry starting with a number is numerical. In other spreadsheet packages, the computer assumes that any information starting with a letter or a number is a label. To ensure a value is numerical, begin with an equal sign, a plus sign, or a negative sign. To ensure that a number is a label, start the entering sequence with a single quote. You cannot calculate with numbers that are designated as text.

Entering Formulas

Formulas are entered into the computer starting with an equal sign, but either a plus or a negative sign as the initial character will also work. If you use a plus or a negative sign, then the computer may add the equal sign for you depending on the software. Formulas only appear in the cell contents. The result of the computation of a formula appears in the cell as displayed. See Figure 12.1. If you want to view the formula in the cell as displayed, then change the format of the cell to text. For printing purposes or if you want to view all formulas, you may choose the view cell formulas option.

Constant and Variable Data

Constants

The computer uses constants and variables to solve problems. A **constant** is a value or a label that is a specific alphabetical character and/or numerical value(s) that only changes when you enter new data into the cell contents. Constants may be any type of data: numerical, alphabetical, or special symbols.

Variable Data

In contrast, a **variable** in a spreadsheet is the name of a cell used as a reference in one or more formulas. The spreadsheet program assigns default cell names as the column letter followed by the row number such as A4 or C2. The end user then uses this name as a reference name for the value of the cell contents in a formula, such as =A1+B1, a formula that perhaps is located in cell C1. In this case, the value used for A1 would be the value found in the cell contents of A1, and the value used for B1 would be the value found in the cell contents of B1. The result of this formula would be found as in the C1 cell as displayed. Both variables and constants may be any data type. For example, a cell may contain a value such as 3.5 or a label such as "Maureen." The cell becomes a holder for these constants. The cell name then becomes a variable when referenced by a formula in another cell, such as =A1+B1. The formula uses the value of the contents of the named cell in the calculation. In the formula =A1+3, A1 is the variable and 3 is a constant, since A1 refers to the value of the cell contents of A1 and 3 neither changes nor refers to another cell.

Data Types

Data Types

Each cell in a spreadsheet is assigned a **data type** and a **data format.** All data are reduced to numerical and text, each with many different formats. Data types are assigned to the cell contents, and data formats are assigned to the cell as displayed. For example, the cell contents may be a number such as 36.45623. The cell contents would be assigned a numerical data type; however, the number may be formatted to be displayed as a number with only two decimal places: 36.46. The cell contents in the computer are used in calculations. The cells as viewed on the screen are formatted and displayed as the user would like to see them.

Numerical Data

Numerical Data

Numerical data include all types of real numbers. Formats of numbers include general, number, currency, accounting, date, time, percentage, fraction, and scientific formats. These are the only formats that may be used in calculations. See Table 12.1 for examples of each format. Others formats are available in some spreadsheet programs. Some of these numeric formats may not be used for calculations even if they contain only numbers such as telephone or social security number formats.

General Format

The cells as displayed use the general format as a default format, which means that the numbers are displayed as they appear in the cell contents up to the width of the cell. If the cell is too small for the number, then number signs (#) will appear in the cell to indicate a cell width error. Numbers do not spill over into the next empty cell(s). When the number is very large or very small in value, the cell contents will be displayed in scientific notation format. Cells as displayed should be formatted in a way that is the easiest to understand and analyze. Formatting the cells as displayed also makes the spreadsheet more aesthetically pleasing.

Number Format

The number format has options to add commas in numbers and to choose the number of decimal places. The user also may choose the format of negative numbers by selecting between the negative sign, red numbers, black numbers with parentheses, and red numbers with parentheses.

Currency and Accounting Format

Currency format is the same as the number format with the exception that an optional currency sign is added in front of the number. You may choose the currency sign according the currency of the country. Commas are displayed in the currency format. Accounting format is the same as the currency format with the exception that the currency sign and the decimal points are aligned in columns of cells.

Date Formats

Dates are stored as numbers in the cell contents of the computer. They are calculated as the number of days from a certain point in history, many times from the first of the twentieth century. Dates are numbers because the calculation of the number of days between two dates is often needed. By using numbers for dates, the problem of crossing from December 31 of one year to January 1 of the next year is eliminated. For example, September 1, 2001, equals 37,135 and January 8, 2002, equals 37,264; therefore, there are 129 days between these two dates.

When the date format is used, the numerical value of the date in the cell contents is not apparent to the user because the date as displayed on the screen appears as a date and not as a number. To see the number you would use the number format. There are many choices in the date format as to how the date is viewed on the spreadsheet. See Table 12.1.

Time Format

Time is also stored as numerical data and is referenced from midnight. There are several optional formats for time. See Table 12.1.

Table 12.1 Number Formats

Number Formats		
Format	Cell Contents	Cell as Displayed
General	234.5436	234.5436
Number	234.5436	234.54
	−234.5436	–234.54
	−234.5436	234,54
	−234.5436	(234.54)
	−234.5436	(234.54)
Currency	234.5436	$234.54
	−234.5436	–$234.54
	−234.5436	234.54
	−234.5436	($234.54)
	−234.5436	($234.54)
Accounting	234.5436	$ 234.54
	−234.5436	$(234.54)
Date	37330	3/15
	37330	3/15/02
	37330	15-Mar
	37330	15-Mar 02
	37330	March 15, 2002
	37330	M-02
Time	0.39	9.25 AM
	0.39	9:25:30 AM
	0.39	9:25:30
Percentage	0.23569	23.57%
Fraction One Digit	0.23569	1/4
Fraction Two Digits	0.23569	4/17
Fraction Three Digits	0.23569	70/297
Fraction as Halves	0.23569	0
Fraction as Quarters	0.23569	1/4
Fraction as Eighths	0.23569	2/8
Fraction as Sixteenths	0.23569	4/16
Fraction as Tenths	0.23569	2/10
Fraction as Hundredths	0.23569	24/100
Scientific	2341567.324	2.34E+06
	0.0000002345	2.35E–07

Percentage Format

Fraction Format

The percentage format is viewed as a percentage with the percent sign. The numeric value in the cell contents is multiplied by 100 before displaying it with the percentage sign. For example, the number 0.1 in the cell contents would be displayed as 10%. The number of decimals is a user choice. The fraction format displays the number in fraction form. The type of fraction is a user choice. See Table 12.1 for several choices.

Scientific Format

Most people recognize all of these number formats with the exception of the last one, which is the scientific format. Examples of the scientific format are 2.3E5 or 5.4E − 3. In scientific notation, the E stands for "times 10 to the power of." Therefore, 2.3E5 is the same number as 2.3×10^5, or 230,000.0, and 5.4E − 3 is the same number as 5.4×10^{-3}, or 0.0054.

Text Data Type

Text Data Type

Text is considered a character data type and is called labels when using spreadsheet software. Formatting character data is the same as in any other software program that uses text. Text cannot be used for calculations even if the text consists of only numbers, unless the numbers are converted through the use of a function.

Text can be compared and arranged in alphabetical order in the following way. The computer assigns each character a number. The alphabet, as it ascends, is in numerical order. See the ASCII character code in Appendix A. ASCII is the most common character representation for personal computers. Numeric representation is necessary because the computer works only with numbers. In the alphabetizing process, the numbers are compared to determine which is larger and are then arranged in ascending numerical order. Since *B* has a larger number representing it than *A, B* is placed after *A; C* would follow *B* by the same method, and so forth. Text may be used in decisions, because the alphabet is in numerical order. *Banana* is larger than *apple* because *b* has a larger number representing it than *a.* When the characters being compared are the same, the next characters in the words are compared. *Joan* is larger than *James* since the letter *o* is attributed a larger number than *a* and they both begin with *J.*

Concatenation

Text may be joined with the & operator in an operation called **concatenation.** When two pieces of character data are joined, the concatenation results in the second being placed at the end of the first, as in "4" & "4" = "44" (not "8"). Concatenation with an additional "(space)" may be used to join a first name with a last name. It also may be used to join pieces of data together to make a code for an inventory item. Notice that quotes are placed before and after the characters to be concatenated. These quotes designate to the computer that they are text values and not function names or numerical values.

Most data in business—names, account numbers, addresses, cities, states, telephone numbers, zip codes—are text even though some information contains only numbers. As a rule, items that would not have mathematical computations performed on them should be designated as text data type. There is another reason for designating a zip code as text. If you are using numerical data, there is no way to retain the leading zeros, that is, the zeros at the front of a number such as 00987. As a result, a zip code on the East Coast could not be entered correctly as a numerical datum. Leading zeros are preserved only with text data type.

Functions

Functions

Functions are small sets of instructions that perform specific tasks and return values such as the SUM function that totals a list of numbers and returns the value of the sum. Most functions are built into spreadsheet software. In addition, there are some spreadsheet packages that allow the user to define functions. Functions are used as all or part of a formula. Because there are basic computational and logical tasks that are used repeatedly in the problem-solving process, by using functions an end user can shorten problem-solving time and improve the readability of the formulas.

Arguments

Form is the same in all functions, such as SQRT(N). Each function has a name, such as SQRT for square root. This name is followed, with no extra spaces, by an open parenthesis. Following the open parenthesis is a list of the data needed for the function calculations. These data are called **arguments.** After the final argument is a close parenthesis. For example, take the square root function in the formula =SQRT(A3). This function will calculate the square root of the number stored in cell A3. SQRT is the name of the function. A3 is the data needed to calculate the square root and, therefore, A3 is the argument. Notice the argument is surrounded by parentheses. In the function SQRT(4), the 4 is the argument, and 2 is the result of the function.

The maximum function, MAX(A1,A2,A3), will find which of three numbers is the largest. The name of the function is MAX. The arguments are data surrounded by parentheses needed to do the calculation. They are A1, A2, and A3. In the function MAX(45,32,78), the arguments are 45, 32, and 78 and the result of the function is 78.

Range of Cells

An argument can be a value, a cell reference, a range of cells, a list of cells, or an expression. An expression is a calculation, such as =C4/100, which has not been given a permanent memory location in the computer. A **range of cells** is a group of contingent cells that are in a column, row, or a rectangular block. Specifying the first cell followed by a colon followed by the last cell designates a range of cells. For example, a vertical range would be C1:C6, a horizontal range would be C1:F1, and a block of cells would be C1:F6. A **list of cells** is a group of cells separated by commas, for example, C1, C5, F2 or C1:C6, F6, E4, D1:D5.

Not all functions need arguments. The function RAND() generates or calculates a random number. Data are not required to do this calculation, so there are no arguments. Parentheses are still required, however.

The names of the functions may vary between different spreadsheet software. This book gives a generic name to each function and places the arguments in parentheses. Spreadsheet programs have many functions; we cover only a few of the most common. Table 12.2 shows a few examples of spreadsheet functions with data and resultants found in most spreadsheet programs, although there are many more. You should take the time to investigate the functions in your spreadsheet software.

Text Functions

Text Functions

Text functions (see Table 12.2) are used to manipulate text. For example, they copy part of the text, find the length or the number of characters in the text, and so forth. *Note:* The following functions use the value of A4 as "Mary Smith" and the function resultant is placed in C4.

CONCATENATE Function

CONCATENATE(TEXT1,TEXT2,TEXT3, . . .) The CONCATENATE function joins several texts together. These may be constants within quotes or cell references. For example, the resultant of CONCATENATE("This student's name is", A4, ".") is "This student's name is Mary Smith." This function is a replacement for the & operator. Notice that the arguments that are constants are placed within quotes.

LEFT Function

LEFT(TEXT,Number) The LEFT function copies the leftmost Number of characters from TEXT. For example, the resultant of LEFT(A4,3) is "Mar" since the letters *M, a,* and *r* are the three leftmost characters in the text in A4.

Table 12.2 Spreadsheet Functions

Spreadsheet Functions						
	A	B	C	D	E	F
1						
2						
3						
4	**Numeric Data:**			**Text Functions**	**Example**	**Resulant**
5	34		−234			
6	54		235	CONCATENATE(TEXT1, TEXT 2, TEXT3,...)	CONCATENATE(A25,A26,A27)	ABCDEFGHI
7	56					
8	76			LEFT(TEXT, NUMBER)	LEFT(A29,3)	Mar
9						
10				LEN(TEXT)	LEN(A29)	10
11	0	33	43			
12	200	45	34	MID(TEXT,NUMBER1,NUMBER2)	MID(A29,6,2)	Sm
13	300	67	22			
14	500	54	56	RIGHT(TEXT, NUMBER)	RIGHT(A29,3)	ith
15						
16				UPPER(TEXT)	UPPER(A29)	MARY SMITH
17	4	23	33			
18	300	45	45	VALUE(TEXT)	VALUE(A31)	12,345.00
19	3		0			
20		67	67			
21	4	22		**Statistical**		
22						
23	Text Data			AVERAGE(LIST)	AVERAGE(A5:A8)	55.00
24						
25	ABC			COUNT(RANGE)	COUNT(A5:A8)	4.00
26	DEF					
27	GHI			MAXIMUM(LIST)	MAX(A5:A8)	76.00
28						
29	Mary Smith			MINIMUM(LIST)	MIN(A5:A8)	34.00
30						
31	$12,345					
32				**Mathematical**		
33						
34				ABS(NUMBER)	ABS(C5)	234.40
35						
36				COUNTIF(RANGE,CRITERIA)	COUNTIF(A5:A8,">40")	3
37						
38				INT(NUMBER)	INT(C6)	5
39						
40				MOD(NUMBER1,NUMBER2)	MOD(B17,A17)	3
41						
42				RAND()	RAND()	0.38
43						
44				ROUND(NUMBER1,NUMBER2)	ROUND(C6,2)	234.57
45						
46				SIGN(NUMBER)	SIGN(C5)	−1
47						
48				SQRT(NUMBER)	SQRT(A21)	2
49						
50				SUM(LIST)	SUM(A5:A8)	220.00
51						
52				SUMIF(RANGE,CRITERIA,SUMRANGE)	SUMIF(A11:A14,"<250",B11:B14)	78

(continued)

Table 12.2 Spreadsheet Functions

Spreadsheet Functions							
	A	B	C	G	H	I	J
1							
2							
3							
4	**Numeric Data:**			**Lookup Functions**	**Example**	**Resultant**	
5	34		−234				
6	54		235	CHOOSE(X,V1,V2,V3,V4,V5)	CHOOSE(A21, 10,30,20,50,40)	50.00	
7	56						
8	76			HLOOKUP(X,RANGE,COLUMN)	HLOOKUP(C17,A11:C14,A19)	67.00	
9							
10				VLOOKUP(X,RANGE,COLUMN)	VLOOKUP(A18,A11:C14,A19)	22.00	
11	0	33	43				
12	200	45	34				
13	300	67	22	**Logical Functions**			
14	500	54	56				
15				NOT(REL_EXP)	NOT(A5<A6)	FALSE	
16							
17	4	23	33	AND(REL_EXP1,REL_EXP2)	AND(A5<A6,C11<C12)	FALSE	
18	300	45	45				
19	3		0	OR(REL_EXP1,REL_EXP2)	OR(A5<A6,C11<C12)	TRUE	
20		67	67				
21	4	22		IF(LOGICAL_EXP,TRUE_VALUE,FALSE_VALUE)	IF(A7>A8,2000,3000)	3,000.00	
22							
23	Text Data						
24				**Financial Functions**			
25	ABC						
26	DEF			FV(RATE,NPER,PMT)	FV(5%/12,5*12,−150)	10,200.91	
27	GHI						
28				PMT(RATE,NPER,PV)	PMT(5%/12,5*12,−3000)	56.61	
29	Mary Smith						
30				PV(RATE,NPER,PMT)	PV(5%/12,5*12,−200)	10,598.14	
31	$12,345						
32							
33				**Date, Time Functions**			
34						**Numeric**	**Formated**
35				DATE(YEAR, MONTH,DAY)	DATE(98, 10, 13)	36,081.00	13-Oct-98
36							
37				NOW()	NOW()	36,909.64	1/18/01 3:14 PM
38							
39				TIME(HOUR,MINUTE,SECOND)	TIME(8, 15,0)	0.34	8:15:00 AM
40							
41				TODAY()	TODAY()	36,909.00	January 18, 2001
42							
43							
44							
45							
46							
47							
48							
49							
50							
51							
52							

LEN Function

LEN(TEXT) The LEN function returns the number of characters in TEXT. For example, the resultant of LEN(A4) is 10 since there are 10 characters in "Mary Smith." Remember that a space is a character.

MID Function

MID(TEXT,Number1,Number2) The MID function copies argument Number2 characters from TEXT beginning with the argument Number1. For example, the resultant of MID(A4,6,4) is "Smit" since the sixth character is S and that character plus three others is SMIT. The number of characters is specified by the third argument and starts with the letter specified by the second argument—in this example, four characters.

RIGHT Function

RIGHT(TEXT,Number) The RIGHT function copies the rightmost Number of characters from TEXT. For example, the resultant of RIGHT(A4,3) is "ith" since *i, t,* and *h* are the three rightmost characters in the text in A4.

UPPER Function

UPPER(TEXT) The UPPER function changes all characters in TEXT to uppercase. For example, the resultant of UPPER(A4) is "MARY SMITH."

VALUE Function

VALUE(TEXT) The VALUE function changes the value of TEXT from a text data type to a numeric data type. TEXT must have a value that is a number. If not, you will get a value error. For example, the resultant of VALUE("$4500") is the number 4,500 and the resultant of VALUE("Maureen") is an error. The as-displayed cell may then be formatted by the user.

Statistical Functions

Statistical Functions

A spreadsheet has many statistical functions (see Table 12.2). Most of these functions are hard to understand unless you take a class in statistics, in which you would investigate such functions. Therefore, our discussion of statistical functions will be limited to those you may use for beginning business classes such as average, maximum values, and minimum values.

AVERAGE Function

AVERAGE(LIST) The AVERAGE function returns the average of the numbers in a list of values. If a cell in the list is empty or contains text, that cell is ignored in the calculation of the average. When calculating the average of 25, 50, and 75, the function is AVERAGE(25,50,75). The as-displayed resultant of this would be the number 50.

COUNT Function

COUNT(LIST) The COUNT function counts the cells in the list that have numeric values. Cells that are empty or contain text are not counted. The resultant of COUNT(25,75,"Maureen",78) is 3.

MAX Function

MAX(LIST) The MAX function calculates the maximum numeric value in the list. The resultant of MAX(45,79,23) is 79. Empty and text cells are ignored.

MIN Function

MIN(LIST) The MIN function calculates the minimum numeric value in the list. The resultant of MIN(45,79,23) is 23. Empty and text cells are ignored.

Mathematical Functions

Mathematical Functions

Math functions calculate values such as square root, absolute value, and a random number. Mathematical functions that are used primarily for scientific purposes have not been included in Table 12.2.

ABS Function

ABS(NUMBER) The ABS function returns the positive numeric value of NUMBER. The resultant of ABS(–34) and ABS(34) are both 34.

COUNTIF Function

COUNTIF(RANGE,CRITERIA) The COUNTIF function counts the number of cells in RANGE that meets CRITERIA. CRITERIA is in the form of a number such as 45 or –32, a relational expression such as “>50” or “<=75,” or a text entry such as “Present” or “56.” For example, COUNTIF(B4:B8,“<25”) returns the number of cells in the range B4 to B8 that have a value of less than 25. Like data types for the range based on the criteria are the only cells that are used. Notice that relational expressions are placed in quotation marks. Operands are data used in an operation. For example, 3 and 5 are the operands in the formula =3+5. Also note that the left operand of the expression “<25” is not present. This operand is assumed to be each cell in the range. The right operand of the expression may be a number or text. If it is a number, then the computer only compares numbers; if it is text, then the computer will only compare text. If a text number is used as the right operand, then a single quote must be placed in front of the number, such as ‘00111 for a zip code—for example “<’20050.” Remember text compares character by character; therefore, a text 6 is greater than a text 21 because 6 is greater than 2. If you want to compare like numbers, they must have all digits including leading zeros. The text 06 is less than the text 21.

INT Function

INT(NUMBER) The function INT returns whole numbers without rounding. For example, the resultants of INT(34.234) and INT(34.987) are both 34. The INT function is used for integer division. In integer division, the resultant is the whole number in the quotient. For example, the resultant of INT(26/3) is 8. This function in conjunction with the MOD function is used to calculate the number of months and remaining days from a number of days, or calculate the number of hours and minutes worked from a total number of minutes worked. See MOD function for an example.

MOD Function

MOD(NUMBER1,NUMBER2) The MOD function is modulo division of NUMBER1 divided by NUMBER2. In modulo division, the resultant is a whole-number remainder. For example, the resultant of MOD(26,3) is 2 because 26 divided by 3 is 8 with a remainder of 2. The MOD function and the INT function are used to calculate two types of division required for selected business processes. They are used to calculate either the hours and minutes someone has worked given the total number of minutes or the number of weeks and days worked given the total number of days. For example, if Jane Smith has worked 19 days during the month, then, assuming a 5-day work week, she has worked INT(19/5) = 3 weeks and MOD(19,5) = 4 days. Therefore, she has worked 3 weeks and 4 days.

RAND Function

RAND() The RAND function is a random number generator that generates and displays a number that is equal to or greater than zero and less than one. To generate a number inclusively between two numbers, use the formula RAND()*(b–a)+a, where *a* is the smallbest number and *b* is the largest number. This will produce a decimal number inclusively between *a* and *b,* such as 9.456 or 6 if *a* is equal to 6 and *b* is equal to 10. If you desire a whole number inclusively between two numbers, use the formula INT(RAND()*(b−a+1))+a. If *a* is 6 and *b* is 9, the resultant of this formula would be numbers such as 6, 7, 8, or 9. There will be no partial numbers. This formula may be used for simulations, raffles, games, or any other time you need a random number. This value will change every time the spreadsheet is updated. If you want to retain the generated number, then change the cell contents to a value through the use of COPY and PASTE SPECIAL.

ROUND Function

ROUND(NUMBER1, NUMBER2) The ROUND function rounds NUMBER1 to NUMBER2 decimals. For example, the resultant of ROUND(3.7854,2) would be 3.79. NUMBER2 must be positive when rounding to the right of the decimal point and must be negative when rounding to the left of the decimal point.

SIGN Function

SIGN(NUMBER) The SIGN function returns the sign of the number. If the number is positive it returns a +1, if negative a –1, and if zero a 0. For example, the resultant of SIGN(10–12) would be a –1. This function is used to retain the sign of a number when using the ABS function or for use in the criteria for logical functions.

SQRT Function

SQRT(NUMBER) The SQRT function returns the square root of NUMBER. For example, the resultant of SQRT(16) is 4. NUMBER must be a positive number.

SUM Function

SUM(LIST) The SUM function returns the total of the cell contents in the list. The SUM function ignores cells that contain text data. For example, the resultant of SUM(4,5,6) is 15 and SUM(4,"Maureen",5,6) is also 15.

SUMIF Function

SUMIF(RANGE,CRITERIA,SUMRANGE) The SUMIF function sums one range and uses a parallel range for the criteria. Parallel ranges are two separate ranges where each cell in one range is related in some way to the corresponding cell in the second range. For example, if the two ranges are A5:A10 and B5:B10, A5 and B5 have related data such as a county in the A5 and the population for the county in the B5. Similarly, A6 has another county name and B6 has that county's population, and so forth. An example of the SUMIF function is if RANGE has the values 30000, 20000, and 25000 and SUMRANGE has the values 300, 200, and 250, then the resultant of SUMIF(RANGE, "<26000", SUMRANGE) is 450. Only two values in RANGE meet the criteria, 20000 and 25000. SUMIF sums the parallel values in SUMRANGE which are 200 and 250. See Table 12.2. SUMRANGE is optional. If SUMRANGE is omitted then RANGE is used for calculating the total.

Lookup Functions

Lookup Functions

CHOOSE Function

CHOOSE(X,VALUE1,VALUE2, VALUE3, . . .) The CHOOSE function selects a value for the cell from a series of values in the argument list of the function, starting with the second argument, VALUE1, according to the selection value of the first argument, X, which is the series sequential selection value. For example, the resultant of CHOOSE(3,34,25,46,54,36,67) is 46, since 46 is the third value in the list of values. If the selection value were 4, the resultant would be 54. The selection value must be greater than zero and less than or equal to the number of values from which to choose. In this case, the selection value must be between 1 and 6, inclusive, since there are only six values. This function may be used for selecting payroll deduction for medical plans or for other payment options.

HLOOKUP Function

HLOOKUP(VALUE,RANGE,ROW) The function HLOOKUP is a table lookup function to select a cell value, based on its column and row placement from a range of values. It uses VALUE to find the correct column and ROW selects the correct row in the range. The resultant is the value of the cell where these two intersect on the spreadsheet. In Table 12.2, the resultant is 67, because this value is in the cell identified by the column beginning with 33, which is equal to the VALUE of C17, and the third ROW, the value of A19. VALUE must be equal to or greater than the top leftmost cell of the range. When VALUE is equal to or greater than the value of the top cell of the present column and less than the value of the top cell in the next column, the criteria for the selection of the column is to use the present column. If VALUE is greater than or equal to the top cell in the last column, then the last column is used.

VLOOKUP Function

VLOOKUP(VALUE,RANGE,COLUMN) The function VLOOKUP is a table lookup function to select a cell value, based on its row and column placement from a range of values. It uses VALUE to find the correct row, and COLUMN selects the correct column in the range. The resultant is value of the cell where these two intersect on the spreadsheet. In Table 12.2, the resultant is 22, because this value is in the cell identified by the row beginning with 300, which is equal to the VALUE of A17, and the third COLUMN, the value of A19. VALUE must be equal to or greater than the top leftmost cell of the range. When VALUE is equal to or greater than the value of the left cell of the present row and less than the value of the left cell in the next row, the criteria for the selection of the row is to use the present row. If VALUE is greater than or equal to the left cell in the last row, then the last row is used.

Logical Functions

Logical Functions

The resultant values of the logical functions (Table 12.2) NOT, AND, and OR are the same as the resultant of a relational expression, TRUE or FALSE. The arguments of these functions are relational expressions. They are used when more than one condition requires the selection of a cell value. For example, a store may require a driver's license or a check-cashing card on file for a customer who wants to cash a check. When the customer has a valid driver's license or a check-cashing card on file, the check can be cashed. The function would be written as OR(A6="Yes",B6="Yes"), where A6 contains the value "Yes" or "No" to indicate whether the customer has a driver's license number on file and B6 contains the value "Yes" or "No" to indicate whether the customer has a check-cashing card on file. The resultant would be TRUE or FALSE according to the value of A6 and B6; then either A6 or B6 are "YES," the resultant is TRUE, otherwise the resultant is FALSE.

The IF function uses these logical functions along with relational expressions to choose between values for the cell in which the formula is located. Any of these functions may be nested, which means that you may use them as arguments within another function.

NOT Function

NOT(REL_EXP) The NOT function changes the resultant of REL_EXP to the opposite value. When the resultant of REL_EXP is TRUE then the NOT function returns FALSE and vice versa. For example, the resultant of NOT(5<6) is FALSE because 5<6 is TRUE and NOT TRUE is FALSE.

AND Function

AND(REL_EXP1,REL_EXP2) The resultant of the AND function is TRUE only when both relational expressions are TRUE, otherwise the resultant is FALSE. For example, the resultant of AND(5<6,7<6) is FALSE since only one of the relational expressions is TRUE.

OR Function

OR(REL_EXP1,REL_EXP2) The resultant of the OR function is FALSE, only when both relational expressions are FALSE, otherwise the resultant is TRUE. For example, the resultant of OR(5<6,7<6) is TRUE because at least one of the relational expressions is TRUE.

IF Function

IF(LOGICAL_EXP,TRUE_VALUE,FALSE_VALUE) The IF function allows the user to create a formula to have the computer make a decision by choosing between two pieces of data for the value of the cell in which the formula in located. For example, the resultant of IF(4<5,34,45) would be 34 since the resultant of the logical expression is TRUE and 34 is the TRUE_VALUE. The resultant of IF(4>5,34,45) would be 45 since the resultant of the logical expression is now FALSE and 45 is the FALSE_VALUE. You may use logical functions as the criteria for selection of the value by nesting them. For example, the resultant of IF(OR(4<5,6<5),34,45) would be 34 since one of the relational expressions in the OR function is TRUE, the resultant of the OR function is TRUE, and resultant of the IF function is consequently 34, the TRUE_VALUE. Figure 12.2 shows a flowchart for an IF function.

Financial Functions

Financial Functions

There are many financial functions (see Table 12.2) available in a spreadsheet program. Most are used in a finance class, but three will be covered in this book. These three you may use to calculate the future value of a current investment, the payments on a house, or how much you can afford to pay for a car.

FV Function

FV(RATE,PERIOD,PMT,PV) The FV function returns the future value of an investment that starts with a given present value amount, PV. Payments, or PMT, are invested at a fixed percentage rate, or RATE, every periodic time unit, or PERIOD. Units must be consistent. If your payments are monthly, then the period must be in months and the interest rate must be monthly. See Table 12.2 for an example. Chapter 14 uses this function in one of the case studies.

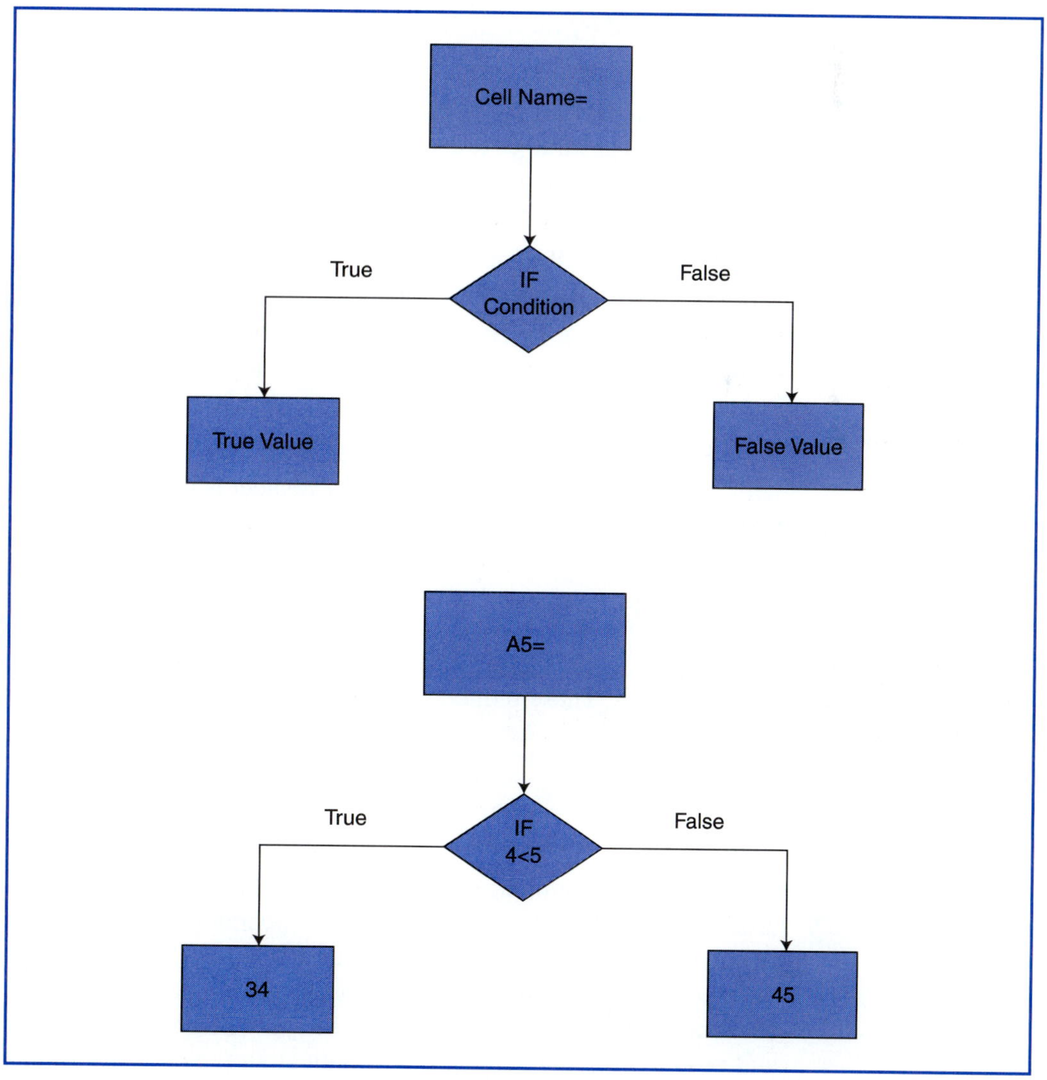

Figure 12.2 Example of Flowchart for an IF Function

PMT Function

PMT(RATE,PERIOD,PV,FV) The PMT function returns the payment necessary on a loan, PV, at RATE invested for so many PERIODs or the future amount FV, invested at RATE for so many PERIODs. Units must be consistent. Remember, if your payments are to be monthly, then the period must be in months and the interest rate must be monthly. See Table 12.2 for an example. Chapter 14 uses this function in one of the case studies.

PV Function

PV(RATE,PERIOD,PMT) The PV function returns the present value of an investment with a payment of PMT at RATE interest for so many PERIODs. Units must be consistent. This function could be used to calculate the amount of money you will have at the end of a time period. For example, this function would calculate the amount of money you would have in five years if you put $150 in your savings account every month at 4% interest. Remember, if your payments are monthly, then the period must be in months and the interest rate must be monthly. See Table 12.2 for an example. Chapter 14 uses this function in one of the case studies.

Date and Time Functions

Date and Time Functions

DATE Function

DATE(YEAR,MONTH,DAY) The DATE function returns the numeric value of the date designated by the YEAR, MONTH, and DAY. This function would be used to calculate the sequential date number for a specific date.

NOW Function

NOW() The NOW function returns the numeric value of the current date and time. You may format this value as a date format or a time format. This date and time will be recalculated every time the spreadsheet is updated. This function would be used to print the present date and time. You may put this function in two different cells and format one as a date format and the other as a time format.

TIME Function

TIME(HOUR,MINUTE,SECOND) The TIME function returns the numeric value of the time designated by HOUR, MINUTE, and SECOND. You may format this value as a time format. This function would be used to calculate the sequential time number for a specific time.

TODAY Function

TODAY() The TODAY function returns the current date in numeric form. This date will be recalculated every time the spreadsheet is updated. This function would be used to print the present date. You would need to format this cell as a date format.

Database Functions

Database Functions—See Chapter 14

Even though a spreadsheet program is not a database program, it does have some database functions. These will be explained in Chapter 14 in one of the case studies.

Operators

Operators

The user must communicate information to the computer as to how to process data. This task is accomplished through the use of operators. **Operators** are the data connectors within formulas. They direct the computer as to how to process the data. Operators also are interpreted by the computer as to what type of processing—mathematical or relational—needs to be executed. Consequently, the types of operators used in spreadsheet formulas and problem solving include mathematical and relational. Without these operators, little processing can be accomplished.

Operand and Resultant

The **operand** and the **resultant** are two concepts related to the operator. Operands are data that the operator connects and processes via the operator. The resultant is the answer produced when the operation is completed. For example, in the expression 5 + 7, the + is the operator, 5 and 7 are the operands, and 12 is the resultant. Operands may be values or cell references. The data type of the operands and the resultant depend on the operator.

Mathematical Operators

Mathematical operators include addition, subtraction, multiplication, division, and powers. The computer has a symbol for each of these. See Table 12.3.

Relational operators include the following: equal to (=), less than (<), greater than (>), less than or equal to (<=), greater than or equal to (>=), and not equal to (<>). An end user will use relational operators to make decisions. The resultant of a relational operation is either TRUE or FALSE. When using relational operators in an IF function, the end user designates one value for the cell when a relational expression is TRUE, and another value when the expression is FALSE. Using relational operators is the only way for the computer to make decisions. For example, when a customer's credit card balance is less than $500 (TRUE), then the customer may charge another purchase because the current balance is evaluated as low enough. When the balance is not less than $500 (FALSE), then the customer may not charge another purchase. The expression would be set up as BALANCE<500. The operands are BALANCE and 500; the operator is <; the resultant is either TRUE or FALSE depending on the value of the balance. The end user would use this expression in a decision-making function such as an IF function, for example, IF(C5<500,"Okay to charge","Not okay to charge"), where C5 contains the value of the balance of the charge account.

Hierarchy of Operations

Hierarchy of Operations

Mathematical and relational operators have a **hierarchy** (or precedence), an order in which their operations take place. See Table 12.3. Functions are computed first, mathematical operators are second in hierarchy, and relational operators are last.

Table 12.3 Operators and Hierarchy of Operations

Order of Operations	Operand Data Type	Resultant
( ) Reorders the hierarchy: all operations are completed within the parentheses using the same hierarchy.		
1. Function		
Mathematical Operators		
2. Power (^) 3. Division (/), Multiplication (*) 4. Addition (+) Subtraction (−)	Numerical Numerical Numerical	Numerical Numerical Numerical
Relational Operators		
5. Equal to (=), Less than (<), Greater than (>), Less than or Equal to (≤), Greater than or Equal (≥), Not equal to (<>)	Numerical or character string	True or False

A hierarchy exists within the mathematical operators, as follows: first all powers, second all multiplication and division, and third all additions and subtractions. To reorder the normal processing sequence, parentheses must be added; therefore, operations within parentheses are processed before all functions and operators outside of the parentheses. The processing of the operands as directed by the operators always starts with the innermost parentheses and works outward. Formulas are processed from left to right. Each level of operators within a set of parentheses requires that the computer make another pass through the parentheses until all levels have been evaluated. Knowledge of this hierarchy is important to the end user, because the order of the operations determines the result of the expression.

If the operations are not completed in the correct order, the result of the expression may be incorrect. For example, assuming a 40-hour work week and overtime pay at 1.5 times regular pay, the expression to calculate overtime pay would be to subtract 40 from the hours worked and multiply the result by the regular wage times 1.5. The expression would be written as,

(HOURS – 40) * WAGE * 1.5

As you can see from the hierarchy chart, multiplication is processed before subtraction, so parentheses must be added to direct the computer to perform the subtraction first before the multiplication. If the parentheses are not added, then the computer would perform the multiplication of 40 * WAGE * 1.5 and then subtract the result from HOURS. This result will be incorrect.

Each type of operator requires a certain data type for operands and determines the data type of the resultant. Mathematical operators require numerical data as the operands and have numerical resultants. When any of the relational operators are used, the resultant is TRUE or FALSE. Relational operators use numerical or text data types as the operands; however, the data type of the operands for an operator must be the same.

Formulas

Formulas

Knowledge of constants and variables, data types, operators, operands, and resultants is not valuable until you can use these concepts to create formulas. The problem you are trying to solve may be calculating net pay after taxes including Social Security and medical deductions. It may be an inventory problem with reorder quantities and cash values. It may be a problem of calculating interest or payments for a loan. These tasks require the use of different operators, written as formulas in order for the computer to process the data and produce a result. Most computer problems that require the use of a spreadsheet also require the use of formulas in the solution.

A **formula** is an expression that processes data, the operands, through the use of operators. For example, to find the number of square feet in a room you would multiply the length of the room by the width in the formula:

LENGTH * WIDTH

In a spreadsheet this formula might be written as B3*C3, where B3 is the location of the length and C3 is the location of the width. If this formula is found in D3, then the cell contents of D3 is equal to B3*C3. D3 is the location of the area. The resultant of the expression is displayed on the screen in the cell where the formula is located.

Developing Formulas

Developing and Evaluating Formulas

For the beginning end user, a big part of learning to use a spreadsheet is learning how to write and evaluate formulas. To evaluate a formula or an entire spreadsheet means to test for correctness using actual data. The following examples illustrate how to use the concepts from this chapter to write and evaluate formulas.

Example 1: Setting Up a Numerical Expression

Setting up a Numerical Expression

A client will often give an end user an expression to use in solving a problem. Assume the end user has to modify the following mathematical expression for computer use:

$$X(3Y + 4) - \frac{4Y}{X + 6}$$

The appropriate computer expression to transfer to a formula is shown as

X * (3 * Y + 4) − 4 * Y/(X + 6)

All variables, constants, and operators must be on the same computer line. There must be an operator between variables and/or constants. For the computer, there are no assumed multiplication signs or power signs as there are in mathematics, so the * and the ^ must be used. Parentheses are not considered operators and so may be next to one. Parentheses must be added when hierarchy is a factor. Parentheses also may be added to improve readability. The following steps help to complete the spreadsheet formula based on client data.

1. Write all parentheses, operands, and operators on a single line with the dividend first, followed by the divisor.

   X (3Y + 4) – 4Y / X + 6

2. Insert all implied operators.

   X * (3 * Y + 4) – 4 * Y / X + 6

3. Insert all parentheses when hierarchy is a factor. X + 6 must be calculated before completing the division, so parentheses are inserted here.

   X * (3 * Y + 4) – 4 * Y / (X + 6)

4. Change the variables to cell reference names. Assume that X is located in B4 and Y in C4, then the spreadsheet formula would be

   B4 * (3 * C4 + 4) – 4 * C4 / (B4 + 6).

This formula would be entered into a cell, say D4. The cell contents would contain the previous formula and the cell as displayed would display the calculated value of the formula.

Example 2: Setting Up a Relational Expression as Part of a Formula

Setting up a Relational Expression

You are developing a relational formula for cell D5. The problem dictates that the formula should be as follows: If X is less than Y + 5, where the value of X is located in B5 and the value of Y is located in C5, then the value of D5 is 7; if not, then the value of D5 is 9. The IF function is selected for the problem because it uses relational expressions to calculate the value of a cell. The formula would be set up as follows:

IF(B5<C5+5,7,9)

Because this formula uses a relational expression, a variable or a mathematical expression may be on either side of the operator. B5 and C5 would be the same data type, in this case a numerical data type. The resultant would be a TRUE or FALSE depending on the values of B5 and C5. When the resultant is TRUE then the value of D5 is the value of the second argument, 7; when the resultant is FALSE then the value of D5 is the value of the third argument, 9.

Example 3: Setting Up a Formula that Uses More Than One Relational Expression

Setting Up a Relational Expression

Often a computer decision is based on more than one relational expression. For example, to cash a check, company policy may require that a customer have both credit okay and check-cashing cards on file at the store. B6 contains a "Yes" when the customer has a credit okay and a "No" if not. C6 contains a "Yes" when the customer has a check-cashing card on file at the store and a "No" if not. The formula will be placed in D6. This formula would use the AND function nested within the IF function. The formula would be

IF(AND(B6="Yes",C6="Yes"),"Okay to cash check","Not okay to cash check.")

This formula is interpreted as follows: *If* B6 equals "Yes" *and* C6 equals "Yes" *then* the cell contents of D6 is "Okay to cash check," *otherwise* the cell contents of D6 is "Not okay to cash check."

Example 4: Evaluating a Mathematical Formula

Evaluating a Mathematical Formula

To find out if proposed solutions are correct, it is important for the end user to evaluate, or test, all formulas. Assume the end user has written the formula in cell E8 as,

$$5 * (B8 + C8) - 4 * C8/(D8 + 6)$$

Evaluate the formula when the values of B8 = 2, C8 = 3, and D8 = 6. Notice in the illustration the structure of the evaluation that follows. A dashed line leading to a circle indicates the operator. The solid lines indicate the operands. Following the illustration for this equation is a list of the operations and the resultant of each operation. The number of circles should equal the number of operators.

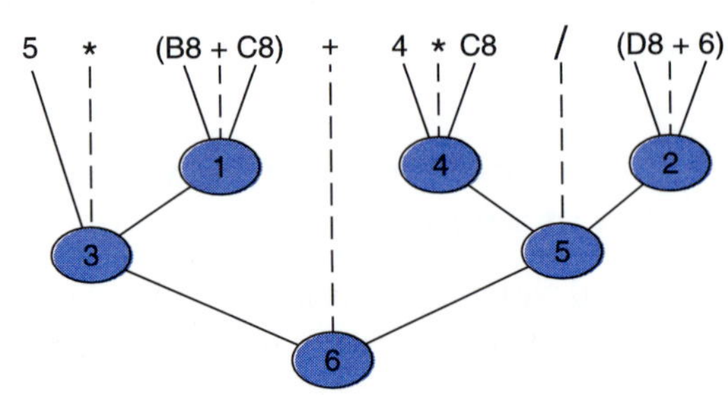

Operation	*Resultant*
1. B8 + C8	5
2. D8 + 6	12
3. 5 * resultant of step 1	25
4. 4 * C8	12
5. Resultant of step 4 / resultant of step 2	1
6. Resultant of step 3–resultant of step 5	24

Illustrating the structure of the expression and listing the operations and results in this way simplifies the evaluation process for the end user. The evaluation must be completed according to the hierarchy of operations. The operations within the parentheses would be completed first, moving from left to right. B6 + C8 would be completed first and D8 + 6 second. According to the hierarchy, the computer would then complete the multiplications and the divisions from left to right. The division would be completed after the multiplications in this expression only because it is to their right. The final operation to be completed would be subtraction, because it is outside of the parentheses and is after the division and multiplication in the hierarchy table.

This evaluation shows how to test a computer expression to see if it matches an equivalent mathematical expression and to ensure that the solution is correct. It gives the end user a correct result that should be compared with the results manually calculated by the client or by whomever requested the computer solution to the problem.

Evaluating a Mathematical Formula Using an IF Function

Example 5: Evaluating a Formula Using an IF Function

Assume the end user has written the formula in C5,

IF(A5−2>B5,F2,G2)

The end user then uses the following values to evaluate the expression:

A5=6   B5=8

The following illustration shows the structure of the evaluation:

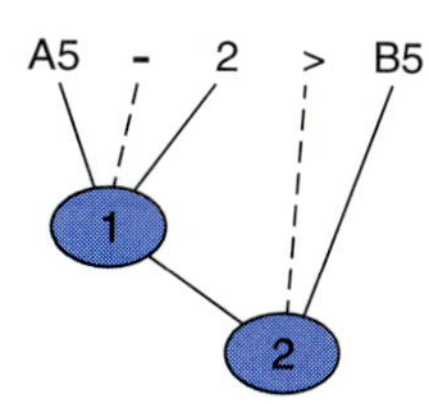

Operation	*Resultant*
1. A5 − 2	4
2. Resultant of step 1 > B5	FALSE

Because the resultant of the relational expression is FALSE, the value of C5 will be equal to the value of G2. According to the hierarchy of operations, the mathematical operation is completed first, then the relational operation.

Evaluating the Formula Created in Example 3

Example 6: Evaluating the Formula Created in Example 3

Assume the end user has written the following formula in D6 and the value of B6 = "Yes" and C6 = "No."

IF(AND(B6="Yes",C6="Yes"),"Okay to cash check","Not okay to cash check.")

The operations are completed in hierarchical order from left to right starting with the innermost parentheses.

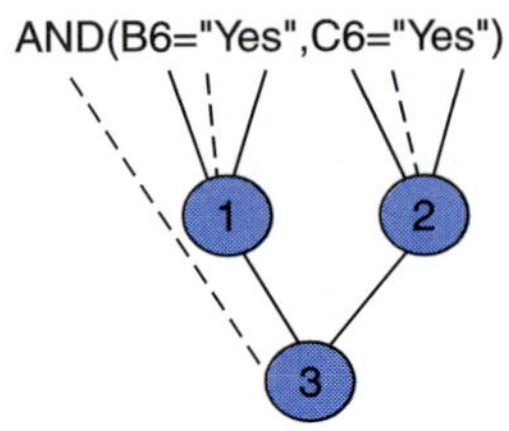

Operation	*Resultant*
1. B6="Yes"	TRUE
2. C6="Yes"	FALSE
3. AND(result of step 1,result of step 2)	FALSE
4. IF result of step 3	Cell contents of D6 is "Not okay to cash check"

The computations within the parentheses are completed first. Therefore, the relational expression B6="Yes" is completed, then the relational expression C6="Yes." The AND function is completed after the argument calculations in the parentheses. Since there are no more calculations to be completed in the arguments of the IF function, the IF function is completed and the results displayed in D6.

Example 7: Developing a Logical Expression for a Given Problem

Developing a Logical Expression for a Given Problem

Many times an end user will be given the policies of a company and then be required to set up a logical expression from these policies. To do this, the end user first needs to list the items on which the condition is dependent, and then develop a logical expression from this list. *Problem:* A large department store has its own charge card. The policy for a customer to charge an item is that the customer must have a valid charge card and either a balance of less than $500 or a current charge of less than $50.

1. The first step is to list the items the charge is dependent upon and their data types:
   a. charge card (text)
   b. balance (numerical)
   c. charge amount (numerical)
2. The second step is to write these items as variables with the conditions on each. Put them on one horizontal line, leaving space between, so that the logical functions may be added. The resultant of each expression must be logical. Remember that the operators must match the data types of the operands. Do not put the functions in as of yet.

   CHARGE CARD = "Yes"   BALANCE < 500   AMOUNT < 50

3. The third step is to put in the logical function names, the commas, and the parentheses: First the OR:

CHARGE CARD="Yes" OR(BALANCE<500,AMOUNT<50)

then the AND:

AND(CHARGE CARD="Yes", OR(BALANCE<500, AMOUNT<50))

Because the policy condition between the balance and the amount is one or the other, the OR operator is required. Since the policy condition between the charge card and the other two items is both, the AND operator is required. Since the AND function has precedence over the OR, the OR function is nested as one of the arguments within the AND function. The precedence of the logical functions are NOT, AND, and OR. NOT has precedence over AND and OR, and AND has precedence over OR.

4. Change the equation into an IF function to be used in the spreadsheet. The formula will be placed in E10. CHARGE CARD value is in B10, BALANCE value is in C10, and AMOUNT value is in D10. The formula would look like this:

IF(AND(B10="Yes", OR(C10<500, D10<50)),

"OKAY TO CHARGE", "NOT OKAY TO CHARGE")

The relational expression just developed is the first argument. The TRUE and FALSE text responses have been added as the second and third arguments. The formula is interpreted as when B10 equals "yes" AND either C10 < 500 or D10 < 50, then the cell contents of E10 will contain "OKAY TO CHARGE," otherwise the cell contents of E10 will contain "NOT OKAY TO CHARGE."

Summary

Spreadsheets are basically electronic calculators. They are tables of columns and rows. At the intersection of a column and row is a cell. The cell is a holder of text, values, and formulas. The spreadsheet recalculates whenever it is updated. The reference name for a cell is the column letter followed by the row number such as A3 or D6.

Each cell is assigned a data type for the cell contents and a format for the cell as displayed. The cell contents contain data as they are entered. The cells as displayed contain the formatted data and the resultant of the formulas. Data types used by a spreadsheet program include numeric and text. There are many formats for numeric and text values.

Functions are small sets of instructions that perform specific tasks. There are many functions available to the user through the spreadsheet program. Each function has a name. The data required to complete the task are surrounded by parentheses and follow the name. Categories of functions include text, statistical, mathematical, lookup, financial, date and time, and database functions.

Formulas are mathematical expressions used in spreadsheet programs. Formulas are developed through the use of values, cell references, operators, and functions. Mathematical and relational operators are used according to a predetermined hierarchy. Formulas are the key to spreadsheets. It is important to learn how to develop and evaluate them.

Key Words

arguments
cell
concatenation
constant
data format
data type
formula
function
hierarchy
list of cells
mathematical operator
numerical data
operand
operator
range of cells
relational operator
resultant
text
value
variable

Questions

1. What is a function?
2. Why are functions used?
3. Find the result of the following operations:
   - **a.** 5 + 4
   - **b.** 10/2
   - **c.** OR(TRUE,FALSE)
   - **d.** MOD(20,3)
   - **e.** 5 < 8
   - **f.** MOD(25,70)
   - **g.** “A” > “H”
   - **h.** NOT(TRUE)
   - **i.** INT(25/70)
   - **j.** AND(FALSE,TRUE)
   - **k.** 20 * 0.5
   - **l.** 35 < = 35
   - **m.** 35/7
   - **n.** OR(FALSE,FALSE)
   - **o.** AND(TRUE,TRUE)
   - **p.** MOD(50,5)
   - **q.** –35 < 67
   - **r.** 4.0 ^ 3
   - **s.** INT(60/9)
   - **t.** 35 < 35
   - **u.** AND(TRUE,FALSE)

Problems

1. Evaluate the following formulas, given the values: A6 =12, B6 =3, C6= 6, D6=2
   a. A6+B6/C6–D6 ^ 2
   b. (A6 + B6)/C6–D6 ^ 2
   c. A6 + B6/(C6–D6 ^ 2)
   d. MOD((A6 + B6), C6)
   e. (A6 + B6)/D6 ^ 2
2. Write the following expressions as spreadsheet formulas using cell A5 for X, cell B5 for Y, and cell C5 for Z.
   a. $Y + 3Z - \frac{Z-3}{Z-1}$
   b. $5Y + \frac{3Z-1}{4(3Z+1)-Y}$
   c. $(X - Y)^2$
3. An employee came into work and clocked in at MORNING-IN (C7), clocked out at NOON-OUT (D7) for lunch, clocked back in at NOON-IN (E7), and clocked out to go home at NIGHT-OUT (F7) (all in minutes since midnight). Set up formulas to calculate the number of hours and minutes the employee worked for the day. (You will develop two formulas to be entered into G7 and H7.)
4. Steve Thompson bought and charged an electric saw on DATE1 (D5) and made the first payment on DATE2 (E5). Write a formula (F5) to calculate how many days (DAYS) have elapsed between the two dates.
5. Eureka Lumber Company gives a 2% discount if the remaining balance is paid within 10 days of purchase. Write a formula using the IF function to verify whether a customer qualifies for this discount. Use the following variable names:

   BUYING-DATE (D4): date the customer purchased the merchandise

   PAID-DATE (E4): date the customer made the final payment
6. A part-time employee worked 20 hours in the first week and 15 hours in the second week of a two-week pay period. He is paid a weekly salary based on a 40-hour week. What is his full-time equivalent for the two weeks (i.e., what percentage of full time did he work)? Write a general formula that could be used to express and store the full-time equivalent of any hours worked per week.
7. Develop a formula using the IF function for the following conditions. A company gives a bonus at the end of each fiscal year. For an employee to get a bonus, the following must be true:
   a. The employee has been working at the company for more than six months with no negative reports.
   b. The employee has earned more than $5,000 during the fiscal year.
8. Develop a formula using the IF function for the following conditions. A retail store has this check-cashing policy:
   a. The customer must have a driver's license.
   b. When the check is for more than $50, the customer must have a check-cashing card on file.

Chapter 13

Spreadsheet Concepts

Overview

Objectives

When you have finished this chapter, you should be able to:

1. Understand the features of a spreadsheet package.
2. Choose a chart type for given data with a given purpose for the chart.
3. Organize information for a well-designed spreadsheet.
4. Develop a solution to a problem using a spreadsheet planning guide.

Spreadsheet software is used when frequent and/or multiple calculations are required to solve such problems as cost analysis, forecasting, and grades. Chapter 12 covered mathematical concepts and functions pertaining to spreadsheets. It also presented various fundamental spreadsheet concepts. Chapter 13 focuses on more spreadsheet concepts, features, and problem development. This chapter explains some features of a spreadsheet package, documents how to plan a spreadsheet, presents how to complete spreadsheet postanalysis, and shows the development of examples of spreadsheet planning.

There are two major problems for people who are starting to use spreadsheets. The first problem is in the development of the formulas. Many people have problems with mathematics and therefore have problems setting up the required formulas. The second problem is in the organization of the spreadsheet. Spreadsheets should be organized and formatted such that the required results may be readily found and analyzed.

Spreadsheet Terminology

Worksheet, Workbook, and Spreadsheet

A spreadsheet allows the user to create a document containing **rows** and **columns** for easy organization and computation of data. Most spreadsheets are three dimensional by allowing for multiple pages or sheets. One sheet or page is called a worksheet, whereas multiple pages are called a workbook. Sometimes the worksheet is referred to as the spreadsheet. In this book, a single page will be referred to as a worksheet; multiple worksheets as a workbook; and the workbook, charts, macros, and so forth as the spreadsheet.

On a worksheet, the intersection of the rows and columns are called **cells.** See Figure 13.1. Each cell may contain multiple characters that become labels containing text data, values containing numbers, or formulas containing mathematical expressions. Different worksheets are used to separate data, for example, different months of a budget or classes of a grade sheet. Separate worksheets are also used to hold tables of data needed in calculation such as tax tables or payroll data. You may also want to keep macros on a separate worksheet.

When a formula references a cell on the same worksheet, the name in the formula is designated by the column letter followed by the row number. Remember CR for column-row. If the formula references a cell on another worksheet, the cell name must include the worksheet name before the column letter. The separator between the worksheet name and the column letter is an exclamation point, for example:

Sheet1!A5 or January!C8

The time saved by using a spreadsheet package does not necessarily lie in the initial calculation but in the recalculations. The spreadsheet is recalculated every time data are changed in cells by adding, deleting, or changing information in the cells. The computer does not keep calculated or formatted values in its memory. The cell contents contains unformatted text, numbers, or formulas. The format selections of the cells are linked to each cell in the memory. It is important to understand the difference between what is in the computer's memory called the cell contents, and what you see on the monitor called cells as displayed.

Errors in Formulas

Errors in formulas are a concern when using spreadsheets. It is important to have a hand-computed test case to evaluate the results. When you evaluate the results, remember the computer uses the cell contents to complete all calculations. Your calculations from the cells as displayed may be different from the computer's calculation. For example, if the cell contents of A5 contains the value 25 and B5 contains the value of 4.6, the resultant of the formula =A5*B5 in C5 is 115. However, if you format these cells with no decimal places, the cell-as-displayed value of A5 is 25 and B5 becomes 5 since the computer rounds. When you hand-compute the product of these cells as displayed, the resultant is 125. If you multiply 25 times 5 you will get a resultant of 125, not 115, that shows on the worksheet, because the computer used the cell content value of 4.6, not the as-displayed value of 5 for B5. Format worksheet cells so that you are viewing accurate, readable information especially during the evaluation period for the development of a worksheet.

Spreadsheet Features

Features of a spreadsheet are divided into four parts: entering, editing, analyzing, and printing information. These features are important to learn in order to use a spreadsheet package efficiently. See Table 13.1.

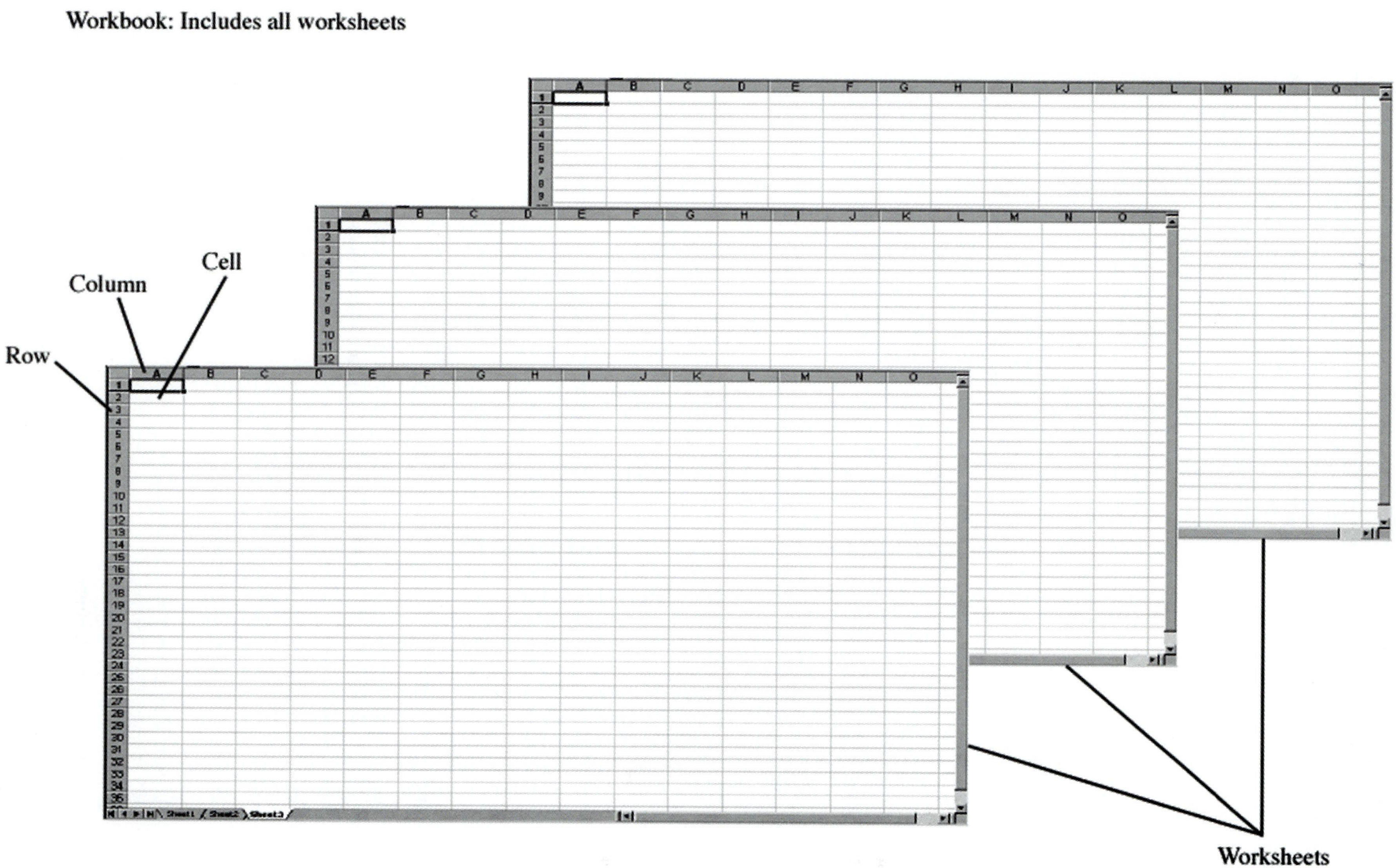

Figure 13.1 Rows, Columns, Cells, Worksheets, Workbooks

Table 13.1 Features of a Spreadsheet Program

Feature	Description
Absolute Reference	Adding a $ before the column and/or row so the reference will not adjust as the formula is copied.
Cell	The intersection of a column and a row.
Cell Comments	Electronic documentation that may be added to a cell.
Charts	Pictorial view of data. Types include bar, column, cylinder, cone, pyramid, line, surface, area, pie, doughnut, stock, scatter, bubble, and radar charts. Each of these may have various options including three-dimensional, stacked, and 100% stacked charts.
Column	A vertical group of cells.
Fill Command	Copies cells; inserts a series of numbers in a range of cells.
Freeze Panes	Keeps specified rows on the left and columns on the top viewed on the monitor while the rest of the worksheet scrolls.
Go To (a cell)	Jumps to a specified cell.
Gridlines	The lines between the cells.
Hide	Makes the column or row of cells disappear.
Insert Command	Inserts cells, rows, columns, worksheets, as well as graphics, charts, hyperlinks, page breaks, and so forth.
Range, Worksheet Names	Allows the user to name ranges of cells and worksheets.
Recalculation	Allows the user to specify how the recalculation is to be performed.
Relative Reference	Allows the adjustment of column letters and row numbers as formulas are copied.
Row	A horizontal group of cells.
Split Screens	Allows the user to view two sections of the worksheet by splitting the screen.
Workbook	Multiple worksheets.
Worksheet	One sheet or page in a workbook.
Worksheet Protection	Locks the cells from being changed.

Entering Data

Some Basic Guidelines

Data are entered into cells. Cursor movement is from cell to cell, not character to character as in other software packages, unless you are in the process of changing information in a cell. When you are planning and creating your worksheet there are two guidelines to follow. The first is to reference as much information as possible. For example, if you are creating a budget and your salary is the same all year, then enter the value for only the first month in cell B4. For all other months, develop a formula to reference the previous salary cell, such as =B4 in cell C4, =C4 in cell D4, and so forth. Then if you get an unexpected raise, you need only change one cell. Since other cells for your salary in succeeding months are referenced to the month that was changed, the other cells will also change. This step saves time and decreases the chance of errors, because you have fewer entries to make and less chance to forget some cells.

The second planning guideline is to copy/paste formulas as much as possible rather than reenter them in other cells. Copying formulas in worksheets is different than copying labels and values. When you copy labels and values, the identical cell contents are duplicated into another cell or **range of cells.** When you copy formulas, however, the row and column references change according to the number of cell position displacements from the original cell(s) to the new cell(s).

Relative and Absolute Reference in Formulas

For example, you have the following formula in cell C5: =A5+B5. When you copy this formula to C6 it becomes =A6+B6, because you are copying the formula to a cell one row down and therefore the row number is increased by one in each of the row references. If you were to copy this formula into C8, the formula would be =A8+B8, because the formula is copied to a cell three rows down and therefore the row reference is increased by three. When you copy this formula to D5, the formula becomes =B5+C5, because the formula is copied to a cell one column to the right and therefore the column letters are increased by one in each of the column references. If the formula were to be copied to cell F5, then the formula would become =D5+E5, because the formula was copied three cells to the right so the column letters increase three cells. The same is true when you copy rows up or columns to the left, except the row and column reference is decreased by the number of rows or columns from the original location of the formula.

If the formula in C5, which is =A5+B5, were to be copied to cell F7, then both the rows and the columns would be changed. The row number would be increased by two and the column letter increased by three. This copied formula =D7+E7 is called a **relative cell reference.** This feature of worksheets is helpful because many times you want the same formula but different references, such as on an instructor's grade sheet that would have the same formula for each student but different references. A relative cell reference in a formula changes the reference but not the basic formula. Using relative cell reference decreases both the time spent and chance of errors while entering formulas.

At times you will require an **absolute cell reference,** in which the cell reference will not change while copying, such as when calculating the percentage of one value of a total value. The formula would be one value divided by the sum of all values. In this formula, you want the cell reference for the individual values to change while copying, but you do not want the cell reference for the total of all values to change. See Figure 13.2 for an example of both relative and absolute copy of cells. To indicate an absolute reference in a formula, add a dollar sign ($) before the row and/or the column of the cell references in a formula.

Examples of absolute cell references are $B$5, $B5, and B$5. When using $B$5, you are instructing the computer not to change the row number or the column letter while copying the formula. When using the cell reference $B5, you are instructing the computer not to change the column letter but only change the row number. Likewise, in B$5 you are instructing the computer to change the column letter and not to change the row number while copying. You will want to use each of these forms at times, but most often the row and column are both absolute.

Figure 13.2 are examples of relative and absolute reference copy of a formula for the number of customers for XYZ Corporation. Examples 1 and 2 illustrate errors that occur while incorrectly making a relative copy of the denominator in the percentage of total calculation. Cell D7 is the cell reference to the total. It must be copied as absolute ($D$7). Relative copy produced a #DIV/0! error for store locations 2 and 3. Examples 3 and 4 illustrate examples of properly copied formulas in column D.

Fill Command

An easy way to copy cells to an adjoining cell(s) is to use the fill down, up, right, or left command. Select the cells from and to which you are copying and then select the fill command from the menu. Select the direction in which you are copying. The fill feature eliminates several steps required when you use copy/paste. In some worksheets, you may point to the small box in the lower right corner of the cell you are copying from and

Figure 13.2 Examples of Relative and Absolute Reference Copy

Example 1

	A	B	C	D	E
1	**Number of customers**	**For XYZ Company**			
2					
3		**Day 1**	**Day 2**	**Subtotals**	**% of Total**
4	Store 1	23	15	=+B4+C4	=+D4/D7
5	Store 2	35	26	=+B5+C5	=+D5/D8
6	Store 3	42	34	=+B6+C6	=+D6/D10
7	Total			=SUM(D4:D6)	
8					
9	Cell content values when copying without using absolute				
10	references in percentage calculation.			**Note:** Error in denominator in formula.	

Example 2

	A	B	C	D	E	F
1	**Number of Customers for XYZ Company**					
2						
3		**Day 1**	**Day 2**	**Subtotals**	**% of Total**	
4	Store 1	23	15	38	21.71%	
5	Store 2	35	26	61	#DIV/O!	
6	Store 3	42	34	76	#DIV/O!	
7	Total			175		
8					**Note:** Resultant error.	
9	As-displayed values when copying without using absolute					
10	references in percentage calculation.					

Example 3

	A	B	C	D	E
1	**Number of Customers**				
2					
3		**Day 1**	**Day 2**	**Subtotals**	**% of Total**
4	Store 1	23	15	=+B4+C4	=+D4/$D$7
5	Store 2	35	26	=+B5+C5	=+D5/$D$7
6	Store 3	42	34	=+B6+C6	=+D6/$D$7
7	Total			=SUM(D4:D6)	
8					
9	As-displayed cell values copying using			**Note:** Absolute reference in denominator.	
10	absolute reference in the calculation of the percentage.				

Example 4

	A	B	C	D	E
1	**Number of Customers for XYZ Company**				
2					
3		**Day 1**	**Day 2**	**Subtotals**	**% of Total**
4	Store 1	23	15	38	21.71%
5	Store 2	35	26	61	34.86%
6	Store 3	42	34	76	43.43%
7	Total			175	
8					
9	As-displayed cell values copying using absolute reference				
10	in the calculation of the percentage.				

drag it through the cells you are copying to in order to copy to the selected adjacent cells. This process is the same as fill.

Another use of the fill feature is to have the computer enter series data for you. For example, an instructor has many students and would like to have a column that will number each student, starting with 1. To do this, the instructor will enter the starting value of 1 in a cell for the first student. He then selects all cells in the number column for every student row. Next, he selects the fill series feature, gives the step a value of 1, and makes the ending value of a number equal to or greater than the number of students in the class. The computer then enters the numbers in each cell starting with 1 and increases the number by one for each of the selected cells until either the stop number is reached or there are no more selected cells. If there are 60 students in the class, for example, this step can save time. If students are added or deleted from the list, the instructor must use the fill feature again.

The fill step number may be any number. If it is 2, the fill will count by 2s; if it is 10, the numbers will be increased by 10. The series may be linear (1, 2, 3 or 2, 4, 6), growth (3, 5, 8 or 4, 6, 9), or by dates. A date series may be by day, weekday, month, or year. The step number would be 7 if you want weekly. Step value for years would be 100 if you wanted every 100 years. The equivalent formula would be the previous cell plus the step value. You would then copy this formula to the same selected cells.

Insert Function Command

When developing formulas, the insert function feature is helpful. This feature will bring up a window listing of all functions. The window will also show an example of the function including arguments and a short description. This saves time when trying to remember the exact form of the function and arguments.

Freeze Panes

When your worksheet is too large for the monitor and you must scroll to see part of it, you may want to use the freeze panes feature. Freeze panes will allow you to select rows and columns to be constantly viewed while you are scrolling the rest of the worksheet. For example, the instructor wants to enter text grades but the test column is off the screen to the right. If he scrolls to see the test column, he loses the as-displayed names of the students as they scroll off the screen. When he uses the freeze panes feature, the students' names will remain in the viewing area while he scrolls to the test column. In most worksheets you designate the scroll area by selecting the upper left cell of the scroll area. All cells in the present viewing area that are above and to the left of the row and column in which the selected cell is located will remain. The rows and columns to the right and below, including the row and column in which the cell is located, will be in the scroll area. Remember that the rows and columns in the freeze area take up viewing room; therefore, you will want to use as few rows and columns as necessary. Scroll your worksheet to the point where the required row(s) and column(s) for the freeze area are showing. Then designate the scroll area to produce the largest viewing area for the rest of the worksheet.

When you use the above features, you not only decrease time in entering data, but also decrease your chance of errors. Even if you are a skilled keyboardist, certain errors may creep in when you enter the same formula multiple times or try to enter data for specific people when you cannot view their names.

Editing Data

Editing Data

After entering data, you typically have some editing to complete. While evaluating the data, you may find some formulas that are incorrect, your client may require something added to the worksheet, you may not like the way the worksheet looks, or the worksheet may just need some tweaking to make it look better. You may need to move data. You may elect to insert rows or columns to move entire rows down and columns to the right. You may decide to delete rows or columns to move entire rows up and columns to the left. Or, you may move one or more cells. Moving cells is like completing a cut and paste. When you move cells, relative and absolute references will be changed by the number of rows and/or columns the cells were moved. This is different from copying cells.

Changing information in a cell is achieved in the same manner as a word processor. You may insert, delete, or change characters. When you are finished, you use the enter key to enter the corrections into the cell contents. You may clear the contents of the cell with or without clearing the format; or you may just clear the format.

Go To

When your worksheet becomes very large, you may want to use the go to feature to move to a specific cell and thus save scrolling time. You may use the indicators on the scroll bars that indicate the top row and left column of the viewing area.

Cell Formats

Number formats are covered in Chapter 12, and label formats are in Chapter 4; however, there are other types of formats available in worksheets for cells, rows, columns, and worksheets. Other formats for cells include background color, borders, alignment, and protection. You may add background color to cells that are often important in worksheet analysis just as you may add borders around cells that you want to emphasize. Be sure to add color only when you are printing the worksheet in color. Otherwise, use shading or patterns as the background. Many colors do not print well in black and white.

In addition to the normal alignments, spreadsheets also have the ability to rotate text in a cell and to center align across a range of selected cell. You may also fill a cell with one or more characters. Enter the character(s) and format the cell with a fill alignment to create a cell with duplicate characters. If you widen the column after a fill alignment, the number of characters will increase; and if you make the column narrower, the number of characters will decrease. For example, if you want a cell filled with dashes (–), type in one dash and then format the cell as a fill alignment. This will create a cell filled with dashes no matter how wide the column.

Cell Comments

Comments may be attached to any cell. They may be viewed, hidden, or printed. Comments are used in the same manner as adhesive notes on a report. They serve to informally communicate information to another person or yourself as a reminder of something or to add supportive information to a cell.

Cell Protection and Security

If your worksheet has sensitive data or has formulas that you do not want anyone to change, you may hide rows or columns and/or protect parts of your worksheet. Protection of cells restricts anyone from changing the contents of the protected cells without entering a password. Rows and columns may also be protected. Row height and column width may be adjusted to fit the as-displayed contents of the cells.

ELECTRONIC DOCUMENTATION

Internal documentation is very important in the maintenance of a project. You may not be the only person working on a project: You may need to turn the project over to someone else who will maintain and change it. Or, you may leave the company and someone else will take over your projects. For these reasons, internal or electronic documentation to the project is important as is the fact that you probably will not remember important facts about the project when you return in six months to a year to update it. Internal documentation is added electronically to the project in the form of comments or remarks about various aspects of the project. In the case of spreadsheets, you may want to add comments to various cells to explain where or how a formula was derived, how constant data were obtained, and so forth.

SECURITY OF A PROJECT

Once a project is completed, it is important that others entering data cannot change constant data or formulas either accidentally or otherwise. For this reason, formulas and constant data should be protected through the use of a password; thus, no one may change the data or formulas unless that person knows the password. Of course, the password should not be given freely. This would defeat its purpose. There should only be a few people who have the right to change data and formulas, and these are the ones who should have knowledge of the password. The password also should be changed on a regular basis.

Sensitive data also need protection in the way of hiding it. Data such as salaries and bonuses may not be public information. This data should be hidden and only seen by the people who have a password to unhide it.

In the case of spreadsheets, you may want to protect columns, rows, or worksheets and hide columns or rows of data. Again, only those who have a need to know or have the okay to change data should know the password(s).

Worksheet Names

Worksheet names may be changed to indicate the type of information found on the worksheet. The background of the worksheet may be changed from white to a background pattern. Worksheets may also be hidden.

Split Screens

When your worksheet becomes very large, you may want to scroll through two parts of it at the same time. To do this, you may split your screen horizontally, vertically, or both. This step saves time in scrolling between the two sections of the worksheet and eliminates trying to remember information from one section while you are scrolling to another section.

Workbook Recalculation

The worksheet is normally recalculated each time it is updated, so the numbers in the worksheet are up to date with all changes. Sometimes, however, when your worksheet is very large, it may take additional time to recalculate each time a data entry is made. In this case, you may turn on the manual calculation option, which means that you have control over when the worksheet is to be recalculated. The danger here is that visual or printed analysis may be accomplished on formulas that have not been recalculated.

Gridlines

Gridlines are those lines that surround each cell. They are there by default; however, you may turn them off. Some people prefer the lines whereas others think they make the worksheet harder to read.

Graphics, Charts, and Hyperlinks

Graphics, charts, and hyperlinks to internet sites or to other files may be inserted to add interest and functionality to the worksheet. Charts will be discussed later in this chapter. Macros may also be added to increase functionality (see Chapters 18 and 19).

Cell or Range Names

Cells and ranges of cells may be given a name. This name is used in formulas instead of the column/row name. For example, you may name A5 Length, B5 Width, and C5 Area. The formula for Area (C5) would be Length*Width. Naming cells increases readability of the formulas and makes the names easier to remember than A5 or B5. Note, however, named cells are absolute references. You may not use named cells in places where you need to copy formulas using relative references.

Try to name cells according to what they represent, such as PAYRATE for the rate of pay and HOURS for the number of hours worked during the pay period. Once you have named the cell(s), you must use the name exactly as you named it. For example, if you use HOURS for hours worked, then you must use HOURS at all times in referring to hours worked. You may not use HRS, Hour, or any other modification to the given cell name.

Just as in other packages, spell check, styles, auto correct, and other common features are available in a spreadsheet package. You may use the track feature to track changes made in a spreadsheet. Changes will be highlighted. Saved changes may create an audit trail if needed. Comments are attached to changed cells as to *what* changes were made, *who* made them, and *when* the changes were made.

Analyzing Information

Analyzing Information

Analysis of the information on a worksheet is important. The calculation of equations is only part of the results when using a spreadsheet program. After the worksheet is planned, created, and data has been entered, analysis on the information should be completed. Tools to help in this analysis include statistical functions, sorting, charts, and database functions. Statistical functions are discussed in Chapter 12. Charts will be discussed later in this chapter.

Sorting

Data may need to be sorted. **Sorting** is arranging the data in order, alphabetically or numerically and ascending or descending according to one or more reference columns. For example, it may be necessary to prepare a list of employees arranged in alphabetical order within each zip code and with the zip codes in numeric order. The zip codes would be the first column to order, the employees' last names would be the second. Sorting is usually completed on parallel columns. Excluding column headers, data associated with the columns to be sorted must be included in the sort range. If any data are excluded, then the sorted results will be incorrect. For example, if a list of employees includes the name, address, city, state, zip code, telephone number, department number, and salary, then the sort range must include all of these columns and all employee rows. Otherwise, the association of the columns not included in the sort range to the sort range columns will be lost. If the salary column was excluded, the salaries will no longer be associated with the right people.

The required results may include analysis on selected data, which may be accomplished through the use of database functions. Database functions include DAVERAGE, DCOUNT, DMAX, DMIN, and DSUM. These are similar to the AVERAGE, COUNT, MAX, MIN, and SUM functions except they process their calculations on selected data. One of the case studies in Chapter 14 includes the use of these functions.

Printing the Worksheet

Printing Worksheets

Page Setup

There are many options when printing a worksheet. Page setup involves the print page only. It has nothing to do with how the cells as displayed are viewed. You may specify whether you want to print grids. Many people do not like the looks of worksheets with grids printed, whereas other people prefer the grids because they find the sheets easier to read. You may specify where you want the page breaks. A large worksheet is broken down into blocks to be printed. You may designate these blocks by specifying the horizontal and the vertical page breaks. You may want the row and column numbers to be printed if you are specifying the location of a cell by the row and column name.

Be sure to specify the area of the worksheet that you want printed. It is best not to assume the computer will print only what you want. Always preview the page before printing it. There are usually adjustments to the margins, size, orientation, and so forth that you want to make. You may scale your worksheet on the printed page by specifying the percentage of normal or you may specify that the worksheet fit on the page. If the worksheet is too large, you may not be able to read it with this option because it will be printed too small.

You may want to center the worksheet on the page horizontally and/or vertically. This will center the worksheet within the margins. Many times the worksheet is different sizes on different pages because of the column width and the total number of columns and rows to be printed. Centering the worksheet ensures that it will not be located on the left side and at the top without consideration of the number of columns and rows to be printed on the page.

Headers and footers are available for printout only. It is nice to have the date and time of the printout. Many times you will print the worksheet several times a day. By having the date and time printed in the header or the footer, you will have a good sequential record of the printed worksheets.

As with the freeze panes feature, when viewing the cells as displayed, you may elect to specify certain rows and columns to be printed on every page. In the example of the instructor, he would want the names of the students to be printed on every page so that he can see who received what grades on all pages.

When a worksheet is printed, it prints the cells as displayed. However, you may select an option to have the cell contents printed too. It is nice to have a printed copy of the formulas for your client and for your project notebook.

Charts

Charts

Charts are a good way to analyze information. It is much easier to see the comparisons and growth of numbers in chart form than in table form. There are many kinds of charts including bar, column, line, pie, scatter, area, doughnut, radar, surface, bubble, stock, cylinder, cone, and pyramid charts. There are varieties of all these chart types, many of which are three dimensional. These charts may be used for multiple purposes. See Figure 13.3 for chart examples featuring sample data for the years 2000, 2001, 2002.

Bar, Column, Cylinder, Cone, and Pyramid Charts

The bar, column, cylinder, cone, and pyramid charts are all similar and are used to compare values across categories such as comparison of wheat, corn, and oats grown in three different states. The bar chart shows data in horizontal bars whereas the column chart shows data in vertical bars. The cylinder chart shows data as three-dimensional cylinders, the cone chart presents the data as three-dimensional cones, and the pyramid chart illustrates the data as three-dimensional pyramids. The bar charts and column charts may be shown as two- or three-dimensional charts.

Stacked and 100% Stacked

All five chart types have a choice of showing data as given, stacked, or 100% stacked charts. Stacked charts show all data values as one bar where each value is stacked on top of the total of the previous values. The final bar value is the total of all values. The 100% stacked chart is the same as a stacked chart except each value is a percentage of the whole. The final bar is 100%.

Line, Surface, and Area Charts

Line, surface, and area charts display data as lines or filled-in areas and are used to show trends across time or categories. For example, you may illustrate the profit for a company over the last year. Multiple lines would show profit over a year for five years. This would produce a line chart with five lines, each representing one year. Line charts have a choice of showing the data as given, a stacked chart, or a 100% stacked chart. These are all displayed as lines. The area chart is a stacked line chart with the area under the lines filled. The area chart displays data as a stacked chart or a 100% stacked chart. Both the line and the area charts may be two or three dimensional. The surface chart displays data across two dimensions in a continuous curve.

Pie and Doughnut Charts

The pie and doughnut charts show percentage of the whole with each section as a pie-shaped part of a circle or a doughnut. Budgets are many times shown as pie or doughnut

Examples of Chart Types

Sample Data

	2000	2001	2002
Company 1	230,340	543,789	568,976
Company 2	334,309	445,907	769,098
Company 3	235,653	245,674	543,765
Company 4	432,566	234,765	756,432

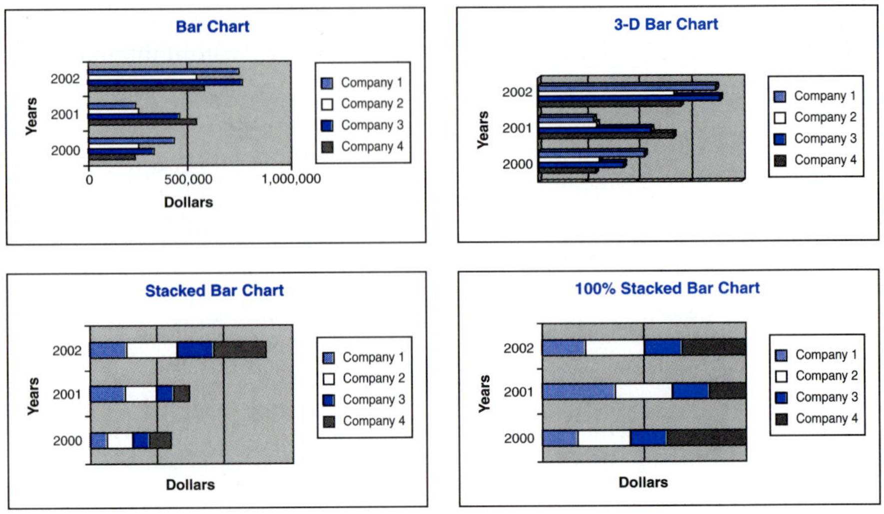

Examples of Chart Types

Sample Data

	2000	2001	2002
Company 1	230,340	543,789	568,976
Company 2	334,309	445,907	769,098
Company 3	235,653	245,674	543,765
Company 4	432,566	234,765	756,432

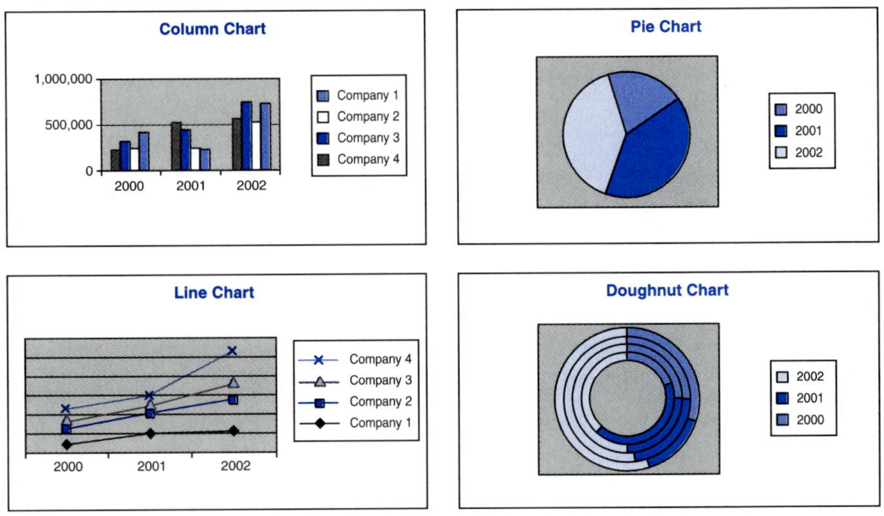

Figure 13.3 Charts

charts. Pie charts use one set of numbers for the whole, whereas doughnut charts may use multiple sets of numbers displayed as nested doughnuts. Pie charts and doughnut charts may be displayed with one or more parts exploded so that there is white space between the wedges. A pie chart may have one wedge linked to another pie chart or a bar chart that further breaks down the value of the wedge into parts.

Stock Chart

A stock chart displays and tracks the values of stocks. There are four options for stock charts: high-low-close, open-high-low-close, volume-high-low-close, and volume-open-high-low-close.

Scatter and Bubble Charts

The scatter and bubble charts display data as points in a two-dimensional space. The points may be connected through the use of smooth or straight lines. The bubble chart shows three-dimensional data in a two-dimensional space. Two values of data for a point designate the placement of the bubble in the two-dimensional space and the third value designates the size of each bubble. These charts are typically used when gathering primary research data.

Radar Chart

The radar chart displays data in relation to a center point. Each point is placed according to direction and value. A radar chart may be displayed with or without data points or with filled-in areas.

Selecting a Chart Type

The type of chart selection is important to the communication of data analysis. Here are some guidelines to follow:

1. Select the chart type according to the communication purpose of the chart.
2. Select three-dimensional charts only if they convey the analysis of the data better than a two-dimensional chart. Three-dimensional charts are interesting but they may be harder to read and understand.
3. Select colors in the chart to emphasize the important data.
4. Scale the data so the analysis is true. If you are comparing numbers in six digits in one set of data to numbers in two digits in another set of data, scale the six digits down to two or three and specify that the data is in 1000s or 10,000s. If not, the six-digit numbers will be displayed properly, but the two-digit numbers may show as a straight line. This will skew the results.
5. Add labels to increase the readability of the chart. Too many labels sometimes can clutter the chart.
6. Display the chart alongside or on top of the worksheet data if possible. People viewing the chart can then check the actual value of the numbers displayed.

Charts are invaluable in the analysis and presentation of data so long as the data are presented correctly.

Setting up the Data

It is important that data are set up correctly on the worksheet to communicate the desired analysis. Many times you will need to copy your values to another location on the worksheet. The series are categorical values in a column or bar chart. The length of each bar or column is indicated by the individual values associated with the categorical values. Figure 13.3 shows four series, one for each company. The length of each of the three bars or columns is indicated by the three values of each series. Each series has a bar or a column for each of the years. In a line chart each series is indicated by a different line; in a pie chart only one series is used. A doughnut chart shows each series on a different ring in the doughnut.

Spreadsheet Design

Spreadsheet Design

The general design of a spreadsheet should be well organized. Place data for each of the following items together: worksheet headings, model, revenues, expenses, other problem data, tables, summary, and data that will be changed often; also add the analysis section, including the database extractions, charts, data for the charts, and any other calculations required for analysis. See Figure 13.4.

Worksheet Headings

Worksheet headings should be at the top of the worksheet and include such items as the name of the company, the name of the worksheet developer, the date and time, the problem title, and any other data that are important to the identification of the worksheet.

Changeable Constants

Below the worksheet headings should be data that change often. This section may or may not be necessary for the problem. However, if you are including an analysis of how the inflation rate or the demand for your product will effect your profit in the next five years, you will want one worksheet location for the inflation rate and another for the demand rate data. Formulas requiring these two numbers will reference one location.

Main Body of Worksheet

Below the numbers that change, design the main part of the worksheet, including the row and column labels, the data text and values, and the formulas other than summary or analysis formulas. These entries will change depending on the type of worksheet you are developing. The main part of a worksheet for a forecast analysis of a business

Figure 13.4 Organization of a Spreadsheet

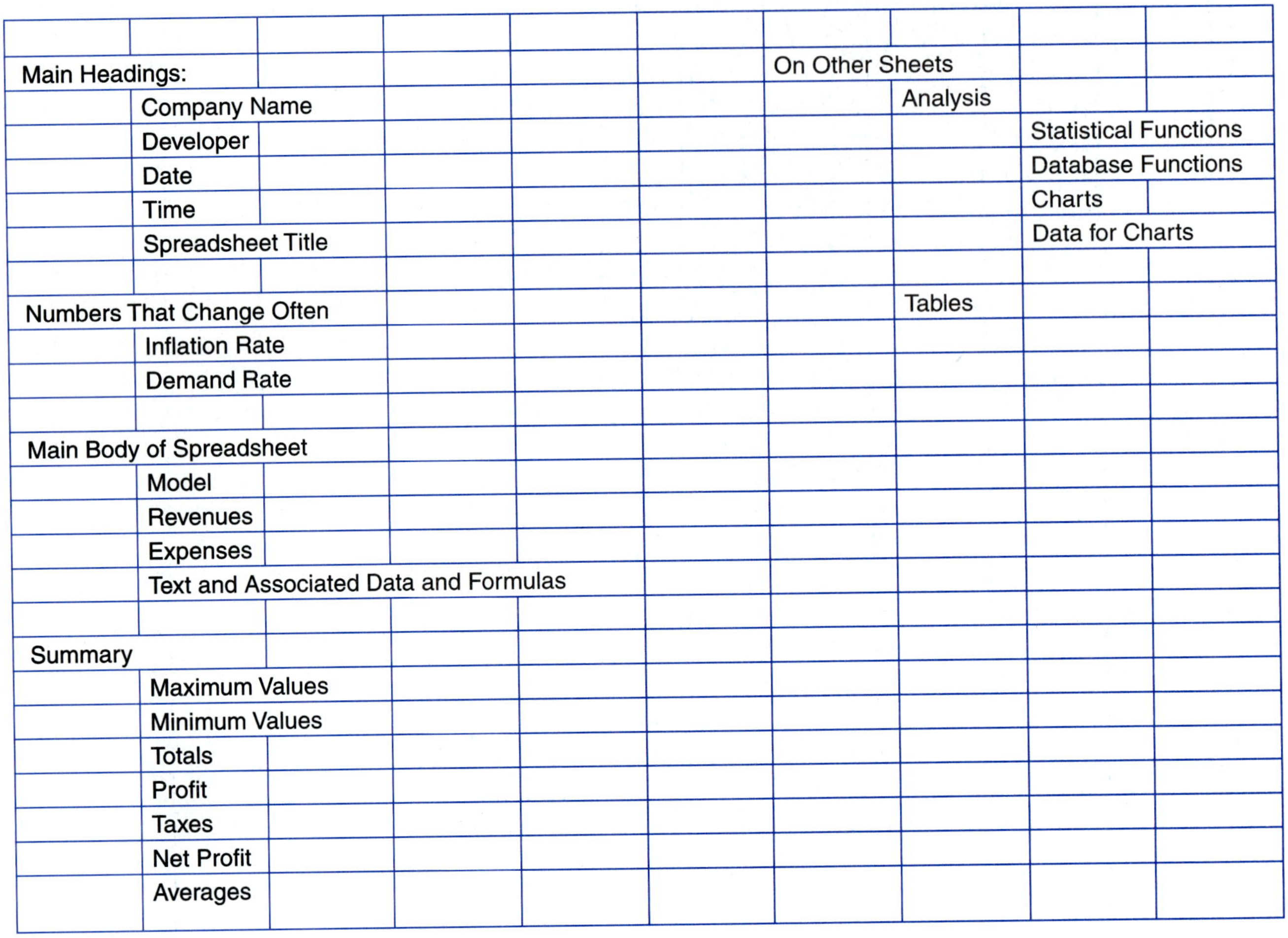

will be very different from a worksheet to record and calculate grades for a class. This section should be organized into subsections which may include a model, revenues, expenses, text with associated data, and intermediary analysis.

The Model

A model may or may not be needed. The **model** includes data about the problem such as the number of clients, the products produced or sold, the demand for the product, or manufacturing statistics. A grade sheet model includes the grade calculations for a test case student that earned perfect scores.

Other Parts of the Worksheet Body

A list of revenues and expenses is required for a budget, cost analysis, forecasting, and other cost accounting applications. It is important to include a complete list of revenues and expenses. If items within either of these lists are omitted, the worksheet will not be accurate. A budget analysis will not be accurate if, for example, the cost of insurance or recreation or an income from stocks is omitted.

When your list of items and associated data is complete, organize this list in some way, such as by column sorting or by categorizing according to year, company, or salesperson. A list of students should be alphabetized; a list of classes you have taken should be categorized into years. The classes may then be alphabetized within each year.

Subtotals

Intermediary analysis is usually in the form of subtotals. The analysis, however, may include an average, a maximum, or a minimum value of a subset of the data. For example, the calculation of a grade point average (GPA) may include the GPA for each semester and the overall GPA.

Summary

The summary section of a worksheet contains the results of the analysis. These may include profit, taxes, net profit, overall grade average, maximum grades on tests and homework, and average grades.

Analysis

The analysis section would include database function analysis, charts and accompanying data, and any other calculations required for analysis. Many times these items are placed on a separate sheet within the worksheet.

Tables

Tables also are usually placed on one or more separate sheets. Table types include tax tables, calendar tables, and medical tables.

Worksheets that are well planned and organized will require less time when entering data and checking the results, and they provide easy readability and quick access to pertinent information.

Spreadsheet Planning Guide

Spreadsheet Planning Guide

The spreadsheet planning guide is for your use while planning a worksheet. See Figure 13.5. Step one helps to identify the problem. As in the other planning guides, this step is a short narrative describing the problem to be solved.

The PAC

Step two utilizes the PAC (problem analysis chart) as described in Chapter 1. It simplifies the separation of pertinent data of a problem from the extras. The given data, the required results, the processes and formulas, and the description of the audience are placed in the appropriate boxes. As part of step two, you should describe the knowledge base of the developer and the audience.

Step three of the spreadsheet planning guide provides a place to list possible solutions for the problem. Step four provides a place to identify the chosen solution and further identifies the requirements to complete it. In step five, you develop the problem solution. Parts of this development include a place to record requirements for printing, files to be imported, analysis to be completed including flowcharts of the IF and CHOOSE functions, worksheet templates, and chart requirements.

The worksheet template includes labels, values that do not change often, and formulas. The template should be organized for easy entry into the computer. The following steps may help you to develop the template.

1. Use step five to plan your worksheet. Use extra pages of the worksheet if you need more columns and/or rows.
2. Enter the main headings into the cells as you would want them on the computer.
3. Label data that will be changed often, and designate the cell that will contain the values. Use one cell for the label and the cell to the right for the value of the related datum.
4. In the main section of the worksheet, bracket the different areas for like data, such as the rows for revenues and expenses to help organize your worksheet. If your worksheet will be large, you may want to use a different sheet for each section, one for the revenues and another for the expenses, for example.
5. Label the rows and columns for the main section.
6. Add the values that will not change often.
7. Add the formulas. Remember to begin formulas with an equal sign and to add the dollar signs to all absolute references in your formulas. If a formula is to be copied, write the formula once and then indicate the cells to copy the formula to by using a circled C in the first cell where the formula will be copied to and an arrow from the circled C through all cells where the formula will be copied. (See Figures 13.6 through 13.8 at the end of this chapter.)

Figure 13.5 Spreadsheet Planning Guide

SPREADSHEET PLANNING GUIDE

Name of Document: ______________________________ Date: ______________

Location of Electronic File: ______________________________

Name: ______________________________

Name of Client: ______________________________

Step 1: Identify the Problem by Writing the Problem Statement.

Step 2: Understand the Problem.

The PAC:

Given Data	Required Results
Processes and Formulas	The Audience

Figure 13.5 (continued)

Required Knowledge of the Problem to Develop the Document:

Required Knowledge of the Audience:

Step: 3 **Identify Valid Alternative Methods to Solve the Problem.**

Step 4: **Select the Best Method to Solve the Problem from the List of Alternative Solutions.**

Step 5: **Plan Your Solution.**

Software to be used: ____________ Spreadsheets: ____________

Margins for Printing:

Top: ____________ Top Printer: ____________
Bottom: ____________ Bottom Printer: ____________
Left: ____________ Left Printer: ____________
Right: ____________ Right Printer: ____________
Header: ____________ Top Printer: ____________
Footer: ____________ Bottom Printer: ____________

(continued)

Figure 13.5 Spreadsheet Planning Guide

***Step 5:* Plan Your Solution. (con't)**

Files to be imported:

File	Description	Use	Location

Rows to be printed on every page: ______________________________

Columns to be printed on every page: ______________________________

Paper Size: ______________________ Paper Color: ______________________

Orientation: ______________________ Color/B&W: ______________________

Gridlines: ______________ Row and Column Headings Printed: ______________

Header Contents:

Footer Contents:

Analysis required:

Figure 13.5 (continued)

Number Format: G = General N = Number C = Currency A = Accounting F = Fraction P = Percentage D = Date T = Time S = Scientific
Text Format: B = Bold I = Italic U = Underline

Page 1

	Format	A	Format	B	Format	C	Format	D	Format	E	Format	F
1												
2												
3												
4												
5												
6												
7												
8												
9												
10												
11												
12												
13												
14												

Figure 13.5 Spreadsheet Planning Guide

Page___

Number Format: G = General N = Number C = Currency A = Accounting F = Fraction P = Percentage D = Date T = Time S = Scientific
Text Format: B = Bold I = Italic U = Underline

	Format		Format		Format		Format		Format		Format	

Figure 13.5 (continued)

Data to Be Charted	Location of Data	Chart Type

(continued)

Figure 13.5 Spreadsheet Planning Guide

Step 6: Evaluate the Solution

List the Criteria for Evaluating the Completed Document: Include test numbers for evaluating the formulas.

Postanalysis Required:

8. Add labels and formulas in the summary lines.
9. Add any formulas for the analysis requirements.
10. Evaluate your plan for completeness of information, organization, deletion and addition of rows and columns, and so forth.
11. Check your formulas for accuracy.

Step six involves the evaluation process. List the criteria for evaluation, including test results with the results of your worksheet, and list the required postanalysis. The postanalysis is always an important part of worksheets, because most problems are not solved without one. The postanalysis should answer questions such as:

1. What happens to the profit when both inflation and demand for our product increase? (Use when completing a business analysis.)
2. How can we increase our savings? (Use for a budget analysis.)
3. Should we buy another business?
4. Should we expand our store to include more square footage?
5. How should we finance our car?
6. How much profit can I project during the upcoming sale?
7. How should we expand our product line?
8. What grade do I need on the final exam to get an A in my class?

Postanalysis is the essence of worksheets.

After finishing your planning guide, you should be ready to enter your worksheet plan into the computer. If your plan is complete, you should have very few modifications after the initial entry to make your worksheet correct. Lastly, add borders, color, background, and so forth to make the worksheet more aesthetically pleasing and easier to read and understand.

Some Common Formulas

Common Formulas

There are a few common formulas used in worksheet problems. These are used to increase a number by a percentage, to total numbers, and to calculate a percentage of a sum. Additional information about formulas is presented in Chapters 12 and 14.

Total of a Group of Numbers

To find a total of a group of numbers:

If there are only two or three numbers, then =A1+B1. If there are more than two or three numbers to sum, then use the SUM function =SUM(A1:E1) or SUM(A1:E1, G5, A3:E3).

Increase or Decrease a Number by a Percentage

To increase a number by a percentage:

The formula to increase a number by a percentage is =A10*(1+A4), where A10 is the number to be increased and A4 is the percentage increase in decimal form such as 0.1 for 10%. If the number is to be decreased, then the percentage would be a negative number.

If the increase is to be compounded, the formula is =A10*(1+A4)^A5, where A5 is the number of compounding periods. For example, if you invested $1,000 for four years at 0.05% compounded yearly, A10 is 1,000, A4 is 0.05, and A5 is 4. The resultant will be the amount of money you will have at the end of the four years.

Calculate a Percentage of a Sum

To calculate a percentage of a sum of values:

The formula to calculate a percentage of a sum is =E5/SUM(E1:E10), where E5 is one of the values in a range. The resultant would be the percentage of the value of E5 to the sum of all numbers in the range. For example, if you would like to know what percentage your rent (E5) is of your total expenses (SUM(E1:E10)), you would use this formula. The numerator of the formula does not have to be part of the range, for example, if you want to know what percentage your rent (E5) is of your income (E15:E20). Your rent (E5) is not part of your income so it would not be part of the range (E15:E20). The resultant cell as displayed is formatted as a percent.

Sample Problems

Calculating a Student's GPA

The following are sample worksheet problems. Because they are small problems, only step five of the planning guide is used. Problem 1 involves the calculation of the overall GPA for a student. Problem 2 is the amortization of a house loan. Problem 3 is the calculation of a sale item that is decreased each day over a five-day period.

Sample Problem 1: Calculating a Student's GPA

Develop step five of spreadsheet planning guide to calculate a student's overall GPA. Following is a list of the courses taken, the units, and the letter grade.

History	3	A
Calculus	4	B
Economics	3	B
Archery	1	A
Word Processing	3	A
Biology	5	C

Figure 13.6 shows step five of the spreadsheet planning guide for this problem.

Sample Problem 2: Amortization Chart

Amortization Chart

Develop step five of the spreadsheet planning guide for an amortization chart of a $30,000 loan borrowed at 8% interest for 10 years. Payments will be monthly. Figure 13.7 shows step five of the planning guide for this problem.

Sample Problem 3: Worksheet Template

Worksheet Template

The local hardware store has a five-day sale each month of six items. Each day the price is dropped 10% from the previous day's price; however, the sale price may not drop below the wholesale price. The store would like a worksheet template on which they can enter the six items and the associated data each month, and have the computer calculate the prices per day for each of the sales items. Develop step five of a spreadsheet planning guide for this template. See Figure 13.8.

Number Format: G = General N = Number C = Currency A = Accounting F = Fraction P = Percentage D = Date T = Time S = Scientific
Text Format: B = Bold I = Italic U = Underline

Page 1

	Format	A	Format	B	Format	C	Format	D	Format	E	Format	F
1	B/U	MATT'S GRADE POINT AVERAGE			D	= TODAY( )						
2												
3	B/C	CLASS	B/C	UNITS	B/C	GRADE	B/C	GRADE POINTS				
4	L	HISTORY	N/0	3	C	A	N/0	= B4*IF(C4 = "A", 4, IF(C4 = "B", 3, IF(C4 = "C", 2, IF(C4 = "D", 1, 0))))				
5		CALCULUS		4		B						
6		ECONOMICS		3		B						
7		ARCHERY		1		A				ALTERNATIVE FORMULA:		
8		WORD PROCESSING		3		A				FOR D4: = B4* VLOOKUP(B4, $E$10: $E$14, 2)		
9		BIOLOGY		5		C						
10									L	A	N/0	4
11	L/C	GPA =		= SUM(D4: D9)/SUM(B4: B9)					L	B	N/0	3
12									L	C	N/0	2
13									L	D	N/0	1
14									L	F	N/0	0

Figure 13.6 Spreadsheet Planning Guide for Sample Problem 1

Number Format: G = General N = Number C = Currency A = Accounting F = Fraction P = Percentage D = Date T = Time S = Scientific
Text Format: B = Bold I = Italic U = Underline

Page 1

	Format	A	Format	B	Format	C	Format	D	Format	E	Format	F
1	B/U	LOAN AMORTIZATION					B/D	= TODAY( )				Name
2				PRINCIPAL =	N/2							
3				INTEREST RATE =	P/2							
4				YEARS =	N/0							
5				PAYMENT =	N/2	= PMT(C2, C3/12, C4*12)						
6	B/C	PERIOD	B/C	BEG. BAL.	B/C	INTEREST PAID	B/C	AMT TO PRINCIPAL	B/C	ENDING BAL.		
7	N/0/C	1	N/2	= C2	N/2	= B7*$C$3/12	N/2	= $C$5 - C7	N/2	= B7 - D7		
8		FILL +1		= E7		C		C		C		
9				C								
10												
11												
12												
13												
14	To 126	To Row 126	To 126	To Row 126	To 126	To Row 126	To 126	To Row 126	To 126	To Row 126		

Figure 13.7 Spreadsheet Planning Guide for Sample Problem 2

Number Format: G = General N = Number C = Currency A = Accounting F = Fraction P = Percentage D = Date T = Time S = Scientific
Text Format: B = Bold I = Italic U = Underline

Page 1

	Format	A	Format	B	Format	C	Format	D	Format	E	Format	F
1	B/L	JOHN'S HARDWARE					L/D	= TODAY( )				Name
2												
3			B/C	ITEM 1	B/C	ITEM 2	B/C	ITEM 3	B/C	ITEM 4	B/C	ITEM 5
4	B/L	DESC.	L		L		L		L		L	
5		WHOLESALE PRICE	N/2		N/2		N/2		N/2		N/2	
6		RETAIL PRICE										
7		DAY 1		=IF(B6*.1<B5,		B6*.1, B5)						
8		DAY 2		C		C						
9		DAY 3										
10		DAY 4										
11		DAY 5										
12												
13												
14												

Figure 13.8 Spreadsheet Planning Guide for Sample Problem 3

Summary

A spreadsheet software program allows the user to create an electronic matrix of labels, values, and formulas that is recalculated each time the matrix is updated. The matrix is made up of cells created at the intersections of rows and columns. The cells are named by the column letter followed by the row number. The cell contents contain the entered data, and the cells as displayed contain the formatted labels, values, and the results of the calculated formulas.

Formulas are copied using relative and absolute cell references. Features of a worksheet include those for entering data, editing data, analyzing information, and printing the worksheet.

Analysis of data includes sorting data, using statistical functions and database functions, and creating charts. Using this information, the end user can then complete a post-analysis to finish the solution to the problem.

Charts are pictorial views of numbers. Chart types include bar, column, line, pie, scatter, area, doughnut, radar, surface, bubble, stock, cylinder, cone, and pyramid charts. Within each of these categories of charts are subtypes such as stacked, 100% stacked, and three-dimensional charts.

A worksheet should be organized in order to locate pertinent information and to create an aesthetically pleasing document. Analysis and tables may be placed on separate sheets.

The spreadsheet planning guide is used to plan a worksheet before going to the computer. Sample problems include configuring a GPA, a loan amortization, and sale percentages.

Key Words

Absolute cell reference
Cell
Charts
Column
Gridlines
Model
Range of cells
Relative cell reference
Row
Sort

Exercises

1. What is a worksheet?
2. How is a cell defined?
3. What can be put into a cell?
4. How does the computer distinguish between a text entry and a formula in a cell?
5. Why should you try to copy formulas as much as possible?
6. Why should you try to reference formulas as much as possible?
7. What is the difference between a relative cell reference and an absolute cell reference in a formula?
8. Why would you use a relative cell reference?

9. Why would you use an absolute cell reference?
10. What does the freeze panes feature accomplish?
11. Name three chart types and explain under what conditions they would be used.
12. Why should the placement of information in a worksheet be organized?

Problems

1. You are planning to buy a new car. Your budget shows that you can spend up to $250 a month for a car payment. You have found that car loans are over a five-year period and the best interest rate is 8% yearly. Develop steps five and six of a spreadsheet planning guide to calculate the maximum amount that you can borrow to buy a car. Add to this plan the amortization of a loan for this maximum value.
2. The bookstore at the mall is having a three-day sale on their tote book bags. They have 50 bags to sell. They buy the bags at $6 a piece. They have a 50% markup rate. During the sale the bags will be marked down 10% the first day and 20% the following two days. However, the store still desires to make a 10% profit on each bag and therefore the sale price cannot fall below 10% over the wholesale price. Assume they sell 10 bags the first day, 15 bags the second day, and the remaining bags on the third day. Develop a spreadsheet planning guide to calculate the profit from the bags.
3. Select one of your classes and develop a spreadsheet planning guide to calculate your grade in the class.
4. Develop a spreadsheet planning guide to analyze your options if you win $1,000,000 in the lottery. Is it better to take one lump sum of $400,000 or take $50,000 a year for 20 years.
5. Develop step five of a spreadsheet planning guide to calculate the amount of money you would need to put away per month for 18 years to have $50,000 for expenses when your child goes to college.

Chapter 14

Spreadsheet Case Studies

Overview

Case Study 1: Budget
Case Study 2: Costing
Case Study 3: Database Functions

Objectives

When you have finished this chapter, you should be able to:

1. Problem solve and develop plans to create complex spreadsheets for use in such cases as budgets, costing, and calculations on selected data.
2. Use the spreadsheet planning guide and the six problem-solving steps to develop a solution for a problem that requires the use of spreadsheet software.

Chapter 14 presents three case studies that require the use of spreadsheet software to solve a problem. Case study 1 involves the creation of a budget which also tracks actual revenues and expenses. Case study 2 is a costing problem, in which you calculate how much it will cost to build chairs, at what price the chairs should be sold, and where the break-even point is due to the cost of new equipment. Case study 3 involves the use of database functions to calculate information on selected data. A spreadsheet planning guide is developed for each of these cases.

Case Study 1: Budget

Case Study 1: Budget

Joe is going to college in the fall. His parents promised him that they will help pay for his college education upon several conditions. First, they have agreed to send him a check each month if he creates a budget and sends them a monthly summary sheet that shows actual total income and actual total expenses. Joe has the normal monthly expenses of rent, food, utilities, gas for his car, supplies for school, recreation, and a miscellaneous fund for unexpected expenses. In August and January he has tuition, books, and first of the semester supplies for school. In July he has car registration and car insurance. Joe's parents have offered to keep him on their medical insurance and to pay for any extra medical costs. Another condition is that Joe establish a savings account into which he is to add at least $100 each month. Joe's parents are starting the savings account with $2,000. Each month Joe should restart his checking account with a $200 balance. Any extra money at the end of the month in excess of $200 should be deposited into the savings account. If the budget for the checking account balance is below $200, he may use money in the savings account to balance his budget.

Figure 14.1 presents a spreadsheet planning guide for this case study. Notice the organization of the worksheet beginning on page 6 of the spreadsheet planning guide. Also note that rows 1 through 14 are on pages 6 to 8 extending from column A through column R, and rows 15 to 18 are on pages 9 to 11. Rows 31 to 51 are copied from the budget range. The headings are at the very top. The next big section is the budget. Within the budget section are three parts: Joe's income, his expenses, and a summary line. There are subtotals at the bottom of the income section and the expenses section. The last large section is the actuals, which is what Joe actually receives and spends. There are also three parts to this section: Joe's income, his expenses, and a summary line. The summary lines include the beginning balance, the adjusted ending balance, the amount that is transferred to or from savings, and the adjusted savings account balance. The adjusted ending balance will always be $200.

The income and the expense headings are in column 1. The next 12 columns are the 12 months of the year. The last column contains the total of each income and each expense item. The row following the last entry in the income and in the expense sections are for the monthly totals. The summary section contains rows for the balance forward (the ending balance from the last month), the ending balance for the month, amount to transfer either to or from savings, and the adjusted savings balance. The adjusted ending balance will be $200 and therefore is not shown. Study these equations in the planning guide to understand how the numbers are calculated. Can you think of another set of formulas to use to get the same answers?

The actuals section is almost identical to the budget section with two exceptions. First, the values of the income and expenses are the actual values that occurred during the month. Second, there are two extra rows that calculate the difference between the budgeted total income and the budgeted total expenses for the month and the values that actually occurred.

Examine Figure 14.1. Step one states the problem. Step two uses the problem analysis chart to glean the required information from the problem including the given data, the required results, the formulas, and a description of the audience. Step three lists various methods of solving the problem. Step four identifies the preferred method of solving the problem, and step five presents the solution development. It includes printing instructions, files to be imported, header and footer contents, analysis requirements, chart requirements, and the design of the worksheet template. The worksheet template should include labels, constant values, formulas, cell formats, and the location where cells are copied. When you are reading the worksheet template, be attentive to the rows and columns on the various pages. Notice how the copying is planned. First copy an upper left-side cell down to form a column, then copy the column across to form the rows. Also notice that values are referenced and then copied. For example, the income from Joe's parents is entered in B5. C5 contains the formula =B5. The contents of C5 are then copied to the range D5:M5. When you copy, the format is also copied. Step six lists the criteria for evaluating the solution and a list of postanalysis required to finish the solution to the problem. Pie charts are planned for the budgeted income, the actual income, and expenses.

Case Study 2: Costing

Case Study 2: Costing

Gary's Furniture Manufacturing Company would like to add a new chair to their product line. They need to know how much the chair will cost to manufacture and determine the wholesale cost. They would like to sell this chair for 50% above the cost of manufacturing.

Figure 14.1 Spreadsheet Planning Guide for Case Study 1

SPREADSHEET PLANNING GUIDE

Name of Document: My Budget Date: 8/3/2002

Location of Electronic File: c:\my data\school\personal\

Name: Joe College

Name of Client: Mom and Dad

Step 1: Identify the Problem by Writing the Problem Statement.

Mom and Dad have promised to help pay for my college education. They have agreed to send me a check each month on the condition that I create a budget. I will be getting my own apartment. I will work 20 hours a week. My normal monthly expenses will be rent, food, utilities, gas for my car, supplies for school, recreation, and a miscellaneous fund for unexpected expenses. In August and January, I have tuition, books, and first of the semester supplies for school. In July, my car registration and car insurance are due. Mom and Dad said they will be able to keep me on their medical insurance and that they would pay for any extra medical costs. Mom and Dad want me to establish a savings account so I will have money after I finish school to relocate and to start a career. I am to add at least $100 each month to this saving account. They will start this account with $2,000 to help with my first semester's expenses. Each month I will start with a $200 balance in my checking account. If I have checking account money over $200 at the end of the month, I should put the extra over $200 into my savings account. If the ending balance is below $200, then I should transfer money from my savings account to balance my budget. Mom and Dad need to know the required amount of their monthly check to me.

Step 2: Understand the Problem.

The PAC:

Given Data	Required Results
Income: Parents, work, other Expenses: Rent, food, utilities, gas, supplies, fun, misc., tuition, books, supplies for semester, car registration, and auto insurance	Budgeted amounts compared with actual amounts spent Savings amounts How much do I need from Mom and Dad each month?
Processes and Formulas	**The Audience**
Summations of income and expenses Subtractions of budgeted amounts and actual amounts	Mom and Dad

(continued)

Figure 14.1 Spreadsheet Planning Guide for Case Study 1

Step 2: Understand the Problem. (con't)

Required Knowledge of the Problem to Develop the Document:
What my projected income and expenses will be each month.

Required Knowledge of the Audience:
Nothing extra.

Step 3: Identify Valid Alternative Methods to Solve the Problem.

a. Charts:
   1. pie charts or column charts
   2. monthly values, running totals for year, or just year-end totals
b. Intermix budget with actual values or separate the budget from the actual values.
c. Place budget on one computer spreadsheet page and actuals on another sheet or both on one spreadsheet page.

Step 4: Select the Best Method to Solve the Problem from the List of Alternative Solutions.

a. Charts: Will use pie charts to show running totals of budgeted and actual values for income and expenses.
b. Separate the budget from the actual values.
c. Place both on same page.

Step 5: Plan Your Solution.

Software to be used: Spreadsheets

Margins for Printing:

Top:	1.0	Top Printer:	0.25
Bottom:	1.0	Bottom Printer:	0.5
Left:	1.5	Left Printer:	0.25
Right:	1.5	Right Printer:	0.25
Header:	0.5	Top Printer:	0.25
Footer:	0.6	Bottom Printer:	0.25

Figure 14.1 (continued)

Files to be imported: **None**

File	Description	Use	Location

Rows to be printed on every page: 1–3

Columns to be printed on every page: A

Paper Size: 8½ × 11 Paper Color:

Orientation: Landscape Color/B&W B&W

Gridlines: Yes Row and Column Headings Printed: No

Header Contents:

	Joe's Budget	

Footer Contents:

Page XX of XX		

Analysis required:

a. Yearly totals
b. Monthly totals
c. Monthly balances
d. Compare actuals with budgeted amounts
e. Track savings account

(continued)

Figure 14.1 Spreadsheet Planning Guide for Case Study 1

Number Format: G = General N = Number C = Currency A = Accounting F = Fraction P = Percentage D = Date T = Time S = Scientific
Text Format: B = Bold I = Italic U = Underline

Page 1

	Format	A	Format	B	Format	C	Format	D	Format	E	Format	F
1	B/U/L	JOE'S BUDGET		AND ACTUALS					D/C	= TODAY( )		
2												
3	B/L	BUDGET										
4	B/C	INCOME ITEMS	B/C	AUGUST		SEPTEMBER		OCTOBER		NOVEMBER		DECEMBER
5	L	MOM & DAD	N/2		N/2	= B5						
6	↓	WORK	↓			(C) ↓		(C) →				
7		OTHER										
8		TOTAL INCOME		= sum(B5:B7)		(C) →						
9												
10	B/C	EXPENSE ITEMS		COPY FROM		RANGE B4:N4 →						
11	L	RENT	N/2		N/2	= B11						
12	↓	FOOD	↓		↓	(C) ↓		(C) →				
13		UTILITIES										
14		GAS										

Figure 14.1 (continued)

Number Format: G = General N = Number C = Currency A = Accounting F = Fraction P = Percentage D = Date T = Time S = Scientific
Text Format: B = Bold I = Italic U = Underline

Page 2

	Format	G	Format	H	Format	I	Format	J	Format	K	Format	L
1												
2												
3												
4	B/C	JANUARY	B/C	FEBRUARY	B/C	MARCH	B/C	APRIL	B/C	MAY	B/C	JUNE
5												
6		Continue	Ⓒ →									
7												
8												
9												
10		Continue	Copy →									
11												
12		Continue	Copy →									
13												
14												

Figure 14.1 Spreadsheet Planning Guide for Case Study 1

Number Format: G = General N = Number C = Currency A = Accounting F = Fraction P = Percentage D = Date T = Time S = Scientific
Text Format: B = Bold I = Italic U = Underline

Page 3

	Format	M	Format	N	Format	O	Format	P	Format	Q	Format	R
1												
2												
3												
4	B/C	JULY	B/C	AUGUST								
5			N/2	=SUM(B5:M5)								
6		Continue → Copy		©								
7												
8												
9												
10		Continue Copy →										
11			N/2	=SUM(B11:M11)								
12		Continue → Copy		©								
13												
14												

Figure 14.1 (continued)

Number Format: G = General N = Number C = Currency A = Accounting F = Fraction P = Percentage D = Date T = Time S = Scientific
Text Format: B = Bold I = Italic U = Underline

Page 4

	Format	A	Format	B	Format	C	Format	D	Format	E	Format	F
15	L	SUPPLIES	N/2		N/2	(C)						
16		FUN						(C)				
17		MISC										
18		TUITION				0						
19		BOOKS/SUPPLIES				(C)		(C)				
20		CAR REG.		0								
21		CAR INS.		0								
22		SAVINGS		100.00		= B23						
23		TOTAL EXP		=SUM(B11:B22)								
24								(C)				
25		BEG. BAL		200.00		= B25						
26		END. BAL		=B25+B8-B24		(C)						
27		AMT TO/FROM SAVINGS		=B26-200		(C)						
28		ADJ. SAVINGS		= 2000 + B23 + B27		= B28 + C23 + C27						

Figure 14.1 Spreadsheet Planning Guide for Case Study 1

Number Format: G = General N = Number C = Currency A = Accounting F = Fraction P = Percentage D = Date T = Time S = Scientific

Text Format: B = Bold I = Italic U = Underline

Page 5

	Format	G	Format	H	Format	I	Format	J	Format	K	Format	L
15		Continue										
16		Ⓒ →		→		→		→		→		→
17												
18				0								
19				Ⓒ		Ⓒ →		→		→		→
20		0		↓								
21		0		↓								
22												
23												
24		Continue Copy →		→		→		→		→		→
25												
26												
27												
28												

Figure 14.1 (continued)

Number Format: G = General N = Number C = Currency A = Accounting F = Fraction P = Percentage D = Date T = Time S = Scientific
Text Format: B = Bold I = Italic U = Underline

Page 6

	Format	M	Format	N	Format	O	Format	P	Format	Q	Format	R
15				Ⓒ								
16		Continue Ⓒ →										
17												
18												
19												
20		0										
21		0										
22												
23												
24		Continue Ⓒ →										
25												
26												
27												
28												

Figure 14.1 Spreadsheet Planning Guide for Case Study 1

Number Format: G = General N = Number C = Currency A = Accounting F = Fraction P = Percentage D = Date T = Time S = Scientific

Text Format: B = Bold I = Italic U = Underline

Page 7

	Format	A	Format	B	Format	C	Format	D	Format	E	Format	F
29	B/L	ACTUAL INCOME AND EXPENSES										
30												
31–55		COPY A4:N28 to HERE										
56	L	DIFF. of INCOME	N/2	= B8 - B35		(C) →						To M56 AND M57
57	L	DIFF. of EXPENSES	N/2	= B24 - B51								

Figure 14.1 (continued)

Data to Be Charted	Location of Data	Chart Type
BUDGET INCOME	DATA: N5:N8 LABELS: A5:A8	PIE
BUDGET EXPENSES	DATA: N11:N22 LABELS: A11:A22	PIE
ACTUAL INCOME	DATA: N32:N34 LABLES: A32:A34	PIE
ACTUAL EXPENSES	DATA: N37:N49 LABELS: 137:A49	PIE

(continued)

Figure 14.1 Spreadsheet Planning Guide for Case Study 1.

> ***Step 6:*** **Evaluate the Solution.**
>
> *List the Criteria for Evaluating the Completed Document:* Include test numbers for evaluating the formulas.
>
> **a.** Does each month's checking account start with $200?
> **b.** Does the savings account get updated by $100 or more each month?
> **c.** Does the total of the yearly amounts equal the total of the monthly amounts?
> **d.** Can I show Mom and Dad how much to send me each month?
> **e.** Do my actuals come close to my budgeted amounts?
> **f.** Can Mom and Dad easily understand the spreadsheet?
> **g.** Is the spreadsheet easy to maintain?
>
> *Postanalysis Required:*
>
> **a.** What is the monthly amount of money required from Mom and Dad?
> **b.** At the end of the year, how will I need to adjust my budget?
> **c.** Will I have at least $1,200 in my savings account at the end of the first year?

They need to purchase new equipment at a cost of $5,000 for making the chair. The wood for the legs and the back costs $40 per chair. The material for the seat costs $10. Labor costs are $30 per hour. In the assembly line, the person who makes the legs can turn out 20 per hour. The person who makes the seats and backs can finish 8 each per hour. Sixteen seats can be upholstered in one hour. The finishing costs of this chair are $4 per chair, and it takes one hour to sand and finish.

Create a spreadsheet planning guide that will produce the cost to make the chair, the wholesale cost, and how many chairs it will take before they break even due to the purchase of new equipment.

Figure 14.2 presents the spreadsheet planning guide for case study 2. The cost of the materials is given. Labor costs must be calculated from the hourly labor cost. The total cost of manufacturing of a chair is the total of the materials and labor. The wholesale value is the manufacturing cost increased by 50%. The break-even point is calculated by dividing the cost of the equipment by the difference between the wholesale cost and the manufacture cost.

Case Study 3: Database Functions

Case Study 3: Database Functions

Judy's Ice Cream Shoppe has 20 employees. Four of these are full time and 16 are part time working from 10 to 20 hours per week. The full-time employees make a weekly salary of between $500 and $600 per week. Her part-time employees are paid hourly at $6.50 to $10 an hour depending upon how long they have worked at the store. Judy would like to know the following information about her employees.

1. What is the average number of hours the part-time employees work?
2. How many of the part-time employees work 10 hours?
3. How many of the part-time employees work 20 hours?
4. What are the total hours worked by the part-time employees?
5. What is the average wage for the full-time employees?
6. What is the average hourly rate for the part-time employees?

Figure 14.2 Spreadsheet Planning Guide for Case Study 2

SPREADSHEET PLANNING GUIDE

Name of Document: Chair Cost Date: 6/16/2002

Location of Electronic File: my data\work\garys furniture\

Name: Gary's Furniture Manufacturing Company

Name of Client: Joe Costing

Step 1: Identify the Problem by Writing the Problem Statement.

Gary's Furniture Manufacturing Company would like to add a new chair to their line of furniture. They need to know how much the chair will cost to manufacture and the wholesale cost. They would like to sell this chair for 50% above the cost of making the chair. They need to purchase new equipment for manufacturing the chair at a cost of $5,000. The wood for the legs and the back costs $40 per chair. The material for the seat costs $10. Labor costs are $30 per hour. In the assembly line, the person who makes the legs can turn out 20 per hour. The person who makes the seats and backs can finish 8 per hour. Sixteen seats can be upholstered in one hour. The finishing costs of this chair are $4 per chair and it takes one hour to sand and finish. They would like to know the cost to make the chair, the wholesale cost, and how many chairs it will take before they break even due to the purchase of new equipment.

Step 2: Understand the Problem.

The PAC:

Given Data	Required Results
Sell chair for 50% above cost Purchase equipment: $5,000 Wood for legs/back: $40 Material for seat: $10 Finishing costs: $4 Labor costs: $30 per hour Legs: 20/hour Seats/back: 8/hour Seats upholstered: 16/hour Finishing: 1 hour	Cost of chair to manufacture Wholesale cost Break-even number of chairs to sell
Processes and Formulas	**The Audience**
Calculate cost of labor Calculate total costs Calculate wholesale cost: =manufactured cost *1.5 Calculate break-even point: =5,000/(manufactured cost *0.5)	Owners of Company

(continued)

Figure 14.2 Spreadsheet Planning Guide for Case Study 2

Step 2: Understand the Problem. (con't)

Required Knowledge of the Problem to Develop the Document:
Costs of manufacturing a chair

Required Knowledge of the Audience:
Knowledge of the chair manufacturing business

Step 3: Identify Valid Alternative Methods to Solve the Problem.

a. In a labor cost formulas, reference hourly labor cost to a cell or use it as a constant in each formula.
b. Separate material costs from labor costs or combine them.
c. Put required results at the top of the spreadsheet or at the bottom.

Step 4: Select the Best Method to Solve the Problem from the List of Alternative Solutions.

a. In labor cost formulas, reference hourly labor cost to a cell.
b. Separate material costs from labor costs.
c. Put required results at the bottom of the spreadsheet as summary lines.

Step 5: Plan Your Solution.

Software to be used: Spreadsheets

Margins for Printing:

Top:	1.0	Top Printer:	0.25
Bottom:	1.0	Bottom Printer:	0.5
Left:	1.5	Left Printer:	0.25
Right:	1.5	Right Printer:	0.25
Header:	0.5	Top Printer:	0.25
Footer:	0.6	Bottom Printer:	0.5

Files to be imported: **None**

File	Description	Use	Location

Figure 14.2 (continued)

Rows to be printed on every page: none

Columns to be printed on every page: none

Paper Size: 8½ × 11 Paper Color: White

Orientation: Landscape Color/B&W B&W

Gridlines: Yes Row and Column Headings Printed: No

Header Contents: None

Footer Contents:

	Page XX	

Analysis Required:

a. Cost to manufacture
b. Wholesale cost
c. Break-even number of chairs to be sold

(Please note: The remainder of Step 5 is on page 308.)

Step 6: Evaluate the Solution.

List the Criteria for Evaluating the Completed Document: Include test numbers for evaluating the formulas if appropriate.

a. Is the spreadsheet easy to read?
b. Are the numbers correct?
c. Is the spreadsheet organized?
d. Are the owners satisfied?

Postanalysis Required:

a. Change of results if labor costs increase.
b. Should we add this to our line of furniture?

(continued)

Figure 14.2 Spreadsheet Planning Guide for Case Study 2

Number Format: G = General N = Number C = Currency A = Accounting F = Fraction P = Percentage D = Date T = Time S = Scientific
Text Format: B = Bold I = Italic U = Underline

Page 1

	Format	A	Format	B	Format	C	Format	D	Format	E	Format	F
1	B/L	GARY'S FURNITURE					D/C	= TODAY( )				
2	B/L	COST OF MANUFACTURING NEW CHAIR										
3												
4	B/C/U	COSTS										
5	B/C	MATERIALS			B/C	LABOR	R	LABOR COST =	N/2		L	PER HOUR
6	B/C	ITEM	B/C	COST	B/C	ITEM	B/C	COST				
7	L	LEGS/SEAT	N/2	40.00	L	LEGS	N/2	= E5/(20/4)				
8		SEAT		10.00		SEATS/backs		= E5/8				
9		FINISHING		4.00		SEAT		= E5/16				
10						FINISHING		= E5				
11		SUB TOTALS		= B7 + B8 + B9				= SUM(D7:D10)				
12		TOTAL COST		= B11 + D11								
13		WHOLESALE PRICE		= B12 * 1.5								
14		BREAK EVEN POINT		= 5000/(B12*.5)								

The employee's names and data are as follows:

Name		*Hours*	*Pay*
1.	Ann	10	6.50
2.	Barbara	14	7.00
3.	Dan	40	500.00
4.	Dave	40	600.00
5.	Del	16	6.50
6.	Don	12	7.50
7.	George	20	10.00
8.	Jim	40	650.00
9.	Joe	20	8.00
10.	John	10	7.25
11.	Josh	10	8.50
12.	Laura	15	6.50
13.	Martha	10	6.50
14.	Mary	16	10.00
15.	Nancy	40	675.00
16.	Norm	20	10.00
17.	Sara	12	9.00
18.	Tamara	20	8.75
19.	Tom	12	6.75
20.	Tony	16	6.50

Figure 14.3 shows the spreadsheet planning guide for case study 3.

In this case, database functions should be used. The solution to this problem uses the following functions, as described.

DAVERAGE Function

DAVERAGE(RANGE,COLUMN_LABEL,CRITERIA_RANGE) calculates the average of the values found in the column with the label COLUMN_LABEL and rows specified by the range of CRITERIA_RANGE. See Figure 14.3.

DCOUNT Function

DCOUNT(RANGE,COLUMN_LABEL,CRITERIA_RANGE) counts the number of the values found in the column with the label COLUMN_LABEL and rows specified by the range of CRITERIA_RANGE. See Figure 14.3.

DSUM Function

DSUM(RANGE,COLUMN_LABEL,CRITERIA_RANGE) calculates the total value of the values found in the column with the label COLUMN_LABEL and rows specified by the range of CRITERIA_RANGE. See Figure 14.3. Other database functions you may be interested in are as follows:

DMAX Function

DMAX(RANGE,COLUMN_LABEL,CRITERIA_RANGE) calculates the maximum value of the values found in the column with the label COLUMN_LABEL and rows specified by the range of CRITERIA_RANGE. See Figure 14.3.

DMIN Function

DMIN(RANGE,COLUMN_LABEL,CRITERIA_RANGE) calculates the minimum value of the values found in the column with the label COLUMN_LABEL and rows specified by the range of CRITERIA_RANGE. See Figure 14.3.

Storing data on a computer is accomplished by saving data in files. In a database this file contains the database. A database is all of the data needed to develop a project. For example, a company would have all of the information for the company in a data-

Figure 14.3 Spreadsheet Planning Guide for Case Study 3

SPREADSHEET PLANNING GUIDE

Name of Document: Employees   Date: 2/3/2002

Location of Electronic File: my data\work\Judys Ice Cream\

Name: Mary Stone

Name of Client: Judy's Ice Cream Shoppe

Step 1: Identify the Problem by Writing the Problem Statement.

Judy's Ice Cream Shoppe has 20 employees. Four of these are full time and 16 are part time working from 10 to 20 hours per week. The full-time employees make a weekly salary of between $500 and $600 per week. Her part-time employees are paid hourly at $6.50 to $10 an hour depending upon how long they have worked at the store. Judy would like to know the following information about her employees.

- What is the average number of hours the part-time employees work?
- How many of the part-time employees work 10 hours?
- How many of the part-time employees work 20 hours?
- What are the total hours worked by the part-time employees?
- What is the average wage for the full-time employees?
- What is the average hourly rate for the part-time employees?

The employee's names and data are as follows:

Name	Hours	Pay
1. Ann	10	6.50
2. Barbara	14	7.00
3. Dan	40	500.00
4. Dave	40	600.00
5. Del	16	6.50
6. Don	12	7.50
7. George	20	10.00
8. Jim	40	650.00
9. Joe	20	8.00
10. John	10	7.25
11. Josh	10	8.50
12. Laura	15	6.50
13. Martha	10	6.50
14. Mary	16	10.00
15. Nancy	40	675.00
16. Norm	20	10.00
17. Sara	12	9.00
18. Tamara	20	8.75
19. Tom	12	6.75
20. Tony	16	6.50

Figure 14.3 (continued)

Step 2: Understand the Problem.

The PAC:

Given Data	Required Results
Database information as provided: 4 full time, 16 part time Part time: $6.50 to $10 an hour Full time: $500 and $600 per week Part time: 10 to 20 hours per week	Avg. hours: part time # of part time who work 10 hrs a week # of part time who work 20 hrs a week Total hours worked by part time Avg. wage for full time Avg. hourly wage for part time
Processes and Formulas	**The Audience**
Use database functions for average, count, and sum	Owners of Judy's

Required Knowledge of the Problem to Develop the Document:
Data on employees.

Required Knowledge of the Audience:
Payroll information.

Step 3: Identify Valid Alternative Methods to Solve the Problem.

a. Use two sheets or one for spreadsheet.
b. Place criteria in a separate location or with database functions.
c. Other calculation method other than the use of database functions.

(continued)

Figure 14.3 Spreadsheet Planning Guide for Case Study 3

Step 4: Select the Best Method to Solve the Problem from the List of Alternative Solutions.

a. Use two sheets
   1. sheet one called Formulas for criteria and required results.
   2. sheet two called Database for the database of employee information.

b. Criteria will be in a separate location below the database function formulas on sheet one.

c. Database functions are the most efficient way of solving this problem.

Step 5: Plan Your Solution.

Software to be used: Spreadsheets

Margins for Printing:

Top:	1.0	Top Printer:	0.25
Bottom:	1.0	Bottom Printer:	0.5
Left:	1.5	Left Printer:	0.25
Right:	1.5	Right Printer:	0.25
Header:	0.5	Top Printer:	0.25
Footer:	0.6	Bottom Printer:	0.5

***Files to be imported:* None**

File	Description	Use	Location

Rows to be printed on every page: None

Columns to be printed on every page: None

Paper Size: 8½ × 11 Paper Color: White

Orientation: Landscape Color/B&W B&W

Gridlines: Yes Row and Column Headings Printed: No

Figure 14.3 (continued)

Header Contents: None

Footer Contents:

	Page XX	

Analysis Required:

a. What is the average number of hours the part-time employees work?
b. How many of the part-time employees work 10 hours?
c. How many of the part-time employees work 20 hours?
d. What are the total hours worked by the part-time employees?
e. What is the average wage for the full-time employees?
f. What is the average hourly rate for the part-time employees?

(Please note: The remainder of Step 5 is on pages 314–317.)

Step 6: Evaluate the Solution.

List the Criteria for Evaluating the Completed Document: Include test numbers for evaluating the formulas if appropriate.

a. Are the numbers correct?
b. Is the spreadsheet easy to read?
c. Can the owners find the required information?
d. Are the owners happy with the spreadsheet?

Postanalysis Required:
Payroll analysis for employees

(continued)

Figure 14.3 Spreadsheet Planning Guide for Case Study 3

Number Format: G = General N = Number C = Currency A = Accounting F = Fraction P = Percentage D = Date T = Time S = Scientific
Text Format: B = Bold I = Italic U = Underline

WORKSHEET: FORMULAS Page 1

	Format	A	Format	B	Format	C	Format	D	Format	E
1	B/U/L	JUDY'S ICE CREAM SHOPPE			D/L	= TODAY( )				
2	B/L	EMPLOYEE ANALYSIS								
3										
4	B/L	REQUIRED INFORMATION								
5	L	AVERAGE HOURS: PT EMPLOYEES	N/2	=DAVERAGE(DATABASE! A5: DATABASE!C25, "HOURS", A13: C14)						
6	↓	# WORKING 10 HOURS:	↓	=DCOUNT(DATABASE! A5: DATABASE!C25, "HOURS", A15: C16)						
7	↓	# WORKING 20 HOURS:	↓	=DCOUNT(DATABASE! A5: DATABASE!C25, "HOURS", A17: C18)						
8	↓	TOTAL HOURS: PT EMPLOYEES	↓	=DSUM(DATABASE! A5: DATABASE!C25, "HOURS", A13: C14)						
9	↓	AVERAGE WAGE: PT EMPLOYEES	↓	=DAVERAGE(DATABASE! A5: DATABASE!C25, "PAY", A19: C20)						
10	↓	AVERAGE Hourly WAGE: PT EMPLOYEES	↓	=DAVERAGE(DATABASE! A5: DATABASE!C25, "PAY", A13: C14)						
11										
12	B/L	CRITERIA								
13	C	NAME	C	HOURS	C	PAY				
14			R	<25						

Figure 14.3 (continued)

Number Format: G = General N = Number C = Currency A = Accounting F = Fraction P = Percentage D = Date T = Time S = Scientific
Text Format: B = Bold I = Italic U = Underline

WORKSHEET: FORMULAS Page 2

	Format	A	Format	B	Format	C	Format	D	Format	E	Format	
15	C	NAME	C	HOURS	C	PAY						
16			N/0	10								
17	C	NAME	C	HOURS	C	PAY						
18			N/0	20								
19	C	NAME	C	HOURS	C	PAY						
20			N/0	40								
21												
22												
23												
24												
25												
26												
27												
28												

Figure 14.3 Spreadsheet Planning Guide for Case Study 3

Number Format: G = General N = Number C = Currency A = Accounting F = Fraction P = Percentage D = Date T = Time S = Scientific

Text Format: B = Bold I = Italic U = Underline

WORKSHEET: DATABASE Page 3

	Format	A	Format	B	Format	C	Format	D	Format	E	Format	F
1	B/U/L	JUDY'S ICE CREAM SHOPPE					D/C	= TODAY()				
2	B/L	EMPLOYEES RECORDS										
3												
4	B/L	DATABASE										
5	C	NAME	C	HOURS	C	PAY						
6	L	ANN	N/0	10	N/2	6.50						
7		BARBARA		14		7.00						
8		DAN		40		500.00						
9		DAVE		40		600.00						
10		DEL		16		6.50						
11		DON		12		7.50						
12		GEORGE		20		10.00						
13		JIM		40		650.00						
14		JOE		20		8.00						

Figure 14.3 (continued)

Number Format: G = General N = Number C = Currency A = Accounting F = Fraction P = Percentage D = Date T = Time S = Scientific
Text Format: B = Bold I = Italic U = Underline

WORKSHEET: DATABASE Page 4

	Format	A	Format	B	Format	C	Format	D	Format	E	Format	F
15	L	JOHN	N/0	10	N/2	7.25						
16		JOSH		10		8.50						
17		LAURA		15		6.50						
18		MARTHA		10		6.50						
19		MARY		16		10.00						
20		NANCY		40		675.00						
21		NORM		20		10.00						
22		SARAH		12		9.00						
23		TAMARA		20		8.75						
24		TOM		12		6.75						
25		TONY		16		6.50						
26												
27												
28												

base. A database is divided into tables. A table contains information on one type of data such as employee data or sales data. A table is divided into numbered records. Each record contains data on one entity of the table. For example, records might contain the data on each employee, each sales, and so forth. A record is divided into fields. Each field contains one piece of data in the record such as the employee name and salary. The database would be analogous to a file cabinet, a table to a drawer in the file cabinet, records to folders in a drawer, and fields to the data within the folder. Databases are made up of tables, a table of records, and a record of fields.

For this case, two worksheets are used. Sheet 1, called Formulas, presents the formulas for the required outcome of the problem and the criteria ranges for the database functions. Sheet 2, called Database, contains the employee information. To use database functions, you must set up a range that contains the information for the database functions in use in order to complete the formulas. The labels are in the row directly above the data. This range is equivalent to a table in a database. The column labels become the field names and the rows become the records.

Database functions also require a criteria range. You must set this range up carefully. First, the labels (field names) of the database range must be exactly as they are in the database. It is best to copy these labels to ensure that they are identical. Next, enter the criteria in the following rows. Figure 14.4 shows examples of criteria ranges. Example 1 shows one criterion: Cost is less than 25. This includes all records where the cost is less than 25 to complete the function calculations. Example 2 shows two criteria where they both must be true to include the record in the function calculations. Notice that they are on the same row. This is the same theory as the AND function. Example 3 shows two

Example 1:

Item	Cost	Quantity
	<25	

Example 2:

Item	Cost	Quantity
	<25	<10

Example 3:

Item	Cost	Quantity
	<25	
		<10

Example 4:

Item	Cost	Quantity
	>=10	<5
	<10	

Figure 14.4 Examples of Criteria Ranges for Database Functions

criteria where one of the criteria must be true in order to include the record in the function calculations. Notice that the criteria are on separate rows, which is the same theory as the OR function. Example 4 shows three criteria using both the AND and the OR logic. In this case, for the record to be included, the cost must be greater than or equal to 10 and the quantity must be less than 5, or the cost must be less than 10. The database function will include all records where the cost is less than 10 along with all records that are less than 5 with a cost greater than or equal to 10. It will not use records where the cost is greater than or equal to 10 but the quantity is greater than or equal to 5. Notice that there are no extra lines between the labels and the criteria. If you add an extra row, the function will use all records since there is no criteria. Notice that the field name in the database function has quotes surrounding it.

The pitfalls when using these functions lie in the setting up of the database and the criteria range. Take care when adding blank rows. The computer uses blank rows as part of the database or the criteria range. Be careful when entering the field names in the criteria range, and when entering the criteria. When using an AND, the criteria are on the same row. When using an OR, the criteria are on different rows.

Summary

This chapter presents three case studies to be completed using a spreadsheet software package. Case study 1 is a budget problem, case study 2 calculates the cost of manufacturing an item, and case study 3 uses database functions to calculate information on selected data. The completed document planning guide for each case is presented.

Problems

1. Create your personal budget that shows your income and expenses. Include in your budget the percent of each income item of the total income, the percent of each expense of the total expenses, and the percent of each expense of the total income. In the summary row, include the beginning balance, the ending balance, the amount over or under $100, the net balance, the beginning savings balance, and the ending savings balance after the net balance has been calculated. Excess budget balance should be placed in your savings account, and any deficit should be subtracted from your savings account assuming you have enough money in your savings. A chart showing the percentage comparisons of expenses and another showing the percentage comparisons of income should be developed. Develop a spreadsheet planning guide for this problem.
2. You are treasurer of the computer club. The club would like to make money selling computer supplies to students. They would like to start with floppy disks. The club can buy the disks for $0.40 each and would like to make at least $1,000 a semester to help students finance trips to computer conferences at the beginning of each semester. The school requires that 10% of all sales goes to the associated student body. The computer club would like a chart of the profits. They plan to sell 1,500 disks in the fall and 800 in the spring. Develop a spreadsheet planning guide to forecast the amount of money the computer club would make each semester for the next five years.

3. Using data from problem 2, the computer club would like to compare how much more or less they would make if they had a 10% increase in demand and a 10% decrease in demand. They also would like to know how far the demand would have to drop in order to break even. Add to the spreadsheet planning guide a demand factor that would allow an increase and decrease in the demand of disks during the five years.
4. You need to build a bookcase for all of your school books. You have calculated that the bookcase will take 30 board feet to build. The cost to finish the bookcase is $0.30 a board foot. You consider three different woods, one at $2.00 a board foot, another at $1.00 a board foot, and another at $3.00 a board foot. You do not have the equipment to build this bookcase; therefore, you have asked a friend to build it for you. The friend is charging $8.00 an hour to build it. The different woods take different times to build because of the time in finishing. The $1.00/board foot bookcase will take five hours to build, the $2.00/board foot bookcase will take six hours to build, and the $3.00/board foot bookcase will take four hours to build. Develop a spreadsheet planning guide to find the total cost of the bookcase using each of these three woods. Include in the plan a chart comparing the costs.
5. You would like to buy a new car. You plan to go to five lending institutions and compare the cost of the loans. Develop a spreadsheet planning guide to create a worksheet template for these comparisons.
6. Your computer instructor would like you to develop a worksheet with student names, student ID numbers, final grade points and earned letter grades for the semester, and number of days absent. He would like to analyze the data to find any correlation between the final grade earned and the number of days absent. He would like the following information.
   a. The number of students who received As or Bs
   b. The number of students who received As or Bs and who were absent less than five times during the semester
   c. The number of students who received Ds or Fs
   d. The number of students who received Ds or Fs and were absent less than five times during the semester
   e. The number of students who received As or Bs and were absent more than 12 times during the semester
   f. The number of students who received Ds or Fs and were absent more than 12 times during the semester
   g. The average grade points of those students who were absent less than five times during the semester.
   h. The average grade points of those students who were absent more than 12 times during the semester.
   i. A list of students with less than five absences during the semester.
   j. A list of students with more than 12 absences during the semester.

   Develop a spreadsheet planning guide to use as a template for this problem.
7. Your computer instructor would like you to develop a worksheet template for students to use to compare four computer systems. Find an advertisement for a computer system to create the items on the worksheet for the students to compare. He would like the students to create a chart to compare the prices of the four computers. Develop a spreadsheet planning guide for this problem.

UNIT FIVE

RELATIONAL DATABASE MANAGEMENT SYSTEMS

Chapter 15

Concepts of Relational Database Management Systems

Overview

RDBMS
Tables
Primary, Secondary, and Foreign Keys
Normalizing Tables
Schema
Creating Tables
Queries
Form Design
Interface Design
Reports
RDBMS Planning Guide
Example RDBMS

Objectives

When you have finished this chapter, you should be able to:

1. Understand the parts of a relational database created in a RDBMS.
2. Normalize relational database tables.
3. Create the schema for a relational database.
4. Design queries for a relational database.
5. Design forms for a relational database.
6. Design reports for a relational database.
7. Develop a relational database for a specific problem.

Relational database management system (RDBMS) software is a data organizer. The primary function of a RDBMS is to store large quantities of data, organize the data, and print reports on all or selected parts of the data. This software is the key for many businesses. Business use of RDBMS includes inventory management, client and sales tracking, and personnel management. Personal use of RDBMS includes address lists, CD collections, recipe collections, home inventory, and book collections. When a problem arises that requires the organization of large amounts of data, the primary software solution is to use RDBMS.

The use of spreadsheets is often confused with the use of RDBMS. When a problem calls for many calculations and numerical analysis of data, and requires very little data to be selected and organized, a spreadsheet should be used. If the problem calls for electronic data collection and organization, and reports on all and/or selected parts of the collected data, then a RDBMS should be used. See Figure 15.1 for a comparison of a spreadsheet and a table from a RDBMS.

The RDBMS is often the last software package that people learn to use, for several reasons. First, the software is not automatically included in many office suites and people do not want to spend the extra money for the package. Second, RDBMS software is not as easy to learn as other software packages because, in order to use the software efficiently, you need to know database theory of how to set up data. Third, data must be organized in some way before entered into the computer. If you are planning to enter a CD collection, then you should have the CDs organized and labeled in some way so you can find the desired CD. Fourth, it takes time to enter the data. If you are computerizing your CD list, then you need to enter not only the names of the CDs, but also the names of the music pieces on each CD. Fifth, you must update the data often. When you buy a new CD you will need to include this new data in the CD database.

Once you have entered data into the computer, however, you may print reports on any or all of the data. You may want to print the names of all the CDs, the names of all the music pieces, or the names of all the CDs of one artist. It is definitely worth the time and effort to learn RDBMS theory and software and to take the time to organize and enter your data.

RDBMS

Entities, Entity Sets, and Attributes

A **database** is developed to store data. Just as the name implies, it stores data about items required to be retrieved at a later date. These items are called *entities.* An *entity* may be an inventory item, an employee, a place, a thing, et cetera. Each entity has *attributes.* The

Spreadsheet

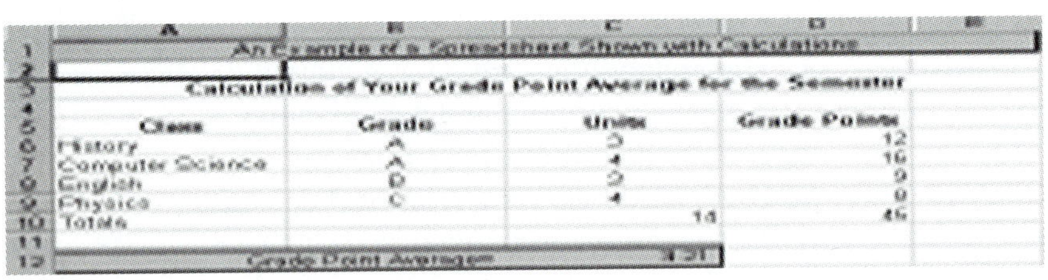

Database Table

Class	Units	Grade
History	3	A
Computer Science	4	A
English	3	B
Physics	4	C
	0	

Figure 15.1 Comparison of a Spreadsheet to a Database Table

attributes are data items that are required to be stored about the entity. For example, the attributes of a client entity might be last name, first name, street address, city, state, zip code, sales rep, and so forth. An *entity set* is a collection of related entities. An entity set may be inventory items, employees, clients, and so forth.

Tables, Records, and Fields

This terminology is standard for database theory. However, you will find other terms used informally by the developers of specific RDBMS. In this text we will refer to more informal names. An attribute is called a **field.** An entity is called a **record.** An entity set is called a **table.** A database is a collection of related tables. For example, you may have a CD table. Each entity or record contains the attributes or fields about one CD. Each attribute or field contains one piece of data about the entity, such as the name of the CD or the producer. Fields may contain entered numbers, text, images, hyperlinks, dates, times, or may be calculated from other fields.

Other Database Components

Saved with the database are other components than the tables including queries, forms, reports, and macros. Queries are tables that contain selected data from the tables. Forms display data pertaining to one record on the monitor. Reports are the printed output of the tables in the database. Macros are short sets of instructions to automate the database.

Naming and Saving a Database

When starting a new database, you first name the database before you start developing it. Data are automatically saved as you add records to the tables. There is no need to save often or before you close as you did in other software packages. As you design your tables, forms, queries, and reports, you will automatically save each of them as part of the database. However, unless you want to save the database under another name, you do not need to go through a save procedure. All tables, queries, forms, reports, and macros are saved together under one database file name.

Tables

Tables

To reiterate the terminology of a database, data are organized into one or more tables or entity sets. A **table** is a group of related records or entities. Each record is an entity in the table. A **record** is a group of related fields or attributes. Each field or attribute is a specific piece of data pertaining to the record. Each record in the table has the same fields that are created in the design of the table. Each record is given a number. Each field is given a name. Each table, query, report, and form is also given a name. Name each according to what data they contain. The database is given a file name.

As an example, let us examine a CD collection in which only the CD names, producers, and dates of publication will be organized. See Figure 15.2. The database will be called CD Collection. There will be only one table called CDs. Each record, a horizontal row of data, will contain data in the four separate areas, called fields, that are the name of the CD, the artist, the publisher, and the date of publication. These fields are named as follows:

Field Description	*Field Name*
ID Number	CDNO
Name of CD	Name
The Producer	Producer
Date of publication	Date

Records are numbered starting with a 1. An individual field is the same number of characters in each record. For example, if 25 characters have been specified for the field

Database File Name: CD Collection

Table Name: CDs

Fields: →	ID Number	Name	Producer	Date
Record 1				
Record 2				
Record 3				
⋮				
Record *N*				

Figure 15.2 CD Collection Table

called Name, then each record has a maximum 25 characters to enter the name of the CD. You may have a derived field or computed field. The data in this field are derived or computed from other fields. For example, the retail cost may be computed from the wholesale cost and the percentage markup.

Tables are holders of data to be organized and printed. In the planning stages of a database, it is important that all data required for the printed reports be part of a table. Therefore, when developing a solution to a problem that requires a database, start with the information required for the reports. This may sound backwards, but, you need to know where you are going in order to know how to start. When you have your reports planned, then you may define your tables. The third step is to plan how to get from the data to the report. Remember to plan your output, then your input, and finally your processing.

Primary, Secondary, and Foreign Keys

Primary Key

One field may be designated as a **primary key.** A primary key field contains unique data, that is, data that will not be repeated in the same field of another record. For example, the CD ID number would be a primary key in the CDs table. It is used in many projects to designate an identification number or an account number. You do not have to designate a primary key field. Many tables do not have a field that is unique. If you designate a field as a primary key, the RDBMS will not allow you to enter a value that is repeated from another record.

Secondary Key

Secondary keys are not necessarily unique. They are primarily used to search for a specific record when you do not know the primary key. For example, in the CD example you may not know the ID number, but you may know the name of the CD. Therefore, you could search on the CD name.

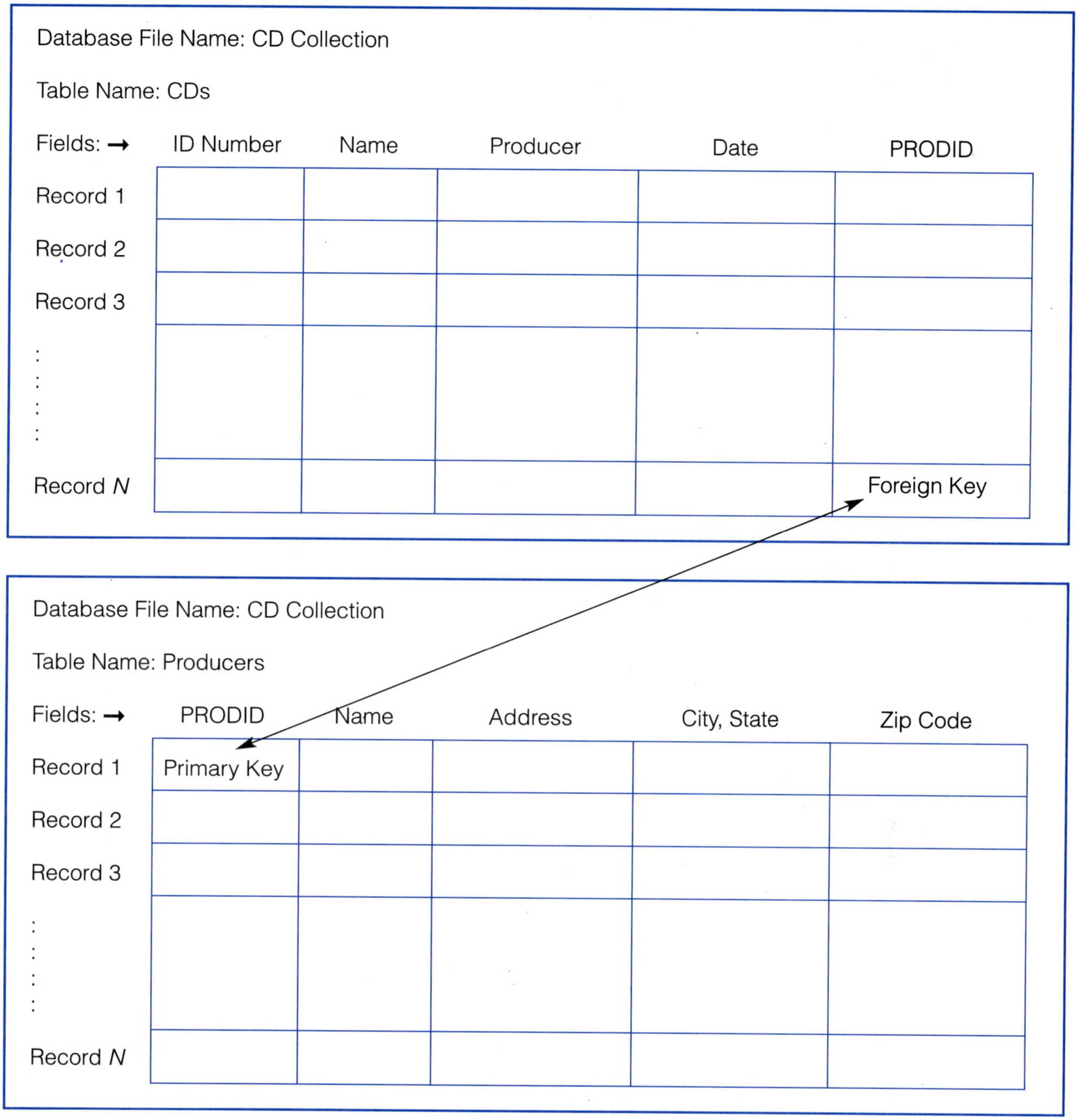

Figure 15.3 Primary and Foreign Keys for CDs Table and Producers Table

Foreign Key

A foreign key is a relational field to another table. The key is a primary key in another table and determines the relationship to it. For example, you may have information about the producers of the CD in the second table. The producer's identification number would be the primary key in the Producers table. To find the producer information for a CD, you must also have the producer's identification number in the CDs table. This number would be a foreign key in the CDs table whereas it is a primary key in the Producers table. The field name is the same in the two tables. See Figure 15.3.

Normalizing Tables

Normalizing Tables

For most problems, data should be separated into multiple but related tables. Let us revisit the CD collection. This time there are more fields required including the name, artist, and time length of each piece of music on each CD. Also required is the address information for the publisher. Figure 15.4 shows the table if all this added information were to go into one table, and lists the attributes or fields in a single list. This table also has several problems. First, how many fields should be reserved for the music selections? Each CD has a different number of selections. Another problem is data repetition, such as the publishers' addresses. This repetition creates possible errors in entry and in table maintenance. Therefore, database tables should be normalized. To **normalize** tables is to separate data into additional but related tables so that they are as efficient as possible when entering, using, and updating data.

Other problems that may occur in database design are null data and data redundancy. Null data have no value, as all value is absent. Primary keys cannot contain null data. A null data field is not a blank field, because a blank field contains spaces, which are characters. Null values should be eliminated if possible. Data redundancy occurs when multiple values of an attribute exist within a table and the multiple values are not required to determine the relationship between two tables. Data redundancy often leads to three anomalies in tables.

Insertion Anomaly

1. *Insertion anomaly* occurs when you cannot add a record because there are too much data for one field, or the number of fields for one data item is different in different records, such as in music selections. This creates an unflat table, or a table that requires a different number of fields for each record.

Update Anomaly

2. *Update anomaly* occurs when the same data must be changed in more than one record, as in the case of the publishers' addresses. Repeated data must be updated in different records.

Deletion Anomaly

3. *Deletion anomaly* occurs when there is a loss of critical data when you delete a record. In the case of the CD collection, assume the publishers' information was to be kept in the original table. If there was only one CD that had a specific publisher and that CD was deleted, then you would lose the address information for that publisher. Conversely, if the address information is in a separate publisher information table, even if there were no CDs in your collection that were created by that publisher, the address information would still remain in the publisher information table.

Normalization takes care of these problems. The first normalization takes care of unflat tables or the insertion problem. The second normalization takes care of repeated data or the update problem. The third normalization takes care of key data entered into a nonkey field of the file or the deletion problem.

When normalizing a table, the first step is to create a list of fields or attributes required for the output reports. Figure 15.5a shows the original field list—the list after the first and second normalizations. There is no need for a third normalization. The original table will show all fields. Notice that fields that hold multiple data are simply named as to the type of data, in this case, Selection, Artist, and Time. The list is then modified to separate fields such as Artist into Artist First Name and Artist Last Name, and to group like fields together, in this case, the CD data, the Selection data, and the Producer data.

First Normalization

The next step is to develop the first normalized form of your database. You will be creating a new table that has an identical field to one in the original table in order to show the relationship between the two tables, in this case, SELID. The field in the Selections

CDs Table

	Name	Selection	Artist	Producer	Date	Time	Address	City	State	Zip Code	Telephone
Record 1											
Record 2											
Record 3											
: : : : : :											
Record *N*											

Attributes or Fields
Name
Selection
Artist
Producer
Date
Time
Address
City
State
Zip Code
Telephone

Figure 15.4 Attributes of the CDs Table

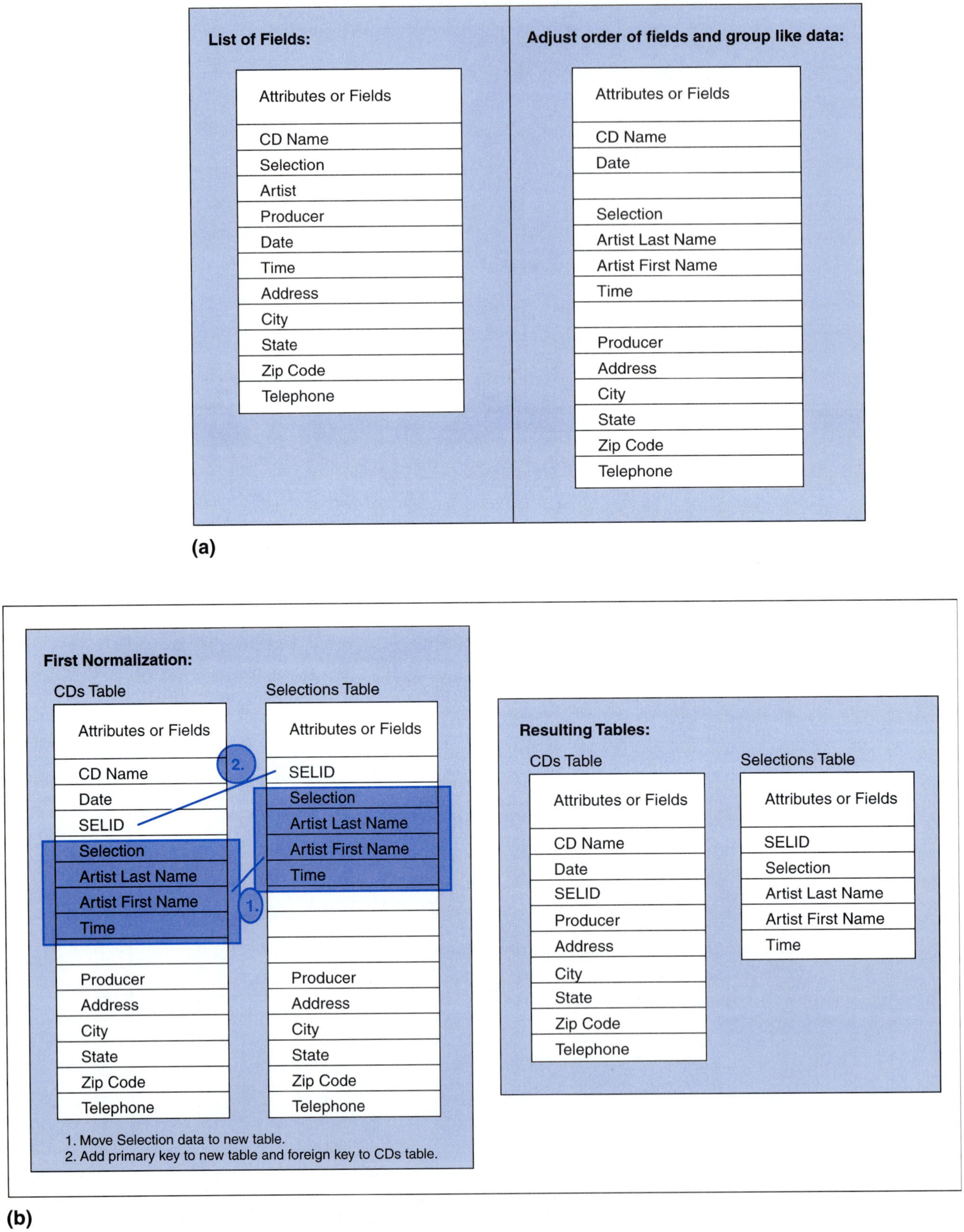

Figure 15.5 (a) Normalization of CD Collection Table Original Data; (b) Normalization of CD Collection Table First Normalization; (c) Normalization of CD Collection Table Second Normalization and Final Tables

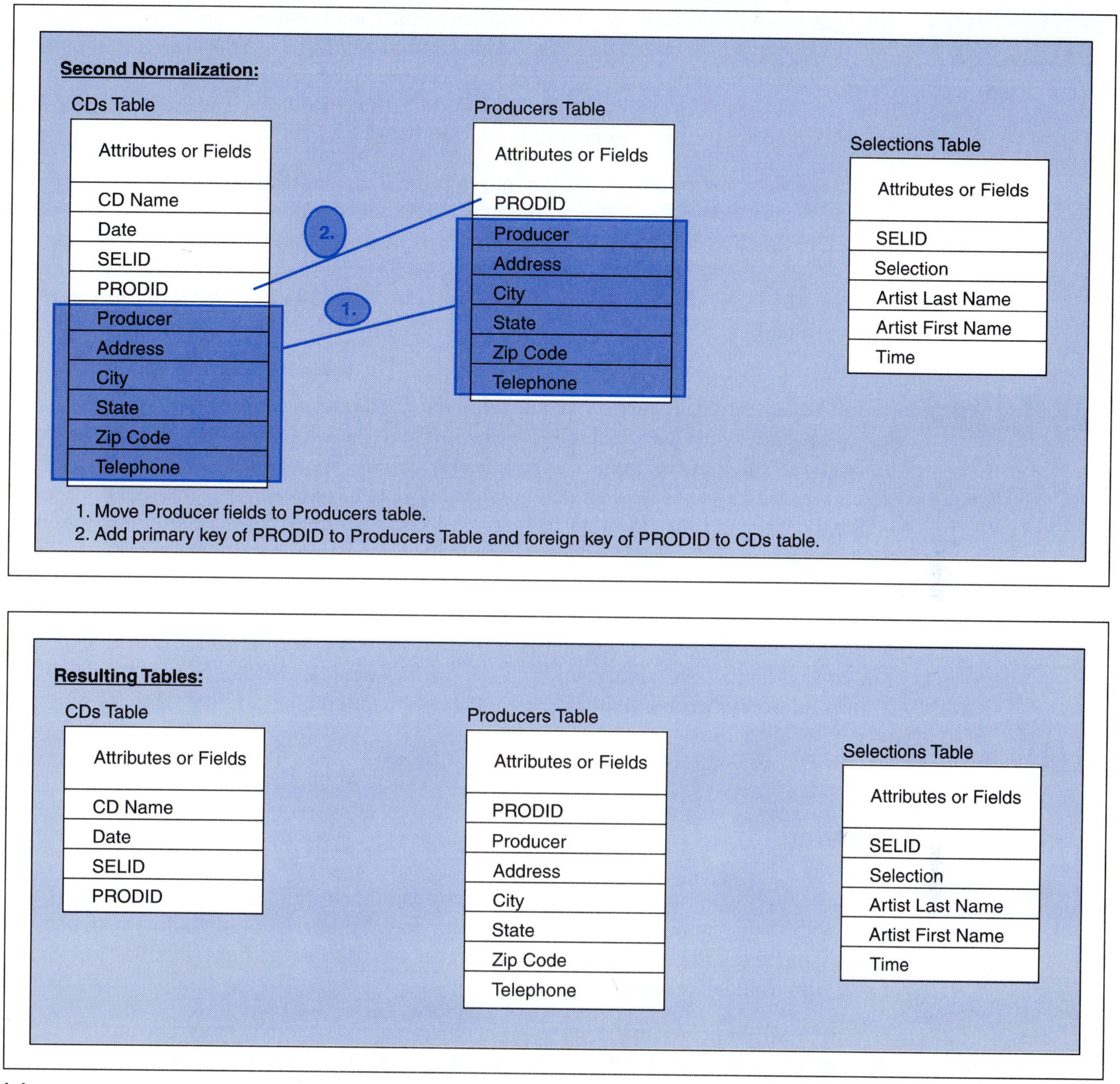

(c)

Figure 15.5 (a) Normalization of CD Collection Table Original Data; (b) Normalization of CD Collection Table First Normalization; (c) Normalization of CD Collection Table Second Normalization and Final Tables

table becomes the primary key. The field in the CDs table becomes a foreign key. The steps to complete the first normalization are as follows:

1. Move related fields that have more than one value to the new table; in this case, move the fields associated with the selections to the new table, named Selections.
2. Add a primary key to the new table and the same named field as a foreign key to the original table; in this case, add a primary key of SELID to the Selections table and a foreign key of SELID to the CDs table.

Second Normalization

This will produce a new table and a modified table. See Figure 15.5b.

The next step is to develop the second normalized form of your database. You will be creating a third table with one field that is identical to a field in the original table to show the relation between the two tables, in this case, PRODID. The steps to complete the second normalization are as follows:

1. Move the related fields that are in more than one record to a new table; in this case, move the Producer fields to the Producers table.
2. Add a field in the new table that will be a primary key and the same named field in the modified table as a foreign key; in this case, add a primary key of PRODID to the Producers table and a foreign key of PRODID to the CDs table.

There are now three tables.

Third Normalization

The last step, if required, is to develop the third normalized form of your database. You would be creating a fourth table with one field that is identical to a field in the original table to show the relation between the two tables. To complete the third normalization, copy the key data field and corresponding data to another file. The relational field is already created in the original table as the key data field. In our CD collection case there is no data and no primary key to complete a third normalization.

You should now have your tables in the most efficient form as possible. If any of the normalizations require more than one new table, you must repeat the steps for that normalization. Complete all required new tables in each normalization before continuing on to the next normalization. You will probably rarely use all three normalizations for a solution to a problem; however, you should examine the original table for the possibility of all three.

Schema

Schema

The **schema** of your database shows the relationship between the tables. See Figure 15.6. Start with the normalized list of attributes for each table. Then draw a line between the tables connecting the relational fields. Mark on each end of the line a number 1 or an infinity sign to indicate the following:

- 1 to 1 indicates that one record in one table relates to one record in another table.
- 1 to infinity (∞) indicates that one record in the table on the one side references to many records in the table on the infinity side.
- Infinity to infinity indicates that there are many records in one table that are related to many records in the other table.

Figure 15.6 shows the schema for the CD example. Notice that there are three tables: the CDs table, the Selections table, and the Producers table.

Creating Tables

Data are entered into the tables through the use of forms or a data sheet view. The form shows one record on the monitor at a time. The data sheet shows multiple records but only as many fields as will fit on the monitor. You must scroll for other fields. Tables must be created by designating the fields and their attributes. Each field in a table has field at-

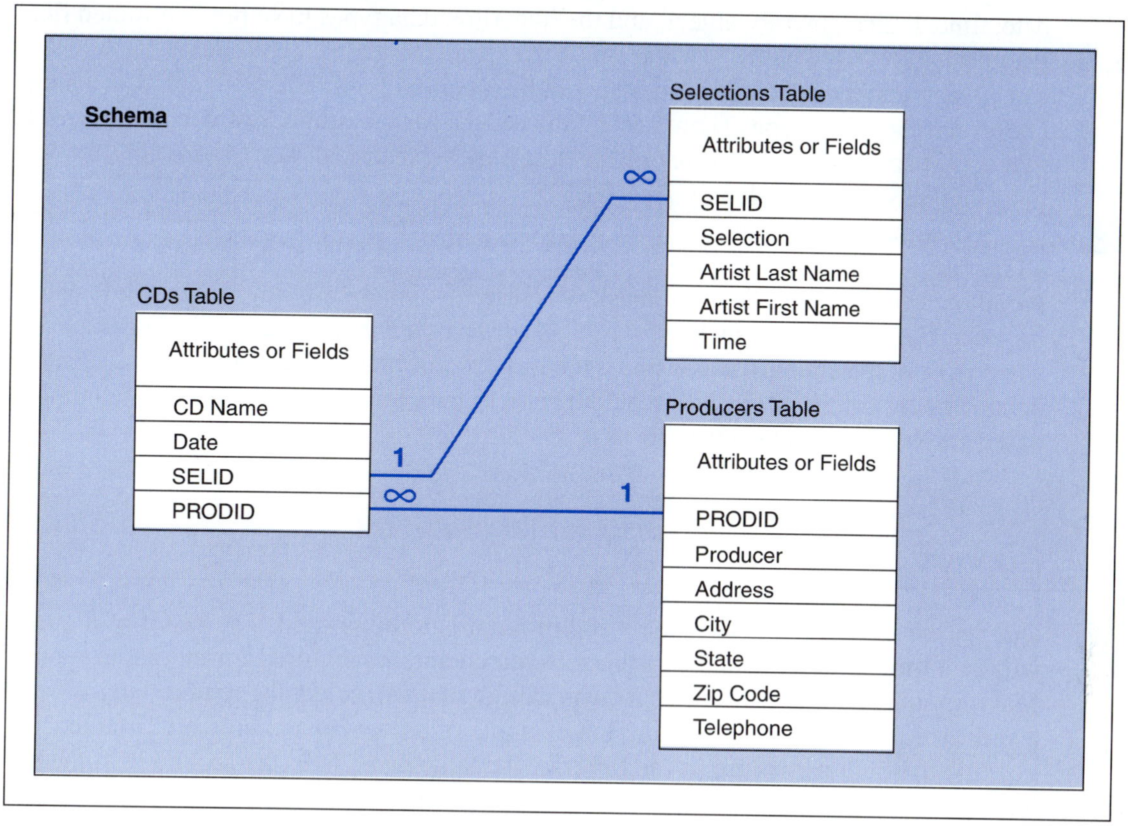

Figure 15.6 Schema of the CD Collection Database

tributes including the field name, the data type, the description of the field, the number of characters in the field called the field size, and the number of decimal places for numbers, format, input mask, and default value. These attributes define the field.

Naming Fields

The field name should be long enough to readily identify the contents, but short enough so it is easy to remember and does not take up much space as the field header in the form or in the data sheet. The field description describes the contents of the field. The field size is the maximum number of characters any entry will require. If the field contains a name, the field size may be 20 characters if all records have names shorter than 21 characters. The computer will not allow you to enter more characters than the size of the field. If you have a name that is longer than 20 characters, you must increase the size of the field by changing the design of the table.

Data Types

There are many data types from which to choose, just as there are in spreadsheets. The spreadsheet data types that are also available in a RDBMS include text, number, currency, date, and time. New data types in RDBMS include logical, memo, objects, and hyperlinks. A logical data type is a yes or a no in the field. You may use it for your checks—yes if the check has been returned and no if not. A memo data type designates a field that can store more data than a text field. A memo field has no field size. An object may be placed in a field such as a picture, which would be an object linking and embedding (OLE) or an object data type. Hyperlinks to an internet site may also be a data type. These data types allow for the organization of many different types of data. For example, a real estate office may want to include a picture of a house in its database of properties. Or you may be doing research and you want to save the hyperlink to a website of the information you have found. There are limitations on some field sizes. The field size for the date, time, logical, memo, object, and the hyperlink data types have predetermined field lengths.

The number of decimal places should be specified for a field designated as a number or currency data type. There are default values for the number of decimal places if you do not specify it. The format of the data may be specified. See Figure 15.7 for formats that may be available in your RDBMS.

Input Mask

An **input mask** allows the user to specify characters that are the same in a field in all records such as the parentheses and dashes in a telephone number or the dashes in a social security number. An input mask decreases the number of keystrokes while entering data. Default values may be specified, such as a state in an address list. For example, when most of the clients for a business are in a specific state, such as California, then the default values for the State field would be CA. Again, this feature decreases the number of keystrokes in the data entry process.

Queries

Queries

Queries are the way to select fields and/or records to be printed. The result of a query will be a **query table,** containing the selected data items required for an output report. Making a query entails setting up a query design that will select the required items from a specified table. Figure 15.8 shows an example of a query made on the CD table. Notice that the field names are in the top row, the table name is in the second row, the selected fields are in the third row, and criteria of publish date is greater than 1990. These data will create a query table with records from the CD table that have been published after 1990. You may then print this table through the use of reports.

Text	Predefined Formats
Memo	Predefined Formats
Number	General Number (3456.456)
	Currency ($3,456.45)
	Fixed (3456.45)
	Standard (3,456.45)
	Percent (34.56%)
	Scientific (1.34E+6)
Date	General (6/11/02 3:45:34 PM)
	Long (Sunday, August 20, 2002)
	Medium (20-Aug-02)
	Short (6/11/02)
Time	Long (3:45:34 PM)
	Medium (3:45 PM)
	Short (3:45:34)
Logical	Yes/No
	True/False
	On/Off

Figure 15.7 Database Formats for Fields

Field Name:	Name	Artist	Producer	Date
Table:	CDs	CDs	CDs	CDs
Sort:	X			
Show:	X	X	X	X
Criteria:				>1990
OR:				

Figure 15.8 Example of a Query

The criteria rows are similar to the criteria range created in a spreadsheet when using the database functions. Notice the first row is the AND, and the second row is the OR. When you want your selection to be based on two or more criteria and they all have to be met, then you place each criterion in the first row under the associated field name. When only one of the criteria must be met, then you place each criterion on different rows. Be careful when you start mixing the ANDs and the ORs to be sure you are asking for the correct records to be selected. Check your resulting table carefully. If you identify more or less records than you had expected from the query, then you need to correct the design of the query.

Structural Query Language (SQL)

The queries in Figure 15.8 are developed through the use of an interface to the powerful structural query language (SQL). SQL exists to facilitate the retrieval of selected data needed for reports. You may program your own methods to retrieving data that you need by learning to use SQL. Many RDBMSs allow the users extensive use of SQL, which decreases the user friendliness of the application but increases its flexibility.

The types of queries you will want to perform are designated by the project. You may want special sums, or averages, or special updates. Just about any application that is used with a RDBMS requires some type of query.

Form Design

Form Design

Forms allow the user to see all or some of the fields of a record on the monitor. The table is transversed through the use of buttons to go to the next, the previous, the last, or the first record. Derived fields may be added. Fields may be placed and moved to any location on the monitor. The data may be viewed or updated. New records may be added. Each field is labeled and has an input box that holds the data.

The form must be well designed to ensure productivity of the end user. The rules of design hold true here, so review Chapter 4 guidelines for design. Fields should be located on the form for easy reading and entering of data. If a source document is being used, the fields should be located on the monitor in the same order as on the source document. Key information should be located in one area. The form should be pleasing to the eye and provide easy readability and access to pertinent information. Add graphics only to enhance the locating and reading of data. Remember that the user of this form will be viewing it every day. You want that person to enjoy looking at it.

Interface Design

Most solutions to business problems are designed to be accessed through an interface. A form is set up as an interface with buttons to automate the use of the database. This form is sometimes called a switchboard, because it switches from one activity to another through the use of buttons. Chapter 19 presents information on the design and implementation of interfaces.

Reports

Reports

Reports are the real reason why you have completed everything else. **Reports** are printed documents of the records in a specific database table or a query table. You may choose any or all of the fields to be included in your report. For example, in the case of the CD collection, the report may include only the CD names and artists. You may sort them in any way you please: by CD names or artists, by date, or by publisher, depending upon the requirements of the problem. To design a report, specify the report headings, the footers, the headers, the contents of each column, the width of the column, the format of the data, the column headings, how the data will be sorted, and if there will be subtotals to be calculated. You may also specify images to be imported on the document and other line art as required by the specifications of the problem.

Specify the column width as greater than, equal to, or less than the field length; however, if the data do not fit into the column they will word wrap within the column. To avoid this, make the columns at least as wide as the field length, but stay within the width of the paper on which you are creating the report. The number of characters across the page is dependent upon the font, the characters, and the font size that you are using. Try to specify extra space for each column. Columns are specified in inches. You may have as many columns as you desire, but, the data must fit into the columns.

RDBMS Planning Guide

RDBMS Planning Guide

Figure 15.9 presents the RDBMS planning guide. Steps one through four and step six are similar to other planning guides. Step five presents the database development process. First create a list of required reports. Starting with a list of reports and the corresponding data for the reports helps you understand what data are needed for the database. Step five presents a form to list the reports and the related data for each report.

The next step is to list all data and create the field names. Step five presents a table to enter the data items and field names. You will then need to normalize the original table and separate the data as required by the normalization. After you have normalized the database, then create the schema. The next step is to design each table. In this step, the fields and their attributes are specified. Step 5 presents a form to help you design your tables. You will need one of these forms for each table. After your tables are designed, you will then design each of your database forms by designating the background, what fields will be on the form, and where they will be placed.

The next step is to design your queries. Use the form in the planning guide to help you. The last step is to design your reports. Specify margins, headers, footers, report headings, column contents, column widths, and anything else required for a specific report.

Example RDBMS

Example RDMS

Figure 15.10 presents an example of a RDBMS planning guide for a personal address list. The problem is as follows:

Figure 15.9 RBDMS Planning Guide

RELATIONAL DATABASE MANAGEMENT SYSTEMS PLANNING GUIDE

Name of Database: ______________________________ Date: ______________

Location of Electronic File: ______________________________

Name: ______________________________

Name of Client: ______________________________

Step 1: Identify the Problem by Writing the Problem Statement.

Step 2: Understand the Problem.

Audience:

Required Outcomes of the Database:

Required Knowledge of the Problem to Develop the Database:

Required Knowledge of the Audience:

Step 3: Identify Valid Alternative Methods to Solve the Problem.

Step 4: Select the Best Method to Solve the Problem from the List of Alternative Solutions.

(continued)

Figure 15.9 RBDMS Planning Guide

Step 5: Plan Your Solution.

Software to be used: RDBMS

List of Required Reports:

Report Name	Data to be Included in Report

Figure 15.9 (continued)

Table Development.

Original Table:		First Normalization—New Table(s)		Second Normalization—New Table(s)		Third Normalization—New Table(s)	
Item	Field Name	Item	Field Name	Item	Field Name	Item	Field Name

Figure 15.9 RBDMS Planning Guide

Schema.

Field Name

Field Name

Field Name

Field Name

Field Name

Field Name

Field Name

Figure 15.9 (continued)

Table with Attributes.

Table Name: ____________________

Field Name	Description	Data Type	Field Length	No. of Decimals	Format	Input Mask	Default Value

Figure 15.9 RBDMS Planning Guide

Form Design.

Background: ______________________

Table: ______________________

Figure 15.9 (continued)

Queries.

Table Name: ____________

Field Name							
Table:							
Sort:							
Show:							
Criteria:							
OR:							

Field Name							
Table:							
Sort:							
Show:							
Criteria:							
OR:							

(continued)

Figure 15.9 RBDMS Planning Guide

Step 5: Plan Your Solution. (con't)

Report Layouts:

Report Name:____

Table or Query Name:____________________________________

Margins:

Top: __________________ Top Printer: ____________

Bottom: ________________ Bottom Printer: ____________

Left: __________________ Left Printer: ____________

Right: _________________ Right Printer: ____________

Header: ________________ Top Printer: ____________

Footer: ________________ Bottom Printer: ____________

Paper Size: ________________ Orientation: ________________ Color/B&W: ____________

Sort by: ____

Subtotals on following fields: ______________________________

Images to be imported:

File	Description	Use	Location

Header Contents:

Footer Contents:

Report Heading:

Figure 15.9 (continued)

Report Layout.

Column Heading:					
Field Name:					
Column Width:					

Step 6: **Evaluate the Solution. List the criteria for evaluating the completed document.**

Figure 15.10 RDBMS Planning Guide for Address Example

RELATIONAL DATABASE MANAGEMENT SYSTEMS PLANNING GUIDE

Name of Document: Addresses Date: 4/25/2002

Location of Electronic File: c:\my data\home\

Name: Jill Homeowner

Name of Client: Same

Step 1: Identify the Problem by Writing the Problem Statement.

Jill would like to computerize her address list. The data she keeps on her friends and family include name, address, phone number, e-mail address, fax number, birthday, anniversary, a check if a card is sent during the December holidays, an X if a birthday card is sent, and the names and birthdays of the immediate family members. She would like to have a listing of all information, a listing of names, addresses, e-mail, and phone numbers, and labels printed for any of the cards sent. She would like to have labels printed for the December holiday cards and another set of labels printed for all other cards, printed in date order.

Step 2: Understand the Problem.

Audience: Jill Homeowner

Required Outcomes of the Document:
Reports:

a. listing of all information
b. listing of names, addresses, e-mail addresses, and phone numbers
c. labels printed for the December holiday cards
d. labels printed for all other cards, printed in date order

Required Knowledge of the Problem to Develop the Document:
Address list information

Required Knowledge of the Audience:
Address information

Step 3: Identify Valid Alternative Methods to Solve the Problem.

a. Use a spreadsheet.
b. Use a relational database.

Step 4: Select the Best Method to Solve the Problem from the List of Alternative Solutions.

a. Use a relational database.

Figure 15.10 (continued)

Step 5: Plan Your Solution.

Software to be used: RDBMS

List of Required Reports:

Report Name	Data to be Included in Report
1. Directory	name, address, city, state, zipcode, phone
	fax, birthday, family members and their
	birthdays, anniversary
2. Phone	name, address, city, state, zipcode, phone
3. Holiday Labels	name, address, city, state, zipcode, hsend
4. Card Labels	name, address, city, state, zipcode, csend

There are no queries or forms for this problem.

(continued)

Figure 15.10 RDBMS Planning Guide for Address Example

Table Development.

Original Table:		First Normalization—New Table(s)		Second Normalization—New Table(s)		Third Normalization—New Table(s)	
Item	Field Name	Item	Field Name	Item	Field Name	Item	Field Name
Last Name	LAST	Family ID	FID	None		None	
First Name	FIRST	Family members	FNAMES				
Title	TITLE	Birthdays	FBIRTHDAYS				
Address	ADDRESS	Fcsend	FCSEND				
City	CITY						
State	STATE						
Zip Code	ZIPCODE						
Telephone	TELEPHONE						
E-mail	EMAIL						
Fax	FAX						
Birthday	BIRTHDAY						
Csend	CSEND						
Hsend	HSEND						
~~Family members~~	~~FNAMES~~						
~~Birthdays~~	~~FBIRTHDAYS~~						
~~Fcsend~~	~~FCSEND~~						
Family ID	FID						

Figure 15.10 (continued)

Schema.

ADDRESSES

Field Name
LAST
FIRST
TITLE
ADDRESS
CITY
STATE
ZIPCODE
TELEPHONE
EMAIL
FAX
BIRTHDAY
CSEND
HSEND
FID (1)

FAMILY

Field Name
(∞) FID
FNAMES
FBIRTHDAYS
FCSEND

Field Name

Field Name

Field Name

Field Name

Field Name

(continued)

Figure 15.10 RDBMS Planning Guide for Address Example

Table with Attributes.

Field Name	Description	Data Type	Field Length	No. of Decimals	Format	Input Mask	Default Value
Table Name: Addresses							
LAST	Last Name	Text	10				
FIRST	First Name	Text	10				
TITLE	Title	Text	9				
ADDRESS	Address	Text	15				
CITY	City	Text	10				
STATE	State	Text	3				CA
ZIPCODE	Zip Code	Text	10				
TELEPHONE	Telephone	Text	15			(xxx) xxx-xxxx	
EMAIL	E-mail Address	Text	15				
FAX	Fax	Text	15				
BIRTHDAY	Birthday	Date			Short due		
CSEND	Send Card	Logical			Yes/No		No
HSEND	Send H. Card	Logical			Yes/No		Yes
FID	Rel. Field	Text	4				
Table Name: Family							
FID	Rel. Field	Text	4				
FNAMES	Family Name	Text	10				
FBIRTHDAYS	Birthday	Date			Short date		
FCSEND	Card Send	Logical			Yes/No		No

Figure 15.10 (continued)

Step 5: Plan Your Solution. (con't)

Report Layouts: Report 1

Report Name: Directory

Table Name: Addresses/Family

Margins:

Top:	0.75	Top Printer:	0.25
Bottom:	0.75	Bottom Printer:	0.5
Left:	0.75	Left Printer:	0.25
Right:	0.75	Right Printer:	0.25
Header:	none	Top Printer:	0.25
Footer:	0.5	Bottom Printer:	0.25

Paper Size: 8½ x 11 Orientation: Landscape Color/B&W: B&W

Sort by: LAST

Subtotals on following fields: None

Header Contents: None

Footer Contents:

Date	XX	

Report Heading:

Address Directory

Report Layout: Report 1

Heading:	Name	Address	City	State	Zip Code
Field Name:	TITLE&FIRST&LAST	ADDRESS	CITY	STATE	ZIPCODE
Column Width:	30	10	10	7	10

Telephone	E-mail	Fax	Birthday	Send Holiday	Send Birthday
TELEPHONE	EMAIL	FAX	BIRTHDAY	HSEND	CSEND
15	15	15	10	14	16

(continued)

Figure 15.10 RDBMS Planning Guide for Address Example

Multiple Lines after Each of Above Lines:

Family Member	Birthday	Send Card			
FNAMES	FBIRTHDAYS	FCSEND			
10	10	11			

Report Layouts: Report 2

Report Name: Phone

Table Name: Addresses

Margins:

Top: 0.75 Top Printer: 0.25

Bottom: 0.75 Bottom Printer: 0.5

Left: 0.75 Left Printer: 0.25

Right: 0.75 Right Printer: 0.25

Header: none Top Printer: 0.25

Footer: 0.5 Bottom Printer: 0.25

Paper Size: 8½ x 11 Orientation: Landscape Color/B&W: B&W

Sort by: LAST

Subtotals on following fields: None

Header Contents: None

Footer Contents:

Date	XX	

Report Heading:

Addresses and Telephone List

Heading:	Name	Address	City	State	Zip Code	Telephone
Field Name:	TITLE&FIRST&LAST	ADDRESS	CITY	STATE	ZIPCODE	TELEPHONE
Column Width:	30	10	10	7	10	15

Figure 15.10 (continued)

Report Layouts: Report 3

Report Name: Holiday Labels

Table Name: Addresses

No Margins Specified

Paper Size: Labels Color/B&W: B&W

Sort by: LAST

Subtotals on following fields: None

Header Contents: None

Footer Contents: None

Report Heading: None

Label Layout:

TITLE&FIRST&LAST
ADDRESS
CITY, STATE ZIPCODE

Report Layouts: Report 4

Report Name: Card Labels

Table Name: Addresses

No Margins Specified

Paper Size: Labels Color/B&W: B&W

Sort by: Birthday

Subtotals on following fields: None

Header Contents: None

(continued)

Figure 15.10 RDBMS Planning Guide for Address Example

Step 5: Plan Your Solution. (con't)

Footer Contents: None

Report Heading: None

Label Layout:

TITLE&FIRST&LAST
ADDRESS
CITY, STATE ZIPCODE

Step 6: Evaluate the Solution. List the criteria for evaluating the completed document.

a. Do the reports have all of the data?
b. Are the reports easy to read?
c. Are the mailing labels printed correctly?

Jill would like to computerize her address list. The data she keeps on her friends and family include name, address, phone number, e-mail address, fax number, birthday, anniversary, a check if a card is sent during the December holidays, an X if a birthday card is sent, and the names and birthdays of the immediate family members. She would like a listing of all information, a listing of names, addresses, e-mail addresses, and phone numbers, and labels printed for any of the cards sent. She would like to have labels printed for the December holiday cards and another set printed of all other cards, printed in date order. See Figure 15.10 for the RDBMS planning guide for this example.

Database maintenance is a continual and complex job and many times is handled by a database administrator or a database manager. The more complex the database, the bigger the need for a single person to have the responsibility of maintaining it. Even at home, the database must be maintained. It is best to have one person in charge of that maintenance.

Summary

Relational database management systems (RDBMS) are data organizers. They allow the end user to enter data, organize data, and print reports. Databases created through the use of a RDBMS have multiple parts including tables that hold all the data, forms that display data, queries that select data, reports that output organized data, and macros that help to automate the database.

Tables are designed through the analysis of the required reports. The data are then normalized into tables for most efficient entry, use, and update of the database. A table is a group of related records. A record contains fields of individual pieces of data. The database schema shows the relationship between tables.

When designing a database, all the parts are designed individually. The tables are designed by designating fields and their attributes. Forms are designed by creating a place on the monitor for each field. Queries are designed to select specific fields and records to be placed in a query table. Reports are designed in accordance with the problem requirements.

Problems that require the use of a RDBMS tend to be more complex than those that require other software. However, since the use of a RDBMS is key to any business, it is most important to learn to design databases.

Key Words

Attributes
Database
Entity
Field
Input mask
Normalize
Primary key
Query table
Record
Relational database management system (RDBMS)
Report
Schema
Table

Questions

1. Name and explain the parts of a database.
2. Explain the use of a primary key.
3. When would you use a primary key?
4. Why would you *not* use a primary key? Give an example.
5. Why is a database table normalized?
6. Explain the process of normalizing your database table.
7. Explain a schema. Give an example of each type of table relationship.
8. Name and describe four attributes of a field. Include examples of each attribute in your answer.
9. Explain a query.
10. In Figure 15.6, how would you change the query to reflect the following:
    a. Include in the report only the name, the artist, and the producer.
    b. Include only Tom Blow's CDs in the report.
    c. Include only Tom Blow's CDs that were produced after 1985.
    d. Include all CDs that were produced after 1995 and all that belonged to Tom Blow.
    e. Include all CDs that were produced after 1995 and all belonging to Tom Blow that were produced after 1985.

Problems

1. Bill Hammer owns a hardware store. He has a special catalog for his customers who have indicated that they would like to receive one. He has the name, address, and favorite department of each customer. He would like to have mailing labels printed for these customers. Bill also would like to have a listing according to favorite departments so he can add specials to the most popular departments. Develop a RDBMS planning guide for this problem.
2. Susan Students has an audiotape collection that she would like to catalog. She prefers to have a report on the following:
    a. an alphabetical listing of the names of the tapes and associated information (artist and favorite listening place)
    b. an alphabetical listing of the artists and their tapes
    c. a listing of the tapes according to where she likes to listen to them most (the car, bedroom, family room, walking outside)
    d. a listing of all music selections and the tape on which each is found

    Develop a RDBMS planning guide for this problem.
3. You are the secretary of the computer club. You would like to computerize your membership list. You have the name, address, telephone number, and e-mail address for each member. You would also like to add the committee to which each member is assigned and the time when that committee meets. You would like to have a report listing all members' information, a report that lists names and e-mail addresses, a form that lists all information on members, and mailing labels. Develop a RDBMS planning guide for this problem.

Chapter 16

Rational Database Management Systems Case Studies

Overview

Case Study 1: Christmas Tree Sales
Case Study 2: Home Inventory
Case Study 3: Equipment Rental Control

Objectives

When you have finished this chapter, you should be able to:

1. Problem solve and develop plans to create complex relational databases for use in such cases as inventory control, equipment rental control, and nursery inventory.
2. Use the RDBMS planning guide and the six problem-solving steps to develop a solution for a problem that requires the use of RDBMS software.

Chapter 16 presents three case studies that require the use of RDBMS software to find a solution to a problem. Case study 1 involves tracking holiday tree sales. Case study 2 is a database for a home inventory. Case study 3 creates a database for tracking equipment rentals. A RDBMS planning guide is developed for each of these cases.

Case Study 1: Tree Sales

Case Study 1: Christmas Tree Sales

Our problem is as follows: The Ever-So-Green Holiday Tree Company sells trees during the December holidays. The company is developing a new marketing strategy. Instead of relying on its customers to come to its place of business, the company has hired a salesperson to contact local businesses and take preorders. The company needs a database to track the customers and their orders. The data on the trees include type of tree, size, grade, flocked or not, flame proofed or not, and if a tree stand is needed. The date of delivery needs to be included with the customer data. The company needs a report of the customers, the quantity of each type of tree, and a daily report of trees to be delivered. Figure 16.1 presents the RDBMS planning guide for case study 1.

This case study involves the ordering of trees by customers. After the trees are ordered, the data should be organized to know who the customers are, what they ordered, how many trees of each kind to order, and when to deliver the trees. Steps one through four and six are similar to other planning guides. The problem is developed in step five.

Figure 16.1 RDBMS Planning Guide for Case Study 1

RELATIONAL DATABASE MANAGEMENT SYSTEMS PLANNING GUIDE

Name of Database: Tree Sales Date: 9/10/2002

Location of Electronic File: c:\my data\work\EverSoGreen\

Name: Joe Green

Name of Client: Ever-So-Green Holiday Tree Company

Step 1: Identify the Problem by Writing the Problem Statement.

The Ever-So-Green Holiday Tree Company sells trees during the December holidays. Instead of relying on its customers to come to its place of business, the company has hired a salesperson to contact local businesses and take preorders. The company needs a database to track the customers and their orders. The data on the trees include type of tree, size, grade, flocked or not, flame proofed or not, and if a tree stand is needed. The trees are flocked, flame proofed, and the stands are put on after the trees are delivered to Ever-So-Green by the wholesalers. The date of delivery needs to be included with the customer data. The company needs a report of the customers, the quantity of each type of tree, and a report of trees to be delivered by day.

Step 2: Understand the Problem.

Audience:
The salespeople and managers of Ever-So-Green Holiday Tree Company.

Required Outcomes of the Document:
The required reports are as follows:

a. report of the customers
b. quantity of each type of tree that has been ordered
c. report of all sales
d. report of trees to be delivered by day

Required Knowledge of the Problem to Develop the Document:
Knowledge of the tree business

Required Knowledge of the Audience:
Knowledge of the tree business

Step 3: Identify Valid Alternative Methods to Solve the Problem.

a. Use a spreadsheet with database functions.
b. Use a relational database with normalized tables.
c. Use a relational database with one table.

Figure 16.1 (continued)

Step 4: **Select the Best Method to Solve the Problem from the List of Alternative Solutions.**

Use a relational database with normalized tables.

Step 5: **Plan Your Solution.**

Software to be used: RDBMS

List of Required Reports:

Report Name	Data to be Included in Report
1. Sales	name, address, city, state, zip code, date of
	delivery, tree information
2. Tree Quantity	tree type, grade, size
3. Delivery	customer information, tree information, by
	delivery date

There are no forms or queries for this case study.

(continued)

Figure 16.1 RDBMS Planning Guide for Case Study 1

Table Development.

Original Table:		First Normalization—New Table(s)		Second Normalization—New Table(s)		Third Normalization—New Table(s)	
Item	Field Name	Item	Field Name	Item	Field Name	Item	Field Name
First Name	LAST	None		Table 2		None	
Last Name	FIRST			Rel. Field	TID		
Address	ADDRESS			Tree Type	TYPE		
City	CITY						
State	STATE			Table 3			
Zip Code	ZIPCODE			Rel. Field	GID		
Telephone	TELEPHONE			Tree Grade	GRADE		
Date of Delivery	DATE						
~~Tree Type~~	~~TYPE~~			Table 4			
~~Tree Size~~	~~SIZE~~			Rel. Field	SID		
~~Tree Grade~~	~~GRADE~~			Tree Size	SIZE		
Flocked	FLOCKED						
Flame Proofed	FLAME						
Stand	STAND						
Rel. Field	TID						
Rel. Field	GID						
Rel. Field	SID						

Figure 16.1 (continued)

Schema.

SALES

Field Name
FIRST
LAST
ADDRESS
CITY
STATE
ZIPCODE
TELEPHONE
DATE
FLOCKED
FLAME
STAND
TID
GID
SID

TREE TYPE

Field Name
TID
TYPE

TREE SIZE

Field Name
SID
SIZE

Field Name

TREE GRADE

Field Name
GID
GRADE

Field Name

Field Name

(continued)

Figure 16.1 RDBMS Planning Guide for Case Study 1

Table with Attributes.

Field Name	Description	Data Type	Field Length	No. of Decimals	Format	Input Mask	Default Value
Table Name: Sales							
FIRST	Customer Name	Text	10				
LAST	Customer Name	Text	10				
ADDRESS	Address	Text	15				
CITY	City	Text	10				
STATE	State	Text	3				
ZIPCODE	Zip Code	Text	10				
TELEPHONE	Telephone	Text	15			(xxx) xxx-xxxx	
DATE	Delivery Date	Date			Short Date		
FLOCKED	Flocked	Logical	15		Yes/No		Yes
FLAME	Flame Proofed	Logical			Yes/No		Yes
STAND	Stand	Logical			Yes/No		Yes
TID	Rel. Field	Text	5				
GID	Rel. Field	Text	5				
SID	Rel. Field	Text	5				
Table: Tree Type							
TID	Rel. Field	Text	5				
TYPE	Tree Type	Text	10				
Table: Tree Size							
SID	Rel. Field	Text	5				
SIZE	Tree Size	Text	10				
Table: Tree Grade							
GID	Rel. Field	Text	5				
GRADE	Tree Grade	Text	10				

Figure 16.1 (continued)

Step 5: Plan Your Solution. (con't)

Report Layouts: Report 1

Report Name: Sales

Table Name: Sales/Tree Type/Tree Grade/Tree Size

Margins:

Top:	0.75	Top Printer:	0.25
Bottom:	0.75	Bottom Printer:	0.5
Left:	0.75	Left Printer:	0.25
Right:	0.75	Right Printer:	0.25
Header:	none	Top Printer:	0.25
Footer:	0.5	Bottom Printer:	0.25

Paper Size: 8½ x 11 Orientation: Landscape Color/B&W: B&W

Sort by: LAST

Subtotals on following fields: None

Header Contents: None

Footer Contents:

Date	XX	

Report Heading:

Sales by Customer

Report Layouts: Report 1

Heading:	Name	Address	City	State	Zip Code
Field Name:	FIRST&LAST	ADDRESS	CITY	STATE	ZIPCODE
Column Width:	30	10	10	7	10

Telephone	Tree Type	Tree Grade	Tree Size	Flocked	Flame Proofed
TELEPHONE	TYPE	GRADE	SIZE	FLOCKED	FLAME
15	5	12	12	12	14

(continued)

Figure 16.1 RDBMS Planning Guide for Case Study 1

Step 5: Plan Your Solution. (con't)

Stand	Delivery Date				
STAND	DATE				
10	10				

Report Layouts: Report 2

Report Name: Tree Quantity

Table Name: Sales/Tree Type/Tree Grade/Tree Size

Margins:

Top: 0.75 Top Printer: 0.25
Bottom: 0.75 Bottom Printer: 0.25
Left: 0.75 Left Printer: 0.25
Right: 0.75 Right Printer: 0.25
Header: none Top Printer: 0.25
Footer: 0.5 Bottom Printer: 0.25

Paper Size: 8½ x 11 Orientation: Landscape Color/B&W: B&W

Sort by: TYPE/GRADE/SIZE

Subtotals on following fields: TYPE/GRADE/SIZE Summary Lines only

Header Contents: None

Footer Contents:

Date	XX	

Report Heading:

Quantity of Trees

Column Heading:	Tree Type	Tree Grade	Tree Size		
Field Name:	TYPE	GRADE	SIZE		
Column Width:	15	15	15		

Figure 16.1 (continued)

Report Layouts: Report 3

Report Name: Delivery Dates

Table Name: Sales/Tree Type/Tree Grade/Tree Size

Margins:

Top:	0.75	Top Printer:	0.25
Bottom:	0.75	Bottom Printer:	0.5
Left:	0.75	Left Printer:	0.25
Right:	0.75	Right Printer:	0.25
Header:	none	Top Printer:	0.25
Footer:	0.5	Bottom Printer:	0.25

Paper Size: 8½ x 11 Orientation: Landscape Color/B&W: B&W

Sort by: DATE

Subtotals on following fields: Break at Date Change

Header Contents: None

Footer Contents:

Date	XX	

Report Heading:

Delivery Dates

Report Layout: Report 3

Delivery Date should be the subheading for each time the date changes.

Heading:	Name	Address	City	State	Zip Code
Field Name:	FIRST&LAST	ADDRESS	CITY	STATE	ZIPCODE
Column Width:	30	10	10	7	10

Telephone	Tree Type	Tree Grade	Tree Size	Flocked	Flame Proofed
TELEPHONE	TYPE	GRADE	SIZE	FLOCKED	FLAME
15	5	12	12	12	14

(continued)

Figure 16.1 RDBMS Planning Guide for Case Study 1

Step 5: **Plan Your Solution. (con't)**

Stand					
STAND					
10					

Step 6: **Evaluate the Solution. List the criteria for evaluating the completed document.**

a. Is the information correct?
b. Are the reports readable?
c. Are data missing?
d. Are the clients happy with the reports?

The first process in the development is to list the desired reports and the data needed to develop the reports. The next process is to list all the data necessary to make the reports, and then normalize the data into separate tables. In this case, second normalization is the only one required.

The schema is then developed. There are four files: Sales, Tree Type, Tree Grade, and Tree Size. The relationship between Sales and the other three are all many to one. There will be many sales of one tree type, one tree grade, and one tree size. The fields and their attributes for each table is created next. Notice the input mask on the telephone number, and the default values on flocked, flame proofed, and stand. It is assumed that for most sales the trees will be flocked, flame proofed, and will require a stand. There are no forms or queries needed for this case study.

The last process is to plan the reports. There are three reports required for this problem. The first is the sales report. The data will come from all four tables. The second report will be taken from the Tree Type, Tree Grade, and Tree Size tables. Only the summary lines will be printed showing the number of each type, grade, and size of tree. The last report is the delivery report. The data will come from all three files and will be ordered by date of delivery. There will be a section break after each day.

Case Study 2: Home Inventory

Case Study 2: Home Inventory

Our problem is as follows: John has just purchased homeowners insurance. His insurance agent has indicated that he should have an inventory of everything he owns in case of a disaster. He has just purchased a new computer with a RDBMS installed on it. John would like to use this for his inventory. He would like to keep the following information on his possessions:

1. Item
2. Original cost
3. Room where item is located
4. Retail store information where item was purchased
5. Appraised value of jewelry, artwork, and antiques
6. Appraiser's name, address, and phone number

John would like the following reports:

1. Alphabetical listing of the items and all associated data
2. List of the stores
3. List of the appraisers
4. Form for the monitor to view each item
5. List of items worth over $500

Figure 16.2 presents the RDBMS planning guide for case study 2.

Case study 2 involves an inventory for a household. This is a typical problem that arises for personal use of RDBMS. Steps one through four and six are similar to other planning guides. Step five develops the plan for this case study, which requires four reports and one screen form. After normalization, three tables include Inventory, Store, and Appraiser tables. The schema is developed next. There are three tables with a relationship between the Inventory table and the other two of many to one. There are many inventory items that were purchased at the same store and that had the same appraiser.

Figure 16.2 RDBMS Planning Guide for Case Study 2

RELATIONAL DATABASE MANAGEMENT SYSTEMS PLANNING GUIDE

Name of Document: Home Inventory Date: 6/3/2002

Location of Electronic File: c:\my data\home\

Name: John Homeowner

Name of Client: Self

Step 1: Identify the Problem by Writing the Problem Statement.

John has just purchased homeowners insurance. His insurance agent has indicated that he should have an inventory of everything he owns in case of a disaster. He has just purchased a new computer with a RDBMS installed on it. He would like to use this for his inventory. He would like to keep the following information on each item:

1. Item
2. Original cost
3. Room where item is located
4. Retail store information where the item was purchased
5. Appraised value of jewelry, artwork, and antiques
6. Appraiser's name, address, and phone number

John would like the following reports:

1. Alphabetical listing of the items and all associated data
2. List of the stores
3. List of the appraisers
4. Form for the monitor to view each item
5. List of items worth over $500.

Step 2: Understand the Problem.

Audience:
Insurance agent and John

Required Outcomes of the Document:
Reports on the following:

- **a.** alphabetical listing of the items and all associated data
- **b.** list of the stores where items were purchased
- **c.** list of the appraisers
- **d.** form for the monitor to view each item
- **e.** list of items worth over $500

Required Knowledge of the Problem to Develop the Document:
Knowledge of items in home, their prices, and appraisal values

Required Knowledge of the Audience:
Knowledge of insured items

Figure 16.2 (continued)

Step 3: Identify Valid Alternative Methods to Solve the Problem.

a. Use a spreadsheet with database functions.
b. Use a database with normalized tables.
c. Use a database with one table.

Step 4: Select the Best Method to Solve the Problem from the List of Alternative Solutions.

Use a database with normalized tables.

Step 5: Plan Your Solution

Software to be used: RDBMS

List of Required Reports:

Report Name	Data to be Included in Report
Inventory	item, original value, room, appraised value,
	store information, appraiser information
Stores	store information
Appraisers	appraiser information
Items over $500	items, original value, appraised value
Form to show one item:	
Inventory	Item, original value, room, appraised value,
	store, appraiser

(continued)

Figure 16.2 RDBMS Planning Guide for Case Study 2

Table Development.

Original Table:		First Normalization—New Table(s)		Second Normalization—New Table(s)		Third Normalization—New Table(s)	
Item	Field Name	Item	Field Name	Item	Field Name	Item	Field Name
Item	ITEM	None		Table 2:		None	
Room	ROOM			Store Purchased	STORE		
Original Value	VALUE			Store Address	SADDRESS		
Appraised Value	APPVALUE			Store City	SCITY		
~~Store Purchased~~	~~STORE~~			Store State	SSTATE		
~~Store Address~~	~~SADDRESS~~			Store Zip Code	SZIPCODE		
~~Store City~~	~~SCITY~~			Store Phone	SPHONE		
~~Store State~~	~~SSTATE~~						
~~Store Zipcode~~	~~SZIPCODE~~						
~~Store Phone~~	~~SPHONE~~			Table 3:			
~~Appraiser~~	~~APPRAISER~~			Appraiser	APPRAISER		
~~App. Address~~	~~AADDRESS~~			App. Address	AADDRESS		
~~App. City~~	~~ACITY~~			App. City	ACITY		
~~App. State~~	~~ASTATE~~			App. State	ASTATE		
~~App. Zip Code~~	~~AZIPCODE~~			App. Zip Code	AZIPCODE		
~~App. Phone~~	~~APHONE~~			App. Phone	APHONE		
Rel. Field	SID						
Rel. Field	AID						

Figure 16.2 (continued)

Schema.

INVENTORY

Field Name
ITEM
ROOM
VALUE
APPVALUE
SID
AID

STORES

Field Name	Field Name	Field Name
STORE		
SADDRESS		
SCITY		
SSTATE		
SZIPCODE		
SPHONE		
SID		

APPRAISERS

Field Name	Field Name	Field Name
APPRAISER		
AADDRESS		
ACITY		
ASTATE		
AZIPCODE		
APHONE		
AID		

(continued)

Figure 16.2 RDBMS Planning Guide for Case Study 2

Table with Attributes.

Field Name	Description	Data Type	Field Length	No. of Decimals	Format	Input Mask	Default Value
Table: Inventory							
ITEM	Inventory Item	Text	10				
ROOM	Location	Text	10				
VALUE	Original Value	Number	10				
APPVALUE	Appraised Value	Number	10				
SID	Rel. Field	Text	5				
AID	Rel. Field	Text	5				
Table: Stores							
SID	Rel. Field	Text	5				
STORE	Store Name	Text	10				
SADDRESS	Store Address	Text	15				
SCITY	Store City	Text	10				
SSTATE	Store State	Text	3				
SZIPCODE	Store Zip Code	Text	10				
SPHONE	Store Phone	Text	15			(xxx) xxx-xxxx	
Table: Appraisers							
AID	Rel. Field	Text	5				
APPRAISER	Appraiser Name	Text	10				
AADDRESS	App. Address	Text	15				
ACITY	App. City	Text	10				
ASTATE	App. State	Text	3				
AZIPCODE	App. Zip Code	Text	10				
APHONE	App. Phone	Text	15			(xxx) xxx-xxxx	

Figure 16.2 (continued)

Form design.

Background: Default

Table: Inventory/Store/Appraisers

Item Name: [ITEM]

Room Where Located: [ROOM]

Original Value: [VALUE] Store Where Purchased: [STORE]

Appraised Value: [APPVALUE] Appraiser: [APPRAISER]

Queries.

Table Name: Inventory

Field Name:	ITEM	ROOM	VALUE	APPVALUE	SID	AID	
Table:	Inventory	Inventory	Inventory	Inventory	Inventory	Inventory	
Sort:							
Show:	X	X	X	X			
Criteria:			>500				
OR:				>500			

(continued)

Figure 16.2 RDBMS Planning Guide for Case Study 2

Step 5: Plan Your Solution. (con't)

Report Layouts: Report 1

Report Name: Inventory

Table Name: Inventory/Stores/Appraisers

Margins:

Top: 0.75 | Top Printer: 0.25

Bottom: 0.75 | Bottom Printer: 0.5

Left: 0.75 | Left Printer: 0.25

Right: 0.75 | Right Printer: 0.25

Header: none | Top Printer: 0.25

Footer: 0.5 | Bottom Printer: 0.25

Paper Size: 8½ x 11 Orientation: Landscape Color/B&W: B&W

Sort by: Item

Subtotals on following fields: None

Header Contents: None

Footer Contents:

Date	XX	

Report Heading:

Home Inventory

Report Layout: Report 1

Heading:	Item	Location	Value	App. Value	Store
Field Name:	ITEM	ROOM	VALUE	APPVALUE	STORE
Column Width:	12	12	10	10	12

Address	City	State	Zip Code	Telephone	Appraiser
SADDRESS	SCITY	SSTATE	SZIPCODE	STELEPHONE	APPRAISER
15	12	8	12	12	12

Figure 16.2 (continued)

Address	City	State	Zip Code	Telephone	
AADDRESS	ACITY	ASTATE	AZIPCODE	APHONE	
15	12	3	10	12	

Report Layouts: Report 2

Report Name: Stores

Table Name: Stores

Margins:

Top: 0.75 Top Printer: 0.25
Bottom: 0.75 Bottom Printer: 0.5
Left: 0.75 Left Printer: 0.25
Right: 0.75 Right Printer: 0.25
Header: none Top Printer: 0.25
Footer: 0.5 Bottom Printer: 0.25

Paper Size: 8½ x 11 Orientation: Landscape Color/B&W: B&W
Sort by: STORE
Subtotals on following fields: None
Header Contents: None

Footer Contents:

Date	XX	

Report Heading:

Home Inventory: List of Stores

Report Layout: Report 2

Heading:	Store	Address	City	State	Zip Code
Field Name:	STORE	SADDRESS	SCITY	SSTATE	SZIPCODE
Column Width:	15	12	12	8	12

(continued)

Figure 16.2 RDBMS Planning Guide for Case Study 2

Step 5: Plan Your Solution. (con't)

Telephone					
STELEPHONE					
12					

Report Layouts: Report 3

Report Name: Appraisers

Table Name: Appraisers

Margins:

Top: 0.75	Top Printer: 0.25
Bottom: 0.75	Bottom Printer: 0.5
Left: 0.75	Left Printer: 0.25
Right: 0.75	Right Printer: 0.25
Header: none	Top Printer: 0.25
Footer: 0.5	Bottom Printer: 0.25

Paper Size: 8½ x 11 Orientation: Landscape Color/B&W: B&W

Sort by: Appraiser

Subtotals on following fields: None

Header Contents: None

Footer Contents:

Date	XX	

Report Heading:

Home Inventory: List of Appraisers

Report Layout: Report 3

Heading:	Appraiser	Address	City	State	Zip Code
Field Name:	APPRAISER	APPADDRESS	APPCITY	APPSTATE	APPZIPCODE
Column Width:	15	12	12	8	12

Telephone					
APPTELEPHONE					
12					

Figure 16.2 (continued)

Report Layouts: Report 4

Report Name: Items Over $500

Table Name: Inventory Query

Margins:

Top:	0.75	Top Printer:	0.25
Bottom:	0.75	Bottom Printer:	0.5
Left:	0.75	Left Printer:	0.25
Right:	0.75	Right Printer:	0.25
Header:	none	Top Printer:	0.25
Footer:	0.5	Bottom Printer:	0.25

Paper Size: 8½ x 11 Orientation: Landscape Color/B&W: B&W

Sort by: ITEM

Subtotals on following fields: None

Header Contents: None

Footer Contents:

Date	XX	

Report Heading:

Home Inventory: List of Items over $500

Report Layout: Report 4

Heading:	Item	Value	Appraised Value		
Field Name:	ITEM	VALUE	APPVALUE		
Column Width:	15	12	12		

Step 6: Evaluate the Solution. List the criteria for evaluating the completed document.

a. Are the reports correct?
b. Are the reports easy to read?
c. Is any information missing?
d. Should anything be added?

The fields and their attributes for each table were developed next. Notice the input masks on the telephone numbers. The screen form for one inventory item was developed. The items were placed on the screen in the best viewing order. Report four required a query to select all items that cost or were appraised at more than $500. The reports were then planned. Report 1 is a listing of the inventory and requires the use of the Stores and Appraisers tables. Report 2 is a listing of the store information from the Stores table. Report 3 lists the appraiser's information from the Appraisers table. Report 4 uses the query table to list those items that cost or were appraised at more than $500.

Case Study 3: Equipment Rental Control

Case Study 3: Equipment Rental Control

Dave's Equipment Rental needs to have a control on the rental equipment. All data are kept by manual records and sometimes get lost in the shuffle of busy days. Dave would like the following reports:

1. Customer report: customer name, ID, address, and amount of money owed to Dave
2. Equipment report: equipment number, description, area stored in, original cost, date purchased, and vendor information
3. Equipment rental report: equipment information, customer information, and date checked out (List only equipment checked out.)
4. List of equipment that has not been checked out for the last 60 days
5. A way to see information about one piece of equipment on the computer, including the name of the equipment, the equipment number, the location of the equipment, last time checked out and in, and by whom.

Figure 16.3 presents the RDBMS planning guide for case study 3.

Case study 3 involves the tracking of equipment rentals. Steps one through four and six are similar to other planning guides. Step five develops a plan for the solution. There are four reports and one screen form. Step five of the RDBMS planning guide presents the data required for each of these reports. These data are then transferred to the table development form to be normalized. The result of normalization is four tables. The Rented table includes the customer ID and the equipment ID for the rental of one piece of equipment. The Customer table includes information on the customer such as address, phone, and amount of money owed to Dave's Equipment Rental. The Equipment table includes information about the equipment such as the equipment description, the purchased price and date, the purchase vendor ID, the date that the equipment was last checked out and in, and the location of the equipment in the warehouse. The Vendors table includes information about the vendors such as address, phone, and contact person.

The schema is developed next. There are four tables. The Rented table has a relational field with the Customers and the Equipment tables. This Rented table and the Customers table have a many to one relationship since one customer could check out many pieces of equipment. The Rented table and the Equipment table have a one to one relationship since each record in the Rented table indicated one piece of equipment that is rented out. The Equipment and Vendor tables have a many to one relationship since there are many pieces of equipment that are ordered from one vendor.

The fields and their attributes are then determined. The one screen form is planned as to where each piece of data will be located. There are two reports that require queries. Report 3 requires that only the equipment that is to be checked out be included. Report

Figure 16.3 RDBMS Planning Guide for Case Study 3

RELATIONAL DATABASE MANAGEMENT SYSTEMS PLANNING GUIDE

Name of Database: Rentals Date: 3/24/2002

Location of Electronic File: c:\my data\work\Daves Rentals

Name: Norm Consultant Service

Name of Client: Dave's Equipment Rental

Step 1: Identify the Problem by Writing the Problem Statement.

Dave's Equipment Rental needs to have a control on the rental equipment. All data are kept by manual records and sometimes get lost in the shuffle of busy days. Dave would like the following reports:

1. Customer report: customer name, ID, address, and amount of money owed to Dave
2. Equipment report: equipment number, description, area stored in, original cost, date purchased, and vendor information
3. Equipment rental report: equipment information, customer information, and date checked out. List only equipment checked out.
4. List of equipment that has not been checked out for the last 60 days
5. A way to see information about one piece of equipment on the computer, including the name of the equipment, the equipment number, the location of the equipment, last time checked out and in, and by whom

Step 2: Understand the Problem.

Audience:
Dave and his employees

Required Outcomes of the Document:
The following reports are required:

a. Customer report: customer name, ID, address, and amount of money owed to Dave
b. Equipment report: equipment number, description, area stored in, original cost, date purchased, and vendor information
c. Equipment rental report: equipment information, customer information, and date checked out (List only equipment checked out.)
d. List of equipment that has not been checked out for the last 60 days
e. A way to see information about one piece of equipment on the computer, including the name of the equipment, the equipment number, the location of the equipment, last time checked out and in, and by whom

Required Knowledge of the Problem to Develop the Document:
Knowledge of the rental business

Required Knowledge of the Audience:
Knowledge of the equipment

(continued)

Figure 16.3 RDBMS Planning Guide for Case Study 3

Step 3: Identify Valid Alternative Methods to Solve the Problem.

a. Use a relational database.
b. Use one table.
c. Use normalized tables.
d. Use a spreadsheet and database functions.

Step 4: Select the Best Method(s) to Solve the Problem from the List of Alternative Solutions.

a. Use a relational database.
b. Use normalized tables.

Step 5: Plan Your Solution.

Software to be used: RDBMS

List of Required Reports:

Report Name	Data to be Included in Report
1. Customer	customer name, customer ID, customer
	address, customer phone, money owed
2. Equipment	equipment number, description, area stored,
	original cost, date purchased,
	vendor name, vendor address,
	vendor phone, vendor contact
3. Rental	equipment number, description, customer
	name, customer ID, customer address,
	customer phone, date checked out
	List only equipment checked out.
4. Unused	equipment number, description, area stored,
	original cost, date purchased
	List only equipment that has not been
	checked out for the last 60 days.
Form:	
Equipment	equipment number, description, area stored,
	last time checked out, last time
	checked in, customer ID, customer
	name

Figure 16.3 (continued)

Table Development.

Original Table:		First Normalization—New Table(s)		Second Normalization—New Table(s)		Third Normalization—New Table(s)	
Item	Field Name	Item	Field Name	Item	Field Name	Item	Field Name
~~customer name~~	~~CNAME~~	Table 1: Rented		Table 2: Customers		None	
~~customer ID~~	~~CID~~	Customer ID	CID	customer name	CNAME		
~~customer address~~	~~CADDRESS~~	Equipment ID	EID	customer ID	CID		
~~customer city~~	~~CCITY~~			customer address	CADDRESS		
~~customer state~~	~~CSTATE~~			customer city	CCITY		
~~customer zip code~~	~~CZIPCODE~~			customer state	CSTATE		
~~customer phone~~	~~CPHONE~~			customer zip code	CZIPCODE		
~~money owed~~	~~OWED~~			customer phone	CPHONE		
~~equipment ID~~	~~EID~~			money owed	OWED		
~~equipment desc.~~	~~DESCRIPTION~~			Table 3: Equipment			
~~location~~	~~LOCATION~~			equipment ID	EID		
~~original cost~~	~~COST~~			equipment desc.	DESCRIPTION		
~~date purchased~~	~~PURCHASED~~			location	LOCATION		
~~vendor name~~	~~VNAME~~			original cost	COST		
~~vendor address~~	~~VADDRESS~~			date purchased	PURCHASED		
~~vendor city~~	~~VCITY~~			date checked out	OUT		
~~vendor state~~	~~VSTATE~~			date checked in	IN		
~~vendor zip code~~	~~VZIPCODE~~			vendor ID	VID		
~~vendor phone~~	~~VCONTACT~~			Table 4: Vendors			
~~vendor contact~~	~~VPHONE~~			vendor ID	VID		
~~date checked out~~	~~OUT~~			vendor name	VNAME		
~~date checked in~~	~~IN~~			vendor address	VADDRESS		
~~vendor id~~	~~VID~~			vendor city	VCITY		
				vendor state	VSTATE		
				vendor zip code	VZIPCODE		
				vendor phone	VPHONE		
				vendor contact	VCONTACT		

Figure 16.3 RDBMS Planning Guide for Case Study 3

Schema.

RENTED

Field Name
CID
EID

CUSTOMERS

Field Name
CNAME
CID
CADDRESS
CCITY
CSTATE
CZIPCODE
CPHONE
OWED

VENDORS

Field Name
VID
VNAME
VADDRESS
VCITY
VSTATE
VZIPCODE
VPHONE
VCONTACT

(untitled)

Field Name

EQUIPMENT

Field Name
EID
DESCRIPTION
LOCATION
COST
PURCHASED
OUT
IN
VID

(untitled)

Field Name

(untitled)

Field Name

Figure 16.3 (continued)

Table with Attributes.

Field Name	Description	Data Type	Field Length	No. of Decimals	Format	Input Mask	Default Value
Table 1: Rented							
CID	Customer ID	Text	5				
EID	Equipment ID	Text	5				
Table 2: Customers							
CNAME	customer name	Text	10				
CID	customer ID	Text	5				
CADDRESS	customer address	text	15				
CCITY	customer city	text	10				
CSTATE	customer state	Text	3				CA
CZIPCODE	customer zip code	Text	10				
CPHONE	customer phone	Text	15			(xxx) xxx-xxxx	
OWED	money owed	Number		2	currency		
Table 3: Equipment							
EID	equipment ID	Text	5				
DESCRIPTION	equipment desc.	Text	15				
LOCATION	location	Text	10				
COST	original cost	Number		2	currency		
PURCHASED	date purchased	Date			short date		
OUT	date checked out	Date			short date		
IN	date chekced in	Date			short date		
VID	vendor ID	Text	5				

Figure 16.3 RDBMS Planning Guide for Case Study 3

Table with Attributes.

Field Name	Description	Data Type	Field Length	No. of Decimals	Format	Input Mask	Default Value
Table 4: Vendors							
VID	vendor ID	Text	5				
VNAME	vendor name	Text	10				
VADDRESS	vendor address	Text	15				
CCITY	vendor city	Text	10				
VSTATE	vendor state	Text	3				
VZIPCODE	vendor zip code	Text	10				
VPHONE	vendor phone	Text	15			(xxx)xxx-xxxx	
VCONTACT	vendor contact	Text	10				

Figure 16.3 (continued)

Form design.

Background: Default

Table: Equipment/customers

Equipment Number: [EID]

Equipment Description: [DESCRIPTION]

Location of Equipment: [LOCATION]

Last Checked Out: [OUT]

Last Checked In: [IN]

Last Checked Out By: [CNAME]

Customer ID Number: [CID]

(continued)

Figure 16.3 RDBMS Planning Guide for Case Study 3

Queries.

Query for Report 3

Field Name:	CNAME	CPHONE	DESCRIPTION	EID	OUT	IN	
Table:	Customer	Customer	Equipment	Equipment	Equipment	Equipment	
Sort:							
Show:	X	X	X	X	X		
Criteria:					>IN	<OUT	
OR:							

Query for Report 4

Field Name:	EID	DESCRIPTION	LOCATION	COST	DATE	OUT	
Table:	Equipment	Equipment	Equipment	Equipment	Equipment	Equipment	
Sort:							
Show:	X	X	X	X	X		
Criteria:						<TODAY()-60	
OR:							

Figure 16.3 (continued)

Step 5: Plan Your Solution. (con't)

Report Layouts: Report 1

Report Name: Customers

Table Name: Customers

Margins:

Top:	0.75	Top Printer:	0.25
Bottom:	0.75	Bottom Printer:	0.5
Left:	0.75	Left Printer:	0.25
Right:	0.75	Right Printer:	0.25
Header:	none	Top Printer:	0.25
Footer:	0.5	Bottom Printer:	0.25

Paper Size: 8½ x 11 Orientation: Landscape Color/B&W: B&W

Sort by: CNAME

Subtotals on following fields: None

Header Contents: None

Footer Contents:

Date	XX	

Report Heading:

Dave's Equipment Rental: Customer List

Report Layout: Report 1

Heading:	Customer ID	Name	Address	City	State
Field Name:	CID	NAME	CADDRESS	CCITY	CSTATE
Column Width:	12	15	12	12	8

Zip Code	Telephone	Money Owed			
CZIPCODE	CTELEPHONE	OWED			
12	12	10			

(continued)

Figure 16.3 RDBMS Planning Guide for Case Study 3

Step 5: Plan Your Solution. (con't)

Report Layouts: Report 2

Report Name: Equipment

Table Name: Equipment

Margins:

Top:	0.75	Top Printer:	0.25
Bottom:	0.75	Bottom Printer:	0.5
Left:	0.75	Left Printer:	0.25
Right:	0.75	Right Printer:	0.25
Header:	none	Top Printer:	0.25
Footer:	0.5	Bottom Printer:	0.25

Paper Size: 8½ x 11 Orientation: Landscape Color/B&W: B&W

Sort by: DESCRIPTION

Subtotals on following fields: None

Header Contents: None

Footer Contents:

Date	XX	

Report Heading:

Dave's Equipment Rental: Equipment List

Report Layout: Report 2

Heading:	Equipment ID	Description	Location	Original Cost	Date Purchased
Field Name:	EID	NAME	LOCATION	COST	PURCHASED
Column Width:	12	15	12	12	12

Vendor Name	Address	City	State	Zip Code	
VNAME	VADDRESS	VCITY	VSTATE	VZIPCODE	
12	15	12	8	10	

Telephone	Contact				
CTELEPHONE	CONTACT				
12	12				

Figure 16.3 (continued)

Report Layouts: Report 3

Report Name: Rented

Table Name: Report 3 Query Table

Margins:

Top:	0.75	Top Printer:	0.25
Bottom:	0.75	Bottom Printer:	0.5
Left:	0.75	Left Printer:	0.25
Right:	0.75	Right Printer:	0.25
Header:	none	Top Printer:	0.25
Footer:	0.5	Bottom Printer:	0.25

Paper Size: 8½ x 11 Orientation: Landscape Color/B&W: B&W

Sort by: EID

Subtotals on following fields: None

Header Contents: None

Footer Contents:

Date	XX	

Report Heading:

Dave's Equipment Rental: Equipment Rented Out

Report Layout: Report 3

Heading:	Equipment ID	Description	Date/Out	Date/In	Customer Name
Field Name:	EID	DESCRIPTION	OUT	IN	CNAME
Column Width:	12	15	12	12	15

Customer Address	City	State	Zip Code	Telephone	
CADDRESS	CCITY	CSTATE	CZIPCODE	CTELEPHONE	
15	12	8	10	12	

Figure 16.3 RDBMS Planning Guide for Case Study 3

Step 5: Plan Your Solution. (con't)

Report Layouts: Report 4

Report Name: Unused

Table Name: Report 4 Query Table

Margins:

Top: 0.75 Top Printer: 0.25

Bottom: 0.75 Bottom Printer: 0.5

Left: 0.75 Left Printer: 0.25

Right: 0.75 Right Printer: 0.25

Header: none Top Printer: 0.25

Footer: 0.5 Bottom Printer: 0.25

Paper Size: 8½ x 11 Orientation: Landscape Color/B&W: B&W

Sort by: EID

Subtotals on following fields: None

Header Contents: None

Footer Contents:

Date	XX	

Report Heading:

Dave's Equipment Rental: Unused Equipment

Report Layout: Report 4

Heading:	Equipment ID	Description	Location	Purchase Date	Original Cost
Field Name:	EID	DESCRIPTION	LOCATION	PURCHASED	COST
Column Width:	12	15	12	12	15

Figure 16.3 (continued)

Step 6: **Evaluate the Solution. List the criteria for evaluating the completed document.**

- **a.** Are the reports correct?
- **b.** Is information missing?
- **c.** Are the reports easy to read?
- **d.** Are the clients happy with the reports?
- **e.** Is the database easy to update?

4 requires only those pieces of equipment that have not been checked out for more than 60 days be included.

There are four reports to be developed. Report 1 is a customer report and a listing of all customers. Data are taken from the Customer table. Report 2 is a listing of all equipment from the Equipment table. Report 3 is a listing of equipment that is out from the Report 3 query table. Report 4 is a listing of all equipment that has not been checked out for the last 60 days. This report used the Report 4 query table.

These three case studies are developed to the point of adding automation to the database. Automation will be presented in Chapter 17.

Summary

This chapter presents three case studies to be completed using RDBMS software. Case study 1 involves the tracking of Christmas tree sales. Case study 2 is a database for a home inventory. Case study 3 creates a database for tracking equipment rentals. The completed document planning guide for each case is presented.

Problems

1. The New Plays Repertory Theater would like to computerize its ticket sales. The theater seats 500 people. The theater company provides seven plays each year and sells season tickets, along with single-night tickets. The season tickets are all for the same performance during the week. Each play has 20 performances. The theater keeps a customer list of those people who buy tickets in order to send play information for advertising purposes.

   Reports that the theater would like to have are as follows:

   - **a.** listing of available seats
   - **b.** listing of all plays and the actors in the plays
   - **c.** listing of customers
   - **d.** labels printed for all customers
   - **e.** list of season ticket holders

   Create a RDBMS planning guide for this problem.

2. You are planning a trip to France. You are compiling documented research on lodging, restaurants, and things to do for the cities you are interested in visiting. The amount of data is beginning to overwhelm you. Therefore, you would like to organize it all on the computer. The reports you would like include the following:
   a. listing of all lodgings and associated information
   b. listing of all restaurants and associated information
   c. listing of all activities and associated information
   d. listing of each city with lodging, restaurants, and activities associated with it

   Develop a RDBMS planning guide for this problem.
3. Sam Manager is the sales manager at the regional office of XYZ Gadgets Inc. He needs to prepare an annual report that includes the following:
   a. listing of salespeople, their territories, their sales, and the number of clients they have
   b. listing of all clients
   c. listing of territories and total number of sales, salespeople, and clients
   d. listing of the total sales per month

   Develop a RDBMS planning guide for this problem.

UNIT SIX:

PROGRAMMING FOR APPLICATIONS

Chapter 17

Integrating Applications for Information Processing

Overview

Objectives

When you have finished this chapter, you should be able to:

1. Develop solutions for problems requiring the use of multiple software packages and the theory of information processing.
2. Understand how to increase productivity through the use of suites.
3. Understand the concept of sharing files.
4. Understand and develop solutions for problems using object linking and embedding (OLE).

The emphasis in the preceding chapters has been directed toward individual types of software including presentation graphics, word processing, desktop publishing, spreadsheets, and relational database management systems. In reality, these products are many times used together to develop a solution to a problem. You may want to design a letter for a client that includes a graphic and an imported spreadsheet. You may want data imported into a spreadsheet from a relational database management system. Keep in mind why each type of software was created:

- the word processor to efficiently accomplish text editing,
- the desktop publisher to efficiently combine graphics and text on a page,
- presentation graphics to easily create electronic slide shows,
- spreadsheets to easily enter, calculate, and analyze numeric data, and
- relational database management systems to easily organize and report large amounts of text and numeric data.

Information Processing

Information or Document Processing

The use of more than one type of software to create a solution to a problem is called **information processing** or **document processing.** It incorporates the sharing of data between software packages. For example, a letter developed in a word processor may require sharing data from a graphics package and from a spreadsheet software package. If this sharing of data is not possible, then you would be required to enter data into more than one package, assuming each package has the capability of accepting the data. Reentering of data is not only time consuming, but it also increases the possibility of errors.

When creating a solution to a problem using document processing, think about how each software package contributes to the final solution. Keep in mind which package will do the best job for each part of the solution. This is true information processing. Also keep in mind that the best solution may be the use of only one type of software. There is no requirement that multiple software packages must be used to complete a solution.

For example, if you have a problem that requires numerical analysis on data, first consider using a spreadsheet. If the problem requires a letter to be prepared containing the spreadsheet, however, then consider using the spreadsheet to analyze the data and then importing it into a word processor, because a word processor is the best type of software to create the letter. You could use the table feature in a word processor to analyze and display the data. Note that a word processor does not accomplish numerical analysis as well as spreadsheet software.

Another example of information processing is job costing a project. A contractor may use a RDBMS to store the data on the components of building a house. When he is creating a bid to build a specific house, he would import data from the database into the spreadsheet package to analyze the costs. He would then import the spreadsheet data into a word processor to complete the bid. He would be using the ideal software to accomplish each portion of the bid process.

Suites

Suites

Software presented in this text is frequently part of a package called a **suite.** A suite is three or more software productivity packages such as word processing, spreadsheets, presentation graphics, and relational database management systems that are packaged together along with other related software such as clipart, paint or draw software, and internet software. A software company may have several combinations of these packages and identify its own suites with slightly different names.

When you purchase a suite, examine the software that is included to be sure you have the desired packages. Many times a suite is bundled with the hardware that you purchase. If the bundled suite does not include all of the software packages that you need, plan to upgrade the suite to the one you desire.

Sometimes you may be working on a computer and it does not have all of the desired software. For example, perhaps the relational database management system is missing. You will need to decide which of your existing software packages will be the best replacement. In this case, the spreadsheet software package may be a good substitute for the RDBMS software. If you do not have a desktop publisher, a word processor is normally a good substitute. Rarely will you have all of the desired software packages on your computer. A good computer skill to learn is how to choose the best software to accomplish the job from the software packages that are available. When you have learned this skill, along with good planning techniques, you should improve your productivity and decrease your frustrations using the computer.

In addition to multiple software packages, a suite has other features that also increase your productivity. Some of these features we have already discussed in the text and they are the commonalties between packages of menu items, look-alike screens, and similar toolbars. Another feature that saves time is the ability to **drag and drop** across applications. You may have both your spreadsheet package and your word-processing package open and displayed side by side on your desktop. You may select items in your spreadsheet and drag and drop them into your word-processed document, or perhaps drag and drop text from your word processor to a cell in your spreadsheet. There is no need to cut and paste.

Another feature of a suite is the file compatibility between software. This is sometimes called cross-application integration. There is no need to worry about saving in a compatible format, because the suite is designed to accept all formats from other software packages included in the suite. Cross-application integration also includes the ability to use one package from another package. For example, you may create a word-processed report using the report form design in a RDBMS from the RDBMS software package; or you may create a spreadsheet chart from the word-processing software package.

Using a suite is convenient in many ways. First, it is usually less expensive than purchasing each package separately. Second, because of the features, a suite increases your productivity. Third, a suite is easier to learn because of the commonalties. Last, for most problems in business, there are very few companion software packages that you will need beyond the suite.

Sharing Files

Sharing Files

Information processing requires file sharing, including drag and drop across applications, cut and paste, and the importing and exporting of files. One document may share all or part of a file. To share part of a file, you are required to either use the drag-and-drop feature or use cut and paste. Realize that cut and paste also means copy and paste. It is best to copy and paste. These features allow you to select all or part of another file for inclusion in the document on which you are working.

Importing Files

Importing files means to have the computer copy all of the information in one file into the active document. When the imported information is inserted in the text, it starts at the point where the cursor is located even if the cursor is on another page. Be sure to check the location of the cursor. If the information is imported as a floating object, then the object is inserted somewhere on the page you are viewing. A floating object may then be moved around on the page. If the object is not floating, then you move the object as you would text, using the space bar and the enter key.

Exporting Files

Exporting files means that you are saving the file in another format other than the default format. Exporting files includes using the Save As feature to save files for use in other versions of the same program, in other software packages, and in other formats such as RTF (rich text format), HTML (hypertext markup language), and PDF (portable document format). RTF saves your file in a file format that retains little of the character, paragraph, and document formats. HTML is the format used for web page development.

PDF Files

PDF is used for electronic printing. It is one way to make your file into a format that almost anyone can read and print. PDF files may be exported from many software packages; however, very few allow you to import PDF files. Adobe Acrobat allows you to view and print PDF files. Adobe Acrobat may be downloaded from the Adobe website. PDF files are becoming a common way to distribute information to many people when you do not know the software available on their computers.

Object Linking and Embedding

Object Linking and Embedding (OLE)

When you import data files, you will use **object linking and embedding (OLE).** Embedding a file is to copy the contents of one file—the file you are importing—into an active file—the file on which you are currently working. An active file is one that is open, viewed on the monitor, and has the title bar of the software package colored (not grayed out). If you modify the original imported file at a later date, the data in the file where it was first imported is not modified. After importing the file, there is no connection between the two files.

Linking a File

At times, however, you will want a connection to the imported file. When this occurs, you should link the imported file to provide the connection you desire between the imported file and the file in which it was imported. When you link the imported file, the location of the file is embedded instead of the complete file. This embedded location points to the storage location where the file can be found. The linked imported file is temporarily copied to the document when it is to be viewed or printed. A low resolution copy may be embedded to retain the space and to show what the file looks like if the link is lost. If the computer can find the linked file, the higher resolution graphic replaces the low resolution copy. A link is lost or broken when the embedded location of the imported file becomes incorrect. If the imported file is moved, then the location of the imported file changes. The embedded location no longer points to where the import file is located. If you have saved the imported linked file on a hard drive of your computer at home and then come to school to view your document, you will have broken the link because the computer at school is not connected to your home computer. Figure 17.1 shows examples of OLE.

To ensure minimal problems of broken or lost links, create a file folder for your project. Save or copy all files to be imported to this folder before you import them. Save your document to this folder also. Import your files from this folder. When you change locations of your files such as from your hard drive to a floppy disk or a zip cartridge, copy the entire folder from one place to the other. In this way, all linked files and project files remain in the same folder as when they were created. Do not move any of these files from this folder or you will find you have broken some of your links. If you do have broken links, your software program has a feature to update them.

Why Link Files?

There are three times when you may want to link files. First, you will link files when you want to modify the imported file at a later date and want the modifications to be made in the file in which it was imported. There are times when you want your file to change when the imported file is modified, for example, in a slide show presentation in which you have a picture that you desire to be changed each time you give a presentation. If the imported picture file is linked to the slide show, whenever the picture file changes, then the picture in the slide show will also change.

Second, you should link your files when there are many places in your document that the file needs to be imported. Graphics tend to be large files. If the same file is embedded many times, your document file becomes quite large. You can decrease this amount by linking the files. Since only a low resolution copy is placed in the document, the total document size decreases. For example, if you have a file that is 3 megabytes in volume and you import it 10 times, it will add 30 megabytes to your document. If the low resolution copy is 0.25 megabyte, it will only add 2.5 megabytes to your file when the file is linked.

Third, you may want to link files when your file becomes quite large. As mentioned, graphics tend to be large files, so when you import many graphics files your working document also becomes large. The larger the file, the longer it takes to move

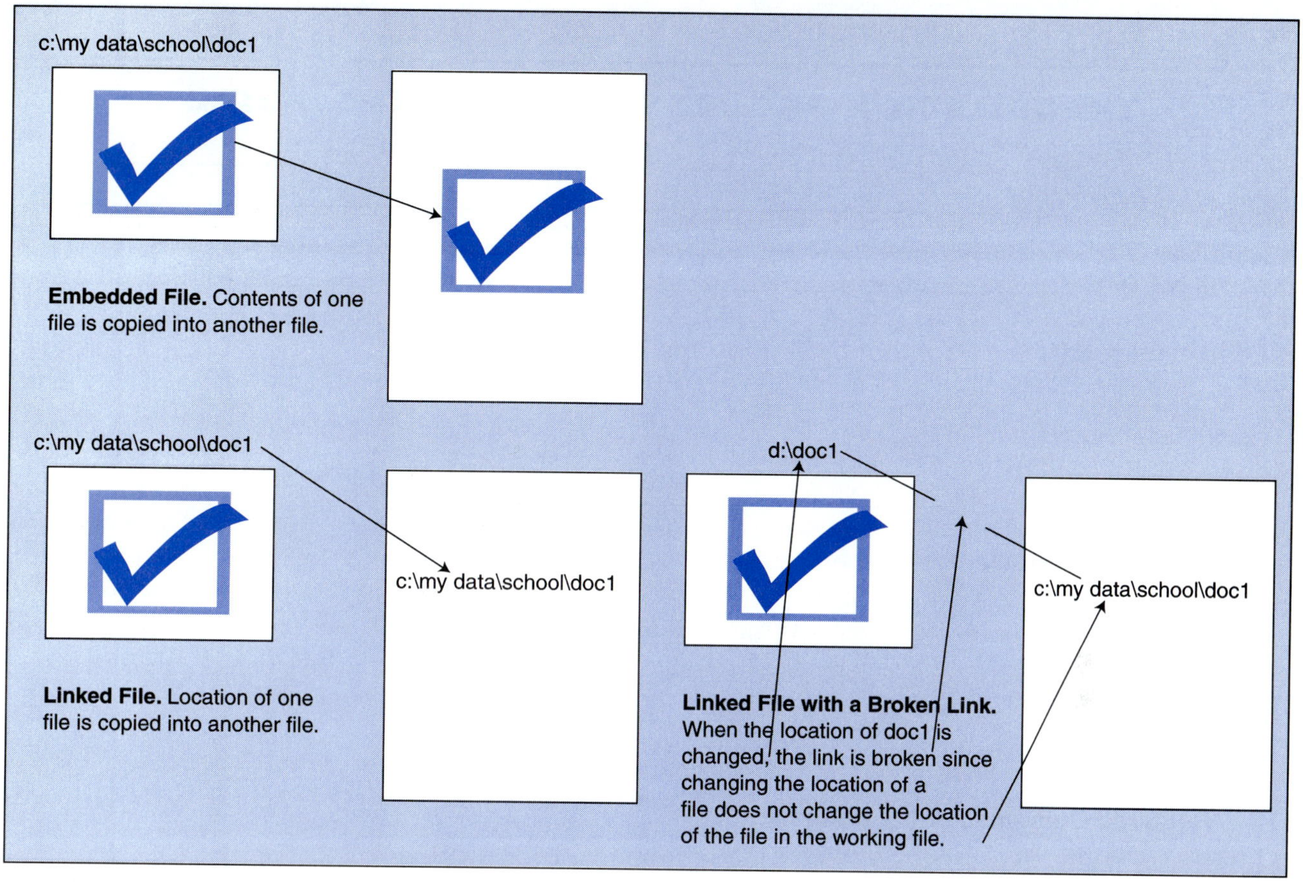

Figure 17.1 Linking and Embedding Files

from one part to another and the greater the chance of problems creeping in during the processing. When you link files, you decrease the size of the imported graphics since only the location of the file and a low resolution image is embedded. Thus, the size of your slide show file will be decreased.

Linking files is often necessary, but you may experience problems if you do not understand how linking works. The link simply points to where the imported file is located. If the file is not in that location, it cannot be imported. Although people tend to embed most files, you should link files under the three previous examples.

Information Processing Planning Guide

The information processing planning guide is a flowchart that shows how files are interconnected. Step five of the planning guides for each part of the solution should be created in addition to the information processing planning guide. If the solution requires a spreadsheet and a letter, step five of a spreadsheet planning guide and a word-processing planning guide should be completed.

Figure 17.2 presents the information processing planning guide. Steps one through four are similar to the other planning guides. Step five is one page and should show a flowchart of the interconnection of files. Step six lists the evaluation criteria for the finished product.

Figure 17.2 Information Processing Planning Guide

INFORMATION PROCESSING PLANNING GUIDE

Name of File Folder: ______________________ Date: ____________

Location of File Folder: ______________________

Name: ______________________

Name of Client: ______________________

Step 1: Identify the Problem by Writing the Problem Statement.

Step 2: Understand the Problem.

Audience:

Required Outcomes of the Document:

Required Knowledge of the Problem to Develop the Document:

Required Knowledge of the Audience:

Step 3: Identify Valid Alternative Methods to Solve the Problem.

Figure 17.2 (continued)

Step 4: **Select the Best Method to Solve the Problem from the List of Alternative Solutions.**

Step 5: **Plan Your Solution. Create a flowchart of the interconnections between files.**

Step 6: **Evaluate the Solution. List the criteria for evaluating the completed document.**

Example 1: Mail Merge

Example 1: Mail Merge

Recall the mail merge case study 2 developed in Chapter 9. The database was already developed for use in that problem. Figure 17.3 shows the problem developed as an information processing project. The letter is printed with the linked computer logo file. The database table is planned as part of the information processing planning guide.

Figure 17.3 Information Processing Planning Guide for Example 1

INFORMATION PROCESSING PLANNING GUIDE

Name of Document: Letter April 3 Date: 4/2/2002

Location of Electronic File: c:\Computer Club\letters\,
Database: c:\Computer Club\Member Information\, File Name: Members

Name: Marcy Smith

Name of Client: Computer Club

Step 1: Identify the Problem by Writing the Problem Statement.

A letter needs to be sent to each of the computer club's members. The letter needs to have the following information included:

- **a.** information about the next meeting
- **b.** information about a club party
- **c.** information about the next fund-raiser
- **d.** information about money to be turned in from the last fund-raiser

These letters requires the club's logo and return address information on the letterhead. Envelopes will need to be printed. Information on members includes:

Information
Last Name
First Name
Street Address
City
State
Zip Code
Telephone Number
Money Owed
Member since

Figure 17.3 (continued)

Step 2: Understand the Problem.

Audience:
Computer club members

Required Outcomes of the Document:
Information communicated to members

Required Knowledge of the Problem to Develop the Document:
Information about events, and members

Required Knowledge of the Audience
Knowledge about the computer club

Step 3: Identify Valid Alternative Methods to Solve the Problem.

a. Individual letters versus mail merge
b. Letterhead or print letterhead
c. Print individual envelopes or use mail merge
d. Standard letter format or a flyer type document
e. RDBMS for member data or database in word processor
f. Link logo or not

Step 4: Select the Best Method to Solve the Problem from the List Alternative Solutions.

a. Use mail merge.
b. Use standard letter format.
c. Print envelopes using mail merge.
d. Print letterhead with letter.
e. Computer club logo will be included on letterhead and envelopes.
f. Computer club logo will be linked.
g. Use a RDBMS for the member data.

(continued)

Figure 17.3 Information Processing Planning Guide for Example 1

Step 5: Plan Your Solution: File Integration Chart

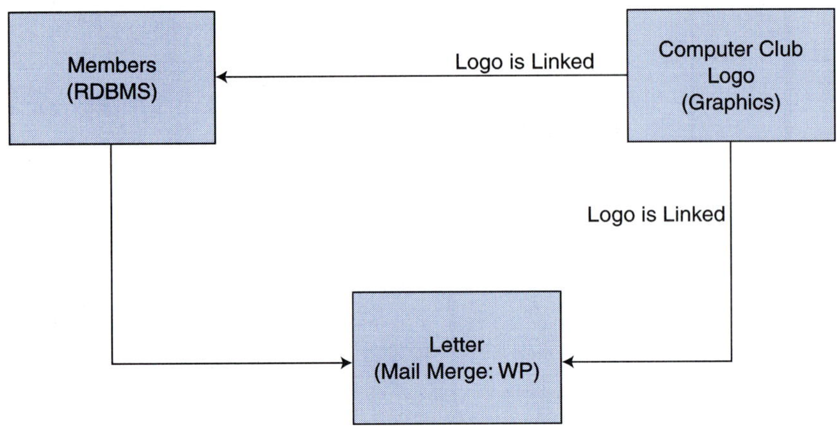

Figure 17.3 (continued)

Original Table:		First Normalization—New Table(s)		Second Normalization—New Table(s)		Third Normalization—New Table(s)	
Item	Field Name	Item	Field Name	Item	Field Name	Item	Field Name
Members Table:		None		None		None	
Last Name	last						
First Name	first						
Street Address	address						
City	city						
State	state						
Zip Code	zipcode						
Telephone No.	telephone						
Money Owed	money_owed						
Member Since	year						

Figure 17.3 Information Processing Planning Guide for Example 1

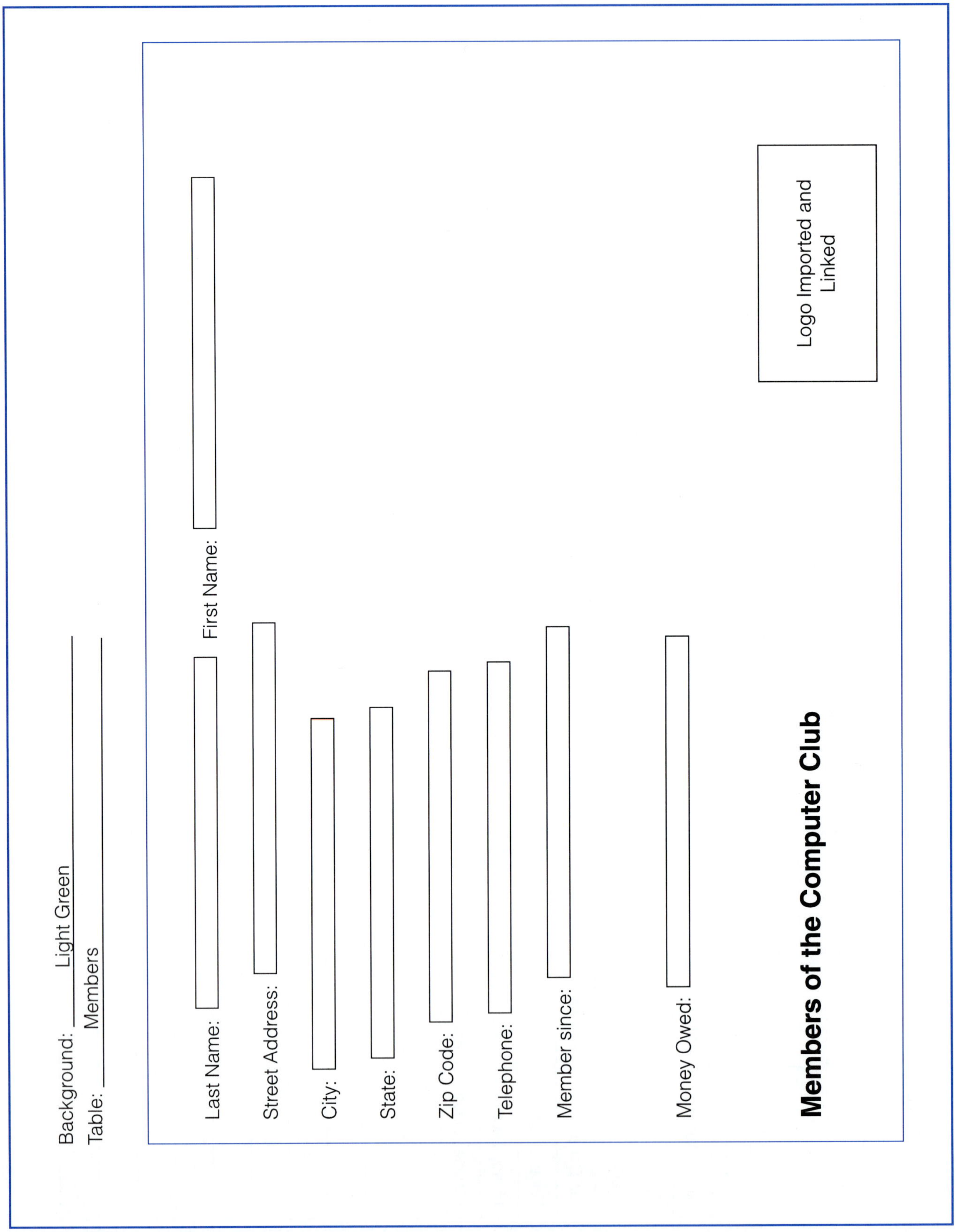

Figure 17.3 (continued)

Step 5: Plan Your Solution. (con't)

Software to be used: Word Processor

Margins for Printing:

Top:	1.0	Top Printer:	0.25
Bottom:	1.0	Bottom Printer:	0.5
Left:	2.0	Left Printer:	0.25
Right:	1.0	Right Printer:	0.25
Header:	none	Top Printer:	0.25
Footer:	none	Bottom Printer:	0.5

Tabs: every 0.5

Files to be imported:

File	Description	Use	Location
Club Logo	Graphics Logo	In letterhead	c:\computer club\graphics

Paper Size: 8½ × 11 Paper Color: White

Orientation: Portrait Color/B&W Color

Number of Comums: one Gutter:

Header Contents: None

Footer Contents:

(continued)

Figure 17.3 Information Processing Planning Guide for Example 1

Step 5: Plan Your Solution. (con't)

Estimated Number of Pages: 1 letter, 78 prints

Sketch(s) of Individual Page Layout(s): ______

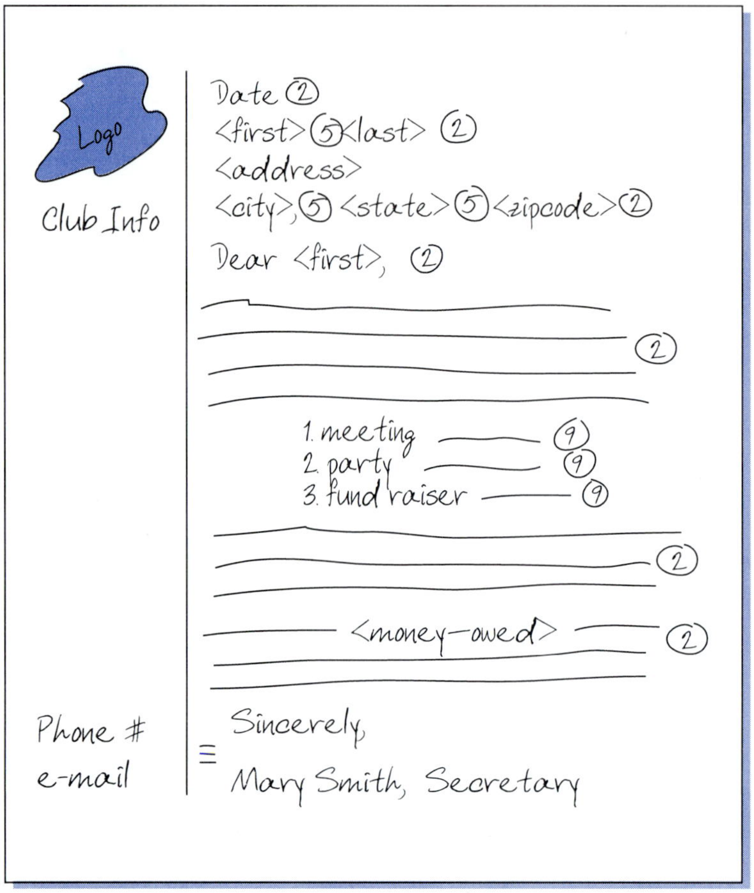

Figure 17.3 (continued)

Step 6: **Evaluate the Solution. List the criteria for evaluating the completed document.**

Criteria for evaluation:

a. Does the letter contain all needed information including times, dates, and locations?
b. Are all members included?
c. Is the letter easy to read?

Example 2: Sales Report

Example 2: Sales Report

Case study 3 in Chapter 9 includes tables and charts as part of the report. In this example we will revisit this problem in which the tables and charts are developed in a spreadsheet program and imported into the word-processed sales report. Figure 17.4 shows the information processing document with step five of the spreadsheet planning guide included.

Example 3: Document Processing

Example 3: Document Processing

Our problem is as follows: The Johnson Lumber Company is required to job cost projects for its customers. The company has just bought a new computer and would like to computerize its costing. The company would like to have its inventory and its client information in a database. The logo for Johnson Lumber is created as a graphics file. The company would like to enter a sales order and then create a spreadsheet and a letter containing the spreadsheet, addressed to the client, which includes the cost of the ordered materials. The company would like to keep the spreadsheet for later reference. Create an information processing planning guide for this problem.

Figure 17.5 presents the information processing planning guide for this example. Step five of the spreadsheet planning guide is included and the table design in a RDBMS. The price is linked from the database to the spreadsheet in case the price changes at the last minute. The customer information is linked to the spreadsheet and to the letter in case there is a change of address and so forth. The letter is a form letter and does not use mail merge because there is only one letter to go out and the spreadsheet will be slightly different for each customer. The spreadsheet will use a template that may be expanded and contracted according to the number of items in the sales order. An envelope is also printed with the letter. The linked data are shown with a gray background.

Information processing is important to the development of good projects. The end user should understand the functions of the different application packages and decide on the best tool for the job to be completed, whether it is word processing, spreadsheets, desktop publishing (DTP), presentation graphics, other graphics software, RDBMS, languages, or any other support software. The efficient use of the integration of these packages should produce a better project in less time.

Figure 17.4 Information Processing Planning Guide for Example 2

INFORMATION PROCESSING PLANNING GUIDE

Name of Document: Sales Report Date: July 15, 2002

Location of Electronic File: c:\my documents\work\sales report

Name: Joe Small

Name of Client: James Big

Step 1: Identify the Problem by Writing the Problem Statement.

As sales manager, I have to develop the computer games sales report for the board of directors this year. This report should be completed with all information on the sales of computer games since July 1 of last year. Information to be included is as follows:

a. sales of computer games per region for the last five years
b. total sales of computer games for the last five years
c. sales of the five different types of computer games per region for this year
d. total sales of the five different types of computer games
e. number of clients per region
f. total number of clients

The report needs to be sent to the members of the board by July 20 for the July 30 board meeting. The related database already exists.

Step 2: Understand the Problem.

Audience:
The members of the board of directors are the audience. Each has some knowledge of the company and of computer games but otherwise no related in-depth knowledge. Most members are over 45 years of age. All members are business men and women and they have an in-depth knowledge of business.

Required Outcomes of the Document:
The outcome of the report is to communicate to the board as to how the sales of computer games have done in the last year compared with the previous five years. Data should be easily communicated since the members are extremely busy people.

Required Knowledge of the Problem to Develop the Document:
a. in-depth knowledge of the present and past sales of computer games
b. knowledge of the company
c. knowledge of computer games and their market
d. knowledge of the sales personnel
e. knowledge of people on the board of directors

Required Knowledge of the Audience:
a. knowledge of the company
b. knowledge of computer games
c. knowledge of business, especially sales

Step 3: Identify Valid Alternative Methods to Solve the Problem.

a. notebook, bound report
b. back to back or one sided
c. columns or none
d. tables from spreadsheet or developed in the word processor
e. paper color, cover color

Figure 17.4 (continued)

Step 4: Select the Best Method to Solve the Problem from the List of Alternative Solutions.

a. bound report, back-to-back facing pages
b. two columns
c. tables developed in a spreadsheet
d. charts imported from a spreadsheet
e. graphics: digital picture of computer game, and company logo

Step 5: Plan Your Solution.

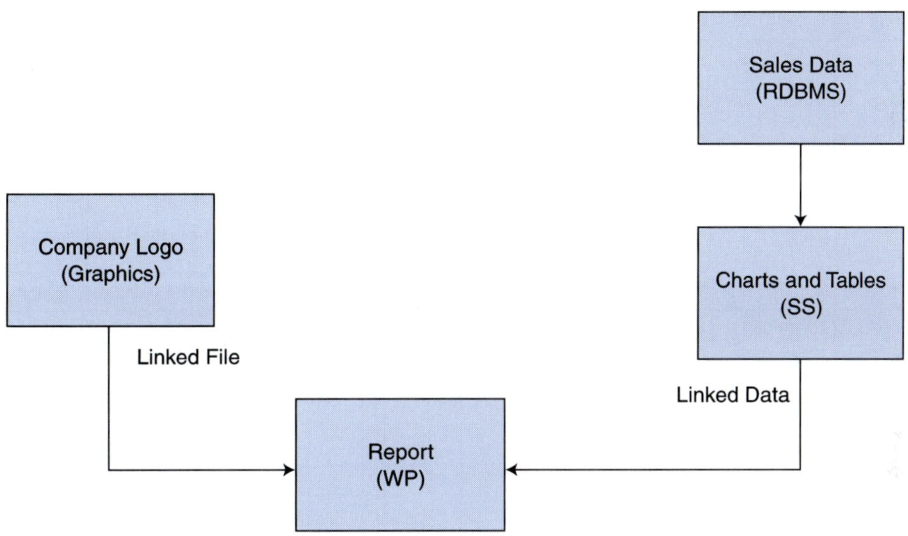

(continued)

Figure 17.4 Information Processing Planning Guide for Example 2

Number Format: G = General N = Number C = Currency A = Accounting F = Fraction P = Percentage D = Date T = Time S = Scientific
Text Format: B = Bold I = Italic U = Underline

Page 1

	Format	A	Format	B	Format	C	Format	D	Format	E	Format	F
1	B/L/U	SALES INFORMATION										
2	B/L	COMPUTER GAMES										
3												
4	B/L	SALES:										
5	B/C	REGION	B/C	YEAR 1	B/C	YEAR 2	B/C	YEAR 3	B/C	YEAR 4	B/C	YEAR 5
6	N/C/0	1	N/0		N/0		N/0		N/0		N/0	
7	↓	2	↓		↓		↓		↓		↓	
8	↓	3	↓		↓		↓		↓		↓	
9	↓	4	↓		↓		↓		↓		↓	
10	B/C	TOTAL	↓	= SUM (B6:B9)	↓	(C) →	↓	→	↓	→	↓	→
11												
12	B/C	REGION	B/C	TYPE 1	B/C	TYPE 2	B/C	TYPE 3	B/C	TYPE 4	B/C	TYPE 5
13	N/C/0	1	N/0		N/0		N/0		N/0		N/0	
14	↓	2	↓		↓		↓		↓		↓	

Figure 17.4 (continued)

Number Format: G = General N = Number C = Currency A = Accounting F = Fraction P = Percentage D = Date T = Time S = Scientific
Text Format: B = Bold I = Italic U = Underline

Page 2

	Format	A	Format	B	Format	C	Format	D	Format	E	Format	F
15		3										
16		4										
17	B/C	TOTAL		=SUM(B13:B16)		(C)						
18												
19	B/C	REGION	B/C	CLIENTS								
20	N/C/0	1	N/0									
21		2										
22		3										
23		4										
24	B/C	TOTAL		=SUM(B20:B23)								
25												
26												
27												
28												

Figure 17.4 Information Processing Planning Guide for Example 2

Charts and Tables to be Imported and Linked to Report

Data	Location of Data	Chart Type
Charts: 1. Region/Year	Data: B6:F9 Labels:: A6:A9, B5: F5	Column
2. Region/Type	Data: B13:F16 Labels:: A13:A16, B12: F12	Column
3. Region/Clients	Data: B20:B23 Labels:: A20:A23	Pie
Tables:		
1. Region/Year	A5: F10	
2. Region/Type	A12: F17	
3. Region/Clients	A19: B24	

Figure 17.4 (continued)

Step 5: Plan Your Solution. (con't)

Software to be used: Word Processor

Margins:

Top: 1.0 Top Printer: 0.25
Bottom: 1.0 Bottom Printer: 0.5
Outside: 1.0 Left Printer: 0.25
Inside: 1.5 Right Printer: 0.25 Binding: 0.25
Header: 0.6 Top Printer: 0.25
Footer: 0.6 Bottom Printer: 0.5

Tabs: every 0.5

Files to be imported:

File	Description	Use	Location
Computer game	Digital Photograph	Cover and inside	s:\reports\graphics\
Logo	Company Logo	Cover and title page	s:\reports\graphics\
This-year chart	Excel Chart	In body of text	s:\reports\sales 02\
Five-year chart	Excel Chart	In body of text	s:\reprots\sales 02\

Paper Size: 8½ × 11 Paper Color: White
Orientation: Portrait Color/B&W Color
Number of Comums: 2 Gutter: 0.4
Back to back or single sided: Back-to-back facing pages
Header Contents:

Computer Games Sales Report 2002		July 30, 2002

Footer Contents:

	XX	

(continued)

Figure 17.4 Information Processing Planning Guide for Example 2

Step 5: Plan Your Solution. (con't)

Estimated Number of Pages: 20 pages

Sketch(s) of Individual Page Layout(s)

- **a.** Cover
- **b.** Title page
- **c.** Table of contents
- **d.** Body of text
  - text pages
  - chart pages
  - table pages
- **e.** Back cover

Figure 17.4 (continued)

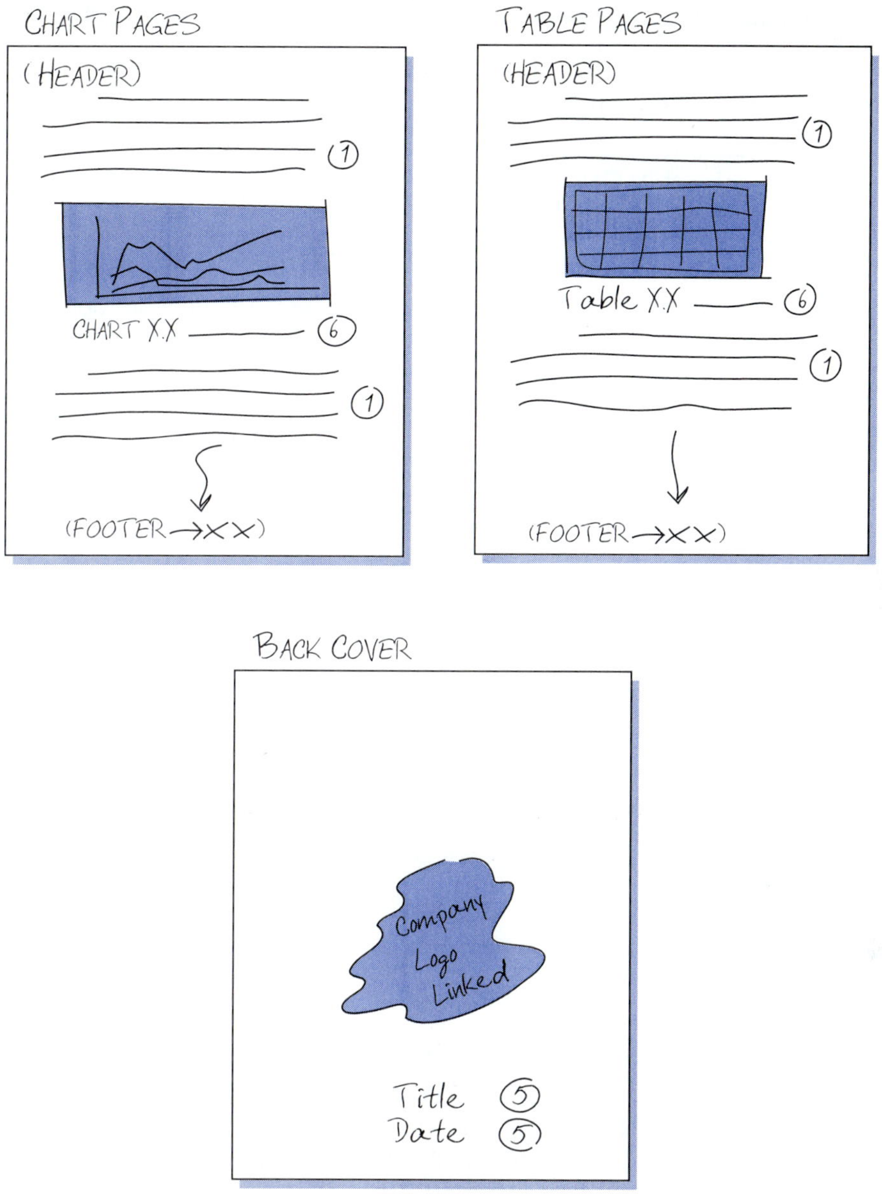

Step 6: Evaluate the Solution.

Criteria for evaluation is as follows:

a. Is the information about the sales of the computer games, past and present, communicated effectively?
b. Is the information easily read?
c. Is the information easily understood?
d. Is the report as short as possible?
e. Is the important information summarized in tables and charts?

Figure 17.5 Document Processing Planning Guide for Example 3

DOCUMENT PROCESSING PLANNING GUIDE

Name of Document: Johnson Lumber Date: 3/5/2002

Location of Electronic File: c:\my data\work\

Name: John Smith

Name of Client: Johnson Lumber Company

Step 1: Identify the Problem by Writing the Problem Statement.

The Johnson Lumber Company is required to job cost projects for its customers. The company has just bought a new computer and would like to computerize its costing. The company would like to have its inventory and client information in a database, and its logo created as a graphics file. The company would like to enter a sales order and then create a spreadsheet and a letter containing the spreadsheet addressed to the client which includes the cost of the ordered materials, and then keep the spreadsheet for later reference.

Step 2: Understand the Problem.

Audience:
Johnson Lumber Company clients

Required Outcomes of the Document

a. A letter to a client will contain a spreadsheet of the cost of materials for a project.
b. Spreadsheet costing will come from database.
c. Prices should be updated in the spreadsheet and the letter as they are changed in the database.

Required Knowledge of the Problem to Develop the Document:

a. Inventory of Johnson's Lumber Company
b. Formulas to complete costing spreadsheet
c. Information required for the inventory and client database

Required Knowledge of the Audience:
Understanding of materials and costs

Step 3: Identify Valid Alternative Methods to Solve the Problem.

a. Reenter data from database or link values from database in spreadsheet.
b. Reenter table from spreadsheet or link spreadsheet in letter.
c. Mail merge or form letter or re-create letter each time.
d. Individual databases or different tables in one database.

Step 4: Select the Best Method to Solve the Problem from the List of Alternative Solutions.

a. Link price values from database to spreadsheet.
b. Link spreadsheet to letter.
c. Use a form letter.
d. Use a spreadsheet template.
e. Create three tables in RDBMS: inventory, vendors, and clients

Figure 17.5 (continued)

Step 5: Plan Your Solution.

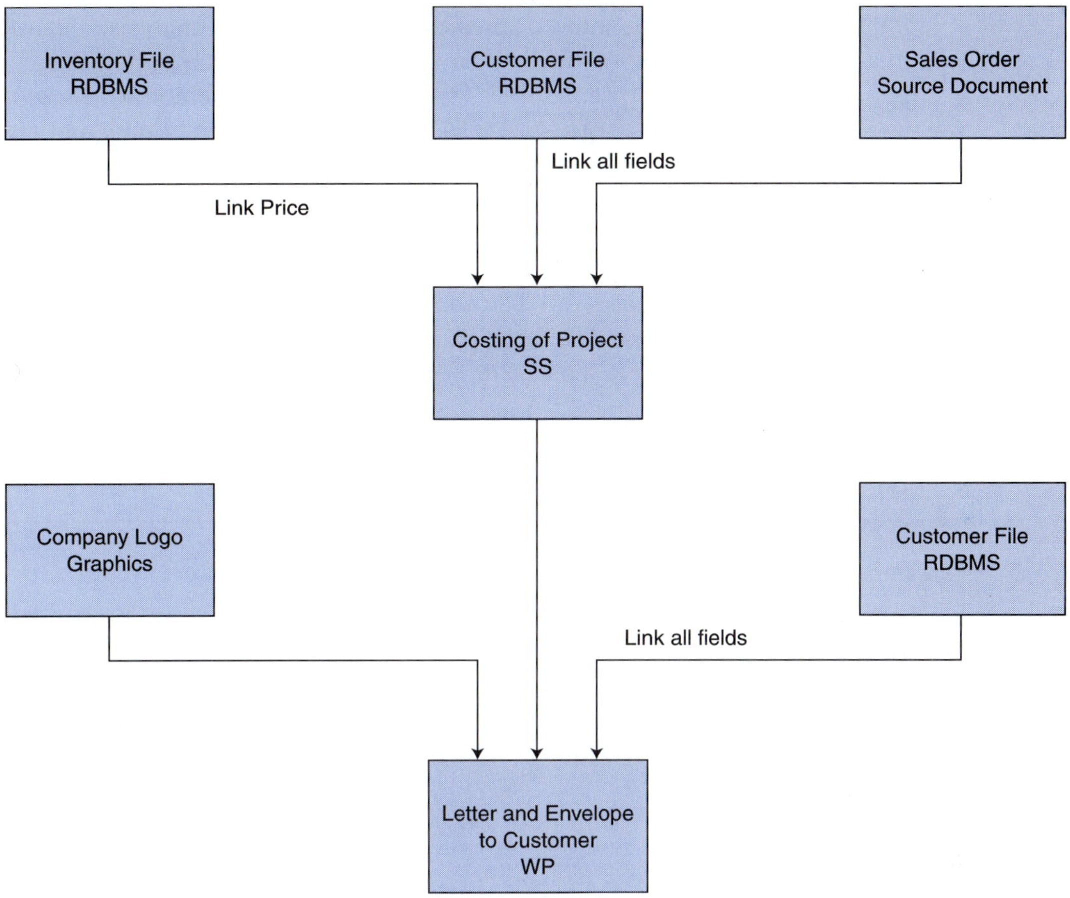

RDBMS = Relational Database Management System Software
SS = Spreadsheet Software
Graphics = Graphics Software
WP = Word Processor Software

Step 6: Evaluate the Solution. List the criteria for evaluating the completed document.

a. Is the total price correct?
b. Does the price change in the spreadsheet and the letter when the price in the database is changed?
c. Is the letter professional and informative?
d. Does the letter look personal even if it is a form letter?
e. Are the owners of Johnson's Lumber Company satisfied?

Summary

Information processing is the use of multiple software packages for a solution to a problem. It involves the use of the best software package to complete each part of a solution, a word processor for text editing, a desktop publisher for graphics and text, presentation graphics to create a slide show, a spreadsheet for numerical analysis, and a RDBMS to organize and report data. A suite is a group of several software packages that have commonalties, drag-and-drop capabilities, and other integrated features.

Information processing requires file sharing in the form of drag and drop, cut and paste, importing, and exporting. When a file is imported, it can be embedded or linked. Embedding an imported file copies the contents of the file into the working document. Linking an imported file copies the location of the file into the working document. The three reasons to link files are (1) when a modified imported file should also be modified in the working document, (2) when there are multiple imports of the same file, and (3) when the file becomes too large. An information processing planning guide helps with planning a solution to a problem that requires document processing.

Key Words

Document processing
Drag and drop
Exporting
Importing
Information processing
Object Linking and Embedding (OLE)
Suite

Questions

1. What is information processing?
2. What is a suite?
3. What are three features of a suite?
4. How can a suite increase your computer productivity?
5. What are the two processes that allow you to import a selected part of a file?
6. What is OLE?
7. What is a problem with using linked files?
8. How can you minimize the problem of lost links?

Problems

1. The Exceptional Consultant Company has just finished a marketing survey for one of its clients. The company would like to produce a letter to that client which will include a summary report of the results, a statistical analysis of the results, and two charts of the results. Create an information processing planning guide and the associated other planning guides for this problem.

2. Joan Green has just been promoted to head of sales at the Best Computer Company. She knows that one of her duties of this job is to make a presentation to the board of directors on the sales of the past year along with projections for the future. Joan would like to keep information about her sales reps, their clients, and the amount of sales for each sales rep and for each client. She plans to develop a slide show to accompany her presentation. Create an information processing planning guide and the associated other planning guides for this problem.
3. You are planning to purchase a new computer and would like to compare four different brands. Find four different advertisements on computers to use for this problem. You must borrow the money for the new computer and need to write a letter to your banker to obtain the loan. Create an information processing planning guide and the associated other planning guides for this problem.

Chapter 18

Programming Concepts

Overview

Types of Problems
Variables and Constants Revisited
Instructions, Algorithms, and Flowcharts
Some Common Tasks
Logic Structures
- **Sequential Logic Structure**
- **Decision Logic Structure**
- **Repetition Logic Structure**
- **Case Logic Structure**

Objectives

When you have finished this chapter, you should be able to:

1. Distinguish between algorithmic solutions and heuristic solutions to problems.
2. Recognize computer language algorithmic instructions and their associated flowchart symbols.
3. Develop short sets of instructions using the four logic structures.

Although programming is not usually considered in context with applications, almost every application has the availability of creating and saving instructions to be used again at a later time. This concept is programming. The terminology may include *macros, scripting,* or so forth, but these terms are all a form of programming. In this text, the word *script* will mean the same as macro or program. It is important to learn programming concepts in order to automate and develop shortcuts to increase your computer productivity and to make your final product convenient and user friendly for the client.

This chapter presents concepts of programming including definitions of algorithms, instructions, logic structures, and flowcharts. Algorithmic and heuristic solutions are two types of solutions for problems. You use algorithmic solutions to develop macros and scripts for your projects. Logic structures are the basic programming techniques used to create macros and scripts. The logic structures that are presented in this chapter include sequential, decision, repetition, and case logic structures. Flowcharts and algorithms are presented to clarify the logic structures and to help you develop programming solutions. Appendix C presents Otto the robot, who uses these logic structures to solve problems for a humanoid environment. Reviewing Appendix C will help you understand the programming concepts presented in this chapter. Chapter 19 presents how to use these programming concepts in application-based projects.

Types of Problems

Algorithmic Solutions

Problems do not always have straightforward solutions. Some problems, such as balancing a checkbook or baking a cake, can be solved with a series of actions. These solutions are called **algorithmic solutions.** Using an algorithmic solution, a set of step-by-step instructions or actions may be written as the solution. These steps are called the algorithm. Some examples of algorithmic solutions include using a recipe, balancing a checking account, instructing someone to the nearest restaurant, or assembling a toy.

Many problems cannot be solved through a set of step-by-step instructions. These solutions require other techniques of problem solving such as reasoning built on knowledge and experience, or a process of trial and error. These types of solutions are called heuristic solutions. Some examples of heuristic solutions are buying the best stock, expanding or downsizing a company, or raising a child. There is no set of instructions that someone can write to buy stocks that will always make money. Children do not come with a manual to tell us how to raise them. Each child is different and there is no algorithmic set of instructions that one can follow. There may be guidelines to follow for these problems, but there are no set rules.

For example, when company decision makers are looking to expand or to downsize, there are no rules to follow to ensure they do not make a mistake. These problems are solved by trial and error with the help of experts. They have had education and experience to construct the guidelines as to how to start out on a solution path that is sound. The solution must continually be tested along the route, and adjustments and modifications made at the first sign of error. The solution path is not constructed via step-by-step instructions.

Think of how you would go about getting a good grade in every class. Is the procedure always the same? Can you write yourself a set of instructions to follow to ensure that you receive an A in every class? Probably not. One class may require a term report along with tests and homework whereas another class may require only tests. Even the tests you take are different and you may study differently for different classes. This requires a heuristic solution. You may have guidelines to follow, but you may make adjustments to your study habits after the first test or after you receive a grade for your first homework paper.

The science of using a computer to solve problems requiring heuristic solutions is called artificial intelligence or expert systems. In this book, we concentrate only on problems and problem solving via algorithmic solutions since these are best solved on a computer using application software.

Variables and Constants Revisited

Constants and Variables

Chapter 12 presented information about constants and variables used for spreadsheets. Instructions also use constants and variables. Constants are values that do not change during the execution of the program, such as 3.5, 69, and–432.9. These are also called values in spreadsheets. Variables are names given to memory locations that hold the resultants of expressions, stored constants, stored labels, and so forth. The value of variables may change during the execution of a script. Variables in programming are similar to the names of the cells in spreadsheets.

Chapter 14 presented a section on naming cells. The same guidelines hold true for naming variables in a script. Try to name the variables according to what they represent, such as HOURS for hours worked or NETPAY for the net pay, to increase readability of your script.

Variables may be assigned to a memory location that is only known by the script that is being executed, or it may be made public so that all other scripts may use the value. You want as many variables as possible to be local. Only those variables, of which other scripts must have knowledge, should be made public to allow for greater flexibility in the naming of variables. When more than one person is working on a project, only the public variables are of concern to everyone. Local variables need only be known to the person who is developing the associated script. If you find that a number is not correct or has a zero value that is being used in a calculation, you may want to check if the value came from another script and, if so, it should be a public variable. Scripts should be as cohesive as possible in that they should be written and executed with as little knowledge from other scripts as possible. Public variables couple the scripts together.

Instructions, Algorithms, and Flowcharts

Instructions, Algorithms, and Flowcharts

Scripts consist of a set of instructions to direct the computer how to accomplish something, such as delete a record, add a record, print a spreadsheet, or create a user-defined menu. These instructions are saved with the spreadsheet, the database, or the document. They are associated with one project; however, you may copy them to a new project or create a template of macros or scripts with which you may start each solution. You do not want to reprogram the scripts every time you start a new solution if they are the same sets of instructions. Chapter 19 will further discuss this issue.

Instructions are specific to the language you are using. The instruction must be created according to the syntax of the language. Any variation will cause an error. In this chapter, the algorithmic instruction will be generic. You will need to learn the syntax of the language you intend to use. As you write algorithms and flowcharts, the generic instruction must be as presented. In human communication, an instruction may be worded in many ways. When communicating with a computer, however, the instruction must be exact. The computer is rigid about allowing few variations to computer instructions.

The lack of flexibility in communication with the computer is one reason why writing scripts is difficult for most people when they first start. The computer does exactly what it is instructed to do. If it does not understand the instruction, an error message occurs. Another reason why the writing of scripts tends to be difficult at first is that we need to think in the step-by-step world of the computer.

Many of the things we do are habits, such as counting to 10 and choosing the largest number from three numbers. You need to understand how you accomplish these tasks before you can instruct the computer to do the same. Counting on the computer is adding one to the previous number. To find the largest number from three numbers, the computer must choose the largest of two numbers and then compare that resultant to the third number. The resultant is the largest of the three. Instructing the computer how to accomplish a task requires remembering how you first learned how to do the task.

Algorithms and flowcharts for each logic structure and each basic instruction are developed in the next section. Algorithms are similar to the instructions you will enter into the computer. The **flowcharts** show a graphical representation of the algorithm. Each of these will be presented in detail in the following section. There are several types of instructions including start, stop, input, output, processing, repeating, decision, and case instructions. Each instruction uses a specific flowchart symbol and specific syntax for the algorithm instruction. Table 18.1 presents the flowchart symbols, the associated algorithm, and a brief explanation of the instruction.

Some Common Tasks

Assignment Instruction

Two common tasks on the computer are to count and to find a sum. These use assignment statements to complete the proper calculation. An assignment instruction is like an equation with one exception: There is only one variable name on the left side of the equal sign. The equal sign in an assignment instruction does not really mean "equal to"; it means "replaced by" or "assigned the value of." Given the assignment instruction A = B + C, the instruction means to replace the value of A with the sum of the values of B and C. Another way to read this instruction is: The value of A is replaced by the value of B plus the value of C.

The assignment instruction to count on the computer is:

Counter = Counter + <constant>

For example, to count by ones: Counter = Counter + 1; or to count by twos: Counter = Counter + 2. This reads as: the value of Counter is replaced by the old value of Counter plus two. Counter must be assigned a zero value before starting to count.

The assignment instruction to sum numbers is:

Sum = Sum + <variable>

For example, to sum a group of temperatures:

TempSum = TempSum + Temperature

This would read as: the value of TempSum is replaced by the old value of TempSum plus the value of Temperature. TempSum must be assigned a zero value before starting the summing process.

If you need the product of a series of numbers, then use the following assignment instruction:

Product = Product * <variable>

In this case, Product must be assigned an initial value of one.

Logic Structures

The four logic structures presented here are as follows:

1. **Sequential logic structure:** instructions that continue one after another.
2. **Decision logic structure:** instructions that allow the computer to choose one of two sets of instructions to execute depending upon the resultant of an assigned condition. The IF function is similar to this structure.

Table 18.1 Algorithms and Flowcharts of Instructions

Algorithm Instruction	Flowchart Symbol	Definition
Start [script name]		Start processing a script
Enter [list of data items]		Enter data from keyboard.
Processing		Processing data.
Print [variables or report]		Output of information.
End/Exit		Stops processing a script.
IF/THEN/ELSE	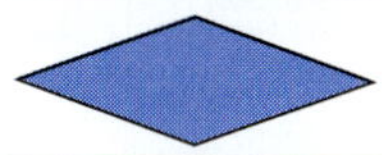	Decision instruction
While/While-end	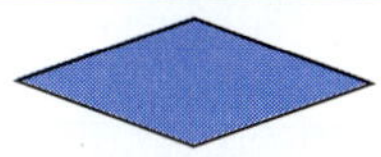	Repetition instruction
Repeat/Until	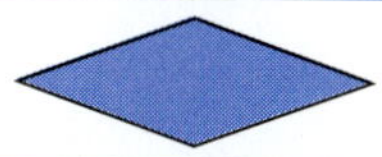	Repetition instruction
Loop: C = Begin to End Step S Loop-end: C		Automatic repetition instruction
Case of: V = expression 1: instructions = expression 2: instructions : : : Otherwise: instructions Case-end	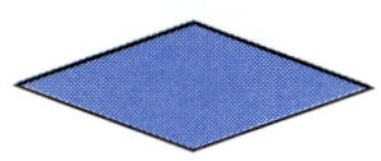	Case instruction

3. **Repetition logic structure:** instructions that allow the computer to repeat instructions.
4. **Case logic structure:** instructions that allow you to choose from several sets of instructions to execute. The CHOOSE function is similar to this structure.

Sequential Logic Structure

Sequential Logic Structure

The sequential logic structure executes instructions one after another in a sequential pattern starting at the top and continuing to the end. Figure 18.1 presents a sequential script to add two numbers. The instructions are to start execution, add the two numbers, and exit the script.

Algorithm:

1. Start Add
2. A = 5
3. B = 6
4. C = A + B
5. Exit

Flowchart:

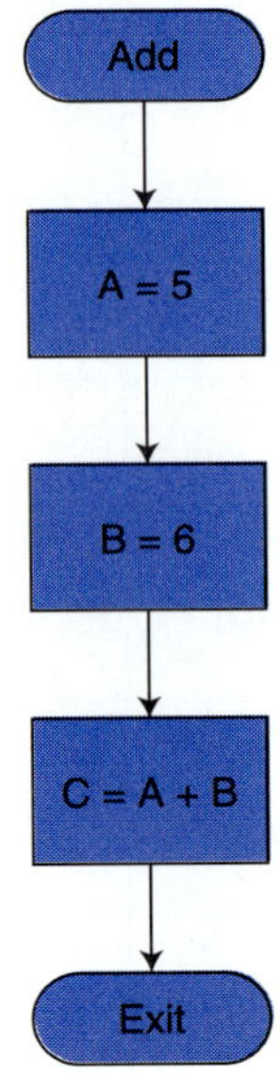

Figure 18.1 Example of Sequential Logic Structure

Decision Logic Structure

Decision Logic Structure

The decision logic structure allows the computer to choose between two sets of instructions to execute according to the criteria. The If/Then/Else algorithmic instruction is as follows:

```
If <criterion>
    Then
        Instructions for True
    Else
        Instructions for False
```

Figure 18.2 presents a decision logic structure followed by an example. The criterion is found in the diamond. There are lines drawn from two of the three lower corners of the diamonds, one for the true instructions and the other for the false instructions. After the true instructions or the false instructions, the lines then meet to continue with the processing in a sequential manner. Notice the brackets and indentations on the algorithm to indicate the true and false instructions. These are added to increase the readability of the algorithm.

If/Then/Else instructions may be nested. For example, if you want to calculate a letter grade from a number grade, you would need to nest the instructions. See Figure 18.3 for an example of this calculation. Notice that the brackets on the algorithm are nested, and that the last decision is for both the D and F resultants. When you get to this decision, if the answer was not A, B, C, or D, then it must be F. You do not need to test for the F.

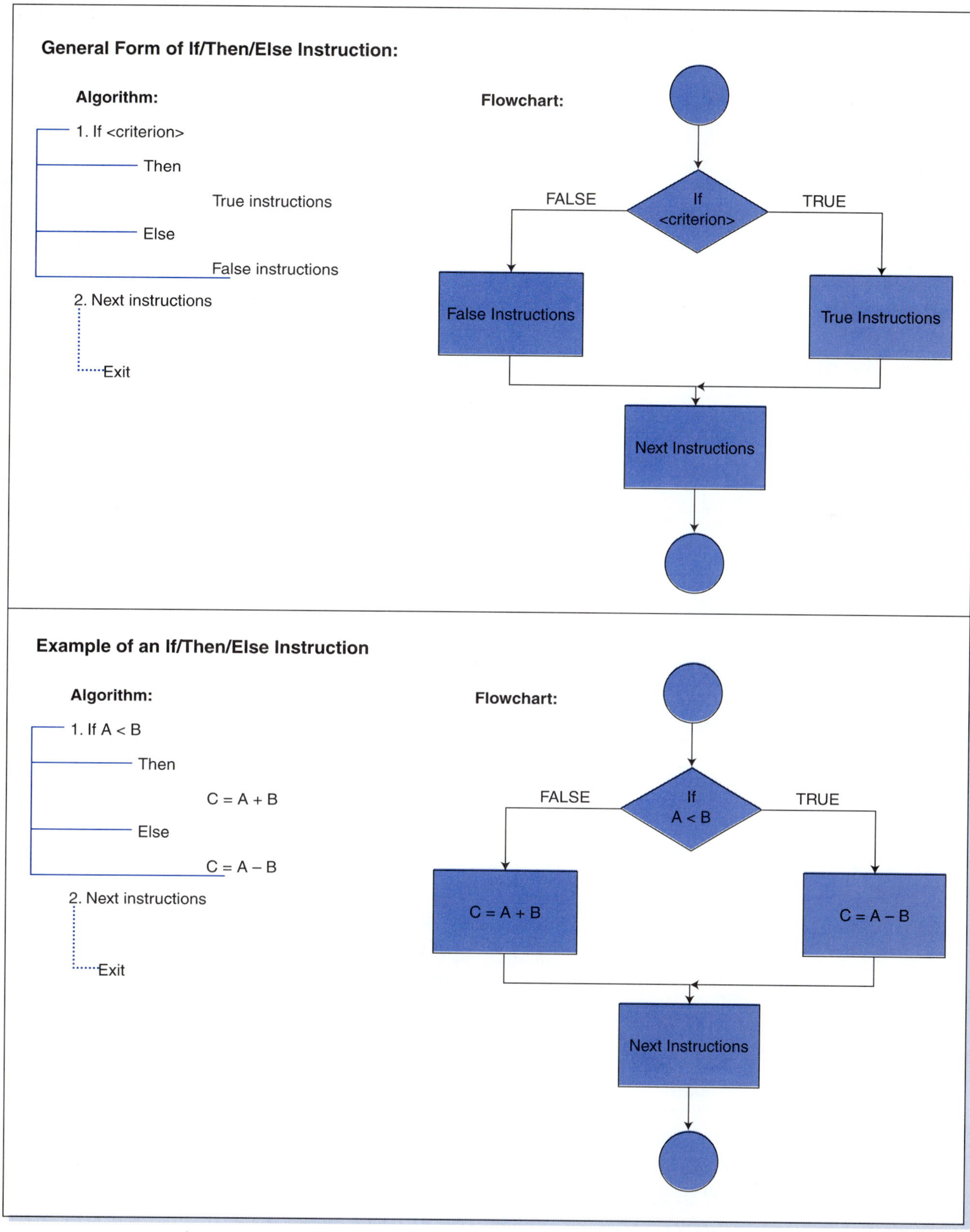

Figure 18.2 Examples of Decision Logic Structure

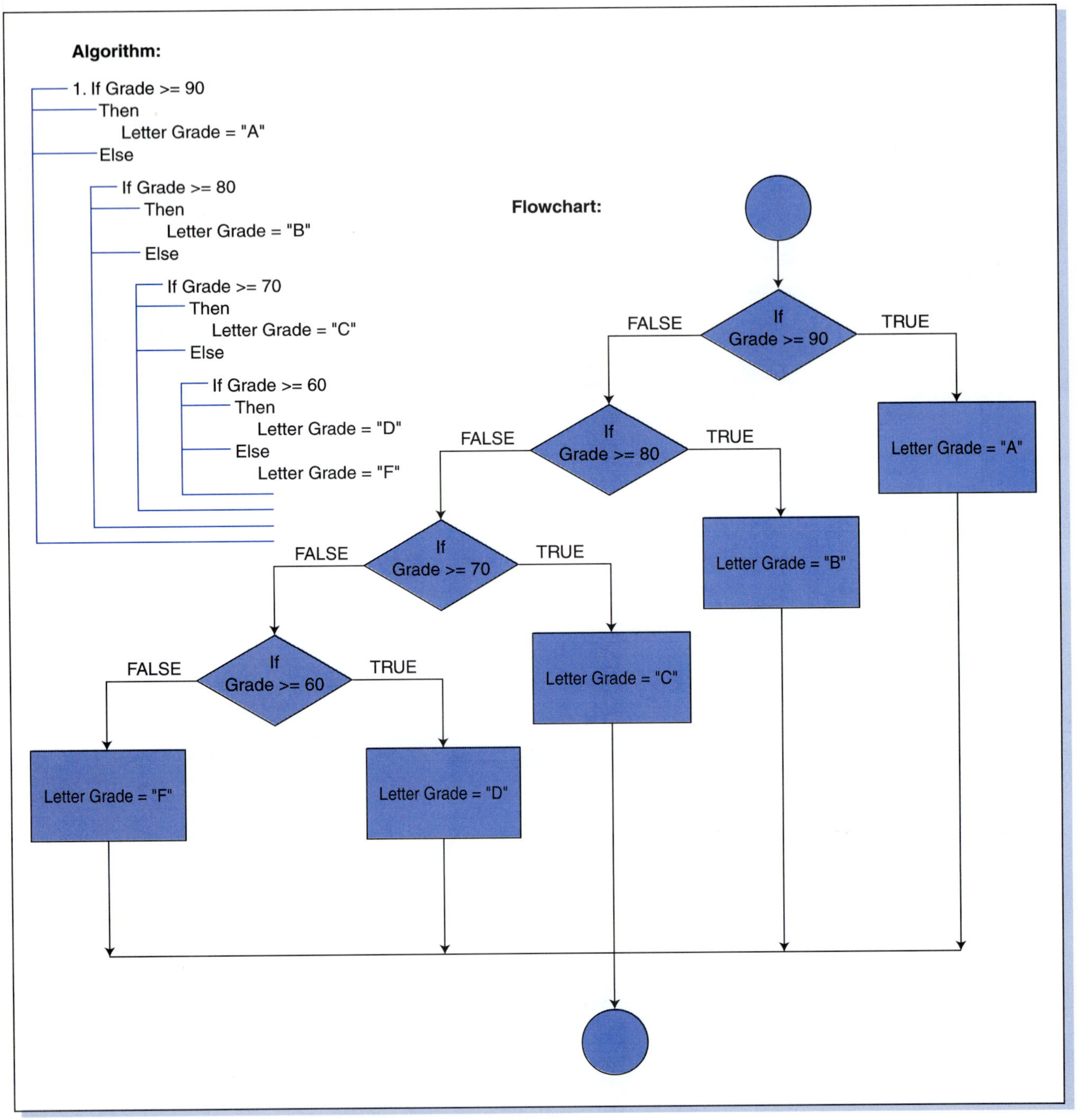

Figure 18.3 Example of Nested If/Then/Else Instructions

You may nest If/Then/Else instructions for either or both of the true instructions and/or the false instructions. Figure 18.4 shows the three scenarios. Notice the brackets and indentations on the algorithm. If the brackets are not nested, something is wrong with your instructions.

Repetition Logic Structure

Repetition Logic Structure

The repetition logic structure allows you to repeat instructions. This structure is sometimes called a *loop,* because it loops back to repeat a series of instructions. There are

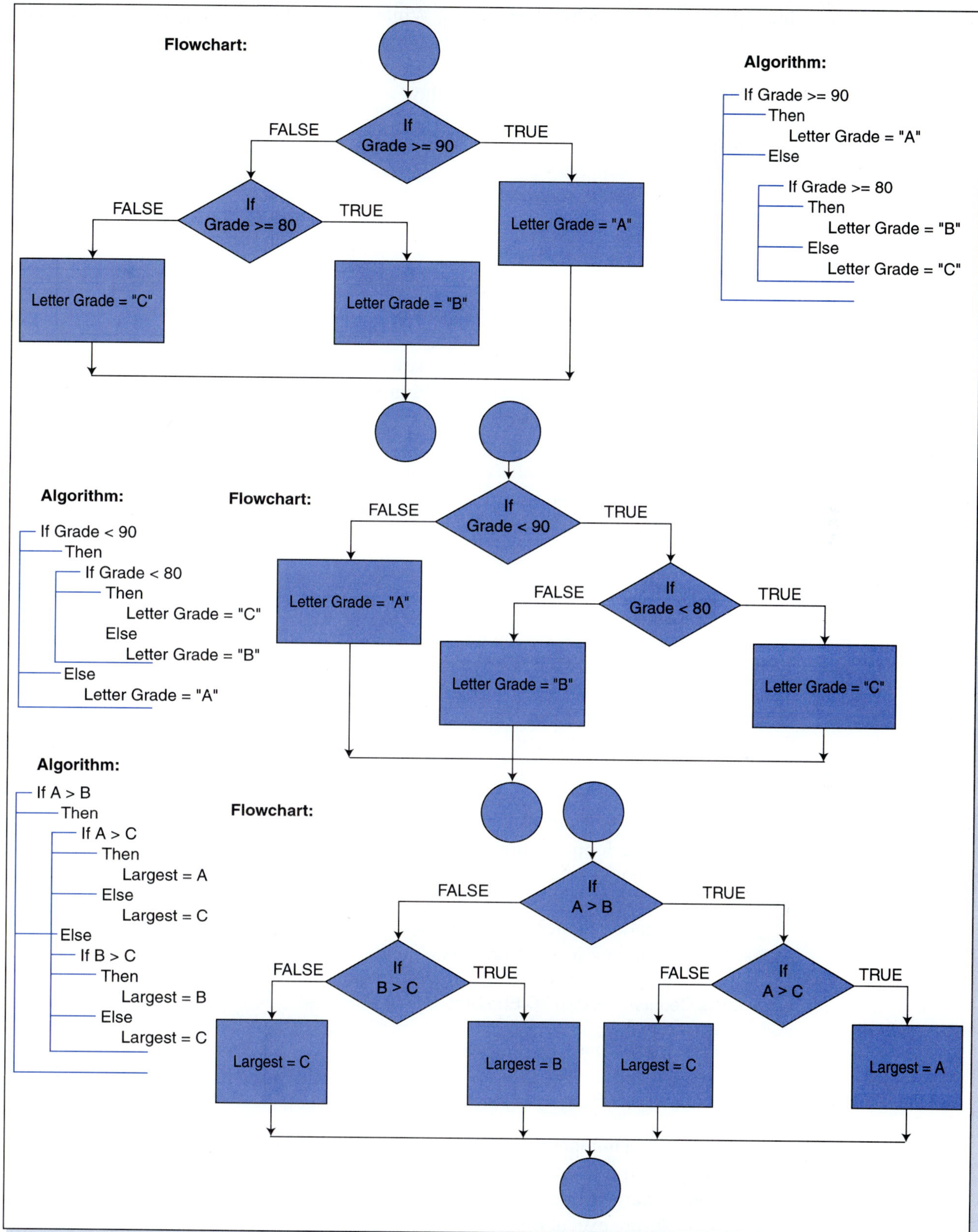

Figure 18.4 Three Types of Nested Decision Instructions

three types of repetition logic structures: While/While-end loop, Repeat/Until loop, and the automatic counter loop.

The While/While-end loop allows the loop to continue as long as the criterion is true. The algorithmic instruction is as follows:

```
While <criterion>

        Instructions

While-end
```

Figure 18.5 shows examples of the While/While-end loop. Notice the brackets and indentations on the algorithm. The criterion is located at the beginning of the loop. The loop must contain an instruction that will change the resultant of the criterion from true to false in order to have the loop stop. When the resultant of the criterion is false, the execution of the script will continue at the next instruction after the While-end. When the criterion is false going into the loop, the instructions in the loop will not be executed. Execution will continue with the first instruction after the While-end. The While/While-end loop should be used when you know the values to calculate the criterion before the loop starts.

The Repeat/Until loop allows the loop to continue as long as the criterion is false. The algorithmic instruction is as follows:

```
Repeat

        Instructions

Until <criterion>
```

Figure 18.6 shows examples of the Repeat/Until loop. Notice the brackets and indentations on the algorithm. The criterion is located at the bottom of the loop. The loop must contain an instruction that will change the resultant of the criterion from false to true in order to have the loop stop. When the resultant of the criterion is true, the execution of the script will then continue at the next instruction after the Until. When the criterion is true going into the loop, the instructions in the loop will be executed once. The Repeat/Until loop should be used when you do not know the beginning values to calculate the criterion before you enter the loop.

The automatic counter loop repeats a set of instructions calculated a number of times. The algorithmic instruction looks like the following:

```
Loop: Counter = Begin TO End Step S

        Instructions

Loop-end: Counter
```

where Counter is a number that begins with Begin and is incremented each time through the loop by S until it is greater than End. Counter is a variable. Begin, End, and S may be a constant, a variable, or an expression. Following are the steps taken by the automatic counter loop during execution.

1. When the automatic counter loop instruction starts, Counter is set to the value of Begin.

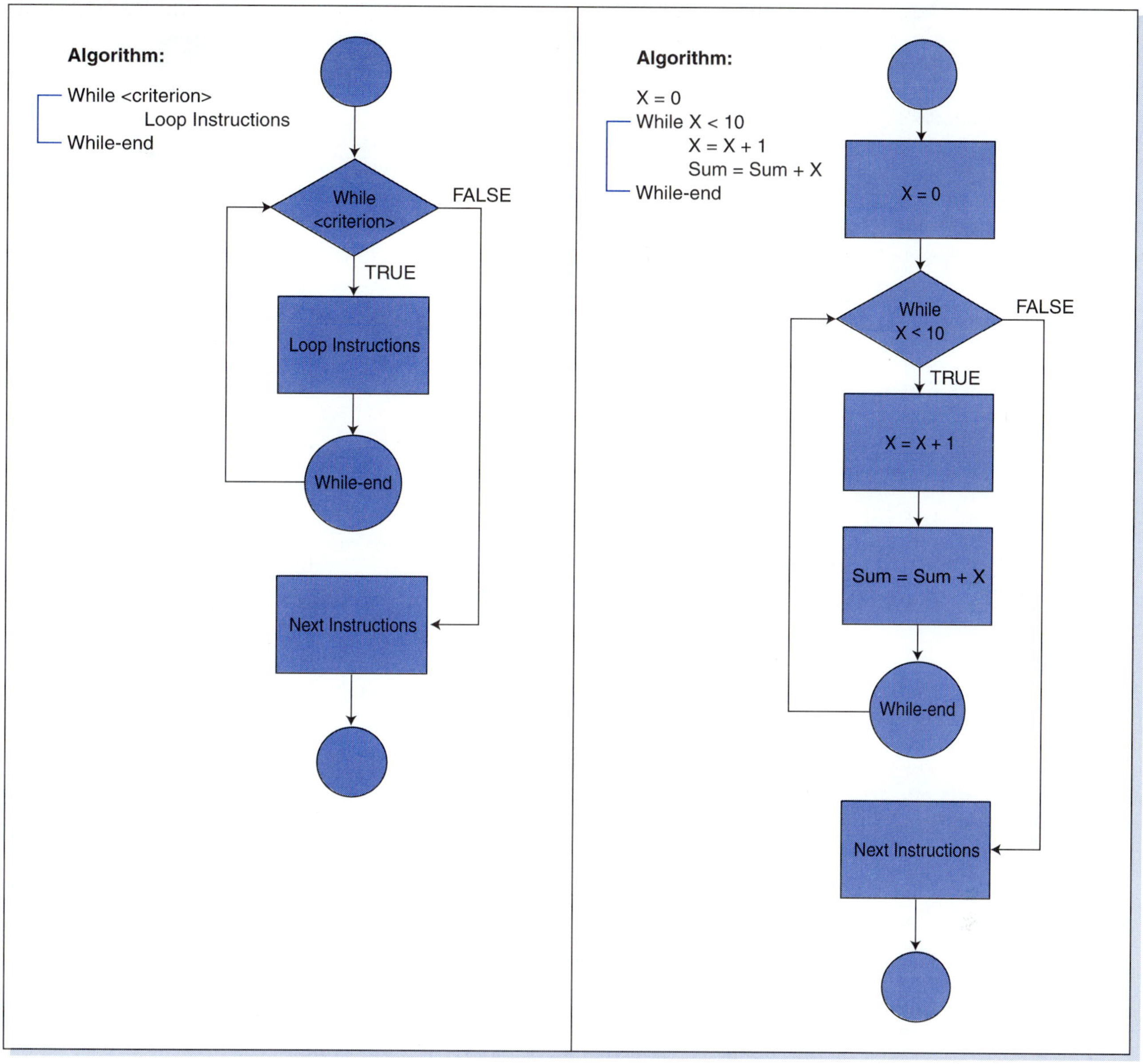

Figure 18.5 While/While-end Repetition Logic Structure

2. Counter is tested. If Counter is greater than the value of End, execution continues with the instruction following the Loop-end. If not, then the loop instructions are executed.
3. At the end of the loop, Counter is incremented by S.
4. Counter is tested. If Counter is greater than the value of End, execution continues with the instruction following the Loop-end. If not, then the loop instructions are executed.
5. Steps 3 and 4 are repeated until Counter becomes greater than the value of End.

Figure 18.7 shows examples of the automatic counter loop. The values of Counter as the loop is executed are included in the figure. Notice the brackets and indentations. S may be positive or negative. When S is negative, Counter starts at Begin and is decremented

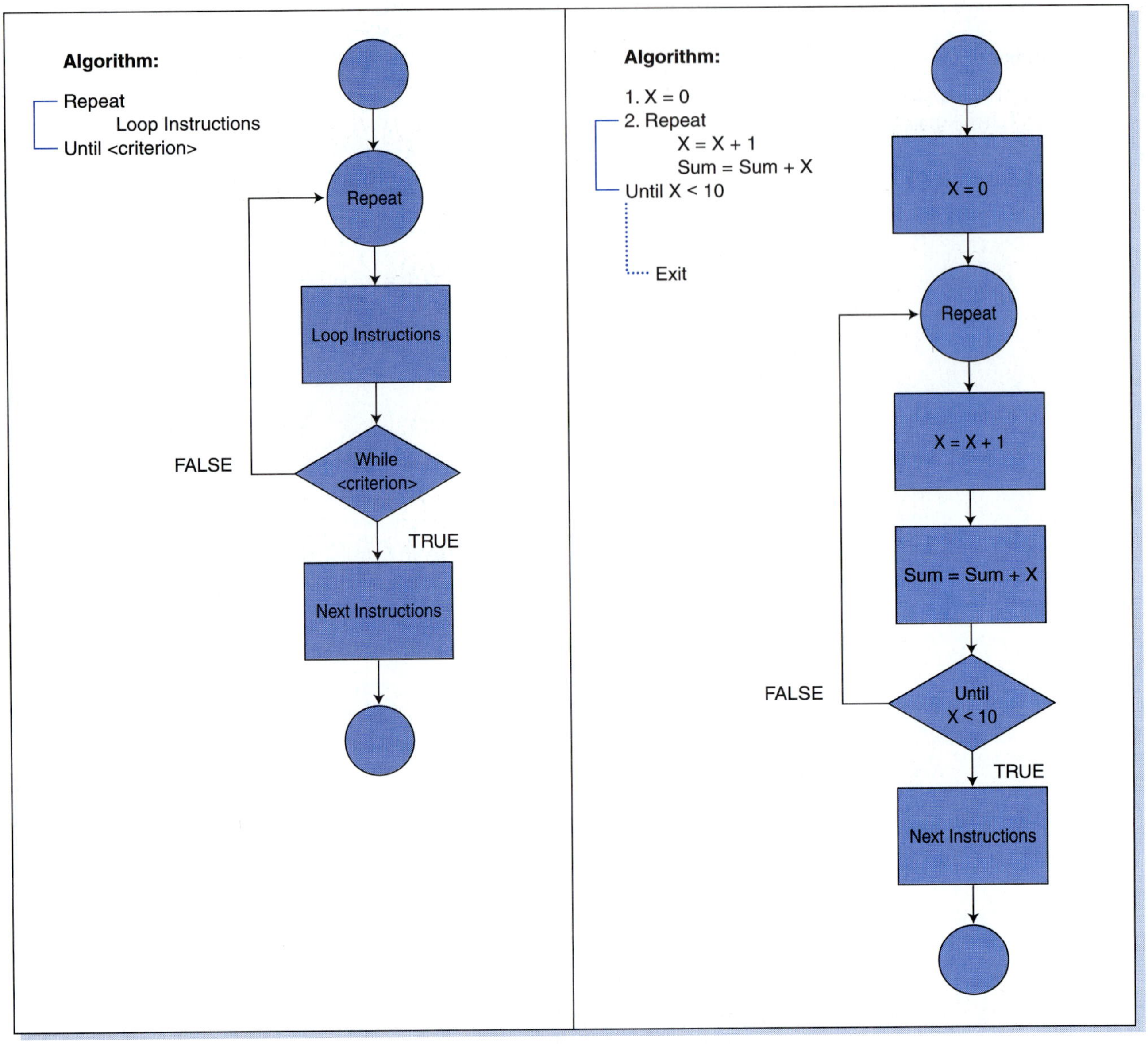

Figure 18.6 Repeat/Until Repetition Logic Structure

each time through the loop until it becomes less than End. The automatic counter loop should be used when you are counting the times through the loop and you know the starting and ending values of the counter.

You may nest loops just as you nested If/Then/Else instructions. You may use any combination of loop types. The innermost loop is completed each time the outer loop instructions are executed. Figure 18.8 presents nested loops with their counters printed. When you are using While/While-end and Repeat/Until loops as part of the inner loops, you must reset the criterion so the loop instructions will be executed. If you use the automatic counter loop, remember the counter is reset each time the loop instruction is started. Figure 18.8 has an example of three nested loops. In this case, the innermost loop is executed completely before the middle loop is incremented. The middle loop is executed completely before the outer loop is incremented. Notice the values of the counters in the table each time through the various loops.

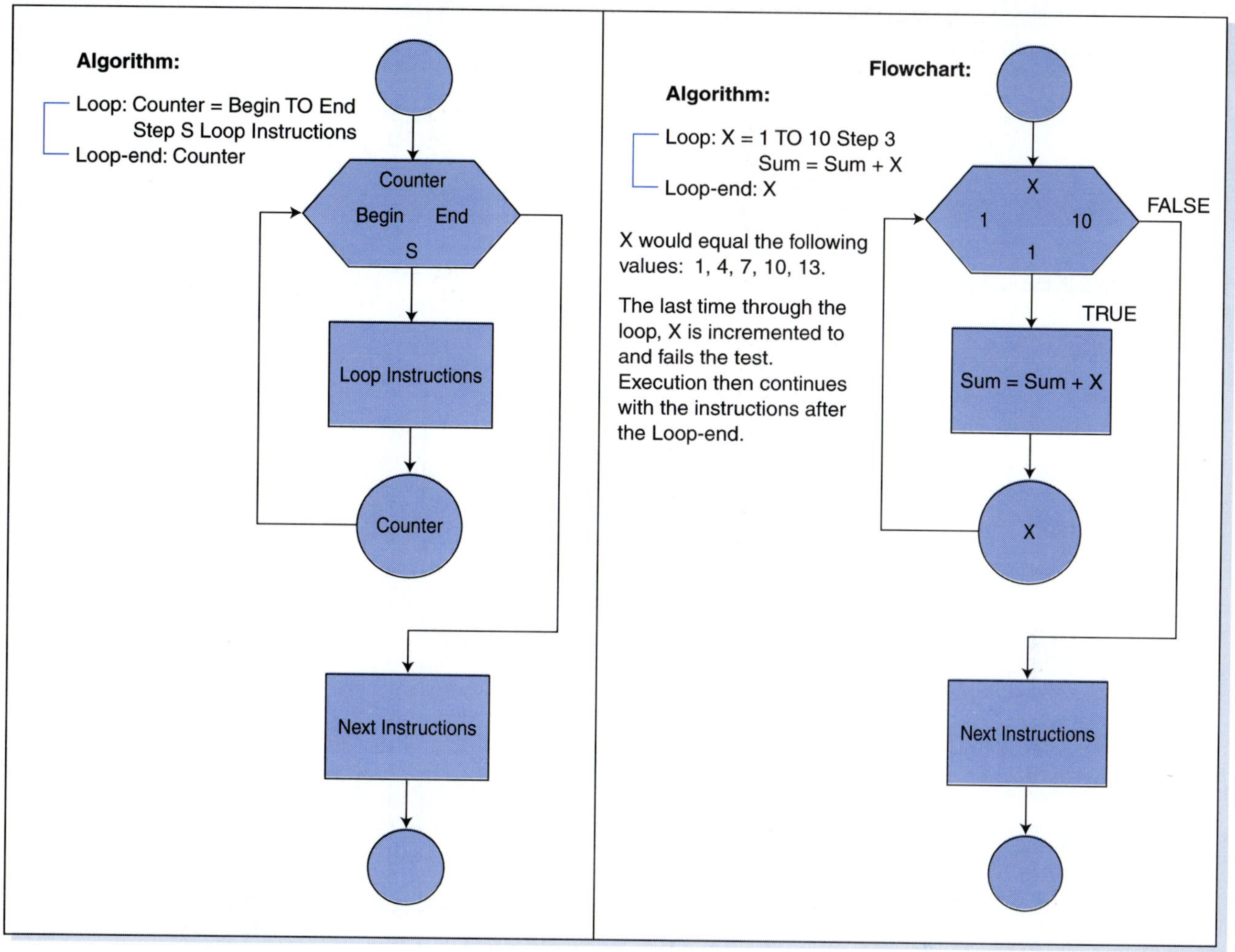

Figure 18.7 Automatic Counter Repetition Logic Structure

Case Logic Structure

Case Logic Structure

The case structure is similar to the CHOOSE function except that a set of instructions are executed instead of one value being calculated. The algorithmic instruction is as follows:

```
Case of <variable>
        = <constant1>
                Instructions when variable = constant1
        = <constant2>
                Instructions when variable = constant2
        = <constant3>
                Instructions when variable = constant3
                :
                :
        Otherwise
                Instructions when variable = anything else
Case-end
```

Figure 18.9 shows an example of the Case/Case-end instruction. Notice the brackets and indentations. This replaces a nested If/Then/Else instruction. The instruction allows the computer to choose one set of instructions according to the value of the variable. This in-

Algorithm:

```
Loop: R = 1 TO 5 Step 2
        Loop:C = 1 to 3 Step 1
                CLoop Instructions
        Loop-end: C
Loop-end: R
```

The values of R and C as they progress through the loops are as follows:

R	C
1	1
1	2
1	3
3	1
3	2
3	3
5	1
5	2
5	3

When C is incremented to 4 it fails the test and drops out of the C loop. R is then incremented and tested. If the test passes then C starts at 1 again.
When R is incremented to 7, execution drops out of the R loop and continues on to the next instruction after Loop-end: R.

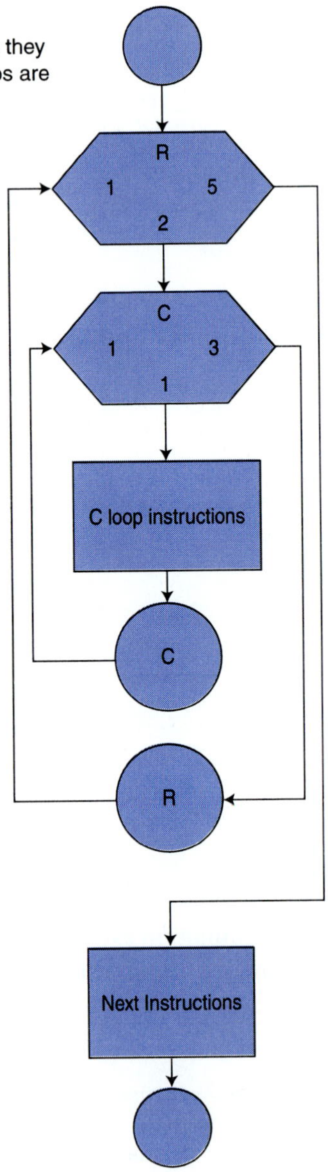

Algorithm:

```
Loop: R =1 TO 2 Step 1
   Loop:C = 1 to 3 Step 1
      Loop: D = 1 TO 4 Step 1
         Print R, C, D
      Loop-end: D
   Loop-end: C
Loop-end: R
```

The values of R, C, and D that will be printed are:

R	C	D
1	1	1
1	1	2
1	1	3
1	1	4
1	2	1
1	2	2
1	2	3
1	2	4
1	3	1
1	3	2
1	3	3
1	3	4
2	1	1
2	1	2
2	1	3
2	1	4
2	2	1
2	2	2
2	2	3
2	2	4
2	3	1
2	3	2
2	3	3
2	3	4

Flowchart:

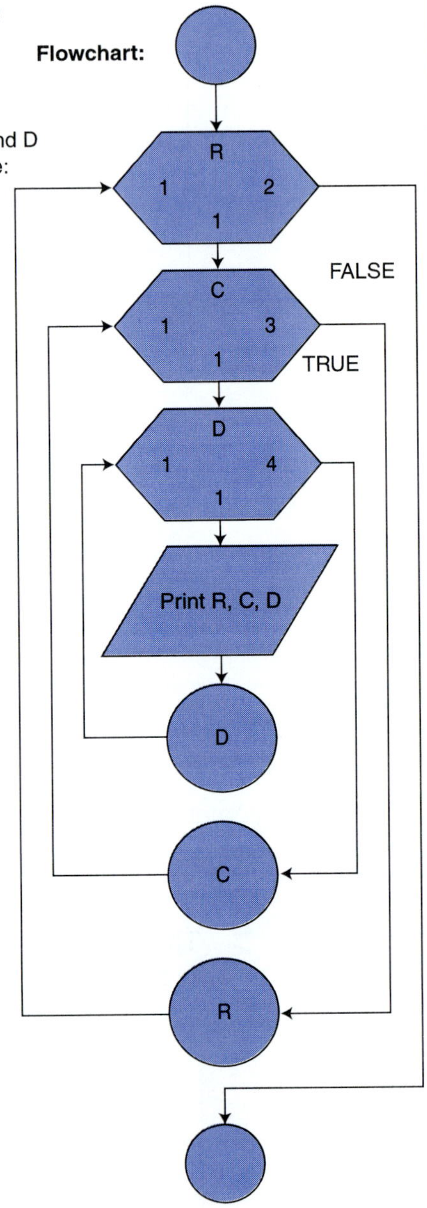

Figure 18.8 Nested Automatic Counter Loops

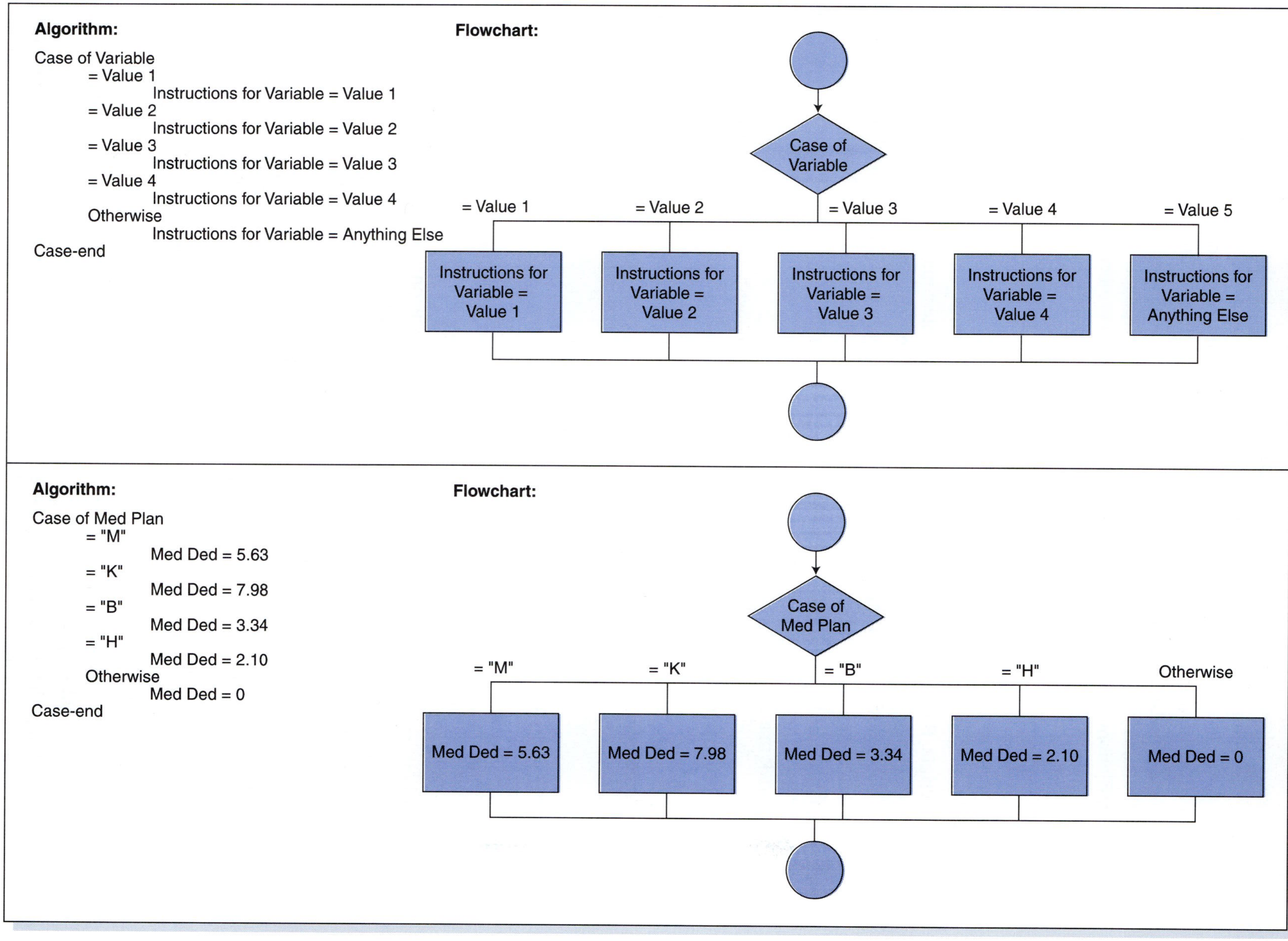

Figure 18.9 Example of Case Logic Structure

struction is used for menus, codes such as medical deduction codes for payroll, and when your solution requires different calculations according to the value of a variable.

You may use the various logic structures in conjunction with one another. The sequential logic structure is rarely used alone. There are, however, very few scripts that you will write where you will not use the sequential logic structure. Decisions and loop are frequently used with the sequential logic structure. The case structure is used less than the others; however, it is nice when the need arises. Chapter 19 presents how these instructions and logic structures fit into the design of a project.

Summary

Most applications programs have programming features which may be called macros or scripts. Programming, however, occurs when you write a macro or a script to develop instructions for the computer, to be saved with your project and used at a later date.

Solutions to problems are either algorithmic or heuristic in nature. Algorithmic solutions require step-by-step instructions to solve a problem such as how to bake a cake or how to find a restaurant. Heuristic solutions require trial and error, previous knowledge, and experience to find a solution to a problem such as how to make money in the stock market.

Writing macros or scripts requires the use of an instruction set. To plan a solution to a problem requiring the use of macros or scripts, flowcharts and algorithms are used. Each computer instruction has an associated algorithmic instruction and flowchart symbol.

The four logic structures used to write macros or scripts are sequential, decision, repetition, and case logic structures.

Key Words

Algorithm
Algorithmic solution
Flowchart
Heuristic solution
Instruction

Logic Structures
- Sequential
- Decision
- Repetition
- Case

Questions

1. What are macros or scripts?
2. What is the difference between an algorithmic solution to a problem and a heuristic solution?
3. Name three problems in your everyday life that would require an algorithmic solution and explain why.
4. Name three problems in your everyday life that would require a heuristic solution and explain why.

5. Name and explain three computer instructions. In your explanation include the algorithmic instruction and the flowchart symbol.
6. Name and explain the four logic structures. In your explanation include the algorithmic instruction(s) and the flowchart of each.

Problems

1. Create the set of instructions required for a solution to one of the problems you gave as an answer in question 3 above.
2. Create a set of guidelines required for a solution to one of the problems you gave as an answer in question 4 above.
3. Create an algorithm and a flowchart to print three numbers, A, B, and C, in order. A, B, and C may be any number.
4. Create an algorithm and a flowchart to switch the memory location values of A and B.
5. Create an algorithm and flowchart to calculate the amount of paint needed for a room. Assume the room has two windows. The walls and ceiling will be painted. The formula for area is length times width. Remember you would not paint the windows. Each can of paint covers 120 square feet. All dimensions are variables.
6. Create an algorithm and flowchart for a script to change a Roman numeral digit to a decimal digit.
7. Create an algorithm and a flowchart to flip a coin 50 times and count the number of heads and tails. Use the random number generator as described in Chapter 12.

Chapter 19

Event-Driven Object-Oriented Programming

Overview

Objectives

When you have finished this chapter, you should be able to:

1. Use object-oriented concepts in the design of a solution to a problem.
2. Design an event-driven object-oriented programming solution.
3. Design a user-friendly, functional user interface.
4. Design the storyboards for an event-driven object-oriented solution.
5. Determine the objects and the scripts needed for an event-driven object-oriented solution.

Developing a project for a client on the computer using application software many times requires that the project be automated. This in turn requires the development of a user interface with areas for data entry, buttons, hot spots, hot objects, and so forth, all with attached scripts. The click of a button is an event on the computer; hence, the development of this type of interface is called event-driven object-oriented programming. This chapter will present concepts and terms used in this programming language.

Interface Design

Graphic User Interface (GUI)

A **graphics user interface (GUI)** is a computer screen designed for easy interaction between the user and the computer. Each item on the screen is an object with related responsibilities. A GUI is developed when using an event-driven object-oriented language such as Visual Basic or Lingo.

RDBMS projects are often designed with a GUI created on a form, usually called the switchboard. Spreadsheets may have a GUI sheet to automate the spreadsheet.

These interfaces contain buttons, entry lines, and other items for anything that is required of the project such as delete a record, add a record, change a record, print a report, print a letter, access the internet, or view a spreadsheet from the switchboard of a database.

Guidelines for Interface Design

The success of an application many times depends on the interface design. Good design is important. You are encouraged to review the design guidelines in Chapter 7. Along with those guidelines are four other basic guidelines to follow:

1. *Never lose sight of the purpose of the project.* Keep in mind the requirements of the projects such as what should be output to the screen or the printer, what data should be updated, and the basic processing requirements of the solution to the problem. These basic items should be placed on the interface.
2. *Keep it simple.* Add artwork and color to make the interface attractive, but, use the guidelines for good design and avoid overdoing the amount of graphics and colors on the screen. Do not lose basic items in the glitz.
3. *Be consistent.* If you are going to use buttons for some items, use them for all items. Do not use some buttons, some hot spots, and some hot objects. Be consistent with colors. If you have more than one interface, do not change the basic design. Remember the users are trying to navigate to accomplish a task.
4. *Design the navigation with the user in mind.* A project must be easy to navigate. Be sure to include on every screen buttons to exit the program, to go back to the main screen menu, and to return to the previous screen. It is important for the user to be able to go back to "home" when lost. If you are designing a switchboard, design a way for the user to return to the switchboard at all times.

The application should have a visual style that is consistent with the purpose of the project. If the project is formal, the style should be formal. The fonts should be selected from traditional fonts and the artwork should be serious and in conjunction with the theme of the project. If the project is informal, then the fun fonts may be used and the artwork can include some cartoons. However, even in the most formal project, a moment of levity many times is appreciated.

Each screen needs to be designed using all or some of the following elements: backgrounds, windows, navigational tools such as buttons, hot spots, input and output boxes, graphics, text, video, sound, and animation. The background of each screen should be similar to all other screens. Again, subtle changes add interest. Navigational tools should be placed in the same area on the screen. Navigational tools do not need to be buttons. Leaves on a tree, fish in a pond, rocks on the beach, and houses on a street can all be navigational tools. Buttons may be a boring sight in your project or they may be your only choice when designing the interface.

User input areas should be large enough for the user to see and located in a convenient, logical place on the screen for entering data. The same holds true for the output. Text should be limited to a few lines per screen or placed in a scrolled text box with a contrasting background for easy reading. Graphics, animation, video, and sound should be added with caution and only to enhance the message or purpose of the screen. These items should add interest or information to data already presented.

A well-designed interface is pleasant to view, functional, and provides easy access to all functions of the program. A well-designed interface allows the user to navigate through the program in a nonlinear mode, including the ability to quit the program at any time.

Event-Driven Object-Oriented Programming

Event-driven object-oriented programs use actions or events to trigger the execution of a set of instructions called a script, a macro, or some other term. An interface is designed such that each item on the screen is an object with assigned properties. The objects may be in the form of a button, a graphic, a user input box, an output box, a pull-down menu, a text box, a video clip, a sound clip, or anything else that has been placed on the screen. The properties of these objects may be such things as location on the screen, name of the object, color, text formats, color palette used, designation of editable text, size, or speed of video or sound. A script may be attached to each object. An overall program script designates any actions that refer to the entire application such as initializations, beeps of the mouse, and designating public variables. Once the application starts, the user has complete control over the order of processing through the use of events, the interface, a pointing device, and a keyboard.

Events

Events

An **event** is a "happening" in the computer. Some typical events are as follows:

on mousedown

on mouseup

on keydown

on keyup

Each language has its own set of events. The only time the script for an event is executed is when the event happens. When a button is clicked, a set of instructions attached to the clicked button is executed when the mouse goes down. A different set of instructions may be executed when the mouse comes up. When a specific key is depressed or released, another set of instructions may be executed. In this case, the computer saves the value of the key. The programmer may use this information in the script. The program is executed through the use of events, many of which are directed by the user.

Interactivity

Interactivity was introduced in Chapter 6 as part of developing slide shows. When you were creating your slide show with interactivity designed into it, you were creating an event-driven slide show. Event-driven object-oriented programming languages add to the concepts presented in Chapter 6.

Interactivity

When using event-driven languages, **interactivity** is between screens and/or between the user and the computer. Each screen becomes an entity to be designed and programmed. Interaction makes something happen. Interaction may cause something to happen on the current screen, to switch to a new or a modified screen, to stop the program from running, or to create a printed document. This interaction produces a nonlinear solution.

For example, if we calculate the interest on an amount of money over several years, we input the amount, the interest, and the number of years. In a procedural solution, the program specifies the order that the user enters the data and changes may or may not be allowed without starting over. In an event-driven object-oriented solution, there would be three user input boxes on the screen. The user may input the data in any order and change any of the data as necessary. The calculation does not take place until the user requests the answer through the use of a button—an event.

Navigational Tools

Interactivity requires that **navigational tools** be built into the program. These tools include hot spots, hot objects, time, and different types of buttons such as a back button, a forward button, a jump button, a menu button, and a quit button. It is important to plan navigation carefully. The user needs to navigate through the program with ease and with as little frustration as possible, and further, to be able to quit at any time.

Tools include interface and screen storyboards, an object dictionary, an interactivity chart for an event-driven object-oriented program, and the algorithms and flowcharts for each script. You have already used interactivity diagrams and storyboards when you developed slide shows.

Designing an Event-Driven Object-Oriented Project

The project planning guide is created with the six problem-solving steps as its base. You may have other planning guides to develop as well as this one, such as a plan for a database or a spreadsheet with which this interface will interact. Figure 19.1 presents the project planning guide. The steps to follow in creating an event-driven object-oriented project are as follows:

Step 1: Identify the problem by writing the problem statement.

Step 2: Understand the problem, including the problem requirements and the audience.

Step 3: List alternative solutions.

Step 4: Select best solution.

Step 5: Plan your solution.

a. Create the storyboards.
b. Define all objects.
c. Define the interactivity between screens.
d. Define the scripts.

Step 6: List the criteria for evaluation.

Steps one through four and six are similar to those in other planning guides. In step five, the storyboards should be completed first. **Storyboards** allow the developer to organize data, objects, and ideas. This may be only the interface design storyboard or screen storyboards as in slide shows. In the box, the developer sketches the objects to be placed on the screen. Fine detail is not necessary but all objects should be placed in enough detail so the programmer may use this document as a plan to start the computerization of the application. The lines allow for notes on the screen such as interactivity guidelines, object sources, animation effects, and so forth. Each storyboard should have a reference number.

Screens are made up of objects. These objects may be developed in the software package or they may be imported from another source. Data that pertain to the object

Figure 19.1 Project Planning Guide

PROJECT PLANNING GUIDE

Name of Folder for Files: ______________________________ Date: ______________

Location of Electronic File: ____

Name: ____

Name of Client: ____

Step 1: Identify the Problem by Writing the Problem Statement.

Step 2: Understand the Problem.

Audience:

Required Outcomes of the Project:

Required Knowledge of the Problem to Develop the Project:

Expected Knowledge of the Audience:

Environment:

Step 3: Identify Valid Alternative Methods to Solve the Problem.

Step 4: Select the Best Method to Solve the Problem from the List of Alternative Solutions.

(continued)

Figure 19.1 Project Planning Guide

Step 5: Plan Your Solution.

Interface Storyboard.

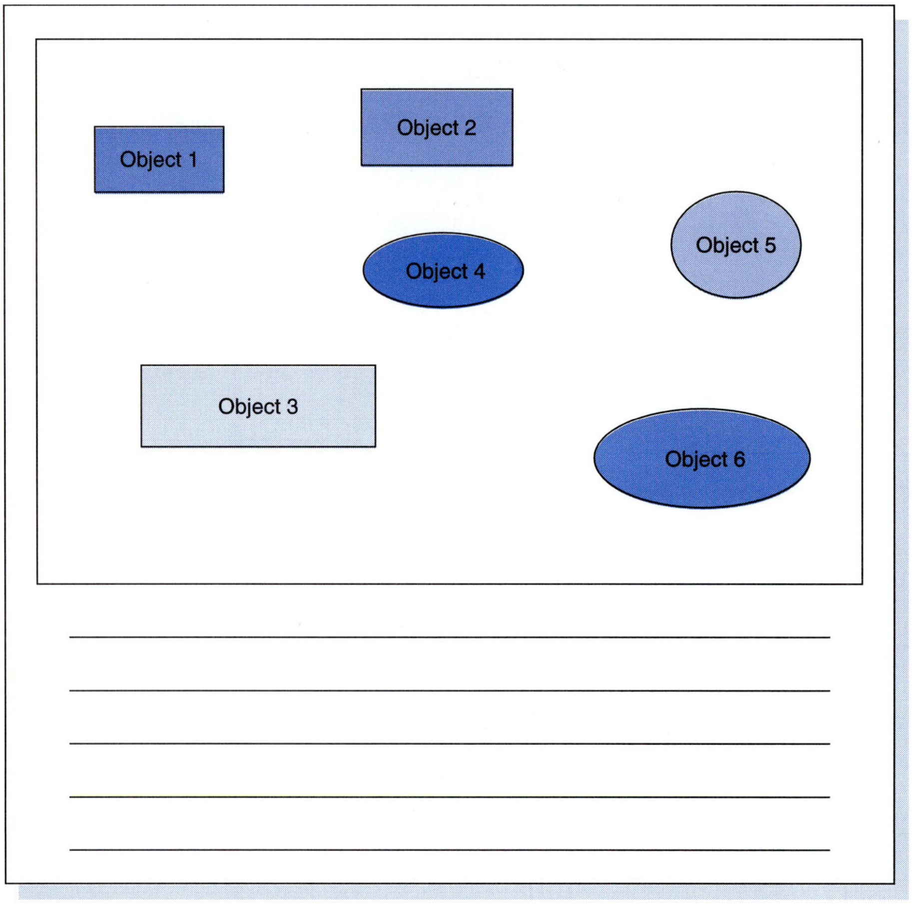

Figure 19.1 (continued)

Individual Screen Storyboards.

Transition: ______________________

Layout: ______________________

Comments: ______________________

____

____

Transition: ______________________

Layout: ______________________

Comments: ______________________

____

____

Transition: ______________________

Layout: ______________________

Comments: ______________________

____

____

Transition: ______________________

Layout: ______________________

Comments: ______________________

____

____

(continued)

Figure 19.1 Project Planning Guide

Object Dictionary.

Object Name	Source/File Name	File Type/Extension	Screen Number(s)	H/I/O*	Script

*H = Hyper, I = Input, O = Output

Figure 19.1 (continued)

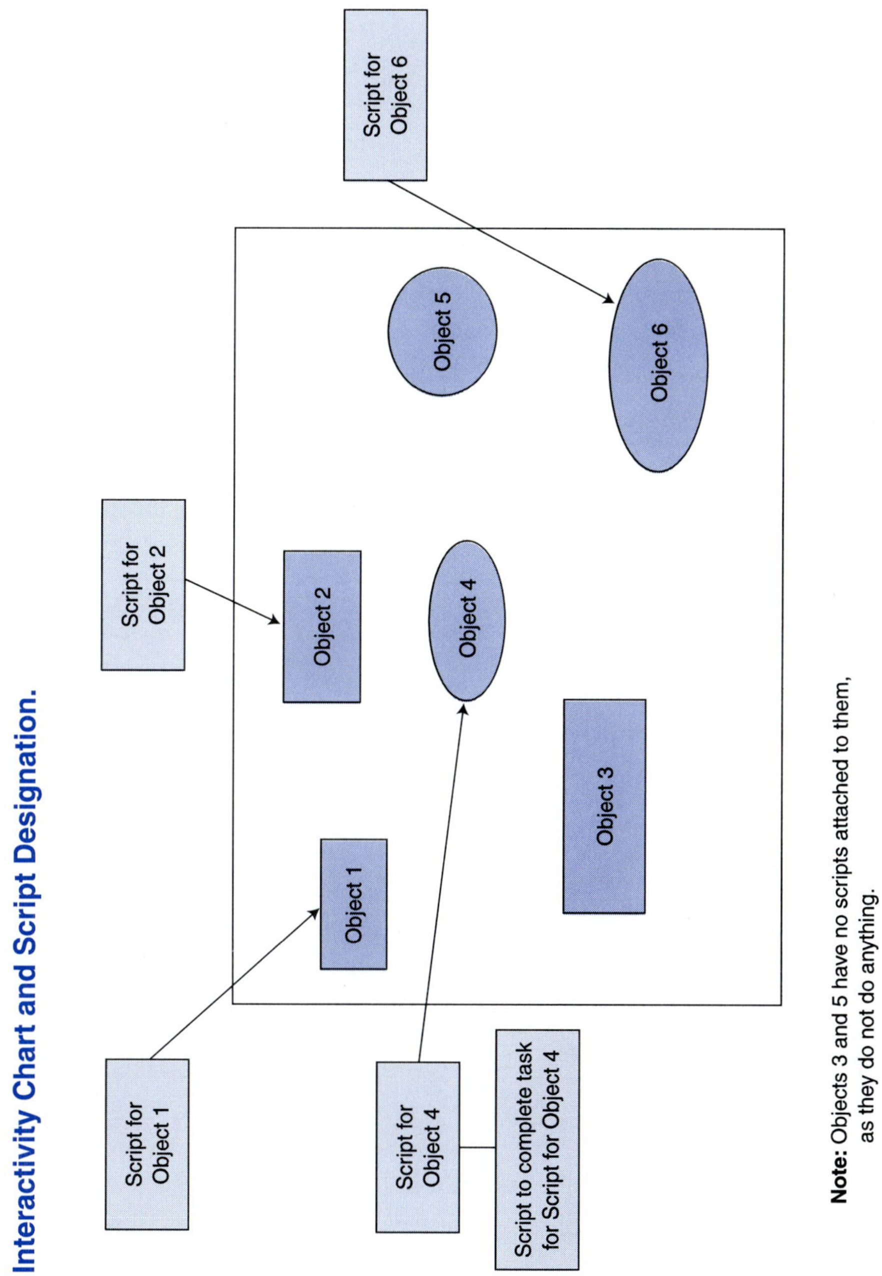

(continued)

Figure 19.1 Project Planning Guide

Step 5: **Plan Your Solution. (con't)**

Algorithms and Flowcharts:

Step 6: **Evaluate the Solution. List the criteria for evaluating the completed document.**

need to be placed in the object dictionary, including the name of the object, the source and/or file name, the file type and extension, the screens on which it appears, whether the object is a hyper object, input object, or output object, and whether there is a script attached to it.

The name of an object identifies it as an object that can later be referred to by the name. The source and/or file name column identifies where the object was created or obtained. The object may be created within the program or obtained from a CD-ROM; or it may be created in another package such as a paint package or an animation package, or from a digital camera, an audio tape, or many other sources. The name of the file is necessary so that the file may be located. The file type and extension column defines the type file, such as a bit mapped or other type of data file. The file extension defines the type of data in the file. The next column lists the storyboards or screens on which the object is found. The last two columns are check columns. The first indicates if this object is a hyper object (H), an input object (I), or an output object (O). The last column indicates if there is a script attached to the object. A yes or a check mark indicates a script. The programmer can refer to this list when creating the screens on the computer to save time in trying to locate objects.

The next part of step five is to design the interactivity between the screens. An interactivity chart starts with the storyboard. There will be an interactivity chart for each screen. The interface design storyboard is the center of the interactivity chart. Surrounding the storyboard are rectangles indicating the script and to which object they are attached. If the script calls another script, the interactivity between these scripts is shown. The interactivity diagram will not show the scripts that are separate from the interactivity such as a script that clicks the mouse when a mouse button is pushed.

Scripts are short sets of instructions attached to objects or to the entire solution. These individual instruction sets are procedural in nature; however, the only time the instruction sets are executed is when an event happens. The logic structures presented in Chapter 18 hold true for these scripts. Variables are made public or they are kept as local variables. If data are required in another script, the variables must be public. There is no other way of coupling scripts. Algorithms and flowcharts should be the last to be developed.

An Example

Our problem is as follows: Develop the switchboard for the library checkout system. Figure 19.2 presents the project planning guide for this problem. The scripts have not been included.

Figure 19.2 Project Planning Guide for Example

PROJECT PLANNING GUIDE

Name of Folder for Files: Library System Date: 6/3/2002

Location of Electronic File: c:\my data\work\

Name: Tom Brown

Name of Client: Little Library

Step 1: Identify the Problem by Writing the Problem Statement.

The Little Library would like to have a computerized checkout system for its books. The library would like to be able to have an interface with buttons to help in the update of the system. The system must be able to check books in and out, change book data, list books, and change client data.

Step 2: Understand the Problem.

Audience:

The Little Library librarians

Required Outcomes of the Project:

To automate the Little Library book check-in system

Required Knowledge of the Problem to Develop the Project:

No new knowledge

Expected Knowledge of the Audience:

Knowledge of the library system

Environment:

The library checkout desk

Step 3: Identify Valid Alternative Methods to Solve the Problem.

a. Develop a switchboard in the database program.
b. Develop a sheet as a switchboard in a spreadsheet program.
c. Use buttons versus hot objects.
d. Use screens already developed or create new screens.
e. Create a new screen for entry of ID numbers or use the switchboard.

Step 4: Select the Best Method to Solve the Problem from the List of Alternative Solutions.

a. Develop a switchboard in the database program.
b. Use buttons and input boxes.
c. Use screens that have already been developed.
d. Use the switchboard screen for entry of ID numbers with the client and/or book data printed on the switchboard.

Figure 19.2 (continued)

Step 5: Plan Your Solution.

Interface Storyboard.

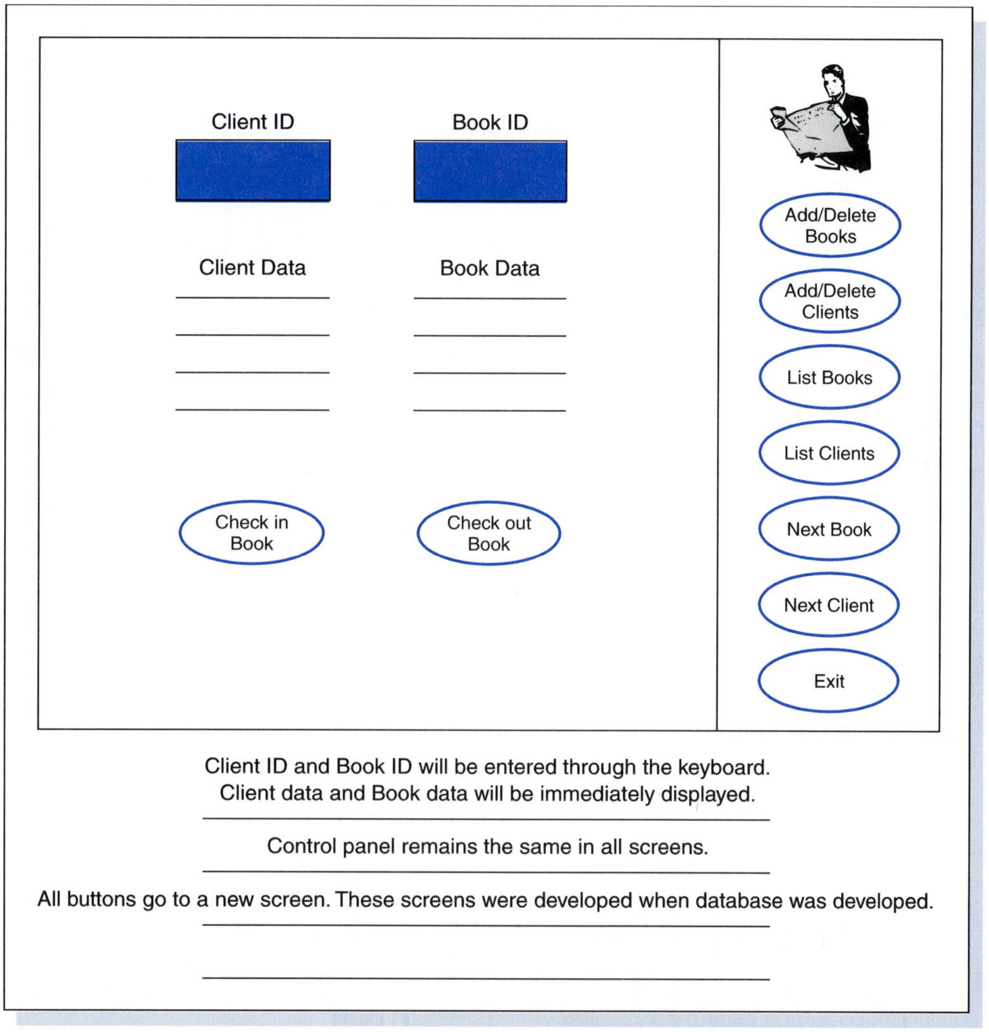

(continued)

Figure 19.2 Project Planning Guide for Example

Object Dictionary.

Object Name	Source/File Name	File Type/Extension	Screen Number(s)	H/I/O*	Script
Client ID			Main	I	Y
Book ID			Main	I	Y
Client Data			Main	O	N
Book Data			Main	O	N
Check In Button			Main	H	Y
Check Out Button			Main	H	Y
Add/Delete Book Button			All	H	Y
Add/Delete Client Button			All	H	Y
List Books Button			All	H	Y
List Clients Button			All	H	Y
Next Book Button			All	H	Y
Next Client Button			All	H	Y
Exit Button			All	H	Y
Man/newspaper Graphic	ManReading	BMP	All		N
Background	Library Picture	TIF	All		N

*H = Hyper, I = Input, O = Output

Figure 19.2 (continued)

Interactivity Chart and Script Designation.

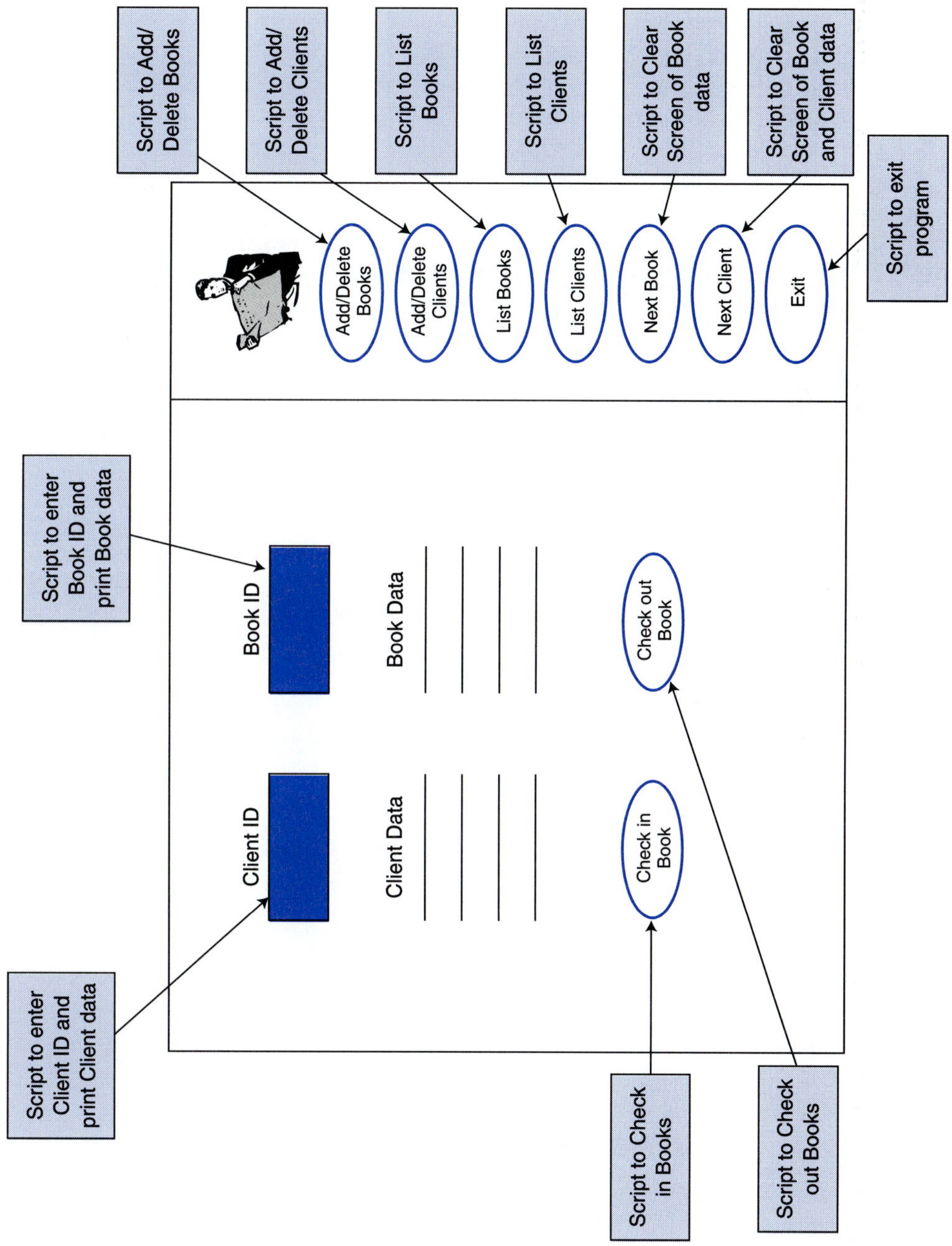

(continued)

Figure 19.2 Project Planning Guide for Example

Step 5: Plan Your Solution. (con't)

The following scripts will need to be developed:

a. Script to enter client ID and print client data on screen
b. Script to enter book ID and print book data on screen
c. Script to check in books
d. Script to check out books
e. Script to add/delete/change data on books
f. Script to add/delete/change data on clients
g. Script to list books (Print book report.)
h. Script to list clients (Print client report.)
i. Script to clear screen of client and book information
j. Script to exit project

Step 6: Evaluate the Solution. List the criteria for evaluating the completed document.

a. Is the system easy to use?
b. Does the system update data correctly?
c. Does the system exit the project correctly?
d. Is the interface designed well?
e. Are the data easy to read?
f. Do the librarians like it?

Summary

Event-driven object-oriented programming uses screen objects that are assigned properties and scripts. Interaction between screens is accomplished by events that occur when the program is executed.

Most programs today use a graphical user interface enabling the user to easily guide through the program. A user interface needs to be functional, well designed, and easy to use. Guidelines for good design should be followed. When designing an event-driven object-oriented project, step five is divided into the following jobs:

- **a.** Create the storyboards.
- **b.** Define all objects.
- **c.** Define the interactivity between screens.
- **d.** Define the scripts.

Tools introduced in this chapter include the interface and screen storyboards, object dictionary, and interactivity script designation chart. A well-designed project allows for better efficiency in programming and maintenance.

Key Words

Event	Object dictionary
Event-driven object-oriented programming	Screen
Graphic user interface (GUI)	Script
Interactivity	Storyboard
Navigational tools	

Questions

1. State the purpose of the following:
   - a. interface and screen storyboard
   - b. object dictionary
   - c. interactivity and script designation chart
2. What is a GUI?
3. Why is a GUI important to the development of solutions to problems today?
4. Describe an example of an event.

Problems

1. Design a solution to the following problems using the project planning guide.
   - a. A restaurant would like to have a scheduling system for its employees. The software will allow the restaurant owner to schedule employees for up to 40 hours in a seven-day week. The restaurant is open from 6:00 A.M. to 10:00 P.M. The system should include a check-in and a checkout system for the employees, a printout of employees' work hours, and the ability to change hours if needed.

b. A college computer lab manager would like to have a system of check in and checkout for the students who use the lab. The system would include the ability to check students in and out of the lab, to check in and out and track all lab materials, to keep track of students' hours, and to track all materials that are checked out. The system would also have the ability to know if a computer is available before allowing a student to check in to the lab.

Chapter 20

Connectivity

Overview

Working in Groups
Working with Others around the World
Telecommuting

Objectives

When you have finished this chapter, you should be able to:

1. Understand the changing workplace.
2. Understand requirements for working in a job that requires connectivity.
3. Understand the pros and cons of telecommuting.

In this day and age of telecommunications, the workplace is changing. You may be working in an office or at home. The office location in which you are working may be remote from the company headquarters from which you receive your paycheck. You may be a freelance worker and have outsource contracts from many companies. In any of these situations, you will probably be communicating with other workers via electronic means. This requires new attitudes and knowledge for both employees and employers, new management styles, and new equipment. Today's workplace requires connectivity both physically and mentally. **Connectivity** is the linking of people together through telecommunications. It requires hardware and software to be physically and electronically connected. It also requires people to be mentally linked through the right attitude, team skills, communication skills, and computer skills.

Working in Groups

Connectivity

With the increasing use of telecommunications comes the expected decrease in turnaround time for projects. Along with this expectation is the increase of project complexity. The solution is to have a team of people, who specialize in one aspect of the project, work together to complete it.

New employee skills are being required of corporations. They want people who have team skills and team members who work well with other people. They want people who have project management skills and good communication skills, both verbal and written. Loss of communications between team members can destroy a project. Corporations want group members who know the processes of putting together a project, who have time management skills, and who know what it takes to accept a project, complete it on time, and make customers happy.

Management styles are changing because of required teamwork. Managers are no longer directing the work of a group of individuals—they are an integral part of the team. Members of the team need to be able to listen to fellow team members' ideas, present their own, and be able to compromise. They need to keep their personal egos away from the workplace. A good team is synergetic and wonderful to work with. Much can be accomplished by good teamwork.

Working with Others around the World

Many times team members may be in other parts of the country or even the world. A person developing a multimedia presentation may work with a graphic artist in Canada, a project manager in New York, a video editor in Los Angeles, a sound editor in France, and a script writer in England. That person may not even be aware of the location of the other team members and may never see them. On the other hand, the developer may have electronic conferences at specified times or may physically meet at specified times and locations during the development of the project.

Working with people around the world requires not only good team skills, but also an understanding of other time zones, cultures, and sometimes languages. This type of a work team can be exciting and fun to be a part of. Whether the other team members are all over the world or in various other parts of the state, the job skills are the same. You need good team skills, communication skills, and telecommunications skills.

Telecommuting

Telecommuting

Many people are telecommuting today. **Telecommuting** is working for a company from your home. Most work is delivered through telecommunications. There are pros and cons to telecommuting. Telecommuting provides flexible working hours, eliminates commuting problems, and decreases expenses for gas, clothes, and so forth. Telecommuting requires self-discipline to work a specified number of hours a day, requires a dedicated place in the home to have as an office, and eliminates the social contact that happens in a company office setting. Telecommuting requires a person to have good team and communication skills and still work in an isolated location. More and more companies are finding that telecommuting is a way to decrease overhead costs. More and more people are finding it desirable because they can live in a remote location and work around family time schedules and other commitments.

New opportunities in the workplace may provide a better quality of life by allowing people the chance to choose where they want to work and live. Connectivity and telecommunications provide the means for these new opportunities.

Summary

The workplace is changing to include remote work locations and working with team members from other places around the world. Corporations are wanting employees with team skills, project management skills, communication skills, and who enjoy using telecommunications as part of their jobs.

Connectivity is linking people together through the use of telecommunications. New job opportunities provide the chance to telecommute, to work in teams with people in other locations, to enjoy flexible work schedules, and to work in a specialized area of your choice.

Key Words

Connectivity

Telecommuting

Questions

1. What are the skills needed for jobs today?
2. How is the workplace changing?
3. What is telecommuting?
4. What skills do you have to enter the world of telecommuting?
5. What skills do you need to improve before entering the world of telecommuting?

Appendix A

ASCII Code

ASCII in Mnemonic	Binary Code	Decimal Code	Octal Code	Hex Code	Remark
NUL	00 00 00 00	0	000	00	Null, tape feed.
SOH	00 00 00 01	1	001	01	Start of heading; also SOM, start of message.
STX	00 00 00 10	2	002	02	Start of text; also EOA, end of address.
ETX	00 00 00 11	3	003	03	End of text; also EOM, end of message.
EOT	00 00 01 00	4	004	04	End of transmission (End); shuts off TWX machines.
ENQ	00 00 01 01	5	005	05	Inquiry (Inqry); also WRU.
ACK	00 00 01 10	6	006	06	Acknowledge; also RU.
BEL	00 00 01 11	7	007	07	Ring the bell.
BS	00 00 10 00	8	010	08	Backspace; also FEO format effector.
HT	00 00 10 01	9	011	09	Horizontal tab.
LF	00 00 10 10	10	012	0A	Line feed or line space (New line); advance paper to next line.
VT	00 00 10 11	11	013	0B	Vertical tab (VTAB).
FF	00 00 11 00	12	014	0C	Form feed to top of next page (Page).
CR	00 00 11 01	13	015	0D	Carriage return to beginning line.
SO	00 00 11 10	14	016	0E	Shift out; changes ribbon color to red.
SI	00 00 11 11	15	017	0F	Shift in; changes ribbon color to black.
DLE	00 01 00 00	16	020	10	Data line escape.
DC1	00 01 00 01	17	021	11	Device control 1; turns transmitter (reader) on.
DC2	00 01 00 10	18	022	12	Device control 2; turns punch or auxiliary on.
DC3	00 01 00 11	19	023	13	Device control 3; turns transmitter (reader) off.
DC4	00 01 01 00	20	024	14	Device control 4; turns punch or auxiliary off.
NAK	00 01 01 01	21	025	15	Negative acknowledge; also ERR, error.
SYN	00 01 01 10	22	026	16	Synchronous file (SYNC).
ETB	00 01 01 11	23	027	17	End of transmission block; also LEM, logical end of medium.
CAN	00 01 10 00	24	030	18	Cancel (Cancl).
EM	00 01 10 01	25	031	19	End of medium.
SUB	00 01 10 10	26	032	1A	Substitute.
ESC	00 01 10 11	27	033	1B	Escape.
FS	00 01 11 00	28	034	1C	File separator.
GS	00 01 11 01	29	035	1D	Group separator.
RS	00 01 11 10	30	036	1E	Record separator.
US	00 01 11 11	31	037	1F	Unit separator.
Space	00 10 00 00	32	040	20	
!	00 10 00 01	33	041	21	
″	00 10 00 10	34	042	22	
#	00 10 00 11	35	043	23	
S	00 10 01 00	36	044	24	
%	00 10 01 01	37	045	25	
&	00 10 01 10	38	046	26	
′	00 10 01 11	39	047	27	Apostrophe.
(	00 10 10 00	40	050	28	
)	00 10 10 01	41	051	29	
*	00 10 10 10	42	052	2A	
—	00 10 10 11	43	053	2B	
,	00 10 11 00	44	054	2C	
-	00 10 11 01	45	055	2D	Hyphen.
.	00 10 11 10	46	056	2E	
/	00 10 11 11	47	057	2F	
0	00 11 00 00	48	060	30	
1	00 11 00 01	49	061	31	
2	00 11 00 10	50	062	32	
3	00 11 00 11	51	063	33	
4	00 11 01 00	52	064	34	
5	00 11 01 01	53	065	35	

ASCII in Mnemonic	Binary Code	Decimal Code	Octal Code	Hex Code	Remark
6	00 11 01 10	54	066	36	
7	00 11 01 11	55	067	37	
8	00 11 10 00	56	070	38	
9	00 11 10 01	57	071	39	
:	00 11 10 10	58	072	3A	
;	00 11 10 11	59	073	3B	
<	00 11 11 00	60	074	3C	
=	00 11 11 01	61	075	3D	
>	00 11 11 10	62	076	3E	
?	00 11 11 11	63	077	3F	
@	01 00 00 00	64	100	40	
A	01 00 00 01	65	101	41	
B	01 00 00 10	66	102	42	
C	01 00 00 11	67	103	43	
D	01 00 01 00	68	104	44	
E	01 00 01 01	69	105	45	
F	01 00 01 10	70	106	46	
G	01 00 01 11	71	107	47	
H	01 00 10 00	72	110	48	
I	01 00 10 01	73	111	49	
J	01 00 10 10	74	112	4A	
K	01 00 10 11	75	113	4B	
L	01 00 11 00	76	114	4C	
M	01 00 11 01	77	115	4D	
N	01 00 11 10	78	116	4E	
O	01 00 11 11	79	117	4F	
P	01 01 00 00	80	120	50	
Q	01 01 00 01	81	121	51	
R	01 01 00 10	82	122	52	
S	01 01 00 11	83	123	53	
T	01 01 01 00	84	124	54	
U	01 01 01 01	85	125	55	
V	01 01 01 10	86	126	56	
W	01 01 01 11	87	127	57	
X	01 01 10 00	88	130	58	
Y	01 01 10 01	89	131	59	
Z	01 01 10 10	90	132	5A	
[	01 01 10 11	91	133	5B	
]	01 01 11 00	92	134	5C	
]	01 01 11 01	93	135	5D	
ˆ	01 01 11 10	94	136	5E	
_	01 01 11 11	95	137	5F	Underline.
`	01 10 00 00	96	140	60	Accent grave.
a	01 10 00 01	97	141	61	
b	01 10 00 10	98	142	62	
c	01 10 00 11	99	143	63	
d	01 10 01 00	100	144	64	
e	01 10 01 01	101	145	65	
f	01 10 01 10	102	146	66	
g	01 10 01 11	103	147	67	
h	01 10 10 00	104	150	68	
i	01 10 10 01	105	151	69	
j	01 10 10 10	106	152	6A	
k	01 10 10 11	107	153	6B	
l	01 10 11 00	108	154	6C	
m	01 10 11 01	109	155	6D	

ASCII in Mnemonic	Binary Code	Decimal Code	Octal Code	Hex Code	Remark
n	01 10 11 10	110	156	6E	
o	01 10 11 11	111	157	6F	
p	01 11 00 00	112	160	70	
q	01 11 00 01	113	161	71	
r	01 11 00 10	114	162	72	
s	01 11 00 11	115	163	73	
t	01 11 01 00	116	164	74	
u	01 11 01 01	117	165	75	
v	01 11 01 10	118	166	76	
w	01 11 01 11	119	167	77	
x	01 11 10 00	120	170	78	
y	01 11 10 01	121	171	79	
z	01 11 10 10	122	172	7A	
{	01 11 10 11	123	173	7B	
|	01 11 11 00	124	174	7C	Alt mode.
}	01 11 11 01	125	175	7D	
~	01 11 11 10	126	176	7E	
DEL	01 11 11 11	127	177	7F	Delete, rub out.

Appendix B

Planning Guides

Given Data	Required Results
Processes and Equations	**The Audience**

Problem Analysis Chart (PAC)

File Structure for: ____________________

Folder Name: ____________________

Storage Media: ____________________

Folder Page: ____________________

Date: ____________

Folder Name	Contains Folders	Contains Folders

File Structure Planning Diagram

SLIDE SHOW PLANNING GUIDE

Name of Document: ______________________________ Date: ______________

Location of Electronic File: ______________________________

Name: ______________________________

Name of Client: ______________________________

Step 1: Identify the Problem by Writing the Problem Statement.

Step 2: Understand the Problem.

Audience:

Required Outcomes of the Slide Show:

Required Knowledge of the Problem to Develop the Slide Show:

Expected Knowledge of the Audience:

Environment of Presentation:

Step 3: Identify Valid Alternative Methods to Solve the Problem.

Step 4: Select the Best Method to Solve the Problem from the List of Alternative Solutions.

Slide Show Overview:

Step 5: Plan Your Solution.

Software to be used: Presentation Graphics

Background:

__________ Premade Background Name: ______________________________

__________ Own Background Description:

Files to Be Imported:

File	Description	Use	Location

Slide Size: __________

Paper Color for Handouts: __________ No. of Slides Per Page: __________

Print in Color/B&W: Handouts: __________ Speaker's Notes: __________

Header Contents:

Footer Contents:

Materials Needed:

Hardware: ______________________________

Software: ______________________________

Projector/Screen: ______________________________

Handouts: ____________________ Number: ____________________

Speaker's Notes: ____________________ Notebook/Computer: ____________________

Other: ______________________________

(continued)

***Step 5:* Plan Your Solution. (con't)**

Interactivity Chart:

Storyboards: Indicate animation on the diagram of the slide:

Transition: ______________________________

Layout: ______________________________

Comments: ______________________________

____

____

Transition: ______________________________

Layout: ______________________________

Comments: ______________________________

____

____

Transition: ______________________________

Layout: ______________________________

Comments: ______________________________

____

____

Transition: ______________________________

Layout: ______________________________

Comments: ______________________________

____

____

Step 6: **Evaluate the Solution. List the criteria for evaluating the completed document.**

WORD-PROCESSING PLANNING GUIDE

Name of Document: ______________________________ Date: ______________

Location of Electronic File: ______________________________

Name: ______________________________

Name of Client: ______________________________

Step 1: Identify the Problem by Writing the Problem Statement.

Step 2: Understand the Problem.

Audience:

Required Outcomes of the Document:

Required Knowledge of the Problem to Develop the Document:

Required Knowledge of the Audience:

Step 3: Identify Valid Alternative Methods to Solve the Problem.

Step 4: Select the Best Method to Solve the Problem from the List of Alternative Solutions.

Step 5: Plan Your Solution.

Software to be used: ______________________________

Margins:

Top: ________________________ Top Printer: ________________

Bottom: ______________________ Bottom Printer: _____________

Left/Inside:________Binder:________ Left Printer: _____________

Right: _______________________ Right Printer:_______________

Header: ______________________ Top Printer: ________________

Footer: ______________________ Bottom Printer: _____________

Tabs:

Files to Be Imported:

File	Description	Use	Location

Paper Size: ______________________________ Paper Color:___________________

Orientation: ______________________________ Color/B&W: ___________________

Number of Columns: ______________ Gutter: ________________________________

Header Contents:

Footer Contents:

(continued)

Step 5: **Plan Your Solution. (con't)**

Estimated Number of Pages:______________________________________

Sketch(s) of Individual Page Layout(s)

Step 6: **Evaluate the Solution. List the criteria for evaluating the completed document.**

DESKTOP PUBLISHING PLANNING GUIDE

Name of Document: ______________________________ Date: ______________

Location of Electronic File: ______________________________

Name: ______________________________

Name of Client: ______________________________

Step 1: Identify the Problem by Writing the Problem Statement.

Step 2: Understand the Problem.

Audience:

Required Outcomes of the Document:

Required Knowledge of the Problem to Develop the Document:

Required Knowledge of the Audience:

Step 3: Identify Valid Alternative Methods to Solve the Problem.

Step 4: Select the Best Method to Solve the Problem from the List of Alternative Solutions.

(continued)

Step 5: Plan Your Solution.

Software to be used: Desktop Publisher

Margins:

Top: ____________ Top Printer: ____________

Bottom: ____________ Bottom Printer: ____________

Left/Inside: ________ Binding: ______ Left Printer: ________

Right/Outside: ________ Right Printer: ____________

Header: ____________ Top Printer: ____________

Footer: ____________ Bottom Printer: ____________

Tabs:

Files to Be Imported:

File	Description	Use	Location

Paper Size: ____________ Paper Color: ____________

Orientation: ____________ Color/B&W: ____________

Number of Columns: ________ Gutter: ____________

Header Contents:

Footer Contents:

Estimated Number of Master Pages:______________________________

Sketch(s) of Master Page Layouts:

	1	2	3	4	5	6	7
1							
2							
3							
4							
5							
6							
7							
8							
9							

(continued)

Step 5: Plan Your Solution. (con't)

Estimated Number of Individual Pages:______________________________

Sketch(s) of Individual Page Layouts:

	1	2	3	4	5	6	7
1							
2							
3							
4							
5							
6							
7							
8							
9							

Step 6: **Evaluate the Solution. List the criteria for evaluating the completed document.**

SPREADSHEET PLANNING GUIDE

Name of Document: ______________________________ Date: ______________

Location of Electronic File: ______________________________

Name: ______________________________

Name of Client: ______________________________

Step 1: Identify the Problem by Writing the Problem Statement.

Step 2: Understand the Problem.

The PAC:

Given Data	Required Results
Processes and Formulas	**The Audience**

Required Knowledge of the Problem to Develop the Document:

Required Knowledge of the Audience:

Step: 3 Identify Valid Alternative Methods to Solve the Problem.

Step 4: Select the Best Method to Solve the Problem from the List of Alternative Solutions.

Step 5: Plan Your Solution.

Software to be used: ______ Spreadsheets ______

Margins for Printing:

Top: ______	Top Printer: ______
Bottom: ______	Bottom Printer: ______
Left: ______	Left Printer: ______
Right: ______	Right Printer: ______
Header: ______	Top Printer: ______
Footer: ______	Bottom Printer: ______

(continued)

Step 5: Plan Your Solution. (con't)

Files to Be Imported:

File	Description	Use	Location

Rows to be printed on every page: ______________________________

Columns to be printed on every page: ______________________________

Paper Size: ______________________ Paper Color: ______________________

Orientation: ______________________ Color/B&W: ______________________

Gridlines: ______________ Row and Column Headings Printed: ______________

Header Contents:

Footer Contents:

Analysis required:

Number Format: G = General N = Number C = Currency A = Accounting F = Fraction P = Percentage D = Date T = Time S = Scientific

Text Format: B = Bold I = Italic U = Underline

Page 1

	Format	A	Format	B	Format	C	Format	D	Format	E	Format	F
1												
2												
3												
4												
5												
6												
7												
8												
9												
10												
11												
12												
13												
14												

Number Format: G = General N = Number C = Currency A = Accounting F = Fraction P = Percentage D = Date T = Time S = Scientific

Text Format: B = Bold I = Italic U = Underline

Page___

	Format		Format		Format		Format		Format		Format	

Data to Be Charted	Location of Data	Chart Type

(continued)

Step 6: Evaluate the Solution.

List the Criteria for Evaluating the completed document: Include test numbers for evaluating the formulas.

Postanalysis Required:

RELATIONAL DATABASE MANAGEMENT SYSTEMS PLANNING GUIDE

Name of Database: ______________________________ Date: ______________

Location of Electronic File: ______________________________

Name: ______________________________

Name of Client: ______________________________

Step 1: Identify the Problem by Writing the Problem Statement.

Step 2: Understand the Problem.

Audience:

Required Outcomes of the Database:

Required Knowledge of the Problem to Develop the Database:

Required Knowledge of the Audience:

Step 3: Identify Valid Alternative Methods to Solve the Problem.

Step 4: Select the Best Method to Solve the Problem from the List of Alternative Solutions.

Step 5: Plan Your Solution.

Software to be used: RDBMS

List of Required Reports:

Report Name	Data to Be Included in Report

Table Development.

Original Table:		First Normalization—New Table(s)		Second Normalization—New Table(s)		Third Normalization—New Table(s)	
Item	Field Name	Item	Field Name	Item	Field Name	Item	Field Name

Step 5: Plan Your Solution. (con't)

Schema.

Field Name

Field Name

Field Name

Field Name

Field Name

Field Name

Field Name

Table with Attributes.

Table Name: ______________________

Field Name	Description	Data Type	Field Length	No. of Decimals	Format	Input Mask	Default Value

Form Design.

Background: ______________________

Table: ______________________

Queries.

Table Name: ____________________

Field Name							
Table:							
Sort:							
Show:							
Criteria:							
OR:							

Field Name							
Table:							
Sort:							
Show:							
Criteria:							
OR:							

***Step 5:* Plan Your Solution. (con't)**

Report Layouts:

Report Name:__________________________________

Table or Query Name:__________________________________

Margins:

Top: ________________ Top Printer: ________________

Bottom: ________________ Bottom Printer: ________________

Left: ________________ Left Printer: ________________

Right: ________________ Right Printer:________________

Header: ________________ Top Printer: ________________

Footer: ________________ Bottom Printer: ________________

Paper Size: ________________ Orientation: ________________ Color/B&W: ________________

Sort by: __________________________________

Subtotals on following fields: __________________________________

Images to be imported:

File	Description	Use	Location

Header Contents:

Footer Contents:

Report Heading:

Report Layout.

Column Heading:					
Field Name:					
Column Width:					

Step 6: **Evaluate the Solution. List the criteria for evaluating the completed document.**

INFORMATION PROCESSING PLANNING GUIDE

Name of File Folder: ______________________________ Date: ______________

Location of File Folder: ______________________________

Name: ______________________________

Name of Client: ______________________________

Step 1: Identify the Problem by Writing the Problem Statement.

Step 2: Understand the Problem.

Audience:

Required Outcomes of the Document:

Required Knowledge of the Problem to Develop the Document:

Required Knowledge of the Audience:

Step 3: Identify Valid Alternative Methods to Solve the Problem.

Step 4: **Select the Best Method to Solve the Problem from the List of Alternative Solutions.**

Step 5: **Plan Your Solution. Create a flowchart of the interconnections between files.**

Step 6: **Evaluate the Solution. List the criteria for evaluating the completed document.**

PROJECT PLANNING GUIDE

Name of Folder for Files: ______________________________ Date: ______________

Location of Electronic File: ______________________________

Name: ______________________________

Name of Client: ______________________________

Step 1: Identify the Problem by Writing the Problem Statement.

Step 2: Understand the Problem.

Audience:

Required Outcomes of the Project:

Required Knowledge of the Problem to Develop the Project:

Expected Knowledge of the Audience:

Environment:

Step 3: Identify Valid Alternative Methods to Solve the Problem.

Step 4: Select the Best Method to Solve the Problem from the List of Alternative Solutions.

Step 5: **Plan Your Solution.**

Interface Storyboard.

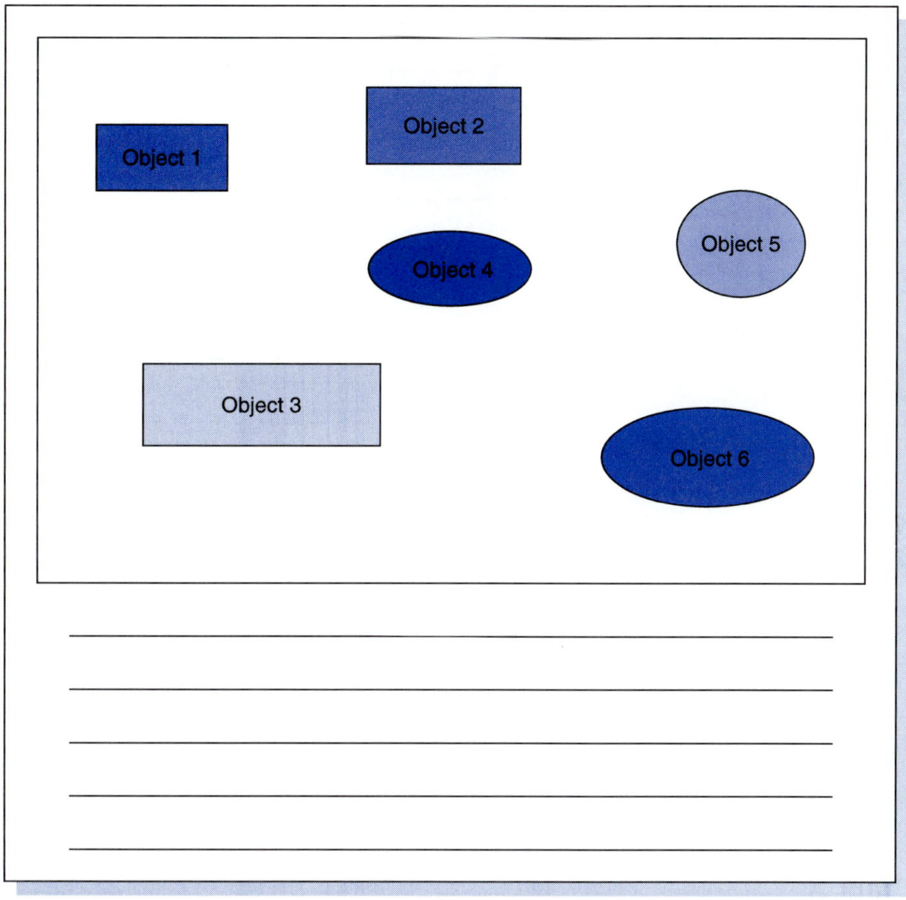

(continued)

Step 5: Plan Your Solution (con't).

Individual Screen Storyboards.

Transition: ______________________________

Layout: ______________________________

Comments: ______________________________

____

____

Transition: ______________________________

Layout: ______________________________

Comments: ______________________________

____

____

Transition: ______________________________

Layout: ______________________________

Comments: ______________________________

____

____

Transition: ______________________________

Layout: ______________________________

Comments: ______________________________

____

____

Object Dictionary.

Object Name	Source/File Name	File Type/Extension	Screen Number(s)	H/I/O*	Script

*H = Hyper, I = Input, O = Output

Interactivity Chart and Script Designation.

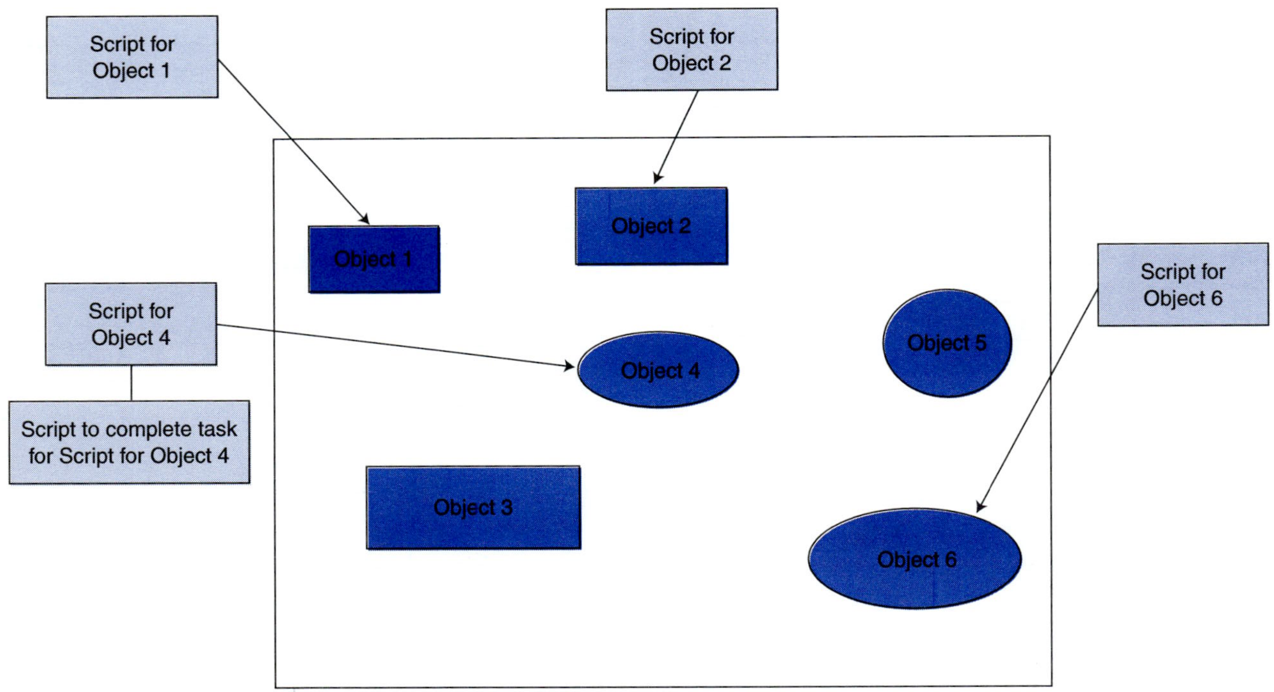

Note: Objects 3 and 5 have no scripts attached to them, as they do not do anything.

Step 5: **Plan Your Solution. (con't)**

Algorithms and Flowcharts:

Step 6: **Evaluate the Solution. List the criteria for evaluating the completed document.**

Appendix C

Otto the Robot

An electronic version of Otto the Robot is found on the CD-ROM in the Instructor's Manual. Thomas Barton and Ayako Kitada, students at College of the Redwoods, created this version. Students may build sets of instructions for the problems at the end of the appendix and then test them for accuracy. In another section, students may choose from any number of mazes and step Otto through the designated maze.

It is fairly easy to understand your knowledge base and the knowledge base of those around you. You can modify your solutions to everyday problems according to these knowledge bases. However, when you are working with a computer, its knowledge base is already defined for you. You may not use any other instructions, actions, or formats. The rules, called syntax, are established for you. To better understand this concept, we move from our own everyday situations to a robot's called Otto.

Otto the Robot has a very limited knowledge base. You must define your solutions to Otto's problems within the limitations of his knowledge base. There are always certain assumptions to be made when solving problems such as a common language. Other assumptions we will make regarding Otto are as follows:

1. Otto always starts from a sitting position.
2. Otto always ends his maneuvers in a sitting position. This means you have to make sure he is sitting down at the end of your solution.

Let us start with a few simple actions in Otto's knowledge base.

> **Action 1:** Stand up. Otto will stand up from his chair in an upright position.
>
> **Action 2:** Sit down. Otto will sit down. You must make sure the chair is behind him or he will sit on the floor.
>
> **Action 3:** Take step. Otto will take one step forward.
>
> **Action 4:** Turn right. Otto will turn right 90 degrees. (How would you make Otto turn to the left?)

With these four actions in Otto's knowledge base, let us solve the following problem: Write a set of numbered, step-by-step instructions to make Otto walk three steps forward and then return and sit in his chair.

1. Identify the problem: Making Otto stand up and walk three steps forward, turn around, walk to his chair, turn around, and sit down.
2. Understand the problem: Do you understand what he is to do? Otto's knowledge base is limited to his four actions.
3. Alternative solutions:
   a. Stand up, walk three steps forward, turn right 180 degrees, go back to chair, and sit down.

b. Stand up, walk three steps forward, turn left 180 degrees, go back to chair, and sit down.

4. Select best solution: Solution a is the best because Otto can only turn right.
5. Plan the solution by listing the set of instructions: (solution a)
   a. stand up
   b. take step
   c. take step
   d. take step
   e. turn right
   f. turn right
   g. take step
   h. take step
   i. take step
   j. turn
   k. turn
   l. sit down
6. Test solution. Have someone test this solution to see if it works.

This is a lot of instructions.

We now add another action that will allow us to repeat the same action several times. This will be the fifth action in Otto's knowledge base.

Action 5: Repeat: [action] x times, where x is a given number such as 3, 6, 8, etc.

Now we rewrite the instructions in problem-solving step five: (solution b):

a. stand up (same as instruction a in solution a)
b. repeat [take step] 3 times (same as instructions b–d in solution a)
c. repeat [turn right] 2 times (same as instructions e–f in solution a)
d. repeat [take step] 3 times (same as instructions g–i in solution a)
e. repeat [turn right] 2 times (same as instructions j–k in solution a)
f. sit down (same as instruction l in solution a)

We now have six numbered instructions that complete the same task as the twelve numbered instructions did in solution a. Will Otto react differently? Overall, no. He will do exactly the same thing. He will stand up, walk three steps forward, turn 180 degrees to the right, walk back, turn 180 degrees to the right, and sit down. The actual number of actions he takes is the same. The only difference is that to move forward he will take three steps with only one instruction instead of requiring three instructions. We can decrease the number of instructions even further: (solution c)

a. stand up
b. repeat [[take step] 3 times, [turn right] 2 times] 2 times
c. sit down

Note the double set of brackets. Use of this technique is called nesting. Just as you might put one basket inside another basket (nested), you are placing repeated instructions inside another repeated instruction. The inside set of brackets includes instructions that are executed before the outer set of bracketed instructions.

The number of actual steps and turns Otto takes is the same. You must decide which set of instructions is easiest to read, easiest to write, and easiest to understand by someone else.

Now let us add some more actions to Otto:

Arm Actions:

Action 6: Raise arms. Raises arms to a forward position perpendicular to his body.

Action 7: Lower arms. Lowers arms to a position at the side of his body.

Arithmetic Actions: Otto has one memory location that may be changed by one of the following instructions. This memory location always starts at zero when the execution of the instruction set begins. This memory location may not be used in the repeat action as the memory number is a specified number and not a variable number.

Action 8: Add one. Adds one to the memory location.

Action 9: Subtract one. Subtracts one from the memory location.

Action 10: Set number to zero. Sets memory location to zero.

Conditional Actions: One thing a computer needs is the ability to make a decision given certain data. With Otto, these tests are using his memory location and sensory devices in his fingertips. Otto can determine when his memory location is zero. He can determine if his hands are touching something. He can determine if his hands are touching a door as the door has a difference sensory return than anything else. These actions include three tests:

Action 11: Test: Is the number in your memory zero?
Yes (one action for yes answer)
No (one action for no answer)

Action 12: Test: Are you touching anything?
Yes (one action for yes answer)
No (one action for no answer)

Action 13: Test: Are you touching a door?
Yes (one action for yes answer)
No (one action for no answer)

As an example of one of these tests, let us say this is instruction 15.

15. Test: Is the number in your memory zero?
 Yes: Turn
 No: Take step

Many times there are several actions that need to take place for the yes actions and/or the no actions, or the action requires going to another instruction either after or before the present instruction. This necessitates a new action.

Action 14: Go to *i,* where *i* is an instruction number, either preceding or following the present instruction. An example would be:

8. Go to 5 or
12. Go to 15

An example of a conditional action using the Go to *i* action is:

18. Take step.
19. Subtract one.

20. Test: Is your memory zero?
    Yes: Go to 21
    No: Go to 18
21. Repeat [turn] two times
22. Continue with other actions

The final action you will need to complete the exercises at the end of this appendix is:

Action 15: Open door.

There are fifteen actions in Otto's knowledge base. Remember that you must use these actions and no other ones. Also, remember that each instruction must be written in the proper form as this is the extent of Otto's knowledge. For example, you must write:

Repeat [take step] 3 times,

And *not:*

Take 3 steps or
Repeat 3 times take step

Remember when you write instructions for Otto that the robot executes the instructions in the order you give them. When you use the go to action, he will execute instruction *i* next and then continue at that point with the execution. Look at problem 1 at the end of this appendix to see some sets of instructions, valid and invalid, and try to determine what Otto will do.

Let us first review the fifteen actions:

Action 1: Stand up. Otto will stand up from his chair in an upright position.

Action 2: Sit down. Otto will sit down. You must make sure the chair is behind him or he will sit on the floor.

Action 3: Take step. Otto will take one step forward.

Action 4: Turn right. Otto will turn right 90 degrees. (How would you make Otto turn to the left?)

Action 5: Repeat: [action] x times, where x is a given number such as 3, 6, 8, etc.

Action 6: Raise arms. Raises arms to a forward position perpendicular to his body.

Action 7: Lower arms. Lowers arms to a position at the side of his body.

Action 8: Add one. Adds one to the memory location.

Action 9: Subtract one. Subtracts one from the memory location.

Action 10: Set number to zero. Sets memory locations to zero.

Action 11: Test: Is the number in your memory zero?
  Yes (one action for yes answer)
  No (one action for no answer)

Action 12: Test: Are you touching anything?
  Yes (one action for yes answer)
  No (one action for no answer)

Action 13: Test: Are you touching a door?
  Yes (one action for yes answer)
  No (one action for no answer)

Action 14: Go to *i,* where *i* is an instruction number, either before or after the present instruction.

Action 15: Open door.

Otto is set up to help you to organize your solutions in a logical order and to realize that the computer cannot read your mind. You must give it a complete set of instructions. One frustrating aspect of working with a computer is that the computer it does exactly what it is instructed to do, not what you thought you instructed it to do.

Problems

1. The following sets of instructions for Otto are incorrect. Find the problem and correct the solution.

a.
1. stand up
2. take step
3. add 1 to memory
4. go to 2
5. sit down

b.
1. stand up
2. repeat [take step] 3 times
3. if touching something
   yes: go to 4
   no: go to 2
4. turn 2 times
5. go to 2
6. sit down

c.
1. stand up
2. take 2 steps
3. turn
4. take 3 steps
5. turn
6. take 3 steps
7. turn
8. take 3 steps
9. turn
10. take 1 step
11. sit down

2. Using Otto's 15 actions, write a set of step-by-step instructions to have Otto complete the following:

a. Direct Otto to walk in a square that is three steps on each side. All turns are to the right. How many solutions are there to this problem?

b. Direct Otto to walk in a square that is three steps on each side. All turns are to the left.

c. Direct Otto to walk to a wall that is an unknown whole number of steps (no partial steps) in front of Otto, and then walk back and sit down in his chair. The back of the chair is taller than Otto and can be touched by Otto's raised hands, when Otto is directly in front of his chair.

d. Direct Otto to walk to a wall that is an unknown whole number of steps (no partial steps) in front of Otto, and then walk back and sit down in his chair. The back of the chair is shorter than Otto's raised hands when Otto is directly in front of his chair, so Otto's hands cannot touch the back of the chair.

e. Write one set of instructions that will direct Otto through any maze with its entrance and exit on the same side. The maze has no dead ends and no intersections. From Otto's starting position, the entrance is two steps forward. When Otto is facing the entrance, the exit is three steps to his right. Figure C.1 shows three example mazes for you to test your solution. Do not make separate solutions for each maze. Your solutions should allow Otto to walk through any such maze as those shown in Figure C.1.

f. Modify your solution in task e (above) to accommodate a change in the place of the exit. Your solution should allow for the exit to be any place on the perimeter of the maze. Figure C.2 shows three example mazes for you to test your solution. Again, do not write separate solutions for each maze. Your solution should allow Otto to walk back to his chair from any exit, such as those in Figure C.2.

Figure C.1 Sample Mazes for Problem 2e

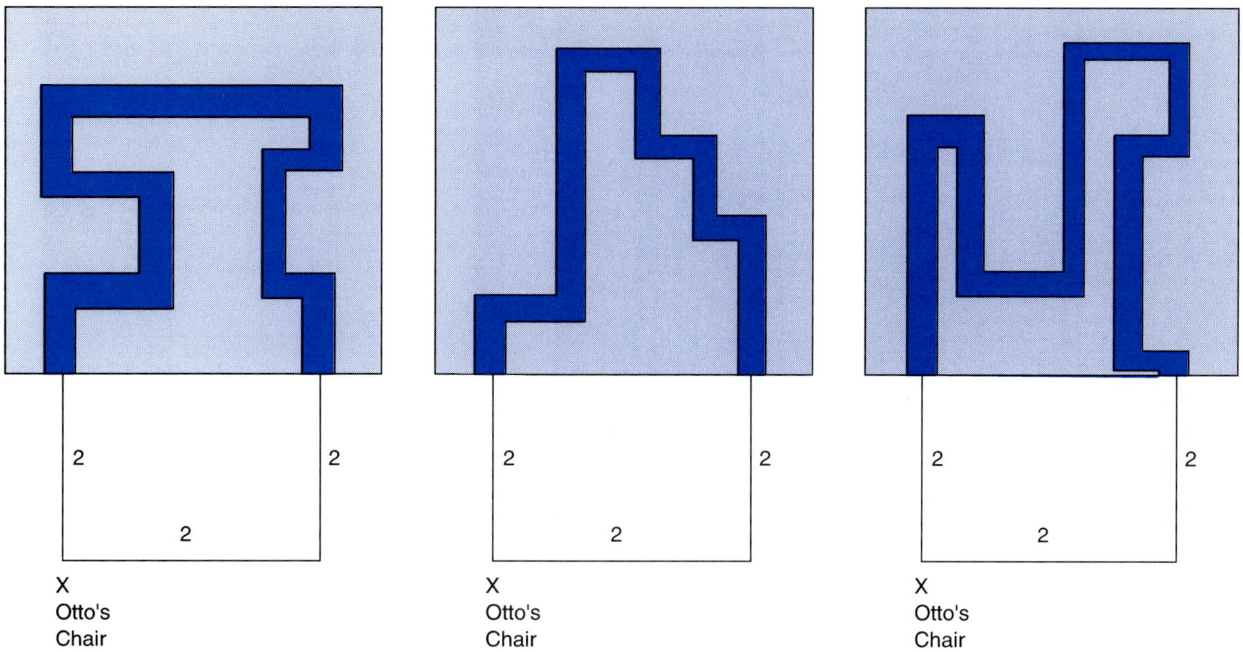

Figure C.2 Sample Mazes for Problem 2f

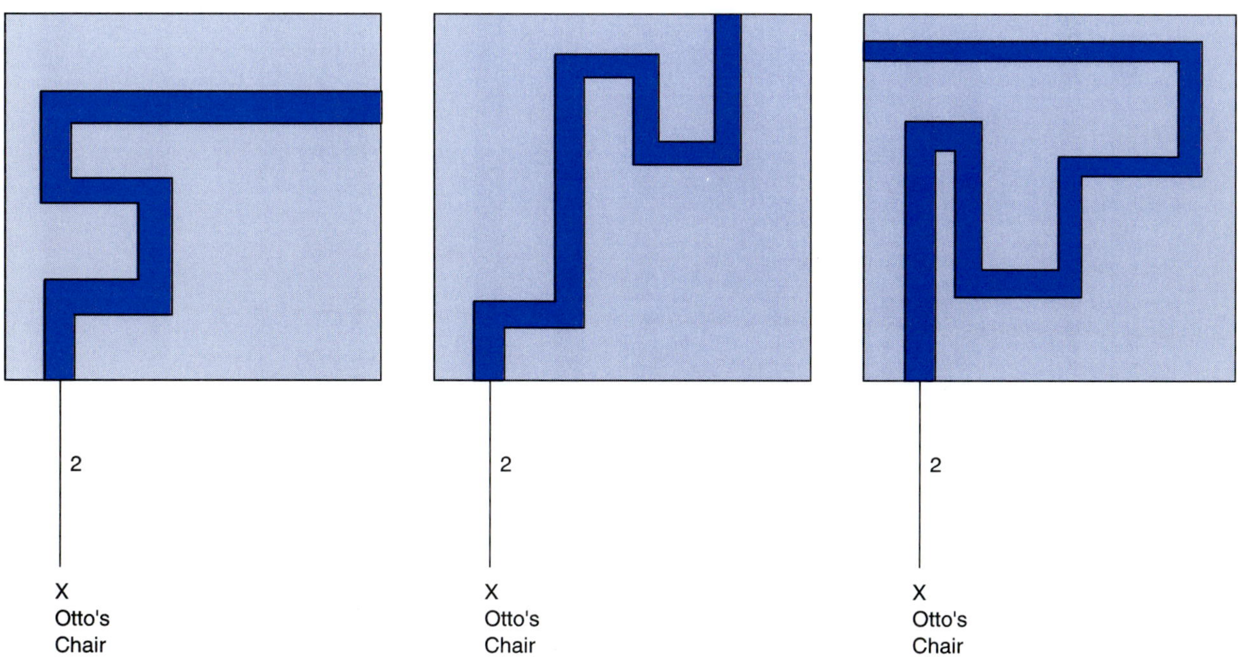

3. How would you modify Otto's knowledge base so as to be able to write a solution for the following tasks? Specify the modifications and then write the set of instructions for each of the tasks.
   a. Direct Otto to walk in a triangle that has three steps on each side.
   b. Direct Otto to walk to a table and pick up a book.
   c. Modify your instruction set in task 2c (to walk to the wall and back) to have Otto detect an object in his path.

Glossary

Absolute cell reference Used in a spreadsheet formula, retains the row numbers or column letters when the formula is copied. It is designated by a $ in front of the row and/or column.

Algorithm A set of step-by-step instructions used to solve a problem.

Algorithmic solution A solution to a problem that uses a set of step-by-step instructions.

Alias An icon on the desktop that is linked to the location of a file.

Alignment Refers to how text or numbers fit into the margins. The alignment types are left, right, center, and justify.

Audience handouts Prepared in a presentation graphics software package, and allows users the ability to print multiple slides on one page for the audience attending a presentation.

Background (of a slide) Refers to the common graphics, color, and buttons placed on every slide developed in a presentation graphics software package. The background is developed separately from the individual slides.

Bit mapped fonts Refers to those fonts that have been developed by defining each character through a designation of pixels.

Bit mapped graphics Developed by designating the attributes of each pixel.

Booklet A group of pages that are folded and stapled on the fold.

Brochure An advertising document that is folded to make a multipanel, small informational sheet that may be mailed or given out to prospective clients.

Cell On a spreadsheet, the location where a row and a column intersect. A cell contains a label, a value, or a formula.

Character formatting Refers to how a character appears in the text. Formatting includes font, size, and other enhancements such as boldface, emboss, engrave, italics, shadow, strikethrough, subscript, superscript, and underline.

Charts Graphical representation of data. Types of charts include column, bar, pie, line, area, and stock.

Clipart Refers to artwork that is purchased or that accompanies software.

Clipboard A section of the computer's memory that holds data that have been cut or copied. The contents of the clipboard are changed only when something new is placed on it or the computer is turned off.

Close The process of shutting a data file to make it unavailable to the user without re-opening it.

Column On a spreadsheet, a set of vertical cells designated by a column letter. A column in a word-processed or desktop-published document refers to the vertical page divisions of text.

Computer desktop The operating system's graphic user interface (GUI). It is the window that you see after you boot up a computer that uses a GUI.

Concatenation The combining of two sets of text by placing the second on the end of the first; for example, "A" concatenated with "B" is "AB."

Connectivity The connection between people through telecommunications.

Copyright The constitutional right to have domain over intellectual property.

Cropping/sizing In graphics, cropping refers to using part of a graphic, and sizing refers to making a graphic larger or smaller.

Cut/Copy/Paste Uses the clipboard to save and retrieve data from a document. Cut removes the data from the document and places it on the clipboard. Copy duplicates the data to the clipboard. Paste inserts whatever is on the clipboard into the current document.

Data A set of unorganized facts.

Data file A place where users save an electronic image of something that has been created on the computer.

Data type Refers to the type values that a datum represents, such as numbers, text, and graphics.

Database Created through the use of relational database management systems software, and contains a group of related tables of data, queries, forms, reports, and macros.

Database form The design of how one record of data will be viewed on the screen. A form may include other items such as images and buttons for automation.

Database query Creates a new table containing selected fields and/or records from the database tables.

Database report A printed document created from data in database or query tables.

Database table Contains data needed to create reports and forms for viewing information; contains one or more records.

Desktop publisher Refers to a software package that allows the easy placement of text and graphics on a page.

Digital photography Involves creating digitized electronic photographs using a digital camera.

Display fonts Refers to the fonts that are fancy, informal, or different. These fonts are normally not used for the body of text but instead for headings, eye catchers, flyers, and so forth.

Document processing Refers to the use of multiple software packages in the development of a project.

DPI Refers to the resolution of graphics, and stands for *dots per inch.*

Drag and drop Refers to the ability to select a portion of a document and move it to another part of the document or to another document.

Draw software Allows the user to create graphics using vector graphics technology. Each item placed on the page is considered an object. Each object is viewed as one entity.

Drop cap The first capital character of a paragraph, usually the first character of a section of text, that is larger than the remaining text and extends below the first line of text in the paragraph.

Electronic slide show A group of electronic graphic panels called slides that are used in conjunction with a presentation.

End users The people who use application software.

Event A happening in the computer such as mouse down, mouse up, and key down.

Event-driven object-oriented programming Used in applications to automate a project. Scripts are written to instruct the computer as to how to execute a task.

Export Refers to saving a file in a different format than the default format.

Fair Use Policy Allows a small amount of copyrighted material to be used for limited purposes.

Field One piece of data in a database table, such as a name or an address. A field is given a name and has the same attributes for all records in a table.

File A set of computer instructions or a set of related data saved in storage and given a file name.

File extensions A dot followed by three letters to distinguish the file type.

File management The organization of files and folders on a storage media.

Find/Replace A feature on most software packages that allows the user to locate specific text in a document or locate specific text and replace it with other text.

Flowchart A graphic representation of an algorithm.

Folder A tool for holding other folders and files on storage media; used to organize saved files.

Font The way in which a set of characters is designed.

Formula On a spreadsheet, a mathematical expression that is entered into a cell.

Function A preprogrammed task that is available in an application or language.

Graphic user interface (GUI) Allows the user to communicate with the computer through the use of icons, menus, and toolbars.

Gridlines Lines that are drawn on the screen to separate cell values in a spreadsheet or to measure and/or place objects in graphics programs.

Group/Ungroup/Regroup Refers to the combining of selected objects to make one object or the breaking of an object into separate objects.

GUI See *graphic user interface.*

Guidelines Used in desktop publishing to position columns, margins, and blue line guides where needed.

Gutter The distance between facing pages or between columns.

Hanging indentation A paragraph in which the first line is further to the left than the rest of the paragraph.

Hardware The physical component of a computer system.

Headers/Footers One or more lines of text that are located within the top margin (header) or the bottom margin (footer).

Heuristic solution Requires trial and error, previous knowledge, and/or previous experience to solve a problem. A set of step-by-step instructions cannot be written for a problem requiring a heuristic solution.

Hierarchy Refers to the order of precedence of mathematical operators.

Horizontal scaling Refers to the stretching or contracting of the horizontal text size without effecting the vertical size.

Horizontal software Written to be used for multiple types of problems. Examples include word processing, spreadsheets, or relational database management systems.

Import(Insert/Place) Refers to the use of all or part of one file within another file. *Insert* and *place* are other names for import.

Information Refers to a collection of organized facts.

Information processing Refers to using the correct methods and software to process data into information.

Input mask Specifies required characters when entering data into database tables. These characters are automatically entered into a field by the computer.

Installation of software The process of copying software files to a computer, and communicating with the software as to the hardware configuration.

Interactivity Refers to how the user interacts with the computer.

Kerning Refers to placing one letter closer to another when using bit mapped fonts.

Landscape A type of printer page orientation; refers to the direction of the printed page, which is wider than it is tall.

Layers Used in graphics software to separate parts of a graphic to work on specific parts.

Leading Extra space between lines.

License Involving software, refers to the written agreement between the user and the software developers as to software utilization.

Line All characters between one cursor return and the next.

Logic structures Writing programs require the use of four types of such structures: sequential, decision, repetition, and case logic structures. Instructions are written in a program sequentially, which uses the sequential logic structure to order instructions. The decision logic structure allows the computer to choose between two sets of instructions. The repetition logic structure allows the computer to repeat instructions. The case logic structure allows the computer to choose a set of instructions to execute from many sets.

Lowercase characters Noncapital letters.

Mail merge Refers to the use of a database file and a form letter to create multiple letters with different data from the database inserted into the letter.

Master pages Used when creating one or more backgrounds for individual pages in a desktop publisher which contain common page items that cannot be changed on the individual pages, such as the page number and blue line layouts.

Mathematical operator A symbol that performs a specific mathematical task such as addition, subtraction, multiplication, or division.

Menu A list of items from which to choose a task.

Menu driven Refers to a software package that uses only menus to process the data.

Model On a spreadsheet, the description of subjects of a problem, for example, the number of people employed, presentation of perfect scores, demand for a product, or numbers of products sold.

Navigational tools Used to move through a project, and include buttons, hot spots, and hot objects.

Nested decision instructions An If/Then/Else instruction that is used for the true and/or false set of instructions of another If/Then/Else instruction.

Nested loops A repetition instruction that is used inside of another repetition instruction.

New Creates a blank sheet such as a blank document, a blank slide or slide show, or an empty spreadsheet.

Normalize To separate the data into related database tables.

Numerical data Designated as numbers that may be used in calculations.

Object An individual part of a graphic, a page, or a slide.

Object linking and embedding (OLE) Allows a piece of data to be automatically changed in one package when changed in another.

OLE See *object linking and embedding.*

Open The process of instructing the computer to retrieve a file from a storage media and to place it on the screen for viewing.

Operating system (of a computer) The hardware and software managers of the computer. The user communicates with the computer through the operating system.

Optical character recognition (OCR) Refers to a software program used with a scanner to digitize text to be used in a computer.

Page orientation Refers to the direction of the printed page. Landscape refers to a page that is wider than it is tall. Portrait refers to a page that is taller than it is wide.

Paint software Allows the user to create a graphic pixel by pixel. Each pixel has its own set of attributes. Paint software creates bit mapped images and is sometimes called raster graphics.

Paragraph All characters from one hard cursor return to the next.

Platform A specific operating system.

Portrait A type of page orientation; refers to the direction of the printed page, which is taller than it is wide.

Presentation graphics A software package that allows the user to create electronic slide shows.

Primary key Designated as one field in a database table. The field must contain unique data.

Print/Print Options/Print Preview Refers to selectable options for printing data files. Print and Print Options allows the user to change how a file will be printed. Print Preview allows the user to view the document prior to being printed.

Problem analysis chart (PAC) A tool to help in the analysis of a problem. It helps to separate the data from the extra words.

Problem solving The logical process of developing a solution to a problem.

Productivity software Another term for *horizontal software.*

Program file A set of computer instructions to process data that are stored on storage media.

Query table The result of a database query. It contains selected records and/or fields from database tables.

Range of cells A contiguous set of cells. The range may be a set of adjacent horizontal cells in one row, a set of adjacent vertical cells in one column, or a rectangular block of cells. A range is designated by specifying the first and last cells in the range.

Record One entity in a database table; contains one or more fields.

Relational database management system (RDBMS) Software that allows the user to enter data into tables, organize the data, and create reports on that data.

Relational operator Compares two values. The operators include =, <, >, <=, >=, and <>.

Relative cell reference In a spreadsheet formula, changes the row numbers and the column letters when the formula is copied from one cell to another.

Resolution Designates the clarity of the graphic and refers to the number of pixels describing the graphic.

Row In a spreadsheet, a horizontal set of cells designated by a row number.

Sans serif fonts Fonts without the extra lines on the top and bottom of characters.

Save/Save As Save As creates a space on a storage media and copies the active document into that space using a file name. Save copies the active document into a space that has already been designated for that file.

Scalable fonts Contain vector instructions as to how to create the characters. Part of these instructions includes variables to create new sizes for the font.

Scanned graphics Artwork that has been digitized through the use of a scanner to be used in a computer.

Schema A graphic representation of the tables and their relationships in a database.

Screen The monitor of the computer.

Script A set of instructions that are attached to an object or that are part of a program.

Sentence All the characters from one period to the next.

Serif fonts Fonts with extra lines on the top and bottom of characters.

Short cut An icon on the desktop that is linked to the location of a file providing for faster file access.

Size Refers to the height or size of a font, usually measured in points.

Slide sorter A feature in a presentation graphics software package that allows the user to scan all of the slides on the monitor at one time and then be able to rearrange them.

Software Instructions written for the computer to accomplish various tasks.

Solution The way a problem can be solved.

Sort To put a selected list of data in numerical or alphabetical order, ascending or descending.

Speaker notes A feature in presentation graphics software that allows the user to create word-processed notes to be used by the person giving the presentation.

Spell checker A feature in most software packages that checks each word in your document with the words in the computer's dictionary to find misspelled works.

Spreadsheet A matrix of cells that are recalculated each time the spreadsheet is updated. The cells may contain labels, values, or formulas.

Storyboard A thumbnail sketch of the design of a screen.

Styles A feature in some software packages that allows the user to name a set of characters and paragraph formatting and designate a style for each paragraph.

Suite A set of software packages that have look-alike features, drag and drop across applications, and integration capabilities. A suite is sold with the software packages bundled together.

Syntax Rules and regulations governing software on the computer.

Tab A function that may be set and used with the tab key. Tabs are designated at a specific ruler location. The types of tabs include left, right, center, and decimal. The user may also designate a tab leader that is associated with a specific tab.

Telecommuting Involves working for a company in a remote location, usually a home.

Template A document that has common data for multiple-use documents. The types of data may include the date, certain formulas, and specific values.

Text A group of characters including letters, numbers, and special symbols.

Text block A group of characters that is treated as an object.

Text fonts Fonts that are easily read and used for a body of text. Text fonts may also be used as display fonts.

Text frame A group of characters that is surrounded by a line frame and is treated as an object.

Text threading The connection of text from one text block to another.

Toolbar Contains buttons representing menu items. Toolbars have specific functions such as drawing, standard, and formatting.

Transitions Created in slide shows to indicate how a slide is introduced onto the screen.

Typography The art of printing with type, and the style and layout of printed material.

Undo/Redo Allows the user to undo or redo what was just done.

Uppercase characters Capital letters.

User friendly Refers to the ease of using the computer.

Value On a spreadsheet, a constant piece of numeric datum.

Vector graphics Graphics created in a draw software package.

Vertical software Software created for a single purpose such as a real estate office or a lawyer's office.

White space Refers to the area of a document that has nothing printed.

Wizard A program designed to take the user step by step through a task.

Word All of the characters from one space to the next space.

Word processor A text editor.

Zoom Refers to the ability to make the document larger or smaller for viewing purposes.

Index

N

O

P

Q

R

S